COLORADO
A SPORTS HISTORY

COLORADO
A SPORTS HISTORY

JAMES WHITESIDE

UNIVERSITY PRESS OF COLORADO

Copyright © 1999 by the University Press of Colorado
International Standard Book Number 0-87081-550-4

Published by the University Press of Colorado
P.O. Box 849
Niwot, Colorado 80544

The University Press of Colorado is a cooperative publishing enterprise supported,
in part, by Adams State College, Colorado State University, Fort Lewis College,
Mesa State College, Metropolitan State College of Denver, University of Colorado,
University of Northern Colorado, University of Southern Colorado, and Western
State College of Colorado.

The paper used in this publication meets the minimum requirements of the
American National Standard for Information Sciences—Permanence of Paper for
Printed Library Materials. ANSI Z39.48-1984

Library of Congress Cataloging-in-Publication Data

Whiteside, James, 1950–
Colorado : a sports history / by James Whiteside.
          p.   cm.
Includes bibliographical references (p.) and index.
ISBN 0-87081-550-4 (alk. paper)
1. Sports—Colorado—History. 2. Sports—Social aspects—
Colorado. 3. Athletes—Colorado—History. I. Title.
GV584.C6W55   1999
796'.09788—dc21   99-41402
                                                  CIP

Designed by Laura Furney.
Typeset by Holly Paulsen.

08 07 06 05 04 03 02 01 00 99   10 9 8 7 6 5 4 3 2 1

For MaryAnn and Blair

CONTENTS

Photos and Illustrations

PREFACE

Why write a sports history of Colorado?

The simplest, and probably the best, answer is why not? After all, sports are fun, exciting, and engage the interest, participation, and money of a great many people. Indeed, a good case could be made for calling the people of Colorado the most sports-conscious in America. In fact, in 1997 the *Sporting News,* a national weekly sports newspaper, named Denver the number-one sports city in the country. Denver, the paper declared, is "a unique setting for sports of all kinds. In addition to the Broncos, Buffs, Nuggets, Avalanche, and Rockies, there is every kind of participatory opportunity imaginable."[1]

Denver is one of only ten cities home to all four major league sports. However, the Broncos, the Rockies, the Nuggets, and the Avalanche are not just Denver's teams; they belong to the whole state. Their fans are fierce and eclectic in their loyalties. As the *Sporting News* noted, on the night in June 1996 when the Colorado Avalanche won the Stanley Cup, the Colorado Rockies showed the game on the Jumbotron television screen at Coors Field where they were playing their own game. Coloradans have become famous for their infatuation with their major league sports teams, an infatuation that sometimes seems obsessive. Much personal and civic self-esteem is bound up with the teams' successes and failures, which somehow become the fans' successes and failures. Reflecting on recent triumphant moments in Colorado sports—the Broncos' 1998 Super Bowl victory, the Avalanche winning the Stanley Cup, Olympic swimmer Amy Van Dyken's four gold medals, Larry Walker's National League Most Valuable Player award—*Denver Post* sports columnist Mark Kiszla wondered, "[H]ow long can the sports magic last?" Kiszla answered his own question, noting that Denver's—he should have said Colorado's—sports euphoria "knows no expiration date. Around every corner, there's another victory parade coming."[2]

However, Coloradans' interest in sports goes far beyond being fans and spectators. Go to any park in the state anytime of the year, and you will find people running, bicycling, in-line skating, and playing tennis, soccer, softball, baseball, football, field hockey, and so on. Skiing, golf, hiking, and mountain climbing are popular as well.

Clearly, any activity, or range of activities, that commands so much popular engagement deserves serious inquiry. Academics feel compelled to come up with complicated questions and explanations, even for the perfectly obvious. For example, what is sport? The historian Allen Guttmann offers a definition, or paradigm, that requires sport to be a competitive physical activity. He also lists other characteristics, including secularism, equality, bureaucratization, specialization, rationalization (the constant refining of rules and equipment), quantification, and obsession with records. Certainly, any modern professional sport fulfills this definition and characteristics. A major league baseball game, for example, is not a religious service (no matter how devout a team's loyalists may be). The players all follow the same rules and are on the field because of their abilities, not because of whom their fathers are, and each has specific skills that contribute to the team's performance. Baseball is played in a highly organized institutional setting, with a powerful business and administrative structure in control. As any fan knows, baseball is also number intensive, as every pitch, hit, catch, and error is duly recorded.[3]

My own view of sport, and its history, especially in Colorado, is not incompatible with Guttmann's, but it is somewhat broader and less formal. In my view, competition in sports does not necessarily require athletes pitting their skills against one another. The clock is often the rival. To be sure, athletes measure their performance against one another in terms of time, but what of the lone recreational cyclist trying to get to the top of the hill faster than she did last week? Is that competition? Against the clock? Against herself? I think so.

The history of sports in Colorado reveals three sometimes over-lapping categories. These categories are themselves somewhat arbitrary, and, as the following chapters will show, the lines between them blur quickly. The first is life and work as sport. Guttmann understands that his definition of modern sports describes sport in the highly urbanized and industrialized settings of late-nineteenth- and twentieth-century America. However, premodern Americans also played games and competed with one another, and did so for their own reasons. For American Indians, competitive sport often was an expression of religion. For them, and for other pre– and early–industrial era Americans, sport also derived from everyday life and work. In the early Colorado mining towns, miners quickly turned aspects of their work into competitive sports.

The second category is sport as personal play and recreation. As leisure time grew by the late nineteenth century, especially for the emerging middle class, Coloradans adapted activities derived from work and amusements into purely ludic games and competitions, played just for the fun of it. Recreational skiing and bicycling best illustrate this phenomenon. Of course, such ludic activities often quickly became competitive. It took no time at all for early recreational skiers to realize that racing to the bottom of the hill made the exercise more interesting.

Finally, by the early twentieth century, sports became business. Again, the story of recreational skiing illustrates sports' evolution from ludic, personal activity to a highly organized, for-profit business. The development of college football from an amateur, middle- and upper-class game into an institutionalized, quasi-professional sport is also a case in point. Likewise, the history of professional spectator sports reveals the industrialization of sport and its close connection to economic and political life, as well as the stresses and uncertainties of life in contemporary culture.

Studying the development of sports in Colorado, from their origins in life and work, through their development as leisure-time activities, to their growth into multimillion-dollar enterprises, tells us a great deal not only about sports but also about Colorado itself. Sports offer a unique and interesting perspective, or "lens," on Colorado's, and America's, history. The story of sports is not just about athletes and coaches. (Indeed, there are few warm and fuzzy stories of athletic heroics and locker-room wisdom here.) Sports history is about business, politics, class, race, gender, mores, and values. As historians Elliott J. Gorn and

Warren Goldstein have noted, "[S]ports arenas are America's living galleries, where we witness all the beauty and grace and passion of which humans are capable. They are also our asylums, filled with delusional fantasies, misogyny, misplaced loyalties, racism, homophobia, and unclear boundaries between self and others." The history of sports in Colorado, then, is about the state's people, their cultures, their politics, and their economic life. The following chapters examine Colorado and sports along those lines.[4]

The hardest problem in researching and writing this book was defining limits. Once you go beyond organized amateur and professional sports and venture into the realm of recreation, the terrain is enormous. Thus, I imposed some rather arbitrary limits on my subject matter. First, a subject had to tell a unique or powerful story about Colorado. Second, I had to be interested in it. These criteria eliminated most forms of outdoor recreation. After all, one can hunt, cast for trout, or climb a mountain (none of which I will ever be caught doing) in any of the other Rocky Mountain states. However, you have to come to Colorado, specifically to Denver, to see a major league sports game (except, of course, the Utah Jazz of the National Basketball Association). On the other hand, while one can go skiing in Wyoming, Utah, New Mexico, Idaho, or Montana, why would one want to? More to the point, Colorado is the center of gravity of recreational skiing in the West. Other widely popular recreational sports, such as tennis and golf, do not tell a unique story about Colorado (although, admittedly, the history of country clubs reveals much about the life and culture of the wealthy).

Some readers may be surprised that I have not included rodeo. After all, rodeo would seem to be the quintessential western sport, and Colorado—its land and its people—embodies the West. Rodeo certainly fits the category of sports based on life and work. However, it is worth remembering that, while the cowboy is a powerful icon of western Americana, the farmer, the miner, the merchant, and the schoolteacher are far more emblematic of Colorado's people and their culture, and in the nineteenth and early twentieth centuries, those folks were most likely to spend their leisure time playing or watching baseball or peddling their bicycles. In fact, rodeo, especially organized and professional rodeo, was rather late in coming to Colorado. The National Western Stock Show, for example, did not begin until 1906. By then the range cattle industry, the cowboy's domain, had long since disappeared.

When I began this project, I thought it would be an interesting and entertaining diversion for one or two summers. Five years later, I have realized the enormity of the task. I have been fortunate to build on the efforts of many historians and journalists. I hope they will approve of the use I have made of their work. Many history colleagues and friends have shared their research, provided good counsel, and critiqued chapters. I am especially indebted to Mark S. Foster and Thomas J. Noel of the University of Colorado at Denver; Duane A. Smith, the dean of Colorado historians, of Fort Lewis College; James E. Hansen II of Colorado State University; and Dolph Grundman of Metropolitan State College of Denver. University of Colorado at Denver students Nancy Widmann, Douglas Reynolds, Whitman Thompson, and Peter Homan contributed useful research from our class "Sports and American Society." Annie Gilbert Coleman, a recent doctoral graduate of the University of Colorado at Boulder, has done important work on the Colorado ski industry. Terry L. Irwin shared his research on mining-town boxing. Jay Sanford shared his encyclopedic knowledge of baseball, his wisdom, and his unrivaled photo collection. I am also grateful to former governor Richard D. Lamm, the Colorado Historical Society's David F. Halaas, the late Richard Conn of the Denver Art Museum, Jim Saccomano, Larry Zimmer, Tim Smile, and, especially, MaryAnn Whiteside for reading and critiquing various chapters.

David N. Wetzel, publications director of the Colorado Historical Society, generously gave permission to use material from my *Colorado Heritage* articles, "It Was a Terror to the Horses: Bicycling in Gilded-Age Denver" (spring 1991) and "Second-Hand Broncos: The Best Worst Team in Football" (winter 1997). Wetzel and *Colorado Heritage* editor Clark Secrest gave me much encouragement for this project.

Gathering photographs has been a surprisingly daunting task. I have enjoyed the help of many individuals and institutions, including Jay Sanford; Eleanor Gehres and the staff of the Western History Department of the Denver Public Library; the University of Colorado Archives; the Colorado State University Archives; the Colorado Historical Society; the Aspen Historical Society; Nancy Manley and the Colorado

Mountain History Collection at Leadville; the Media Relations Office of the Athletic Department at the University of Colorado at Boulder; the University of Nebraska Press for permission to reproduce illustrations from the Bison Books edition of Stewart Culin's *Games of the North American Indians;* Yale University Press for permission to reproduce a photograph from George Bird Grinnell's *By Cheyenne Campfires;* Colorado Ski Country USA; Drew Litton, sports cartoonist at the *Rocky Mountain News;* the *Denver Post;* the Denver Broncos; the Denver Nuggets; the Colorado Rockies; the Colorado Avalanche; Rick Garber of Rich Carlson Associates; Tim DeFrisco; Dan Becker; Mark Junge; and Edna Dercum, the delightful grand dame of Colorado skiing. Deciding which photos to use from among the hundreds I collected was difficult, and not every institution and person who helped is represented in the final selection, but I am grateful for their interest and help.

I am honored that the Colorado Endowment for the Humanities selected this book for its 1999 Publication Prize. It is especially gratifying to have received this award in its inaugural year.

Writing about sports, like writing about politics, has the inherent hazard that anything that can be said is obsolete or incomplete. I have tried to make the book, especially the chapters on collegiate and professional sports, as current as possible. John Elway's retirement in May 1999 more or less represents the book's chronological terminus. As for what I have written about, I thank in advance the ardent sports fans, journalists, and scholars who know vastly more than I about the subjects of this book and who, I am confident, will point out my errors.

COLORADO
A SPORTS HISTORY

1

INTERACTING WITH THE SACRED
AMERICAN INDIAN SPORTS IN COLORADO

Nathan Meeker came to Colorado with a mission. In 1870 the Ohio-born social reformer, agricultural expert, and protégé of Horace Greeley led a group of settlers to the plains of eastern Colorado. The colonists aimed to show that the "Great American Desert" could be irrigated and put into production. Meeker's Union Colony settled near the Cache La Poudre River and soon established the town of Greeley. The colony prospered, but within a few years Meeker, who had never managed his money well, found himself in debt. By 1877 Meeker's debts forced him to look for employment outside the colony, and, using his political connections, he secured appointment as the federal government's agent to the White River Ute Indians in western Colorado. Meeker's new job offered him not only a solution for his financial troubles but another challenging social-reform project as well.

Agent Meeker intended to "civilize" his new wards. He believed that American Indians had to be forced, for their own good, to abandon their traditional nomadic ways and their growing dependency on government subsidies and become self-supporting farmers. A major obstacle to this goal, he quickly realized, was the Utes' attachment to their horses.[1]

The Utes may have been among the first Indians to possess horses, acquiring them, directly or indirectly, from the Spanish as early

1-1. The Ute Indians prized horses as a measure of wealth and status and for racing. Courtesy, the Denver Public Library, Western History Department.

as 1600. The horse became the Utes' main means of transportation and hunting and changed their culture from a seminomadic to a more fully nomadic society. Horses also became objects of trade and a measure of status and wealth among the Utes. The Utes became fond of racing and betting on their horses as well (fig. 1-1). Races usually involved two horses and riders at a time, but the whole community would turn out to see, and bet heavily on, the outcome. With much yelling and flaying of rawhide whips, the contestants ran on a straight course that was several hundred yards long. The contestants often ran several heats before they, and the crowd, agreed on a clear winner. The horses also seemed to enjoy the contests and occasionally refused to stop at the end of the course.[2]

By 1874 the Utes owned about six thousand horses; unfortunately, by that time their territory had shrunk considerably. The Utes once roamed freely throughout Colorado, and into Wyoming, Utah, and New Mexico. By the late 1860s, however, the pressure of white settlement in Colorado forced them onto a reservation that confined them to the western third of the territory. Between 1868 and 1873 the federal government established three Ute agencies, one near the New Mexico border, another at Gunnison (later moved to Uncompahgre), and the third in the north at White River.

Nathan Meeker took charge of the White River agency in the summer of 1878. One of his first decisions was to relocate the agency from its original site several miles west to Powell Park, an area that he deemed more suitable for farming. Here Meeker's vision of an Indian pastoral utopia ran headlong into the Utes' attachment to their horses, love of racing, and nomadic way of life.

When he first inspected Powell Park, Meeker found approximately two thousand ponies grazing on the valley's abundant grass. Two Utes, Quinkent (also known as Douglas) and Canalla (also known as Johnson), owned more than a hundred horses each, making them influential among their people. Meeker also found a half-mile racetrack, which appeared to belong to Canalla. During this initial visit to the valley, Quinkent complained to the new agent that agency cattle were encroaching on his horses' pasture and asked Meeker to fence them out. The scene at Powell Park and Quinkent's complaint strengthened Meeker's attitude about the Utes and their prized horses and made him more resolved to break the connection. Only then could the Utes' increasingly anachronistic lifestyle of nomadism and dependency be reformed. As Meeker put it in a report to Indian Commissioner Edward A. Hayt, it was

> evident that the greatest obstacle to civilizing the majority of these Indians is their ownership of horses, which is proved by the fact that those who work have either few or no horses. An Indian who has a band of horses devotes all his time to them and to racing. Such a one will not work . . . but he is clamorous for goods and supplies.

The task would be formidable, but, as *Rocky Mountain News* publisher William Newton Byers noted, "if the condition of the Utes is capable of any improvement, Father Meeker is the man to accomplish it."[3]

In the spring of 1879, Meeker began to put severe pressure on the Utes to conform to his ideas. He started by ordering Quinkent and his band to plant garden crops and refused to release treaty-promised supplies until they completed the work. Meeker also tried to prevent the men from leaving the agency for the summer hunt by demanding that they appear with their families each week to receive allotments. For a time, the agent believed that he was making some progress with his charges as evidenced, he thought, by Quinkent's request to have two horses broken and trained for farm work. Meeker soon discovered, however, that Quinkent was racing the animals and ordered him to move them from the agency.[4]

In September 1879 Meeker decided to force the issue with the Utes by ordering the agency farmer to begin plowing the Utes' favorite pasture and threatening to do the same to the racetrack. Meeker's determination, as well as his sense that trouble lay ahead, is reflected in his report to Commissioner Hayt: "Plowing will proceed, but whether unmolested I cannot say. This is a bad lot of Indians. They have had free rations so long and have been flattered and petted so much that they think themselves lords of all." Predictably, the Utes reacted angrily to the plowing. At one point, as his plow neared the racetrack, a bullet whizzed past the farmer's head to warn him away. Finally, Meeker and Canalla had an angry argument that led to Canalla's shoving the agent to the ground. The incident convinced Meeker that he had lost control of the agency, and on September 10 he asked for troops to protect him and to enforce his orders. The War Department, with Gov. Frederick Pitkin's backing, approved Meeker's request, and on September 21 Maj. Thomas T. Thornburgh and a detachment of the Fourth Infantry left Fort Steele, near Rawlins, Wyoming, bound for White River.[5]

During these tense days, newspapers and politicians in Denver and elsewhere in Colorado fanned hot tempers and emotions by accusing the Utes of all manner of depredations, including murder, cattle theft, and setting forest fires. By the end of September, relations between Utes and whites reached the flash point.

News of the approach of army troops prompted the Utes to prepare to defend themselves. One band, led by Nicaagat (also known as Captain Jack), who had refused to reside at the agency or to ever cooperate with Meeker, set out to meet Thornburgh's force. On September 29 at Milk Creek, near the reservation boundary, Nicaagat struck, killing Thornburgh and thirteen others and pinning the rest in a siege that lasted nearly a week. Later the same day, at the agency, Quinkent and his followers attacked and killed Meeker and eleven others. Meeker's mutilated body was found with a stake driven through his throat. The Utes also took Meeker's wife and daughter and three others captive.

The arrival of more troops and diplomatic intervention by Ouray, the nominal chief of the Utes in Colorado, quickly brought the White River uprising to an end. However, mere surrender would not placate aroused whites for whom the slogan "The Utes Must Go" became a nonnegotiable demand. In June 1880 a Ute delegation led by Ouray agreed to a new treaty that terminated the existing reservation and required the White River Utes to resettle on the Uintah reservation in Utah. Only a small reservation in the southwest corner of Colorado remained—a gesture to Ouray—for the few Utes who were not forced out.[6]

The White River uprising of 1879 is often treated in histories of Colorado and the American West as another episode in the long and bitter history of conquest and obliteration of Indians and their culture. However, it is also illustrative of other currents in and between Native and white societies in the late nineteenth century.

Nathan Meeker was not ignorant of the importance that the Utes attached to their horses, and he knew what he was doing when he tried to break the connection. As a social reformer, Meeker sincerely believed that pastoralism of the Utes was in their best interest. They could no longer live as unrestrained nomads, as they had in the past; nor could they live indefinitely as dependents of the government without suffering social degeneration. However, his campaign against horses and, especially, horse racing also reflected a strong Victorian-era middle-class bias against that sport and the gambling that accompanied it.

Although eastern horse breeders and racing enthusiasts considered it a gentleman's sport, the reform-minded often saw it as symptomatic of the mounting problems of an industrialized and urbanized America. To be sure, wealthy gentlemen dominated the sport, but all too often they also enjoyed links with, and protection from, corrupt city politicians. The sport also encouraged middle- and working-class men to waste their time and earnings on gambling. The racetrack, then, seemed to be little more than an outdoor saloon with livestock. Middle-class reformers such as Meeker considered horse racing as part of the pathology of an increasingly unwholesome and corrupt society. They saw themselves as bulwarks standing in defense of the true American values of decency and hard work.

Thus, pastoralism and the attempt to banish horse racing was more than an effort to change the socioeconomic foundations of Ute society; it also aimed to transform the Utes culturally, to remold them according to Victorian-era middle-class values.

Although Meeker, in this sense, knew what he was doing, in a larger sense he was operating in the dark, in ignorance of how American Indians integrated sport into the core of their cultural life. In modern urban society—even in the late nineteenth century—sport is entertainment, business, livelihood, or personal enthusiasm. To be sure, sport is often a means of expressing other values, such as work, fair play, success, health, and well-being. Athletes enjoy social prominence, are rewarded for their physical prowess, and are held up as role models, though few people would consider them indispensable to society.

In traditional Indian society, sport was an expression of the life of the community—its values, myths, techniques of survival—as well as entertainment. Among the Utes, the horse was the basis of a way of life, horse ownership a measure of wealth and status, and horse racing a celebration of the animal and of the individual's and the community's intimate relationship with it.

Religion was especially important in Indian culture and was often closely tied to sports. As sports historians Elliott J. Gorn and Warren Goldstein have noted,

> Indian games accompanied fertility ceremonies, burial rites, healing practices, and efforts to control the weather. It was not just that games were part of religious practices; the sacred pervaded the Indians' existence. . . . Games, then, were embedded in ritual; contests could be fun and exciting, but even as tribesmen enjoyed themselves, athletic events kept them connected to their sacred beliefs, which gave meaning to the world and their place in it.[7]

American Indian ball games and races often represented a tribe's understanding of the origins and structure of their society and of the world itself and imitated and honored the spirits' choices in creation. Games and running events were often only part of a larger ceremony that might include ritual dancing, body painting and marking, and dietary and sexual taboos.

Running, too, was embedded with complex cultural, economic, communication, and even military meaning. The Jicarilla Apache relay race was a fertility rite in which competing teams represented the sun and animal food sources associated with it, and the moon and the vegetable foods linked with it. Among some southwestern tribes, running societies and their members were accorded high status, not because of their athletic prowess per se, but because of their important roles in the life of the community.[8]

Other characteristics of Indian sports included broad-based community participation, betting, intense competition, gender distinctions, and informality. Whether as contestants, spectators, or participants in related ceremonies, Indian games attracted the participation of the entire community. Gambling was another common form of participation. Betting helped to legitimate and underscore the importance of the event, as well as heighten interest. Indian sports were also intensely competitive, as the Ute horse races demonstrate. In team sports, however, the competitive emphasis lay more in team and community achievement than in individual triumph. Men and women did not often compete with one another in Indian sports, though women did participate in ritual elements and frequently had games of their own. Finally, the rules of Indian sports tended to be informal. Universally accepted standards of scoring, team size, field boundaries, and other rules were not common. Instead, these matters were usually settled at the time of the event. Elders, or the whole community, served as referees, but the value of good sportsmanship made honest play virtually self-enforcing.

In Colorado the major Indian groups—the Utes, the Cheyenne, and the Arapaho—played most of the sports commonly found among North American tribes, and their games illustrate these general characteristics. Especially notable among the Colorado tribes were hoop and pole games; ball games, including shinny and double-ball; and running.

Hoop and Pole Games

Hoops and rings have powerful religious meaning among American Indians, often symbolizing the earth and heavens, fertility and the life cycle, or war. They were used as amulets, body and hair ornaments, and as tokens of prowess in some activities, such as hunting. Ceremonial hoops and rings were also used for important events such as the Sun Dance among Plains tribes and the Sioux Ghost Dance at the Pine Ridge and Rosebud reservations. Ethnologist George Dorsey in 1896 described the hoop as "the object esteemed next after the great tribal medicine, the flat pipe, among the northern Arapaho." Dorsey described the Arapaho Sun Dance wheel as about eighteen inches in diameter.

> It is made of a rectangular piece of wood, one end of which tapers like the tail of a serpent, the other being rudely fashioned to represent a serpent's head. Near the head of the serpent are several wrappings of blue beads. . . . At four opposite sides of the wheel are incised designs, two of them being in the form of crosses, the other two resembling the conventionalized Thunderbird. Attached by means of short buckskin thongs are also four complete sets of the tail feathers of an eagle. . . . [T]he inside of the wheel is painted red, while the outer periphery is stained black. These designs are similar to those found on gaming wheels, used by Arapaho and other Plains tribes.[9]

Hoop and pole games thus represented the sacred in traditional Indian games. Indians across North America played versions of the game. Darts found at Mesa Verde, fashioned from corncobs and hardwood, suggest a similar game played by the Anasazi. The game was common among the Cheyenne, the Arapaho, and the Utes, though not among the Kiowa and the Comanche, who at times ranged about southeastern Colorado. According to ethnologist James Mooney in 1896, however, Kiowa men played a game using a three-inch ring and darts. Mooney reported that "warriors or hunters purchase the privi-

1-2. A Cheyenne man playing the hoop and pole game. Source: George Bird Grinnell, *By Cheyenne Campfires.* Courtesy, Yale University Press, copyright 1926, 1962.

lege of throwing a dart at the ring, and derive auguries from success or failure in sending their darts through the circle."[10]

Evidently, hoop and pole was an exclusively male game. Ethnologist Stewart Culin, who published the massive *Games of the North American Indians* in 1907, stated categorically that "the game was always played by males. There is no record of women participating." James Mooney, describing the Arapaho game, also noted that "it is a man's game."[11]

The hoop and pole game itself was simple and involved throwing a projectile—a spear, arrow, or dart—at or through a rolling hoop (fig. 1-2). In the Arapaho game, described by Mooney, "there are three players, one rolling the wheel, while the other two, each armed with a pair of throwing sticks, run after it and throw the sticks so as to cross the wheel in a certain position. The two throwers are the contestants, the one who rolls the wheel being merely an assistant." Scoring was determined by success in piercing the hoop in the desired area or knocking it over so that its markings came to rest on the pole. Mooney also noted that "like most Indian games," hoop and pole was "a means of gambling, and high stakes are sometimes wagered on the result."[12]

The hoop, of course, was the central object of the game and of the game's cultural meanings. Hoops varied from approximately six inches to eighteen inches in diameter and were made from a sapling or branch with the ends bound with sinew or rawhide. The ring might be simple, or have spokes or elaborate rawhide netting. Ute hoops were netted with beaded twine. The hoops were usually painted, and carvings and notches on the circumference represented both scoring positions and symbolic meanings.[13]

The hoop and pole game was associated ritually with creation, fertility, and the buffalo hunt. Equally spaced markings, for example, represented the four quadrants of the earth, or the four winds. In George Dorsey's description of the Arapaho Sun Dance wheel, "the disk itself represents the sun, while the actual band of wood represents a tiny water-snake . . . which is said to be found in rivers, in lakes, near ponds, and in buffalo wallows." The wheel, representing the snake, thus "has a derived meaning, and represents the water which surrounds the earth." Blue beads around the snake's neck symbolized the sky or heavens, and four inside markings represented the Four Old Men who "may also be called the gods of the four world quarters" in whose keeping was "the direction of the winds of the earth." They also represented summer, winter, day, and night. The Four Old Men were considered "ever-present, ever-watching sentinels, always alert to guard the people from harm and injury." Dorsey concluded that "the wheel, as a whole, then, may be said to be symbolic of the creation of the world, for it represents the sun, earth, the sky, the water, and the wind." To the Arapaho, the hoop and pole game, though very much an entertaining game of skill and chance, was more importantly a celebration of creation and the earth.[14]

The hoop and pole game also figured in Arapaho and Cheyenne myths of the origins of the buffalo hunt. In his *Traditions of the Arapaho* (1903), George Dorsey relates the story of Found-in-Grass, in which a youth, Spring-Boy, was carried away by a windstorm. An old woman found him and named him Found-in-Grass. The boy convinced the old woman to make him a bow, arrows, and a netted wheel. One morning he directed his new grandmother to roll the wheel toward him while saying that a fat buffalo calf was coming at him. "Sure enough there came running to him a red cow. This cow he shot with his arrows. The operation was repeated, resulting in his shooting a fat buffalo steer and a big fat bull; in this way a supply of meat was procured."[15]

A Cheyenne tale of Sweet Medicine, the tribe's legendary prophet, lawgiver, and hero, is similar to the Arapaho story. The young Sweet Medicine's village was nearly out of food; game was nowhere to be found, stores of dried fruit and meat had been eaten, and new fruit was not yet ripe. Sweet Medicine asked his grandmother to make a wheel of cherry wood and weave a net of buffalo hide on it. Grandmother rolled the wheel in front of Sweet Medicine and called out, "My grandson, here is a yellow buffalo calf!" Three times Sweet Medicine threw arrows at the wheel and knocked it over. On the fourth throw, however, Sweet Medicine's arrow went through the hole in the center of the net, and the wheel turned into a buffalo calf with an arrow in its side. When the calf fell dead, Sweet Medicine invited the people to take the animal's meat.[16]

The hoop and pole game, then, was more than a mere pastime. It symbolized the life of the Indian community, their spiritual connection to the world, and their physical sustenance in the buffalo hunt. Over the years, that connection has weakened, but has not disappeared completely. The Cheyenne writer John Stands-in-Timber wrote in 1967 that "they still make those hoops and use them for playing a game, though many people have forgotten it. . . . [S]ome of the Cheyenne put it on at the Forsyth County Fair in Montana some years ago, to show the people a real old-time Indian custom."[17]

BALL GAMES

A Ute legend tells of a great chief's deep grief for his dead wife. To console the chief, the spirit Ta-vwoats agreed to take him to the land where his wife had gone. To make a trail for the journey Ta-vwoats "took his magical ball and rolled it before him, and as it rolled it rent the earth and mountains . . . and made a way for them to that beautiful land." There the chief "saw his wife and the blessed abode of the Spirits where all was plenty and all was joy, and he was glad."[18]

As this tale suggests, ball games had important cultural meanings for Indians. Sports historian Joseph B. Oxendine, a Lumbee Indian, notes that "ball games served a sporting, spiritual, economic, and overall cohesive force in traditional life. More than any other activity, these games reflected the positive and holistic character" of Indian life. Most significant was the broad participation and identification of the community with ball games, which were often accompanied by religious ceremonies, feasting, gambling, and decoration of bodies and implements. Ball games served to strengthen kinship and community ties, especially when the contests were between villages and tribes. Games also had an economic function, serving as trading as well as sporting events. Contests were held in conjunction with religious observances, or to celebrate some important event such as a successful hunt.[19]

Lacrosse, or racket, probably was, and is, the best known of the ball games played by Indians in North America. Oxendine notes that it was played throughout Canada and the United States, with the exception of the Southwest. Folklore, he says, "supports the prominence of lacrosse in the lives of Indians" of the Plains. However, Stewart Culin, though agreeing about the wide popularity of lacrosse, cites, in his *Games of the North American Indians,* only one reference to lacrosse artifacts from Colorado, and the literature about the major Colorado tribes does not refer to the game.[20]

Shinny, double-ball, and hand-and-foot ball were the ball games most widely played by Indians in Colorado. They illustrate, among other things, wide community participation and gender division in Indian sports. For Indian women, ball games were part of a sphere of life separate from male culture.

Like lacrosse, shinny was played all over North America, though, according to anthropologist Jerald C. Smith, "it appears to have developed in the western region." Citing Stewart Culin and others, Smith argues that the game appeared among tribes living west of the Rocky Mountains, whom whites later derisively called "diggers." These people used sticks to gather roots, and, says Smith, "it is possible that the shinny stick evolved from the digging stick used by these people's

1-3. Ute shinny stick and buckskin ball. Source: Stewart Culin, *Games of the North American Indians,* vol. 2. Courtesy, University of Nebraska Press, Bison Books.

ancestors" (fig. 1-3). However, Smith also notes the Zuni claim that shinny came north from Mexico. Whatever the game's origins, "shinny is an ancient game to be sure."[21]

Like the hoop and wheel games, shinny was not always played for only its own sake, but was associated with other important activities. "When played among members of the same village or tribe," says Jerald Smith, it might function "as a supplemental activity in the celebration of a successful hunt." Likewise, it might be played when different villages or tribes gathered to trade. Shinny matches were often occasions for betting.[22]

Shinny was predominantly a women's sport, though in various Indian cultures it was also "played by men alone (Assiniboin, Yankton, Mohave, Walapai), by men and women alone (Sauk and Foxes, Tewa, Tigua), by men and women together (Sauk and Foxes, Assiniboin), by men against women (Crows)." Among the Utes, both men and women played, but never together.[23]

Shinny closely resembled the modern game of field hockey. Players formed two teams of ten to twenty-five members each and met on a level field, usually 200 to 250 yards in length and about 250 feet wide. Goals, usually stakes or mounds of dirt, were set at each end of the field. The players used sticks, curved at the end and measuring from two to four feet in length, to try to knock a small, two- to four-inch, buckskin ball through the goals (fig. 1-4). Play began with a face-off between two players who tried to get control of the ball and hit it to a teammate. Players could not touch the ball with their hands, but could kick it. Shinny games were rough-and-tumble affairs. Blocking and tripping an opponent, as well as grabbing her stick, was fair play, though contestants could not grab each other. In the Ute game, when one team scored a goal they switched ends of the field. If the

1-4. Ute women playing shinny. The game primarily was a women's sport.
Courtesy, Colorado Historical Society, F 1614.

same team scored the next goal, the game ended. If the other team
scored next, however, they continued to play until one or the other
scored back-to-back goals. Matches thus could last all afternoon or
even all day.[24]

Double-ball, an aerial version of shinny, was even more exclusively a women's sport. Only in northern California did men play the
game. Like shinny, it was an ancient game. Yoke-shaped wooden artifacts found at Mesa Verde, and at Chaco Canyon in New Mexico, are
similar to curved throwing sticks used in the game. Double-ball probably served the same social and economic functions associated with
shinny, though Stewart Culin claimed that the game apparently had
no ceremonial meaning. However, some Indian myths feature women
who use magical double-balls to travel and to escape danger. Culin
himself relates Wichita, Oklahoma, tales of the game's origin and importance to women. Bright-Shining-Woman (the Moon) "gave it to
women among the things they should use to enjoy themselves. She
showed them how to play the game, and told them that the ball was
for their use in traveling." In the stories of "Seven Brothers and the

1-5. Cheyenne double-balls. Ball games often functioned as a sphere of life for Indian women separate from men. Some games represented escape myths in which women fled from unwanted male attention. Source: Stewart Culin, *Games of the North American Indians,* vol. 2. Courtesy, University of Nebraska Press, Bison Books.

Woman" and "Child-of-a-Dog," women use the double-ball to elude pursuers.[25]

Double-balls were made of buckskin and consisted either of two balls joined by a thong several inches long or of a single piece of leather with bulbous pouches at the ends and a narrow middle (fig. 1-5). The balls were stuffed with hair, sand, or perhaps grass. Culin described a Cheyenne double-ball as "two buckskin-covered balls, 3 inches in diameter, somewhat flattened," painted with red and yellow bands, and joined by a 5-inch thong. Players used curved throwing sticks (sometimes notched for beginners) to catch and throw the double-ball toward goals set at each end of a field 300–400 yards in length. The whole village often turned out to watch these vigorous games and to wager on their outcome. In some Indian cultures the games provided young women and men an opportunity to admire and flirt with one another.[26]

Indian women were also fond of hand-and-foot ball games, which resembled the modern game of hackey-sack, popular on college campuses and street corners, and the child's game of paddleball. In the Cheyenne foot game, two teams of nine or ten women formed a circle, alternating team members all the way around. Up to three hundred slender counting sticks were placed in the center of the circle, often in the care of two other women. The object of the game was for each woman in turn to try to keep a large ball in the air by repeatedly kicking it upward. Typically, balls were about eight inches in diameter and were made of deer or antelope hide stuffed with buffalo hair. Sometimes the ball had a long thong attached that the kicker could hold. When a player faltered, she passed the ball to the woman next to her, a member of the other team. Each player, or the neutral women, kept track of her kicks, and, after her turn, she went to the pile of sticks and took the proper number. When all the sticks in the center of the circle were gone, players began to take them from their opponents' piles until, at last, one team had won all of the sticks. The Arapaho played a similar game, but the thonged ball was struck only with the hand.[27]

Like shinny and double-ball, hand-and-foot ball had significance beyond the game itself in the lives of Indian women, a part of life they could enjoy separate from men. Cheyenne historian George Bird Grinnell has noted that the contests were occasions for gambling among the women, and they wagered personal possessions such as bracelets, beads, and earrings. Sometimes, too, "they had a regular feast before the game began."[28]

In mythology, women gained special powers from the hand-and-foot ball. The Arapaho tale of "Foot-Stuck-Child" is an escape story similar to those associated with double-ball. In it a young girl escapes from her husband, from a buffalo, and from a rock that wanted to marry her by using her magic powers and a ball that she kicks hand-and-foot style. "She first threw the ball, and as it came down kicked it upward, and her fathers, in turn, rose up. Then she threw and kicked it for herself. She and her fathers reached the sky in one place. They live in a tent covered with stars."[29]

RUNNING

Running is, perhaps, the essential athletic activity. The most popular modern sports—football, baseball, basketball, tennis, jogging, marathon running, and even bicycling, which adapts the running motion to machinery—are based on it. Traditional Indian sports—lacrosse, shinny, and double-ball—were also based on running. However, in Indian cultures, running, like the other sports, reflected the life of the community. Running was vital to traditional Indian life, especially before the coming of horses, for a variety of reasons apart from sport. As historian Joseph Oxendine has noted, "a multitude of social concerns demanded that Indians travel great distances on foot under considerable time pressure." Hunting, warfare, trade, and communication needs all made running, and runners, important, so Indians viewed races as very important events. As with other sports, foot races often were part of religious events.[30]

Because of his importance to the community, an especially fast and durable runner earned considerable prestige among his people. In some cultures runners even formed guildlike societies within the tribe. However, as anthropologist Peter Nabokov notes, runners "were more than functionary athletes. They were communicators of culture; their units were absorbed into social and religious life. They were highly regarded as safekeepers of accurate information. Their status was high for they helped to keep their worlds intact and in touch." According to Nabokov, "[T]hey also ran to enact their myths and to create a bridge between themselves and the forces of the universe."[31]

Running figured importantly in Indian folklore. In one motif, the spirits settle disputes among themselves by racing, and the outcomes shape the world and man's place in it. One Cheyenne myth, for example, explains humanity's dominance of animals. A great relay race pitted man and his helpers (dog, eagle, and hawk) against the cloven-footed animals (deer, elk, and buffalo). In the final lap, hawk sped to victory. The losers were forever after man's prey in the hunt. Another Cheyenne fable concerns the origin of the buffalo hunt. In old times, "buffalo ate human beings and were very powerful. It was a great risk to go against them." One day a buffalo bull carried off Sister, and her youngest brother went to rescue her. When he found the herd, the buffalo tried to trick him so that his life would be forfeited, but he saw through their traps. Finally, the buffalo challenged the youth to a race, promising to go back with him if he won. If he lost, "people would always be eaten by buffalo and other animals." As he prepared for the race, Thunder Spirit blessed him and gave him a spear decorated with magpie feathers to help him, "because, while Magpie is slow, he is long-winded." When the race began, the youth fell behind, but, using his wits and the medicine given him by Thunder Spirit, he eventually triumphed. "Because of his winning, people now can eat and use all game, but the buffalo can no longer eat people."[32]

Other tales, including trickster fables, aimed to educate and to transmit values. A Cheyenne tale tells of Old Man tricking baby rabbits into his cook pot. As Old Man is about to eat his ill-gotten dinner, Coyote, who appears to be crippled, challenges him to a race with the meal as the prize. Old Man accepts, thinking Coyote too disabled to beat him. Of course, Coyote only feigned his weakness, and by the time Old Man crossed the finish line, the cunning challenger was finishing the last of the rabbit stew. Coyote's tricking Old Man out of dinner was no more unfair than Old Man's tricking the rabbits into the pot.[33]

The tale of Old Man, Coyote, and the rabbit dinner is a lesson in fair play. Indians were hardly unique in using sport to teach that and other values. Contemporary society also tries to associate and transmit important cultural values via athletic activity. However, sport was embedded in, or reflected, the fabric and life of Indian cultures in ways, and in depth and breadth, unmatched in modern times. Sport explained and celebrated creation and mankind's place in it, and thus was a reflection of the mystical core of American Indian life. Broad participation by members of the tribe, as players, spectators, and bettors, mirrored and enhanced the unity of the community and the shared identity of its members. Sports also played a role in defining gender roles and identity in Indian society as women enjoyed their own separate sphere with distinct games, customs, and rituals.

Gambling, a pervasive feature of Indian culture throughout North America, has persisted and flourished, though its connection to other cultural activities may be less intimate. In fact, gambling has become an important industry to many contemporary tribes. By the 1990s Indians operated more than 150 casinos nationwide and earned more than $700 million. In Colorado, both the Ute Mountain and the Southern Ute reservations sported profitable casinos.[34]

The contrasts between traditional and modern sport cut across many lines in society. Modern sport is rapidly losing the role of gender divider as women, as both players and spectators, move into sports domains previously dominated by men. Indian sports events often took place in connection with some other economic activity, whether a trade meeting between groups or a hunt celebration. Modern sport itself is big business. Sport and competition in American Indian cultures was often associated with religion. Although modern fans often display fervid, almost idolatrous, devotion to teams and players, sport is not itself part of religious life. Some complain, in fact, that sport dilutes religion's role and influence in society.

In a sense, though, the sort of devotion to sport and team shown by the modern Colorado Rockies and Denver Broncos fan does link her to one of the key traditional roles of Indian sport, for in her allegiance to a favorite team she creates part of her personal identity and her place in a community.

The arrival and settlement of whites in Colorado in the nineteenth century displaced Indians and altered their culture. Where the Cheyenne, the Arapaho, and the Utes once hunted buffalo, raced horses, ran, and played ball and hoop and pole games, white settlers came to raise wheat and cattle, and to mine gold and silver. They brought their own sporting culture with them.

2

ANYTHING TO RELIEVE THE MONOTONY
SPORTS IN THE COLORADO MINING TOWNS

Late in November 1880, as winter tightened its grip in the Colorado Rockies, a writer for the Central City *Daily Register* pleaded, "Can't we have a temperance lecture . . . ? Anything to relieve the monotony of the times." A few days later, another dispatch from Central City complained of "a dearth of amusements here this winter," and noted that, with the opera house idle and no social clubs, "were it not for the skating rink and good ice the people would die of ennui." These cries for amusement suggest that Central City residents lacked recreational outlets. However, it was a false suggestion because, in fact, mining-town residents in the nineteenth and early twentieth centuries enjoyed a diverse and complex sport and recreational life. The story of sports and recreation in the Colorado mining towns reflects both the traditional and the modern in sports and the large gray area in between, just as the early mining town itself represented a kind of gray area, an urban-industrial presence in a frontier setting. Some activities, such as rock-drilling contests, fire-cart races, and skiing, grew out of important dimensions of life and work in the mining communities, and so reflect the traditional, or premodern, in sports— what might be termed "life and work as play." Nevertheless, because they evolved from the life of the community, which was fundamentally urban and industrial, they soon displayed features of the modern in organization and rules. Other mining-town sports more directly anticipated modern major professional and recreational sports popular at the end of the twentieth century. Baseball and bicycling, horse racing and hockey, gymnastics, boxing, and many more were available, at least in the larger towns, to consume spare time and money.[1]

Beginning with the first gold rush in 1859, succeeding mining booms lured a steadily growing population to Colorado. They came from eastern states, Europe, and eventually Mexico and Asia in search of quick wealth. By mid-1859 some 4,000 to 5,000 men lived and worked in the Gregory Gulch area, where the towns of Mountain City, Central City, and Black Hawk sprang up virtually overnight, and new arrivals came at a rate as high as 500 a day. Population in the territory topped 34,277 in 1860, but the first boom soon faltered, in part because of the Civil War, and population slipped to less than 28,000 in 1866. The great silver booms of the 1870s and 1880s caused a sustained rush to the Rockies. During the seventies, population grew from about 40,000 to more than 194,000, and more than doubled again by 1890 when the census found more than 413,000 persons in Colorado. By 1910 the state's population was almost 800,000.[2]

Mining-town populations tended to be young and predominantly male, especially in the early years of growth. The median age in Central City in 1860, for example, was twenty-seven. Over succeeding decades, the population tended to age, but remained fairly young, with median ages in the 1870s and 1880s between thirty and thirty-nine. As mining-town populations grew and matured, the number of women also increased, making them more important and visible in social and economic life. Indeed, women are usually credited with bringing more civility to the camps. In addition to working in their homes, women also worked in and owned stores, restaurants, boardinghouses, newspapers, saloons, and brothels.[3]

The concentration of most of Colorado's population in the major front-range cities of Denver, Colorado Springs, and Pueblo and in scores of mining camps and towns in the mountain districts made the state, to use historian Duane Smith's term, an "urban frontier." Mining became, and until the early twentieth century remained, the core of Colorado's economy and society. Once the short-lived era of placer mining gave way to large-scale underground operations, Colorado became an integral part of America's industrial capitalist economy. Mining towns soon replicated industrial society's social class structure, with owners and managers, a professional and merchant middle class, and a large working class, as well as the inevitable urban-industrial underclass subculture linked to vice and crime.[4]

Saloons and brothels did a lucrative trade and became the basis for the stereotype of the rip-roaring nineteenth-century mining camp. Indeed, their association with vice gave the words *sport* and *sporting* meanings entirely different from those used today. Drunkenness, gambling, prostitution, and brawling became, in legend, the most widely pursued recreational activities in the camps. It was said of Creede, "It's day all day in the daytime, there is no night in Creede." In Leadville, where the population had soared from essentially zero in 1877 to about 15,000 in 1880, 249 saloons—about one for every sixty residents—supplied liquid refreshment for tired, thirsty miners.[5]

The reality of life and work in the Colorado mining towns was richer and more complex than the stereotype. So, too, were sport and recreation. Some mining-town sports derived from the miner's work and his pride in the skills of his trade. Others grew out of the exigencies of life and community in the camps. Rock-drilling contests and fire-cart races, especially, exemplified these traditional sources— albeit with elements of the modern—in mining-town sports.

ROCK DRILLING

Drilling was the most important of the hard-rock miner's skills and the one in which he took the greatest pride. In order to bring ore out of the depths of the earth, it had to be blasted free. Before pneumatic or steam-powered drills displaced them, skilled miners used hammers and handheld drills to bore holes deep into solid rock for the explosive charges that brought down the ore. Rock drilling required strength, stamina, skill, and not a little courage. A shaky hand on a drill or a mistimed swing of the hammer could mean a bloodied or broken hand or arm. Miners took great pride in their ability to drill holes fast, straight, and deep. There were two styles of drilling: single-jacking and double-jacking. In single-jacking, the miner worked alone, holding and rotating his drill with one hand while swinging a four-pound hammer with the other. Single-jacking was usually used

2-1. Rock-drilling contest, Eldora, Colorado. These contests adapted the miners' work and skills to competitive play. Courtesy, the Denver Public Library, Western History Department.

in narrow confines and for overhead drilling. In double-jacking, two men worked together, one swinging an eight-pound hammer and the other holding the drill. Double-jackers traded positions periodically to conserve their strength. Cornish miners, who were among the earliest skilled miners to work in Colorado, much preferred double-jacking because single-jacking went against the ancient traditions of their trade and because it made for more jobs. So strong was their attachment to double-jacking that when mine managers at Grass Valley, Nevada, attempted to economize by requiring single-jacking, the town's Cornish miners went on strike.[6]

With so much pride and identity vested in their trade's most important skill, miners naturally competed among themselves to prove which man or team was best (fig. 2-1). At first, miners staged contests at individual mines, but soon began to challenge men from neighboring works. Before long, camps and towns organized matches pitting local champions. Fourth of July celebrations were often the settings for local contests, while countywide meets took place later in the summer. Contests between rival towns prompted great interest and partisanship, indicating that the driller's skill was more than a source of personal pride, but of community pride and identity as well. An announcement for a rock-drilling contest in Leadville in 1889 illustrates the place of the miner's sport as a source of community and trade pride:

> These annual friendly contests of brawn and muscle should have a place at the head of the list of athletic sports, since they are grander and more heroic than any in which Americans are wont to engage. They are a nearer approach to the games of the Olympian period, and have a much more useful and worthy purpose, the training of men in an honorable calling and the strengthening of their ambition to excel in it. . . . [R]ock drilling should become our foremost local pastime, and encouraged to the fullest limit. . . . It may indeed be a matter for some surprise that it has not taken a deeper hold upon our people, since this is the greatest mining camp in the world, and since mining is our chief pursuit. It is a little difficult for us to conceive of a more inspiring spectacle.[7]

Heavy betting always heightened interest in rock-drilling matches, and feelings could run high among partisans who backed their favorites "with every dollar that they could lay their hands on." In the late 1880s a match between drillers from Idaho Springs and Central City nearly resulted in a riot, and "it took firm tact and a forceful move on the part of the police to avert trouble." Mining towns sometimes went to great lengths to field the best drillers. One year in the 1880s, Cripple Creek challenged Idaho Springs to a particularly grueling double-jacking contest in which the hammer man was to swing his hammer for the entire ten-minute match. Unfortunately, Idaho Springs' champion team of Rory McGillivray and Tom Sullivan were working out of state when the challenge arrived. Town leaders, however, tracked them down, brought them home, and put them to work in the Shafter Mine just barely more than a month before the contest (the accepted rules of the day required contestants to be employed in the community for at least one month). The Idaho Springs champs won the match against Cripple Creek and thus rewarded their town's pride and investment in them.[8]

To determine the state's best drillers, county champions met in Denver, at the Festival of Mountain and Plain, Colorado's annual celebration of its economic achievements and culture. These state contests, recalled *Boulder County Miner and Farmer* editor Victor I. Noxon, "really put rock-drilling on a clean business-like basis" by subjecting the contests to universally accepted and carefully enforced rules. Double-jack teams used eight-pound hammers and single-jacks a four-pounder. Both used a seven-eighths-inch drill to drive holes into carefully selected specimens of Gunnison granite. Contestants had fifteen minutes to drill as deeply as possible into the stone. The festival in 1899 offered first-place prizes of $750 for double-jacking teams and $250 for single-jacks, along with trophies described as "beautiful works of art."[9]

Drillers trained for weeks before the state contest and arrived in Denver leading contingents of loyal hometown supporters. "Every partisan was for his own. Citizens of Leadville, of Creede, of Victor, of Ouray and elsewhere declared vociferously that his town was the best on earth and offered to wager money that the representatives from the chosen locality would win." Fans cheered their heroes with cries of "Come down on it, old man!" and "You're good for twenty!" One man's supporters promised that if, in pursuing victory, he "killed himself right there," they would ship his body home for burial.[10]

Rock-drilling contests were a mainstay of the Festival of Mountain and Plain for years, long after power drills replaced hand drilling in all but the smallest of mines. Mechanization of the miner's trade had important consequences. Although it made mining more productive and profitable, it ended the individual miner's control over his work and his pride in his trade. It also ruined his health. Rapidly spinning mechanical drills generated clouds of silica dust that the men could not help but inhale. As the dust invaded their lungs, miners often sickened and died of silicosis, or miners' consumption.

Today, students at the Colorado School of Mines, and the occasional odd history professor, give demonstrations of hand drilling. However, these displays are only reminiscences of a skill, and a sport, once vital to a great Colorado industry, to the tradesmen who practiced it, and to the identity and pride of their communities.

FIRE-CART RACING

Fire-cart racing, like rock drilling, was born of a function vital to the life of the community. Perhaps even more than the collapse of gold or silver prices, mining-town residents feared fire. The towns, especially in their early years, were ramshackle collections of wooden buildings. Exposure to alpine sun and wind quickly dried the lumber, making it tinder. Inevitably, some accident, an upset stove or lantern, would start a blaze that spread quickly to adjoining structures, sweeping away entire blocks of stores, saloons, and homes. One such fire, the April 25–26, 1896, blaze that leveled the heart of Cripple Creek, left some five thousand persons temporarily homeless.[11]

As towns and their governments matured, often after hard experience, they installed networks of water lines and hydrants to give firefighters a better chance of containing and dousing flames before they could spread. Few, if any, towns were willing, however, to maintain permanent, full-time fire departments. Instead, the responsibility for fire fighting fell to teams of volunteers who were usually organized and sponsored by merchants who helped with the costs of uniforms, carts, hoses, and ladders. Larger towns such as Leadville, Cripple Creek, Central City, and Georgetown could boast several volunteer squads. Fire-company members came from all walks of life. In the mid-1870s, for example, Georgetown's Hook and Ladder Company Number One included a livery man, a miner, a doctor, a boot maker, a merchant, a dentist, and a grocer.[12]

In addition to their fire-fighting responsibilities, the volunteer fire departments also functioned as social clubs. Monthly meetings not only were for conducting business but also were often followed by dinners and dances. At training sessions the men honed their fire-

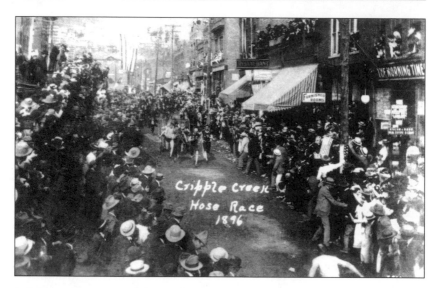

2-2. Fire-cart race, Cripple Creek, 1896. Teams often represented a cross-section of mining-town communities and were important social groups. The races made an important civic function into a competitive sport. Courtesy, Colorado Historical Society, F 27830.

fighting skills and enjoyed a camaraderie born of a shared interest and commitment.

Mining-town firemen were justifiably proud of their service to their communities and of their ability to dash to fire scenes. Friendly, and sometimes not so friendly, rivalries developed among the squads, and they began to challenge one another to see which teams were fastest and most skillful (fig. 2-2). Races often took place on holidays and usually drew enthusiastic audiences. As Aspen historian Malcolm Rohrbough has noted, "[S]pirited competitions between fire companies became a high-light of holiday celebrations, and the social affairs that accompanied them were among the camp's best known and most popular." Contests usually "took place on the main streets of the town . . . and featured liberal distribution of water to contestants and spectators alike."[13]

By 1875 Colorado's fire companies organized a state firemen's association and in that year began to stage annual tournaments with stringent rules governing entries and the conduct of races. Dressed in running outfits consisting of loose trunks over long underwear, teams competed in two types of races. In the first, teams ran a straight or circuitous course of seventy-five to two hundred yards. In the second, the racers sped along a course to a hydrant to which they connected their hoses. The team that ran the fastest course or showed water in the shortest time won. Prizes included trophies, flags, and cash put up by teams, sponsors, and townsmen. Of course, side bets between team members and spectators added to the interest. Fire-cart races were great fun for participants and spectators alike, but they were not without their hazards. A stumble by one man could easily mean lost time, or worse, for the whole team. In the 1877 state tournament at Georgetown, for example, firemen N. T. McClure and James C. O'Connor were injured when McClure stumbled and O'Connor fell over him. Both men were then struck by a third team member. O'Connor's face was severely lacerated, and it was feared that he would lose an eye. Nevertheless, throughout the ordeal, O'Connor was "pluck to the bone, and never uttered a groan, though he must have suffered greatly."[14]

Fire-cart racing and rock-drilling contests were products of the life and work of the mining community and thus reflect the traditional in sports. Rock-drilling contests were born of the hard-rock miner's skills and his pride in them. Fire-cart races grew out of the mining towns' need to protect life and property. Once drillers and firemen began to use their skills competitively, elements of modern sports could be seen in their contests. Organized competition, universally accepted rules, and, especially, intense competition in which the identity and pride not only of the competitors but also of their entire communities were at stake are links tying these traditional sports to the modern. A similar heritage, and change, is found in the origins of one of Colorado's most important recreational sports, skiing.

SKIING

The earliest recorded use of skis, or of devices approximating skis, in Colorado was in 1857 when guide Jim Baker became separated from the Randolph B. Marcy expedition that journeyed from Camp Scott, in present-day southwest Wyoming, across the Colorado Rockies to Fort Massachusetts (later moved and renamed Fort Garland) in the San Luis Valley. In order to move more quickly through the high-country snow and find his party as soon as possible, Baker fashioned a pair of Norwegian-style snowshoes. Baker's experience shows that at least the rudiments of skiing were known in the West by the late 1850s. This method of wintertime mobility appeared first in California and was probably introduced by Norwegians who had joined the gold rush to the Sierra Nevada. The *Marysville Herald* noted in January 1853 that "the miners do all their locomotion on snow shoes." The forty-niners may have introduced snowshoes, as skis were called until about 1900, to trappers and explorers ranging between the Rockies and the Sierra Nevada. Almost certainly, veterans of the California gold rush brought the knowledge of skiing with them when they joined the stampede to Colorado beginning in 1859.[15]

The *Marysville Herald's* description of skiing as a method of locomotion is apt, and in Colorado, as in California, its use was born of necessity, not play. In the winter, when snow and drifts could bury cabins and trees and even stop locomotives on their tracks, skiing often became the best, sometimes the only, way for mining-town residents, and those who lived in remote camps and isolated cabins, to get around. Skiing became the mountain population's wintertime link to each other and to the rest of the world. George Cornwall, a veteran of winters at Irwin, a camp located several miles west of Crested Butte in the Gunnison country's Elk Mountains, recalled that "all travel, except from cabin to cabin right in Camp [sic] was necessarily on snow shoes." Cornwall "thought nothing of skiing twenty miles to Teachouts [sic] ranch . . . for a couple of square meals with fresh meat and potatoes and Mrs. Teachout's biscuit and syrup." As late as 1887, Crested Butte's E. R. Warren reported that "many of the smaller mining camps would be completely isolated from the outside world in winter, were it not for show-shoes."[16]

Nineteenth-century Norwegian snowshoes resembled modern skis only in the most generic sense: they were long and narrow. Hand hewn, mostly from spruce, they were usually approximately four inches wide (though some were as wide as six inches) and from eight to fourteen feet in length, depending on the height and preference of the owner and the condition of the snow. The midsection of the ski, where the foot was bound to it, was about one and one-half inches thick. From the midsection to the ends the ski tapered to about one-half inch in thickness and near the tip to about three-eighths of an inch. To prevent the ski from plowing too deeply into the snow, the tips were curved upward to a point "from 4 to 6 inches above the level of the shoe," which was accomplished by boiling the tips until they were soft enough to bend around a log. One expert advised that "a log of too small diameter should not be chosen; one less than eighteen inches should not be taken." The shape of the tip was a matter of personal taste, "some being beveled and others being quite flat." Leather bindings attached to the snowshoe just forward of center held the skier's foot to the board. The most common types were a toe cup made of a single piece of leather, or "two pieces of leather . . . cut of a width to suit the wearer; about four inches is usual and high enough so that when fastened to the sides of the shoe and laced together, to hold the foot tightly." A heel block that was screwed on across the top of the ski also helped to hold the foot in place. Finally, the bottoms of the skis were sanded smooth and beeswax applied "either with a hot iron or by rubbing on cold, to prevent the snow from sticking to it."[17]

The great length of nineteenth-century skis—up to fourteen feet—was a matter of function. Because skiers used them to travel across country, they had to support the person's weight and all that he carried. Although such long boards might support a heavily laden traveler on the snow, they made maneuvering difficult at best. Early-day skiers used a single long pole, usually seven to nine feet long, to help maintain their balance, as a brake, and, to the extent possible, help them steer. Dragged to one side or placed between the legs, the pole could be used like a rudder to help the skier gradually change directions. Most skiers tried to avoid making quick turns, preferring what *Crested Butte Chronicle* editor George Sibley has called the Early American Ski Technique: "the idea was to stand up straight and go straight." If turning was unavoidable and, indeed, became urgent in the face of oncoming trees, rocks, or precipices, skiers could also resort to "hunkering," which Sibley described as "the art of impressing on the skis the need to turn faster." Cross-country travel in the mountains, even in a straight line, could not avoid uphill climbs. Unfortunately, well-waxed skis always wanted to go downhill. A length of rope, a piece of burlap, or some elk or other animal hide tacked or

2-3. A skiing mail carrier high in the Colorado
Rockies. Skiing took root first as a vital means of
communication and transportation between mining towns and even more remote outlying camps.
Courtesy, Colorado Historical Society, F 7467.

tied to the skis with the grain running to the rear proved an effective
brake on unwanted backward, downhill motion.[18]

Once outfitted, would-be skiers were ready to learn the art of
staying upright and moving forward on their long boards. Crested
Butte's Harry C. Cornwall recalled that they "at first were all clumsy
and falls were numerous but it was not long before we became fairly
skillful and could travel without much trouble."[19]

High in the Elk Mountains of southwestern Colorado, the town
of Crested Butte was a regional metropolis serving outlying camps
such as Gothic, Crystal, and Irwin. When residents of these remote
camps wanted to come to the big town, recalled newspaper editor
John Phillips, "they had to come on skis . . . and it was not an uncom-

mon sight to see fifty or more pairs" stacked outside M. J. Gray's store, where miners and their wives came to shop. Skiing, as a basic mode of wintertime transportation, was vital to trade and communication, as well as human contact in the Colorado mining districts. Mail carriers, clergymen, doctors, and professional packers routinely braved deep snow, cold temperatures, blizzards, avalanches, and dangerous terrain to provide vital services to the most remote camps.[20]

"The most welcome of all in the mining camps far up the Rocky Mountain peaks," noted the *Colorado Graphic* in 1891, "are the mail carriers. Brave, hardy fellows they are that climb the peaks on snowshoes, delivering the mail and many precious packages." According to skiing historian Jack A. Benson, mining-camp residents in the nineteenth century depended on some fifty skiing mailmen for contact with the outside world (fig. 2-3). Men such as Albert A. "Al" Johnson, who carried mail between Crested Butte and Crystal in the 1880s, braved all the hazards of winter in the Rockies to complete their rounds. Johnson, who became known as the "top snowshoer in the Rocky Mountains," regularly challenged and survived the "Snowshoe Express" through treacherous Crystal Canyon. Peter Scott, who came from Maine to Silverton in 1877, "carried the first mail from Silverton to San Miguel via Ophir." Swedish immigrant Swan Nilson had the same route in 1883. On Christmas Eve that year, despite a raging snowstorm, Nilson set out on his route that was to take him first to Ophir, some eighteen miles from Silverton. He never arrived. Search parties turned up nothing, and some people began to think that Nilson had simply absconded with his gift-laden mail sack. In the summer of 1885, Nilson's brother, who had come to Colorado not knowing of his brother's disappearance, pressed the search and in August finally found Swan's body, "perfectly preserved in the snow, his mail sack on his shoulders." Inside the bag was a letter to Swan Nilson from his wife in Sweden. In spite of the hazards that Nilson and other mail carriers faced, pay for the skiing mailmen was low. The annual contract for the route between Georgetown and Hot Sulphur Springs, a ninety-six-mile round-trip over 11,315-foot Berthoud Pass, paid only $1,680. Indeed, complained the *Colorado Sun* in 1892, "there is no class of laborers so poorly paid as . . . the mountain mail carriers." Nevertheless, unemployed miners often welcomed the low wages and the hazards of winter delivery when regular contractors preferred the comforts of home.[21]

John L. Dyer's South Park mail route in 1864 included the towns of Fairplay, Alma, Buckskin Joe, Oro, and Granite. Dyer, who called himself the "Snow-Shoe Itinerant," completed his trek in a week. Mail service, however, was a sideline for Dyer, a Methodist minister who preached and conducted weddings and funerals. On one outing in 1865 Dyer found himself caught in a winter storm as he tried to cross Mosquito Ridge between Alma and Fairplay. He waited out the storm's first blast and then, as snow continued to blow all around, tried to find his way back home. Essentially blind in the storm, Dyer suddenly felt himself slipping over the edge of a ridge. As he fell, he held a ski under each arm and placed his life and soul in the Almighty's hand. Fresh snow softened his fall, and after a long, uncontrolled slide Dyer came to rest only about a mile from his cabin door. The Reverend Mr. Dyer's colleagues, Father James Gibbons and George M. Darley, ministered to Catholics and Presbyterians in San Juan mountain towns, including Telluride and Ouray.[22]

Skis enabled physicians and midwives to tend to the sick, injured, and pregnant through the winter months. In Crested Butte and Gunnison County, Doctors J. R. Rockefeller and Charles Fox Gardiner skied to their patients in the 1880s. Dr. Gardiner recalled, "I had never seen or heard of skis in the East at that time, and I took to the sport because I liked it, and because it was absolutely necessary for me to learn if I had to go on a call to some other camp." In northwestern Colorado, Steamboat Springs men donned their skis and harnessed themselves to a sleigh to pull the region's midwife, Mrs. Settle, to tend to women in childbirth.[23]

Snow blindness and sunburn were among the medical hazards that skiers and others faced outdoors during high-country winters. Dr. Gardiner recalled his first case of snow blindness was that of "a powerful, sand-haired young Swede, who was led along on snowshoes and supported by two companions. I thought he had been powder burnt, but when I tried to lift his eyelids apart to see his eyes, he gave a scream as the light caught his eyes, flung himself on the ground, and acted like a man in convulsions." There was little the doctor could do for the young man. "I had him put in a dark room.

There was no cocaine in those days—only a solution of sulphate of zinc to put in the eyes—but he recovered." Modern sunglasses, which can filter out harmful ultraviolet light, were unheard of in the 1880s. Only rudimentary smoked spectacles offered some relief from the intense glare of sunlight on snow.

Sunburn could be another painful consequence of a day's skiing. To prevent blistered noses and lips, Dr. Gardiner's Crested Butte neighbor, Harry Cornwall, recalled that "we finally painted our faces with gunpowder and water before a day in the sun." Presumably, skiers thus anointed stayed clear of warming fires and other sources of ignition. The only sure method of avoiding sunburn and snow blindness was to ski at night. In the spring, especially, skiing itinerants preferred to travel at night when the snow tended to crust over, holding their weight better and easing movement of the skis. "This made ideal skiing and we could reel off five miles an hour with very little exertion," said Harry Cornwall. Of course, as the Reverend Mr. Dyer had learned, night skiing had its own special hazards.[24]

As Dr. Gardiner practiced his skiing technique in the winter of 1882, he also noted the growing tendency of his neighbors to put life and limb at risk on the long boards just for the fun of it. "About half the people in town would shut up shop early in the afternoon and take their skis" to a mountain "just back of town," which he described as "a slope one thousand feet high at an angle of forty-five degrees." As a novice that winter, Gardiner was envious of youngsters on the mountain who "would give a yell, plunge down the long slide with the utmost ease and skill, managing their little skis like veterans." The doctor also recalled his own first flight down the mountain. As he stood at the top, the mountain was "so steep that it seemed as if you were looking straight down a precipice into space. . . . It was a fearful moment when, taking my courage in both hands, I slipped over this edge and went flying down so rapidly it took my breath away. . . . The valley seemed to rush up to meet me, and it was no time at all before I was gliding over a level field, safe and very proud of myself."[25]

Mining-town women adapted to skiing as readily as men. Like the men, women used their skis for transportation to town, to work, or to a neighbor's cabin, and they enjoyed a trek across country or a dash down a hill (fig. 2-4). The sight of women on skis was certainly

2-4. Mining-town women took to skis as readily as the men for transportation and for play. Courtesy, Colorado Historical Society, F 8277.

not unusual, but nevertheless could be an occasion for mocking condescension. For example, in an article on wintertime sports in the mountain towns, the *Rocky Mountain News* in 1891 reported that "even the girls would go to the top of a hill . . . and assay to run down and jump the 25 foot road at the bottom." However, the article went on to note that "as a rule, a vision of petticoats and upheaving snow was the end of the female efforts" and that the women "would be rescued amid some difficulty and shrieks of laughter." At about the same time reporter Nellie Bly, of Joseph Pulitzer's *New York World*, visited Irwin and tried her hand at skiing. One day, as she practiced on the town's main street, Bly took a spectacular tumble in front of local newspaperman John Phillips. Phillips made no effort to conceal his amusement at the sight and burst out laughing, to which the angry and embarrassed Bly said, "Sir, I have seen enough of you to know that you are no gentlemen." The still much amused Phillips replied,

2-5. Snowshoe racing at Irwin, in Gunnison County, 1883. Mining-town skiers readily adapted a necessary skill to play, and racing made the activity even more enjoyable and challenging. Courtesy, the Denver Public Library, Western History Department.

"Madam, I too have seen enough of you to know that you are no gentleman."[26]

Necessity and fun put mining-camp women on skis, but even in remote camps such as Irwin the most skillful female skier could not completely outrun the conventions of Victorian-era morality. It was unladylike and unseemly for women to compete with one another, and certainly with men, so even in the setting of ski clubs, women's participation was strictly informal and recreational. When the first organized ski races took place in the 1880s women were excluded.

The first Rocky Mountain Snowshoe Championship took place at Irwin in February 1881. On a quarter-mile course laid out on Main Street, twenty contestants competed for a twenty-five-dollar purse. Most of the "racers" fell almost immediately after the start, while "others seemed to take a delight in parting with their shoes when they went over a knoll, turning a somersault in the air and diving into the snow, leaving their feet sticking up as the only visible portion of their body." The street was soon pitted with holes, and finally, according to ski historian Jack A. Benson, the "local judge awarded first-place money to the skier who had fallen the least number of times and, therefore, had done his best to preserve the quality of Irwin's main thorough-fare." In spite of this precarious beginning, organized ski racing became a regular feature of winter life, especially in the Gunnison country (fig. 2-5). Crested Butte, Crystal, Gothic, Tin Cup, and other camps staged their own championships in succeeding years. At Snowmass City in 1882 and 1884, daring, and most likely inebriated, skiers even held cabin-jumping contests.[27]

In February 1886 skiers and civic leaders at Crested Butte set out to stage the grandest ski race yet seen in the Gunnison country. They raised thirty-seven dollars in prize money—twenty dollars for first place—and also purchased medals to bestow on the winners. On race day, February 22, it was estimated that one thousand spectators from all around the region filled the town. Many skied in, but others

2-6. Skiing became an important social activity in the mining towns by the mid-1880s. Colorado's first ski club, the Gunnison County Norwegian Snow-Shoe Club, was formed in 1886. Courtesy, Colorado Historical Society, F 13742.

arrived on a special train chartered for the event. Sixteen contestants from Crested Butte, Irwin, Crystal, Gunnison, Scofield, and Gothic entered the race, including mail carrier Al Johnson and George and Harry Cornwall. The 525-yard course began with a daunting stretch down a thirty-five-degree hill, gradually eased, and ended with a 250-foot flat run to the finish line. The contestants drew lots to form groups of four, and each group ran heats until one man had finished first twice. The final race pitted sixteen-year-old Charles Baney of Crested Butte, Al Johnson and Al Fish of Crystal, and Irwin's Harry Cornwall. A rifle shot signaled the start of the race, and Baney and Johnson quickly took the lead. The two raced neck and neck all the way, appearing to shoot "down the steep declivity like a bullet through the air," at speeds of sixty miles per hour. Young Baney crossed the finish line only two feet ahead of Johnson.[28]

That evening, after appropriate celebrations, the racers and others formed the Gunnison County Norwegian Snow-Shoe Club, the first such club in Colorado, "for the object of encouraging snow-shoeing and all other winter sports" (fig. 2-6). The club quickly agreed to hold a series of races around the county through the rest of the winter. The first meet held under club auspices took place at Gunnison on the fifth of March. A large crowd of between fifteen hundred and two thousand people gathered to watch twelve contestants race in pairs down Tenderfoot Mountain. To encourage attendance, Gunnison's "schools were closed, and the District Court, then in session, adjourned, in order to give the judge and lawyers a chance to see the fun." Club president E. W. Burton, a Gunnison resident, allowed members "to use his store as club headquarters, and borrowed all his wife's flat-irons for the members to use in waxing up their shoes." After a long day of racing, Crested Butte's Percy Ramsden carried off the thirty-five-dollar first prize.[29]

Over the next ten days the Gunnison County Norwegian Snow-Shoe Club staged races at Irwin, Gothic, and even at Scofield, "whose resident population consisted at that time of four men, three women, a baby, two dogs and a cat or two." Owing to the lateness of the season, the March 15 race at Gothic, won by Crystal's F. M. Williams, was the club's last official race. The group had big plans for the next year, intending to "have two or three days' carnival, probably at Gunnison, and races of various kinds. Uniforms will be selected, and the organization of the club completed in every respect."[30]

The Gunnison County Norwegian Snow-Shoe Club disappeared after that first season, as did its grand plans. Nonetheless, skiing continued to gain popularity as a recreational sport. In succeeding years ski clubs formed at Irwin, Silver Plume, Leadville, Dillon, Frisco, and elsewhere, each invariably claiming to be the state's first. They lasted a season or two and disappeared. However, from its roots in the exigencies of life and work in the Rocky Mountain mining camps, skiing by the early years of the twentieth century had become a popular recreational sport in Colorado. Although most skiing enthusiasts continued to live and work in the mining towns, interest in the sport could now be found in the cities of the front range. The *Denver Times* in 1901 recommended skiing as "one of the most exhilarating outdoor sports that can be imagined, besides the spice of danger which adds zest to the sport."[31]

When the miner-skiers of Gunnison County first imposed organization and rules on their favorite recreation, they took the first steps toward its transformation into a modern sport. The next step would be turning skiing into a business. That process began with the arrival of Norwegian Carl Howelsen in Colorado in 1911.

RECREATIONAL SPORTS

Skiing was the major winter recreational sport in the Gunnison country, but elsewhere in Colorado ice-skating became a popular cold-weather activity. As Leadville historian Edward Blair has noted, from that town's birth to the turn of the century, "skating was far and away the most popular winter activity. Over the years the city had a dozen or more popular skating rinks." One such rink, called the Amphitheater, attracted the "respectable elements" among Leadville's population, including women. At Central City, the basement of the burned-out Tappan hardware store served as a skating rink, and at neighboring Black Hawk the town band played for skaters.[32]

Hockey was another seemingly natural winter sport of high-country athletes. The *Denver Times* reported in 1901 that "hockey is all the rage in Leadville," which was congenial ground for the game "as every man, woman and child in the Cloud City knows how to skate."

The city's twenty-seven-member hockey club declared itself "up on the sport . . . and ready to meet all comers" and tried to negotiate games with teams from the Denver Wheel Club, the University of Denver, and Colorado College.[33]

Nineteenth-century Americans considered football a game for young college gentlemen. Because colleges and universities were scarce in the Colorado mining towns, football never really caught on, though men and boys occasionally played pickup games in the streets and schoolyards. Attempts at organization were few. Central City tried to field a team to compete against Denver squads in 1878, with unknown results, and at Durango an organized high school team played its first game in December 1893, defeating the Colorado National Guard's Company K.[34]

More popular than hockey and football was gymnastic exercise, carried to Leadville, Central City, and other towns by a German social and athletic club, the Turnverein. Organized in 1879, Leadville's Turnverein taught gymnastics to large classes, which included women and children. The Turners also introduced physical education into the town's public schools. Among the Leadville Turnverein's organizers was investment banker and industrialist Charles Boettcher, who became a founder of one of Colorado's most important nonmining businesses, the Great Western Sugar Company. Central City's Turnverein dates to 1869. Most of the active members were German miners employed in the Bobtail tunnel, which eventually connected with the Argo tunnel from Idaho Springs. The Central City Germans apparently enjoyed mixing beer drinking with their exercise. One man recalled that at Sunday meetings "they had a beer, and then their trainer led them in acrobatics on trapezes and bars, which were followed by the drinking of more beer and the singing of German songs." These Sunday gatherings provoked some hostility among some Central City residents, which the club tried to assuage by promising "to allow no saloon men to hold places on the board of directors."[35]

Other ethnic sports imported to the mining towns included Cornish wrestling, and curling and cricket meets organized by Caledonian clubs. Few native-born Americans had hard-rock mining experience at the time of the great gold and silver rushes of the 1850s and 1860s, so skilled miners were much in demand. The lure of

2-7. Cornish wrestler John Tippet of Central City, with saloon keeper John Waters and town marshal John Jordan, ca. 1907. The "Cousin Jacks" brought their distinctive wrestling style, as well as their mining skills, with them from Cornwall. Courtesy, the Denver Public Library, Western History Department.

good wages in western mining camps was strong, especially for Cornishmen after that English region's mining industry slipped into depression in the 1870s. As many as one-third of Cornwall's mining population emigrated during the 1870s and early 1880s, and large numbers of them came to Colorado. Leadville's population in 1880 was one-third foreign born and included many "Cousin Jacks," along with German, Canadian, and Irish newcomers.[36]

The immigrants brought their mining skills and their cultures, including their sports, with them. Wrestling was especially important to the Cornish and fit well in the male working culture of the mines. By the 1870s Cornish wrestling was a fixture of mining-town life. What most set Cornish wrestling apart from other styles was the contestants' dress. A photo of Central City champion wrestler John Tippet shows the Cornish wrestler's typical canvas jacket, joined in the front by drawstrings, and close-fitting lightweight pants (fig. 2-7). Before stepping into the ring Tippet would have removed his shoes and fought barefoot. The fights themselves reminded one Central City youth of a cockfight, but in fact they were fought according to long-accepted rules. Three referees, or "sticklers," supervised each match, or "play." Hitting was not allowed, and a fall was awarded when one wrestler forced the other's shoulders and one hip, or "pin," to the ground. The Cornish wrestlers were a tough lot, and individual matches could last for hours. In 1877, for example, a fight at Brownville (located a few miles west of Georgetown) between George Wedge and John Hall went on for more than four hours (winner unknown). A wrestling meet could thus last for several days, and the ultimate winner was the man who defeated all other challengers. The wrestlers fought for trophies and cash prizes, and often received a percentage of ticket receipts (the wrestling arena at Brownville seated 270, with a bar "where soda water and other refreshments" could be purchased). As usual, gambling added to the interest and excitement.[37]

"Extending far back in the mists of Scottish history," says sports historian Benjamin Rader, "rural communities had held annual track-and-field games as a part of their larger festive culture. Scots brought these games with them to America, where they organized Caledonian clubs." One such club, organized by upper-class Scottish and English residents, was active in Leadville in the 1880s. The Leadville Caledonians sponsored curling contests in the winter, in which competing teams tossed polished stones across ice toward a target, and held cricket matches in the summer. The Caledonians' games had a distinctly elite character, for, as one Leadville historian has noted, neither "received much support from the general public, but they did arouse a good deal of enthusiasm among the small group of socialites that supported them." As Rader notes, the Caledonian clubs are most famous for introducing organized track-and-field contests to the United States. There seems to be no record of Caledonian-sponsored track meets in the Colorado mining camps, though pedestrianism—running and walking—did have its enthusiasts.[38]

Running contests often were local affairs, but when one town's champion took on another's all the forces of community identity and pride weighed in with enthusiastic betting to back it up. Some communities went so far as to bring in professional ringers to ensure their investments and their town's self-esteem. Itinerant professionals, often hiding their identities, could make a living challenging local runners. In 1876, for example, a man named Gilbert defeated Silver Plume's C. C. Thompson for a two-hundred-dollar purse. Just before the race, some members of the crowd recognized Gilbert as "a Mr. Crandall of Niles, Michigan, one of the best runners in the Union." The race went on, but side betting was understandably light. Professionalism was even more apparent in walking races, which were preferred to running, in part because of high altitude. Teams of professional walk racers traveled the country giving exhibitions and contesting local challengers. Pedestrianism was a male-dominated sport, but, as historian Duane Smith notes, some women joined the professional teams, and these "celebrated pedestriennes displayed their talents to appreciative male audiences."[39]

Wheeled forms of locomotion also caught the fancy of mining-town residents. Roller-skating flourished in Central City during the 1870s and 1880s. The Central City *Daily Register* declared in 1871 that "for pleasurable, healthful and fashionable exercise, the skating rink at Turner's Hall is an attraction never before equalled" in the town. Skating embodied "music and merriment, health and happiness." The rink's managers were also found to be "gentlemanly teachers." Fourteen years later, the opening of a new rink at Central City was also declared a success. The large crowd that attended "showed that the interest in skating [had] by no means died out in Central . . . and the innocent fun of the evening delighted everybody." Roller-skating's fashionability, healthfulness, gentlemanliness, and innocence suggest that the sport was viewed as one that passed the tests of Victorian-era propriety and thus was an appropriate recreation for women, especially middle- and upper-class ladies. Indeed, roller-rink owners worked hard to attract a female clientele through such devices as "free ladies nights." However, the sport's propriety was inevitably threatened whenever two or more fellows decided to find out who could skate fastest, opening the skating-rink door to gambling and making the establishment and the sport less suitable for refined ladies.[40]

Mining-town women also enjoyed bicycling. Beginning in the late 1880s, a cycling craze swept the United States, and for a time it seemed as if the entire country had sprouted wheels. The bicycle had obvious potential as a means of transportation, but most cyclists used their "wheels" for recreation and racing. Nineteenth-century mountain-biking enthusiasts quickly formed clubs to sponsor social outings and races. Mining-town women took to bicycles as readily as men, though the propriety and health consequences of female cycling became topics of hot debate (see chapter 3). Female cyclists, however, were not the most important subject of debate about bicycling. Nineteenth-century bicycles resemble modern mountain bikes, but they were essentially urban machines. Their weight and easily punctured tires made off-road riding difficult at best. In cities and towns all over America, bicycles challenged horses, wagons, and pedestrians for space on busy streets and provoked a great deal of animosity. They frightened horses and startled, and sometimes ran over, pedestrians. In short, bicycles became a public-policy problem. A Leadville newspaperman categorized cyclists as "the good and the very good, the bad and the very bad and the incorrigibles." He urged compassion only for young children "who are doing the best they can and do not deserve to be shot at." Soon, mining towns joined cities everywhere in passing ordinances to regulate bicyclists on their streets.[41]

Bicycling underscored the Rocky Mountain mining town's character as an urban island in a frontier setting. Because of this urban character, mining-town sports quickly exhibited many of the features of modern sports: competition, organization, and rules. Some sports—rock drilling, ski racing, Cornish wrestling, pedestrianism—required a serious commitment to frequent, sometimes constant, training, and in them the line between sport and business or profession began to blur. That line was crossed even more clearly in boxing, horse racing, and baseball.

2-8. Jack Dempsey was Colorado's most famous boxer.
The "Manassa Mauler" fought saloon matches between
1911 and 1916. Like all of the mining-town sports, boxing matches always occasioned heavy betting. Courtesy,
the Denver Public Library, Western History Department.

BUSINESS AND PROFESSIONAL SPORTS

Boxing may have been the first spectator sport in the male-
dominated saloon culture of the early mining camps. As Duane Smith
notes, "after reading about some of the saloon brawls, one could sur-
mise there were a great many amateur practitioners" of pugilism. The

excitement those spontaneous barroom bouts produced prompted talented fighters and promoters to try to turn a profit from fisticuffs. For example, as early as 1861 Central City's Charles Switz challenged all comers to join him in the ring. Switz held two exhibitions, but both "ended in free-for-all fights involving the excited spectators," who no doubt had a good deal of money riding on the outcome. Boxing was popular enough in the Central City–Black Hawk area to support regular classes in the sport. If trained fighters were not available, promoters such as Cripple Creek's Otto Floto would recruit local drunks to hammer one another in front of a paying and betting audience.[42]

Mining-town boxing matches might be held in a gymnasium, on a theater stage, or outdoors, but saloons remained the heart of the boxing culture where many fighters got their starts. Colorado's most famous saloon fighter was Jack Dempsey (fig. 2-8). Born William Harrison Dempsey in the San Luis Valley town of Manassa in June 1895, Dempsey won the heavyweight title in 1919 and held it until 1926, when Gene Tunney defeated him. Dempsey left home at age fifteen to work in the mines. However, following the lead of brother Bernie Dempsey, who used the ring name of Jack (in honor, or imitation, of Irish middleweight Jack Dempsey the Nonpareil, who died in 1895), he began to fight in saloon matches, often for as little as one dollar. Calling himself Harry Dempsey, or Kid Blackie, the young boxer tramped from town to town in Colorado, Utah, and Nevada from 1911 to 1916 and became famous for his challenge, "I can't sing, I can't dance, but I'll lick anyone in the house." And he usually did.[43]

Leadville's bantamweight champion, William J. "Billy" Irwin, was less famous but more important to his town than Jack Dempsey. Irwin came to Leadville as a boy in 1879 and, except for brief interludes in Aspen and Butte, Montana, spent the rest of his life there. Irwin's boxing career spanned the 1890s, and he fought challengers from all over Colorado, earning a reputation as "an aggressive fighter with a thorough mastery of ring generalship and the grand tactics of the game." After he left the ring, Irwin became prominent in Leadville's civic life, serving as fire chief, deputy county clerk, secretary of the county Democratic Party, and president of the Eagles club. Irwin died of pneumonia in November 1910.[44]

Because of boxing's connection to the mining-camp saloon culture, both fighters and spectators tended to be working class. That alliance, along with the sport's violence and the attendant gambling, made boxing less acceptable than other sports to middle- and upper-class residents, especially as mining-town society matured and became more socially complex and sophisticated. As early as 1861, Central City's newspaper sniffed about "demoralizing" boxing exhibitions and urged the sheriff to stop them. Likewise, when Aspen witnessed its first boxing match in 1885 the *Sun* observed sarcastically, "Aspen's glory is complete—we have had a prize fight."[45]

Moral qualms did not stop mining-town elites from participating in horse racing, another sport that featured gambling. Indeed, horse racing mirrored the evolving social stratification of the mining towns. Throughout the United States in the nineteenth century, members of the wealthy elite, both old money and the new-money upper class created by the growth of industrial capitalism, bred and raced horses because they enjoyed the sport and the social atmosphere of the race season, and because owning fast, expensive horses set them apart from and above the rest of society. Especially in the larger mining camps, those men who scrambled to the top of the social pyramid adopted horse racing as a means of demonstrating their superior social station.

As with most mining-camp sports, the beginnings of horse racing were informal. All that was needed were horses, riders, an agreed-upon course, and stakes for the winners. Of course, gambling by onlookers broadened interest in a race beyond the contestants themselves. Any reasonably flat stretch of ground, including Main Street, would do for a day's races, which usually involved matches between several pairs of horses and riders. Horse racing did not develop beyond this informal level in most camps. However, in larger towns, where a more diverse social and class structure emerged—dominated by mine owners, merchants, bankers, and professionals—horse racing became a highly organized affair, the sport of the elite.

At the height of the silver boom of the 1870s and 1880s, Leadville outpaced every other town to become the center of high-country horse racing. In August 1879, members of Leadville's business and social elite formed the Leadville Trotting and Running Association.

Led by R. E. Goodell of the Little Giant Mining Company, railroad financier James N. Carlille, and Horace Tabor's partner, William H. Bush, the association pooled five thousand dollars and built a race-track, located about three miles west of town. Built on an eighty-acre site, the track featured a grandstand with seating for twelve hundred, a restaurant, and stalls for sixty horses. The *Rocky Mountain News* noted of Leadville and its new horse-racing shrine that "there is so much loose change lying in and about Leadville that the people there can't spend it fast enough and those who attend the races . . . may expect to witness some of the liveliest betting that has ever been done in this state, Denver not excepted." In fact, local horse owners entertained challengers from all over the state and as far away as Chicago for purses as high as six thousand dollars. Anyone with the price of admission might attend and bet on the races, but horse racing at Leadville had become the sport of the carbonate kings.[46]

Baseball, America's game, also made a major imprint on mining-town life in the nineteenth century and, like horse racing, quickly developed from an informal pastime to an organized sport and business. Contrary to myth, Abner Doubleday did not invent the game of baseball in 1839 or in any other year. Baseball evolved from traditional English-village games, including stoolball and rounder. By the early eighteenth century, American colonists played various games resembling baseball, calling them "goal ball," "town ball," and even "base ball." By the early nineteenth century, two versions of the game became prevalent, the Massachusetts game and the New York game. In the Massachusetts version, outs were made by "plugging" or "soaking" the runner, that is, hitting him with the thrown ball. The New York game was slightly more sedate as outs were achieved either by touching the runner with the ball or by throwing the ball to his base. In the early 1840s a group of New York City professional men, clerks, and artisans began playing regular games at a vacant lot at Twenty-Seventh Avenue and Fourth Street in Manhattan. In 1845 one of the group, Alexander Joy Cartwright, organized his fellow "ballists" into the New York Knickerbocker Base Ball Club as both an athletic and a social club. The group agreed to and published formal rules for their game, including three outs per inning; batters, or "strikers," were out if they missed three swings at pitched balls; and fielders scored

outs by catching hits in the air or òn the first bounce, by throwing the
ball to first base ahead of the runner, or by tagging runners between
bases. A game ended when one team scored twenty runs, or "aces."
Later it was decided to award the win to the team ahead at the end of
nine innings. A single umpire sat at a table along the third baseline
and had the job of resolving controversies between players and teams.
He could, if necessary, seek the advice of spectators.[47]

Nineteenth-century baseball equipment differed from that used
by today's players. Bats were shorter and much less tapered. Balls,
though about the same size as the modern version, were softer and
were deliberately stained or allowed to become dirty to be less visible to the "striker." Fielders did not wear gloves, and catchers had
neither masks nor vests to protect them from fastballs or errant swings.
In rural areas, especially, playing fields were a far cry from the lush
and level carpets of green to which modern players are accustomed.
At Pandora, in Savage Basin near Telluride, for example, the infield
was fairly level, but the outfield was littered with tree stumps that
complicated fielding and threatened shins and knees. A Colorado
man recalled that "accidents were frequent—broken teeth and noses,
and sometimes a smash on the forehead sent a man to the ground in
a heap."[48]

American baseball's origins were eastern, urban, and middle
class. Although it was a gentleman's game, it had little attraction to
society's upper crust. They enjoyed their own sports, such as horse
racing and yachting, while the working class rarely had the leisure
time to indulge in an afternoon of ball playing. Two powerful historical events, however, helped transform baseball into a national game.
During the Civil War baseball became a favorite pastime in both Union
and Confederate army camps. Soldiers of all classes and regions, in
effect, took the game home with them. The rapid movement of population across the continent in the decades following the Civil War
spread the game from coast to coast.

No doubt many of Colorado's "fifty-niners" had played or at
least seen a baseball game. Some may have brought bats and balls
west with them. However, none of them had come west to play ball.
They were much more interested in gold fields than outfields. Even
the efforts of *Rocky Mountain News* publisher William Newton Byers

to organize a baseball team in Denver in 1862 succumbed to the gold fever, and the obstacles to organizing baseball in the mining camps were even greater.[49]

That reluctance began to change in the late 1860s and early 1870s as Denver and the mining towns became more settled. Central City organized a team in the summer of 1867, but the members had to play among themselves since they could find no opponents. By the early 1870s, however, Central City's Stars had become worthy opponents to such teams as the Denver Blue Stockings and the Bald Mountain Daisies of Nevadaville.[50]

In contrast to Alexander Joy Cartwright's New York City team of the 1840s, mining-camp baseball began as very much a working-class activity. Most of the players and spectators came from the ranks of the miners, daymen, and other workers. Aspen historian Malcolm Rohrbough describes baseball as an important "unifying social activity" for those who worked with their hands. A Sunday-afternoon game was both entertainment and a social gathering. As the mining towns became more ethnically diverse, baseball also became a way for immigrant workers to try to join American culture, especially in Colorado's coal-mining camps where tens of thousands of eastern and southern European immigrants settled in the late nineteenth and early twentieth centuries. At Walsenburg, Starkeville, Crested Butte (where coal mining displaced silver mining), Erie, and dozens of other coal camps, baseball eclipsed even the traditional Italian game of boccie as the favorite pastime. Although historian Duane Smith's assertion that "it was difficult to deny an individual his place in the community after he had led his town's team to victory" probably overstates Anglo-Saxon Americans' willingness to fully accept immigrants in the mainstream of American life at the turn of the century, to the newcomers baseball was one path leading toward that goal. Ethnic and religious xenophobia and mounting animosity between the upper classes and an increasingly restive working class whose ranks swelled with the foreign-born were powerful forces in late-nineteenth- and early-twentieth-century America. Nonetheless, for some newcomers baseball was a link to American culture and to the community. It helped the immigrant to see himself as a part of the town and its life.[51]

Rivalries among mining towns were intense, and a successful baseball team often became another measure of a town's identity and its sense of superiority to its neighbors. Central City's C. H. Hannington recalled that the Stars and the Daisies "had many a hard fought game, some ending in a free-for-all." Because local nines became important symbols of civic pride, town newspapers kept fans posted not only on scores but also on individual and team batting averages. In Aspen's newspapers, baseball coverage appeared on page two, while mining news was relegated to page three. Local business leaders often sponsored teams and saw to it that they had the best equipment and brightly colored uniforms.[52]

By the 1870s, baseball in America began to change from an amateur sport for middle-class gentlemen to a business employing professional athletes. The organization of the Cincinnati Red Stockings in 1869 marked that change. Composed entirely of salaried players, the Red Stockings that year traveled twelve thousand miles, played before two hundred thousand paying fans, and went undefeated. The Red Stockings barely broke even that first year, but their success on the diamond inspired, or forced, other players and investors to form their own professional teams.

In Colorado the intense rivalry among mining towns and their baseball teams encouraged the movement toward professionalism. Towns and team sponsors competed to lure talented players, often by offering them desirable jobs, cheap or free housing, or other inducements. Increasingly, they also offered to pay them for their baseball services. Some teams resisted the trend, held out as gentlemen amateurs for many years, and suffered the competitive consequences. As their losses against professional and semiprofessional nines mounted, they could console themselves that they had preserved their honor and fought for the honor of the game. After Durango suffered an especially humiliating loss to arch rival Silverton in 1892, the *Durango Herald* complained that its tormenter had "committed a gross breach of hospitality in bringing in professional players to play against amateurs." Staking its claim to higher moral ground, the paper declared, "Durango can afford to lose a game of base ball, but Durango cannot afford to win by questionable methods." Indeed, Durango could have imported its own ringers but refused to do so "through motives that do honor to our club." Such protests and the honor of the game not-withstanding, the day of the professional ballplayer had long since arrived.[53]

No team exemplified mining-town pride and competitiveness, and professionalism in baseball, more than the Leadville Blues. Leadville in the early 1880s needed a boost. The town had been racked in 1880 when the failure of two important mines, the Little Pittsburg and the Chrysolite, brought Leadville's first boom to a painful halt as investment dried up. Then, in May and June, a miners' strike led to the imposition of martial law. By 1882, Leadville still had not fully recovered its morale. One group of young mine owners, merchants, and professional men decided that fielding a top-notch baseball team was the tonic needed to revive the town's flagging spirits and, no doubt, to turn a profit for themselves. In April they organized the Leadville Base Ball and Athletic Association to sponsor the town's new team, the Blues. They meant to "win the state championship and fly the whip pennant in the cloud city."[54]

Winning a championship required stocking the team with pros. Manager Harry Keily brought in Cincinnati Red Stockings and Brooklyn Athletics veteran Harry Kessler to play third base. Jake Knowdell, the catcher, had played for National League teams, including Brooklyn, and Joe Tumulty of St. Louis played shortstop and outfield. The heart and soul of the team, though, was pitcher Dave Foutz, who later became a star for Brooklyn and for the St. Louis Browns, winning 166 games in his major league career (fig. 2-9).[55]

The 1882 Blues played a forty-three-game schedule, lost eight, tied one, and earned the state championship. During one thirteen-game period in August and September, Foutz hit .370, and right fielder Gomer Price connected for a .388 average. The Blues routinely put double digits between their score and their opponents'. They downed Buena Vista 42-1 on July 16 and on July 27 pummeled the Bonanza Whites 47-0. One of their closer games was an 8-1 win over the Colorado Springs Reds. Although the spread was only seven points, the local paper declared that the Colorado Springs nine had suffered "such a drubbing that they will never forget it as long as they are in existence." The Blues' few defeats came at the hands of such worthy opponents as the Longmont Utes, the Kansas City Reds, the

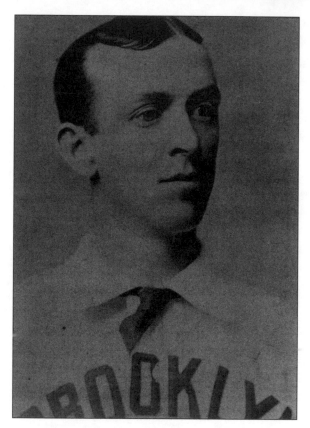

2-9. Dave Foutz led the 1882 Leadville Blues to the state baseball championship. Foutz played on Colorado's first professional team, the 1879 Denver Brown Stockings, before his season in Leadville. He went on to a major league career with St. Louis and Brooklyn. Courtesy, Jay Sanford Collection.

Burlington and Missouris, and the Council Bluffs, Iowa, team. So dominant were the Blues that as the 1883 season approached, Denver poet and journalist Eugene Field "hoped that no effort will be made to organize a Denver baseball club this season." The prospect of being "pounded to death by every scrub and dunghill nine in the country," presumably including Leadville, was just too depressing.[56]

Leadville also helped bring league baseball to Colorado. Until the mid-1880s each team set its own schedule, mainly by issuing and accepting challenges to other nines. In 1885, Leadville, Denver, and Pueblo tried to bring some regularity to their schedules by forming the state's first league. Denver won the championship that year, but the league also collapsed when the Pueblo team fell apart. In 1886, Leadville and Denver joined the newly reorganized Western League, which also included teams in St. Joseph, Missouri; Topeka and Leavenworth, Kansas; and Lincoln, Nebraska. Denver won the pennant that year, which was also Leadville's only season in the league. When a snowstorm on July 4 delayed a game, league officials decided that the climate in the Cloud City was too unpredictable and expelled the Blues from the loop, awarding the franchise for 1887 to Omaha.[57]

The Leadville Blues remained a force in Colorado baseball for almost two decades, but never again achieved the dominance they enjoyed in 1882. They won the state championship again in 1896 and 1897, but in 1899 the team's sponsors disbanded it in the face of rising costs.[58]

Mining-town sports and recreation had changed profoundly by the turn of the century as, indeed, had the towns themselves. In the early days of settlement, the most important sports—rock drilling, fire-cart racing, and skiing—emerged as by-products of life, work, and survival in the camps. As towns grew and their populations became more diverse and stratified, leisure-time activities also became more varied and disconnected from the demands of everyday life. Sports and recreation became not only entertainment but also business.

Mining-town baseball exemplified important features of these social changes. It was intensely competitive, but competition by the last two decades of the nineteenth century took place in an increasingly organized setting with universally accepted (if not obeyed) rules. By then, too, baseball had shifted from its amateur foundations and was becoming a business for its organizers and a profession for its players. In these ways, mining-camp baseball mirrored changes in the game occurring nationally. Those changes also mirrored the transformation of society. Whether in New York City, Denver, or Leadville, America in the late nineteenth century had become an urban-industrial society, and baseball reflected that society's increasingly organized, competitive, and socially stratified character. For all his pitching and hitting skill, Dave Foutz was an employee, working for the men who owned the Leadville Blues. His job was to entertain the crowd, bring home the pennant, and earn a profit for his employers.

Of course, the emergence of baseball and other sports as businesses and professions was but one aspect, albeit an important one, of modern sports. Recreational sports, especially bicycling and skiing, were also important in the development of modern sports and society in Colorado.

3

A Terror to the Horses
Bicycling in Colorado

The old boathouse on the shore of Smith Lake in Denver's Washington Park has been the scene of many gatherings over the years. Picnics, concerts, dances, and parties are mainstays of the park scene during the warm-weather months. However, the crowd gathered there on the evening of July 25, 1989, was unlike anything the boathouse had ever witnessed. Some five hundred angry park users, mostly bicyclists, met that warm summer evening to protest planned changes in the park's roadway. Under the plan, announced twelve days earlier, cyclists were to be diverted from the main road at two points onto narrow paths that would also be open to pedestrians. For years the park's 2.3-mile loop had been a favorite of area cyclists, especially after the Department of Parks and Recreation in 1971 closed most of the roadway to automobile traffic. The smooth, flat circuit was ideal for a leisurely ride, a vigorous workout, or for training for the small number of serious athletes who used it for that purpose. By the late 1980s, hundreds of cyclists of all ages and abilities flocked to the park, especially during evenings and weekends.

On this evening, however, it seemed to the cyclists that the parks department intended to run them out. The department denied any such intent, maintaining that the new traffic plan was meant to make the park a safer place for all of its users. "The biggest problem," said department comanager Carolyn Etter, "is packs of bicycles [sic] who are going at very high speeds and causing accidents. We want all people to have greater ease in getting around the park without the fear or intimidation of bike racers behind them." Apparently, Etter believed that forcing bicyclists and pedestrians to share the same narrow off-road paths would make everyone feel safer and more comfortable.[1]

The proposed new park plan provoked a brief but acrimonious debate. One neighborhood resident claimed that "you're often taking your life into your hands over there. These people who insist on riding their bikes at forty miles per hour are endangering a lot of people. This is not the Tour de France in Washington Park." Indeed, Denver police had timed some cyclists at speeds as high as thirty-one miles per hour, well above the park's twenty-mile-per-hour speed limit. However, such speeds were the exception rather than the rule. One cyclist pointed out that world champion rider Greg LeMonde that week won the Tour de France in a final all-out sprint in which he reached thirty-four miles per hour.[2]

Cyclists could not understand how forcing them off the roadway and onto eight-foot-wide paths clogged with pedestrians would create a safer environment in the park. When challenged to document claims about bicycle-pedestrian accidents, park officials could produce no data to prove how serious the problem really was, or if there was even a problem at all. Cyclists also complained that the plan had been handed down from on high, without adequate public input. "It's irresponsible and undemocratic at best," said attorney Ron Hill, a twenty-five-year veteran of cycling in the park. "This is our park. Let's not let stupid bureaucrats take it away from us for no reason."[3]

Although one runner claimed to have run twenty-five thousand miles in the park without ever being "brushed by a bike," other pedestrian users agreed with city officials that bicyclists were endangering the public. Cyclists admitted that a few riders violated the speed limit, but maintained that careless pedestrians and runners, and motorists in those parts of the park still open to automobiles, were just as dangerous. Some of the most strident rhetoric against bicyclists appeared in the pages of the *Rocky Mountain News*, which termed cyclists' objections to the proposed roadway plan "self-centered drivel." Sports columnist Teri Thompson characterized cyclists as "insufferable yuppies" who "mistakenly and brazenly think of themselves as athletes," and as "the kind of people who run the government in China—totalitarian, inhumane and self-important." Thompson, who was later arrested for possessing and using cocaine, concluded that bicyclists were "just plain bad people." *News* sports cartoonist Drew Litton weighed in with a caricature of a thuggish cyclist deliberately mowing down women, children, and puppies.[4]

The five hundred protesters and the one thousand who signed petitions against the roadway plan finally won their point. The day after the Washington Park rally, the parks department postponed the roadway changes. Once tempers cooled, a citizens group representing all classes of park users gathered to draw up a new scheme. The result was a plan to further restrict automobile traffic and divide the park roadway into separate pedestrian and bicycle lanes. The new plan restored peace to Washington Park.[5]

How had the Washington Park bicyclists managed to defeat city hall? The answer lay in who they were. By the mid-1980s, nearly two hundred thousand bicyclists rode regularly on Denver's streets. An estimated 39 percent of the population between the ages of twenty and forty-four rode at least occasionally. Adult recreational cyclists were a large and powerful constituency in the city. Many of the "insufferable yuppies" who rode in the park were doctors, lawyers, college professors, realtors, stock brokers, business executives, and merchants: middle-class people willing and able to defend their interests, even against city hall.[6]

These 1980s Denver bicyclists doubtless were not aware of it, but in a striking sense they were repeating history. A century earlier, during a period of immense bicycling popularity in Denver, cyclists found themselves embroiled in similar controversies with other citizens and with city hall.

BICYCLING IN GILDED AGE DENVER

During the so-called Gilded Age, roughly from 1875 to 1900, Denver was swept up in a nationwide bicycling boom. Taking to the streets on high-wheeled "ordinaries," or on the more easily mounted and ridden modern "safety" bicycle, Americans by the hundreds of thousands used the "wheel" for transportation and recreation. Bicycling became not only a roundly popular form of exercise but also the focal point of organized social activity. For women, the wheel was a liberating device that gave them unprecedented personal mobility and even freed them, at least while riding, from the constraints of elaborate Victorian-era garb. Swarms of cyclists added to congestion on city streets and became the cause of political and legal conflict.

Denver became one of the most bicycle-crazy cities in the country. The *Rocky Mountain News* first noted cycling activities in January 1869, when the paper reported that a Mr. Thompson had been seen riding a "velocipede" (a generic term describing all manner of early two- and three-wheeled devices) on Blake Street. Thompson made regular appearances for several weeks, attracting "the attention of those who had nothing else to do." He allowed some of his spectators to test their dexterity and balance on his wheel, and the "green hands on the machine created a good deal of fun." The ten-dollar price of a velocipede apparently made bicycling an affordable hobby for many in Denver, to the extent that by that spring a velocipede school was running successfully, teaching new bicycle owners the finer points of remaining upright.[7]

Not all of early Denver's residents were smitten with the wheeled contraption and its riders. Unregulated cyclists quickly became a nuisance to pedestrians, as evidenced by a May 1869 ordinance prohibiting them from riding on the sidewalks. George Hannan, a prominent wheelman and bicycle dealer, recalled in 1893 that in the early days many citizens and civic leaders favored banning bicycles from the streets. "The bicycle was a terror to the horses when it first came into use," Hannan remembered, "and hence the opposition." In fact, at least one wheelman, Al Bennett, the instructor at George Rickard's cycling school, was arrested several times in 1879 because he frightened horses. Indeed, the city council in 1880 nearly passed a measure banning bicycles from the streets and permitting their use on sidewalks only by children under age twelve. The proposal's supporters used the by-then familiar arguments that wheels "scare some horses and endanger the lives of citizens." Opponents pointed out that "horses used to scare at railroad cars, brass bands and sprinkling carts, but these were not suppressed and finally the horses got used to them." A better solution, they argued, would be to prohibit skittish horses.

Mayor Richard Sopris broke a tie vote in the council to defeat the measure and thus keep Denver's streets open to bicycling.[8]

Despite these problems, Denver won notice around the country as a haven for cyclists. The inaugural issue of the *American Bicycling Journal* in 1877 declared that

> no city in the country should be ahead of Denver, Colorado in adopting the bicycle. The magnificent roads, smooth, hard and level as a floor, will doubt- less attract the touring bicyclist from other states, and we feel justified in predicting that to all such the en- terprising and generous-hearted people of Denver will extend most hospitable welcome.

Visitors, in fact, were greeted by a large and growing bicycling com- munity in Denver. By the 1890s, Denver rivaled eastern cities as a cycling center and was prominent enough to lure the 1894 meeting of the League of American Wheelmen, the largest national bicycling organization. By 1900 the city claimed to have more bicycles per capita—forty thousand in a population of one hundred thousand— than any other city in the country. So ubiquitous was the bicycle that it threatened the city's streetcar companies, which claimed in 1900 to be losing $1 million in fares annually. One company went into re- ceivership because "the universal wheel had impaired its earnings to such an extent that it could not meet its interest demands."[9]

Beginning in the early 1880s, Denver's most enthusiastic and wealthiest cyclists made their presence and influence felt by organiz- ing clubs that sponsored races and outings, picnics and balls, all of which the local press followed closely. By the turn of the century some of the clubs had become powerful social and political institu- tions in the city. The first such organization appeared in 1881 when fifteen wheelmen banded together as the Denver Bicycle Club. That group was short-lived and was succeeded in 1884 by the somewhat more substantial Colorado Wheel Club. Member George Harris is credited as the driving force behind the construction of Denver's first bicycles-only racetrack, located at a baseball park on Larimer Street.[10]

The Colorado Wheel Club lasted until 1887 when most of its members left to form the Denver Ramblers, the first successful cy- cling club (fig. 3-1). The Ramblers by the mid-1890s included "some

3-1. The Denver Ramblers bicycling club, formed in 1887. Note the high-wheeled "ordinary" bicycles, which were already giving way to the more practical, but less elegant, "safety" bicycle. Bicycling clubs represented the city's social elite and wielded considerable influence in civic affairs. Courtesy, the Denver Public Library, Western History Department.

of the oldest wheelmen in the state," and occupied a "commodious" clubhouse at 1642 Larimer Street. Another group, the Social Wheel Club, was formed in 1888, but disbanded in 1892 when many of its members elected to form the Denver Wheel Club.[11]

The Denver Wheel Club became one of the city's two powerful cycling organizations. In order to ensure the club's elite, middle-class character, exclude minorities, and isolate it from the corrosive influence of the saloon culture, membership was limited to "white male persons over 18, not engaged as bartenders or professional gamblers." Despite this exclusivity, the club eventually grew to more than two thousand members, including some of the most prominent gentlemen in town. When the organization dedicated its new clubhouse in 1897, it invited seventeen hundred guests to inspect the facility, which included a gymnasium, bowling alleys, a swimming pool, a billiard room, a library, card rooms, a reception room, parlors, a kitchen, and six living rooms (available for rental to members), complete with steam heat and gas and electric lights. Governor Alva Adams led the dedication ceremonies, which included a formal ball. By 1900 the Denver Wheel Club also operated a subsidiary, the Denver Wheel Club Country Club, a cycle park complete with cottages and other recreational amenities, located in Platte Canyon some fifty miles southwest of Denver.[12]

Denver Wheel Club members also played a prominent role in organizing a different sort of cycling organization. Many of the club's members in 1893 helped establish the Cycle Division as part of the Colorado National Guard's Signal Corps. The division soon included "the majority of the fastest riders in the city and state in its rank and file," and it was reported that they had "a very neat arrangement for carrying their rifles on their wheels when mounted."[13]

The Denver Wheel Club's main competitor in the 1890s was the Denver Athletic Club (DAC) Bicycle Division, formed in 1891. By 1894 the DAC and its Bicycle Division included "some of Denver's most prominent businessmen" who boasted of having "the largest and handsomest club house in the country, located at 1335 Glenarm," which remains the site of the DAC more than a century later. The club also owned its own athletic park, located at the southwest corner of City Park, complete with a quarter-mile cycling track where members perfected their racing skills.[14]

Denver's earliest bicycle race probably took place the first time that two energetic wheelmen met on the street. The first organized contest, pitting the *Denver Tribune*'s Deacon Walker, General Nathan Harris, and "a gentleman from Golden," took place on April 1, 1869. General Harris won the half-mile heat and claimed the one-hundred-dollar prize, but the race was not really much of a contest since the other two racers' wheels broke down, throwing them into the dirt street.[15]

The cycling clubs devoted much of their energy to racing, and city newspapers followed local and national racing events and personalities closely. The Denver Cyclists Union, composed of members of the Ramblers and the Social Wheel Club, in 1889 sold five hundred dollars in stock to build a racetrack at Sportmen's Park, at Broadway and

Sixth Avenue. Later, the Denver Wheel Club and the Denver Athletic Club built their own tracks. Other racing facilities were available to nonclub riders. For example, cyclists "could sneak into the horse track of the Gentlemen's Driving and Riding Club in City Park, or the horse track at Overland Park."[16]

Club races were popular and well-attended events, sometimes attracting two to three thousand spectators. Among the largest were the races conducted during the Denver Athletic Club's Field Days, held in the spring, summer, and fall. These events pitted DAC and other club members in one-, two-, and five-mile races. Other contests popular among DAC and Denver Wheel Club members were so-called dinner races. These road races were to Littleton or to Brighton, and the prize was dinner for those racers who finished in the top half of the field, paid for by the losers. One of the largest and most lucrative road races was staged in the spring of 1890. This twenty-five-mile event, sponsored by Denver clubs, attracted 189 contestants who rode a course from Sand Creek, in present-day Commerce City, to a finish line near Platteville. Prizes included a $750 piano, bicycles, and trophies. Probably the most popular regular road race was the one over the "sandpaper track" from Denver to Brighton. Sponsored by the Denver Wheel Club, this dinner race followed the gravel road along the Union Pacific Railroad's track. The trains sometimes became moving grandstands, as race enthusiasts piled aboard to follow the event from start to finish. The winner of the weekend race was entitled to the sobriquet of "Buttermilk Boy," for the refreshments that farmers along the route frequently offered the cyclists. The railroad thwarted the races from 1892 through 1894 by fencing off the road, which it claimed was on its right-of-way. A court fight ensued, but the railroad finally yielded to pressure from members of the Platte Valley Farmers Association, who also used the road.[17]

Onlookers stood to win as much or more from these races than the cyclists because they often were the subject of sizable wagers, which, in turn, invited fraud. The most notorious case of fraud stemmed from a race in 1897 when five men were convicted of rigging a race and swindling seventy-five hundred dollars from George Hannan, one of Denver's most prominent wheelmen.[18]

Bicycle racing in Gilded Age Denver reached its zenith in 1894 when the League of American Wheelmen, the largest cycling organization in the country, held its annual meeting in the city. Thousands of cyclists from all over the country attended the meet, which the Denver Wheel Club hosted. National-championship races took place at the club's track, improved for the occasion, at Sixth and Broadway. A newspaper notice in May announced that "colored men will be allowed to race in the annual bicycle meet at Denver," suggesting that the national gathering forced, at least temporarily, some recognition of African American cyclists. The three-day event drew an average daily attendance of about seven thousand: "The grandstand and bleachers were packed and people flocked to every point of vantage outside of the grounds to see the cracks battle for the championships."[19]

Ironically, the popularity of bicycle racing in Denver soon led local clubs to rebel against the national organization. In deference to Victorian-era religious values, the League of American Wheelmen maintained what Denver cyclists viewed as a "stubborn rule" against racing on Sunday, which was the most popular racing day in the city. By 1896 a "secession" movement was under way as local clubs staged Sunday races in defiance of the league's decree. The rebellion continued until at least 1898, but by that time bicycle racing was past its prime and enthusiasm for cycling itself began to diminish as many wheelmen turned their fancy to a smoke-belching, four-wheeled machine. In September 1900 the *Denver Republican* declared that "bicycle racing has died a natural death in this city, and no amount of galvanizing has been able to restore it."[20]

Racing and club life were very much the province of the elite cycling population before the turn of the century. The less wealthy enjoyed the pleasures of the wheel alone or in the company of friends on city streets, on the several popular "runs" between Denver and neighboring communities, or on off-road bike paths. The roads to Golden and Morrison were good, smooth stretches. Even better was the Brighton road, popular for racing, and the "almost perfect straightaway which leads south of Denver past Petersburg to Littleton." (Petersburg, with a population of two hundred in 1900, was a rail stop near present-day Englewood.) A League of American Wheelmen brochure noted that in pedaling the seven miles to Petersburg, "one

3-2. Two young Denver couples out for a day of bicycling. Bicycling gave women greater mobility and social freedom. Courtesy, Colorado Historical Society, Lilybridge 294.

accumulates but little perspiration and only feels warm enough to partake of a refreshing glass of beer."[21]

Although women did not participate in organized bicycle races, they nevertheless took to the wheel in large numbers and found in cycling unprecedented personal mobility (fig. 3-2). A women's cycling club, the Victorias, was formed in 1891. The twenty-five members were "enthusiastic bicyclists and made a number of tours to points near Denver, with gentlemen for escorts." The club's tours included "three moonlight excursions to Littleton, about twenty ladies going on the trip, with as many gentlemen."[22]

Few men ever claimed bicycling as an exclusively male sport, but the appearance of "cycliennes" prompted a debate over female health, decorum, and dress. The *Cycling West,* a periodical for western cycling enthusiasts, gave much consideration to bicycling's health and social consequences for women. The paper in 1893 reprinted an article from the *New York Mercury* warning that "the female form was not made to ride astraddle. To thus ride is both ugly and unnatural." The writer did not spell out the dire perils of riding "astraddle" for the female anatomy, but did warn that women riders would become less marriageable, for "one look at the ungraceful attitude of the rider would cause most men to seek wives among women who still cling to the side-saddle." The *Cycling West's* editor wisely advised the author "to join the ancient order of lunatics at once." Four years later the paper's "Cyclienne's Column" advised husbands that the price of a bicycle was much preferable to a sheaf of doctors' bills to cure "house nerves . . . blues . . . and that run down feeling so prevalent among the women closely confined to their homes."[23]

Although the *Cycling West* scoffed at the notion that riding would harm a woman's marriage prospects and endorsed casual cycling's salutary effects on female health, it was ambivalent about more strenuous exertions on the wheel by women. In March 1898 it warned women against attempting long rides, especially the rigorous one-hundred-mile "century" rides. Conceding that a woman "might be able to hold out longer than a man, and average more miles a day," nevertheless, "it should be remembered that a high-strung, nervous temperament which may keep her up is in reality her greatest enemy. When she breaks down her nerves are ruined for life." One month later, however, the paper noted that the best long-distance riders were "small, wiry, nervous men" and that "upon this basis . . . the average woman may prove herself a better rider than the average man."[24]

The exploits of Denver's most famous cyclienne, Dora Ellen Thornworth Rinehart, ought to have put this question to rest before 1898. Rinehart, who became known as "Denver's petite but herculean mistress of the road," took up the wheel in September 1895, still "suffering from some of the lingering effects of scarlet fever which she had gone through over a year before." Against her doctor's advice, she decided to try bicycling, not because she believed it would cure her but simply because she would enjoy it. She made her first century ride less than three months later and claimed to have pedaled more than seventeen thousand miles during 1896 (fig. 3-3). In July she "astonished the world" by riding ten centuries in ten consecutive days. Then, in October and November, she completed twenty hundred-mile rides in twenty straight days. Rinehart considered her great-

3-3. A great controversy raged over the propriety and possible adverse health consequences of women riding bicycles. Some "experts" worried that the exertions of bicycling might permanently ruin a woman's delicate nervous system. Denver's Dora Ellen Thornworth Rinehart put such concerns to rest by riding as many as seventeen thousand miles in 1896, including numerous "century" rides. Courtesy, Colorado Historical Society, F 34189.

est feat to have been a 203-mile trip in seventeen hours and thirty-five minutes. On Sundays she preferred to take more leisurely rides with her husband. "I do not like to go on a hard run when my husband is with me," she explained, "for you know it does take so much starch out of a man to ride a century."[25]

Dora Rinehart's usual riding habit consisted of "a divided skirt, sweater, golf hose and low shoes." That the *Cycling West* took note of her cycling apparel is indicative of the importance attached to women's attire, bound as it was to notions of modesty and morality. A brochure titled "Useful Information for the Bicyclist" in 1896 advised ladies not to race, coast, chew gum, wear a man's cap, or use bicycle slang. It also admonished female riders to "dress with becoming modesty," not to go out without needle and thread to repair torn clothing, and never to "wear a garden party hat with bloomers." More grave was the concern of *Ladies Home Journal* editor Edward Bok, who was alarmed at the "vulgar extent" to which wheelwomen were seen riding in skirts "too short for a well grown child of 12 years." Bok conceded that for a woman "to be comfortable at her athletics she must have a skirt shorter than that which she wears on the street or in the house," but that did not mean she should embarrass herself and polite society by wearing "a garment so scant as to leave her limbs exposed." For a woman to wear such revealing garb and to "parade before the eyes of men" was, he pontificated, "nothing short of disgusting."[26]

Denver's cycliennes of the 1890s would have mortified Bok. The *Cycling West*'s "For the Ladies" column in May 1898 noted that "ladies who only possessed ankles, or possibly limbs, now openly confess to having and using such terribly vulgar but convenient articles as legs." Bicycling not only resulted in shorter skirts and exposed legs but also freed women, at least temporarily, from the corseting, lacing, and padding of Victorian dress. Among the first items to fall by the wayside were bustles and hip pads, which proved "decidedly ungraceful on the bicycle." It was noted that "short dresses and abnormal hips are not especially pretty," and their vibrations all too noticeable when riding. Corsets were also among cycling's fashion victims. Although not all women could dispense with them, "slim girls, whose lack of *avoirdupois* will permit it, are discarding corsets from their wheeling wardrobe, saying that they ride better, feel better and look better without them." The revolution in apparel also promised more comfortable and honest relations between men and women. A young gentleman could take great comfort in the knowledge that "when he goes out with a young lady he need feel no anxiety as to the beautiful curves of her figure becoming disarranged, or of having the embarrassing duty thrust upon him of loosening her corset strings to revive her from a faint." And "when he looks at the girl of his choice he knows her figure to be natural."[27]

Although questions about women riders seemed to affect basic social values and relations, other issues became more pressing in the 1890s. Especially important was the hazardous and volatile problem

3-4a and 3-4b. Two cartoons, one from 1899 and one from 1989, illustrate persistent public-policy concerns surrounding bicycling. Sources: *Denver Evening Post* (May 22, 1899); *Rocky Mountain News* (July 27, 1989), courtesy Drew Litton.

of mixing bicyclists with other users of the streets and roads. More than any other issue, that one and efforts to resolve it link the cyclists of the 1890s to their descendants in the 1990s.

Just as a century later, a few delinquents-on-wheels, called "scorchers," brought Gilded Age cyclists into conflict with other citizens and with city hall. By the mid-1890s, "scorching"—riding at speeds in excess of ten miles per hour—was something of an epidemic in Denver, especially in the downtown area. Scorchers particularly favored Eighteenth Street between Court Place and Larimer Street, where they raced, attempted acrobatics, terrified horses, and intimidated pedestrians and sedate, law-abiding citizens. Nineteenth-century scorchers were not the objects of the blanket condemnations of cyclists that the Washington Park speedsters elicited in 1989, though one cartoon depicted them as a herd of thuggish brutes knocking a helpless woman from her wheel and sending her scrambling for safety. The press was careful to distinguish scorchers from the ranks of club cyclists. According to the *Denver Times,* the troublemakers were "not the old wheelmen, but the smart lad with the new wheel who wants to be the 'hot member.' "[28]

The most ferocious condemnations of scorching actually came from Denver's cycling elite, who blamed city authorities for inadequate vigilance. The scorcher, noted the *Cycling West* in 1897, was a "vapid ass" and a "cheerful and complacent idiot" who, in the interests of public safety, ought to be "restricted to four cell walls and a tightly laced straight jacket." The cycling paper singled out for particular scorn "the vicious park scorcher who has all too long been a menace to other people's right of common enjoyment" (figs. 3-4a, 3-4b). These "cyclomaniacs" turned a stroll or a quiet ride into activities fraught with "constant danger to life and limb." These "pinheaded nonentities" existed solely "for the same reason that skunks and mosquitoes do, viz., for the mental and physical irritation of God's more rational creatures." Indeed, there seemed to be no "excuse for the city scorcher's being alive, other than the deplorable one that he has unfortunately not yet been killed." That they allowed scorchers to roam the streets and parks showed how "criminally tolerant of wheeling abuses our municipal authorities are." The time had come to call a halt to the insolence of these "plug uglies of the wheel."[29]

Driving scorchers from the streets was a difficult challenge for city officials. Despite the cycling clubs' condemnation of scorchers, the organizations would not tolerate antibicycle legislation, so the only hope was to establish speed limits, which would be difficult, at best, to enforce. An ordinance passed in 1896 mandated an eight-mile-per-hour speed limit for cyclists and required them to slow to four miles per hour at intersections, and they were to keep to the right-hand side of the road. To enforce the ordinance, the Denver police department commissioned twenty-five prominent wheelmen to patrol the streets and apprehend violators. However, the police soon concluded that the citizen-patrolmen did not give proper attention to their duties. Thus, in July 1896 the department detailed a two-man team of regular policemen to do the job. On their first day this "cycling squad" arrested twenty scorchers. The "scorcher herders" soon won the reputation of being among the fastest riders in town. Indeed, there was some complaint that the "wheelcops" themselves became the worst scorchers.[30]

Scorchers quickly found ways to avoid at least the financial consequences of their crime. An especially effective tactic was to tie up the police courts by parading witnesses who would swear that they "saw the officer . . . drunk while performing his duty," and that the policeman, therefore, could not possibly have accurately judged the cyclist's speed. Indeed, the police in the 1890s never developed an accurate means of determining how fast a cyclist was going, which made successful prosecution of scorchers even more difficult.[31]

Denver authorities in the 1890s failed to completely quash scorching, but the problem eventually solved itself with the decline of cycling's popularity soon after the turn of the century. To their credit, Denver police never resorted to the extreme tactics used in Chicago, where officers used a slingshot device to disable speeding cyclists. The weapon's lead balls, when hurled at the wheels, broke the spokes and brought the bicycle and the wheelman to a sudden stop. A visitor from Chicago reported that "the sling ruins the bicycle, but a rider who has once been brought to his senses by the useful device will never again try to make a record on the public streets."[32]

Denver's comparatively mild antiscorching campaign may have owed to the political clout that the city's cyclists exercised. Some five hundred wheelmen in April 1893 paraded through downtown Denver demanding street improvements and underscoring their potential as a voting bloc. "They want good streets," a newspaper noted, "and they wish to demonstrate that they have sufficient strength to compel recognition of their demands." By the mid-nineties, cyclists pressured public officials and candidates to support a whole agenda that included public financing of bicycle paths, good roads, and the demand that railroads carry bicycles free as personal baggage. Denver was said to be "the only city in the country where the bicycle vote controls elections on municipal issues." The prominence in cycling affairs of major business and political figures, most notably Governor Alva Adams, lent credibility to that exaggerated claim.[33]

One of Governor Adams's special interests was the construction of off-road bicycle paths. A few months before he was elected governor, Adams became a founding member and the first president of the Denver Cycle Path Association. The group, which numbered one thousand by August 1896, raised money and built a path from Denver to Littleton. The path ran south along Broadway to the City Ditch and then meandered along the ditch through the countryside to Littleton. The City of Denver boosted the project by granting the use of the right-of-way along the ditch and appropriating one thousand dollars to start construction. The eleven-mile path cost as much as four hundred dollars per mile to build, but was open by August 1896.[34]

The Denver-Littleton path was an immediate hit with cyclists, especially the stretch along the City Ditch. This section was "the most picturesque part of the entire route, taking the cyclist . . . away from the roadway, away from the necessity of watching for teams and pedestrians, in the very midst of a luxuriant farm life, among fields of waving wheat . . . and resting the eyes upon many a peaceful rural scene."[35]

The Broadway–City Ditch path's popularity and the ease with which the financial and political obstacles to its construction were overcome illustrate the cyclists' influence in the 1890s. However, the path and those who rode it did not receive a warm welcome from people who lived along or near it. Attorney D. C. Webber complained to the *Denver Post* in May 1899 that the path "is an outrage and a disgrace to the city and people." Citing the "constant abuse of the

3-5. Bicyclists on the Palmer Lake Cycle Path. Built in 1897 by a club led by Gov. Alva Adams, the path represented the high point of the bicycling clubs' power. Courtesy, the Denver Public Library, Western History Department.

Broadway cycle path by reckless, irresponsible and often drunken and ruffianly riders," Webber noted that "women and children are so nervous when they go out for a ride that they get no pleasure from it. Every Sunday crowds of [bicyclists] go to the drinking places out South Broadway and return drunkenly carousing and making the whole street perfectly vile with their oaths and vulgarity." Police officers were never around, he alleged, adding that if the police and city fathers could not control the situation, then the cycling clubs should.[36]

Farmers who owned property along the ditch also soon came to resent the cyclists who frequented the path and who sometimes abused the privilege. Soon after the path opened, for example, farmer Clarence E. Brown was hauled into court and enjoined from interfering with the path and its users. Brown had become upset with cyclists "molesting his melon patch and orchard," and decided to take "measures to eliminate the evil himself." Brown stretched a barbed-wire fence across the path where it adjoined his land. On the afternoon of August 24, 1896, "an unsuspecting biker was enjoying the cool shade and the surrounding scenery of the path when he abruptly collided with the barbed wire fence, scratching himself up badly." When the state legislature in 1899 considered a bill to permit construction of bike paths along state highways, the measure provoked substantial opposition from farmers. At a mass meeting in Littleton, farmers protested that cyclists had torn down fences, raided gardens, and generally made nuisances of themselves. The bill did not pass.[37]

Undeterred by such episodes, the bicycle-path movement achieved its greatest success in the last three years of the century. The original cycle-path association gave way in July 1897 to a new Denver–Palmer Lake Cycle Path Association, formed to extend a trail south to that resort town. Alva Adams, now governor, became the association's president. William Cook Daniels, a member of a prominent retailing family, served as vice president, and George Ross-Lewin, an officer of the First National Bank, was treasurer. The association raised money for the project by selling lapel buttons featuring the group's logo and identifying the wearer as a contributor. When completed, the fifty-mile route to Palmer Lake quickly became a favorite of century riders (fig. 3-5). However, the path rose some two thousand feet by the time it reached Palmer Lake, and less ambitious cyclists often preferred to take the train south and then pedal back to Denver.[38]

As the twentieth century began, several signs foretold the collapse of Denver's cycling clubs, the bicycle-path movement, and the cycling fad itself. Two culprits were particularly important: cycling's very popularity and the automobile. One of the oldest clubs, the Ramblers, voted in 1899 to disband. Club president Al Senn said that the day of the wheel club was gone, "a consequence of the fact that the bicycle is no longer a luxury and means of pleasure, a bond to bring a crowd of wholesouled fellows together." Thus, he said, the Ramblers decided "to retire from the stage as gracefully as possible and go the way that wheel clubs are going all over the country." The bicycle had simply become too available, and its mass popularity impaired the clubs' ability to sustain themselves as elite organizations.

That fact was underscored by the Denver Wheel Club's decision to broaden its athletic program and decrease its emphasis on cycling and to merge with the new Centennial Club, which was devoted to football, golf, boxing, and other sports. An important symbolic blow fell in September 1900 when construction for the Denver Tramway Company streetcar system tore up part of the bike path along Broadway. "Only a little of the path is left south of Mississippi Avenue," the *Denver Times* reported.[39]

Even as cycling's mass appeal undermined the clubs, the wheel itself could not sustain the challenge of the automobile. In fact, cyclists welcomed autos, viewing them as complementing their own interests. "When motor carriages shall have arrived at a state of practicality and autocars fitted with pneumatic tires become the prevailing conveyances," the *Cycling West* predicted, "good roads will inevitably result." Cyclists thus could look forward to smoother streets, free of "the seductive cable slot and cycle-wrecking tramway rails." Like the bicycle, automobiles were originally toys of the well-to-do, but by the 1920s they came within the means of average people, who largely abandoned their bikes. The era of the bicycle gave way to the age of the automobile.[40]

BICYCLING IN THE TWENTIETH CENTURY

Through the first six decades of the twentieth century, some adults continued to enjoy bicycling, and racing even sustained a slight pulse, but the wheel principally became a toy and transportation for children and teenagers. That is, until young adults became interested again in the 1960s and launched a new bicycling boom that has sustained popularity through the 1990s.

Several factors contributed to renewed enthusiasm for cycling among adults in the 1960s. Among them were rapidly increasing leisure time and the need for exercise and recreation. Adults of all ages began dusting off their old bikes or buying new ones and took to the streets and parks in fast-growing numbers to break out of the increasingly sedentary pattern of middle-class life and work. Many of the same people became frustrated with mounting traffic congestion in the sixties and began to use bicycles for commuting to work and for other transportation needs. Denver's infamous "Brown Cloud" became another incentive for many to return to the wheel as a personal contribution to improving the environment. In 1965 a new Denver-area cycling association began to lobby the city to designate recreational cycling paths. The group achieved an early success with the opening, in June 1965, of a route through residential neighborhoods linking Cheesman and Washington Parks. Over the next five years the city laid out similar routes in a dozen neighborhoods and parks. To accommodate the growing demands of recreational and commuter cyclists, Denver in 1972 proposed building a citywide system of sixty-four trails, routes, and bike lanes. By 1990 Denver had 180 miles of on- and off-road bike paths and linked its system with those of suburban communities. In all, the off-road bicycle-path system in the Denver metropolitan area includes more than four hundred miles of interlinking trails. The spine of the system is the twenty-mile South Platte River trail, which extends from Eighty-Eighth Avenue in the north to Highway C-470 in the south. A trail parallel to C-470 and E-470 runs from the foothills east to the town of Parker. Another path, along Cherry Creek, runs from the Platte to Cherry Creek Reservoir in Aurora. Other spurs follow Clear Creek and Bear Creek westward. The seventy-one-mile Highline Canal trail bisects the metro area from Chatfield Reservoir to the Buckley Air National Guard Base.[41]

In 1975 the Denver Regional Council of Governments reported that there were some 480,000 bicycle owners in the metropolitan area. By the mid-1980s bicycle ownership in the Denver area reached 660,000 and continued to grow as sales boomed in the succeeding decade. Managing the demands of the expanding cycling population became a permanent part of state and local government. By the 1990s the City of Denver and the Colorado Department of Transportation employed full-time officials to work on bicycling issues, and a thirty-eight-member board advised the governor on integrating cycling into the state's transportation and recreational infrastructure.[42]

Although state and local governments worked hard and invested millions of dollars to meet the needs of recreational and commuter cyclists, the sheer numbers of people taking to the wheel ensured that conflicts would erupt between cyclists and others. The 1989 struggle over Washington Park was symptomatic of the mounting hostility that many, especially motorists, held toward cyclists.

With hundreds of thousands of cyclists out pedaling even occasionally, the Denver area's off-road bike-path network soon became congested, especially as pedestrians, runners, and skaters also took to them in large numbers. Many cyclists found the hazards of riding on streets and highways preferable to the crowded paths. As the numbers of cyclists on the roads grew so, too, did tensions between them and motorists. The conflict between cyclists and motorists in suburban Douglas County highlighted the problem.

State Highway 105 skirts the foothills between the towns of Monument and Sedalia, south of Denver. The route passes through a rolling, verdant valley dotted with horse ranches. Near the north end of the valley, Wolfensberger Road connects Highway 105 to the town of Castle Rock. These two roads became cycling favorites in the late 1980s and 1990s, and the subjects of intense conflict. Ranchers and homeowners along Highway 105 and Wolfensberger Road grew increasingly frustrated and angry with bicyclists who seemed to be taking over their roads. Bicyclists riding two or three abreast blocked lanes. Even when they rode single file, they impeded traffic where the roads narrowed to as little as eighteen feet. Honking horns and ugly words and gestures became commonplace. For their part, cyclists complained of belligerent motorists, some of whom even deliberately tried to run them off the road, and pointed out that state law accorded them the rights and responsibilities of other vehicles.

Some Douglas County motorists simply wished that cyclists would obey traffic laws, but others wanted them banished from the roads entirely. In May 1992 residents along Highway 105 and Wolfensberger Road gathered several hundred signatures on a petition asking the Douglas County commissioners to close the two roads to bicycles. At a hearing on the issue a Sedalia woman summed up the motorists' point of view by asking, "[Would] someone tell me why I should share the road with bicyclists? They impede traffic, stand in the middle of the road and are not licensed vehicles." Another person declared that "when hundreds of bicyclers are on the road, it's a bloody awful mess. About 1% of cyclers give you . . . courtesy, and 99% give you the finger."[43]

Cyclists at the meeting countered that "some people just see bicyclists as aliens in Lycra," with no legitimate reason for taking up space on the road. One cyclist conceded that "some cyclists are going to ride two or three abreast at times," but pointed out that "a lot of motorists are driving too fast for the circumstances." Another cyclist dismissed concerns about highway safety as "a red herring" and claimed that "they're just interested in getting bicyclists off the road."[44]

The county commissioners appointed a citizen task force to study the problem. At the group's first meeting, one member identified the real social fact underlying bicycle-motorist conflict in Douglas County. "This is not ranch country anymore," said lifetime resident Dave Curtis. Douglas County experienced a population boom during the 1980s and 1990s. Located on the southern edge of metropolitan Denver, towns and housing developments in the county provided homes for tens of thousands of newcomers to Colorado as well as migrants from the core of the city. Rapid population growth quickly overburdened the county's infrastructure, including its roads. Most of Douglas County's newcomers were urban-oriented middle- and upper-middle-class people, the segment of society most devoted to cycling. Along with housing tracts, bicycles symbolized the changing character of life and society in Douglas County. Thus, when longtime residents of Wolfensberger Road and Highway 105 tried to banish bicyclists from their roads, they were, in a real sense, fighting to preserve their rural way of life in the face of rapid and threatening change.

One year later the bicycle-motorist conflict in Douglas County shifted to the state capitol and took on statewide implications. In February 1993 state representative Jeanne Adkins, a Parker Republican, used a parliamentary sleight of hand to attach an amendment to "a seemingly innocuous House bill on county responsibilities" to authorize county commissioners to ban bicycles from roads less than thirty-four feet wide and with speed limits greater than forty miles per hour, or where more than one thousand vehicles traveled daily. The continuing conflict in Douglas County lay behind Adkins's maneuver, and she clearly sided with the motorists, though she called her amendment a "public safety issue." A Douglas County spokesperson, however, conceded that there had been no reports of serious accidents in the county for several years.[45]

Opposition to Adkins's gambit was swift and powerful. Republican House leader Tim Foster opposed the measure, as did Boulder

Republican Drew Clark, who said, "It's inappropriate this issue has been slipped in on this bill. The bicycle riders of this state would like to have a chance to comment on this." Westminster Democrat Vi June also sided with bicyclists and explained that her husband "was on the Ride the Rockies event last summer in Douglas County . . . and was run off the road by a fellow in a pickup who not only ran him off the road but flipped him the bird as he went alongside." Although the story seemed frightening, "everyone in the chamber roared with laughter," except Adkins. Representative June argued that "we have to recognize that bicycle riders have rights in this state, and they must be accommodated also."[46]

The House quickly defanged Adkins's amendment and by a large margin adopted a much less restrictive plan, offered by Westminster Republicans Norma Anderson and Shirleen Tucker, which allowed counties to bar cyclists from roads carrying more than fifty thousand vehicles per day. Under that standard virtually all roads in the state would remain open to bicycles. "We don't have a road in this state that does 50,000 in a day," the defeated Adkins snapped.[47]

Like the Washington Park episode, the defeat of this effort to ban bicycles from state roads illustrates the political clout of bicyclists in Colorado. In this case, even the usual lockstep solidarity of statehouse Republicans succumbed to the cyclists' influence.

The disputed roads of Douglas County not only were popular for individual outings but also hosted some of the largest organized cycling events in Colorado. Each June since 1987, the Elephant Rock Century, a one-day, one-hundred-mile event with more than five thousand riders, winds around the county. Another event, the MS 150, a two-day fund-raiser for the National Multiple Sclerosis Society, passes through on the way to Pueblo or Cañon City. Other counties on the edges of metro Denver also see their share of major bike tours. In September the Denver Bicycle Touring Club's annual Front Range Century rolls through Weld, Boulder, and Larimer Counties. Boulder County also hosts the MS Society's annual "Biketoberfest" fundraiser. Colorado's premier bicycle touring event is the *Denver Post*'s annual Ride the Rockies. Since 1985 the tour has taken two thousand cyclists on a six-day, four-hundred-mile ride over several mountain passes. Because of the event's popularity, riders are drawn by lot and often represent several states and foreign countries. The tour is often a boon to the towns it passes through, as riders altogether spend as much as ninety thousand dollars per night for lodging, food, and services.[48]

Professional bicycle racing also enjoyed a period of popularity during the 1970s and 1980s. In 1975 Mo Siegel, head of Boulder's Celestial Seasonings tea company, founded the Red Zinger Bicycle Classic, a two-day event with a budget of twenty thousand dollars. By 1979, the race had expanded from its Boulder base to include events in Aspen, Vail, Estes Park, and Colorado Springs. Future Olympic and professional cycling stars such as Davis Phinney and Connie Carpenter competed in the race, which by 1980 had outgrown the tea company's sponsorship. In April 1980 Siegel relinquished sponsorship to the Coors Brewing Company. Siegel stated that "in order for this bike race to grow it needs more muscle. . . . [W]e're passing the baton to a company that wants to see bike racing grow in this country." For the next seven years Coors did expand the race, which it renamed the Coors International Bicycle Classic, but in so doing it took the event away from its Colorado foundations. In 1985 the race added stages in Nevada and California and attracted Tour de France winner Bernard Hinault. In 1987 Hawaii became part of the race's circuit. By the late 1980s the Coors Classic was one of the most popular cycling events in the world, attracting crowds as large as fifty thousand people to the race's finale in Boulder. In 1987 the problems of large crowds prompted residents of a northern Boulder neighborhood to demand that the race be moved to the University of Colorado campus. The potential for future such conflicts ended the following year when Coors dropped its sponsorship in favor of supporting a Tour de France team. In July 1989 race director Michael Aisner canceled the event. Speaking for cyclists and fans, racer Marianne Martin, a Women's Tour de France winner, said, "[I]sn't it sad? It was such a focus of the racing season. It energized the state, and we will all miss it."[49]

MOUNTAIN BIKING

A different sort of race was born in 1976, on 12,700-foot Pearl Pass between Aspen and Crested Butte. That September a group of motorcyclists from Aspen rode over the pass on a rock-littered mule trail to Crested Butte. As the group moved from bar to bar, recalled Crested Butte's Carole Bauer, "they were strutting around, being macho" about their motorcycling bravado. Not to be outdone, a group from Crested Butte, denizens of Oscar's Bar, decided to ride bicycles, and other conveyances, over the pass to show up the Aspenites. Richard "The Rat" Ullery rode in a bathtub of beer in the back of a pickup truck. Only two in the group made the entire trip on bicycles, old-fashioned paperboy-style bikes with fat tires and heavy frames. However, the stunt caught the attention of a group of Californians who had been tinkering with "clunker" bikes in Marin County. Two years later the Californians joined the Crested Butte group for another assault on Pearl Pass. The event has since become an annual affair, Fat Tire Bike Week, held each July with races, bike rodeos, and bicycle limbo.[50]

The Pearl Pass adventure of 1978 brought together many of the pioneers of a new sport and a new kind of bicycle, the mountain bike. Marin County, California, was the birthplace of the mountain bike. In 1974 members of a Marin cycling club set out to make a bicycle that, with its rider, could survive hair-raising descents down the fire roads of 2,600-foot Mount Tamalpais. They outfitted old Schwinn frames with heavy, wide tires capable of withstanding road hazards and began careening down the mountain. The first descents down Mount Tamalpais were frightful fun, but there were problems. Coaster brakes and wheel bearings often overheated, and the bikes' single-speed gearing made riding up the hill virtually impossible. Mariners Gary Fisher, Joe Breeze, Otis Guy, and Charlie Kelly began adapting multiple gearing, motorcycle handlebars, and brake levers, even drum brakes, to the Schwinns to improve performance and make uphill riding possible. The bikes, however, were still heavy. In 1977 Joe Breeze built a new diamond-shaped frame of chrome-molybdenum steel that was both lighter and stronger. The result was the first true modern mountain bike. Breeze built and quickly sold a small number of his "Breezers." Two years later Fisher, Kelly, and Tom Ritchey, a frame builder, introduced their "MountainBike," which featured fifteen-speed gearing, lightweight-alloy wheel rims, and knobby tires. In 1981 Mike Sinyard, head of Specialized Bicycle Components, bought four MountainBikes and, using them as prototypes, made more modifications and had a new bike, the "Specialized Stumpjumper," built in Japan. The Stumpjumper sold for $650, half the price of the Fisher-Kelly-Ritchey MountainBike, and became the first commercially successful, mass-produced mountain bike.[51]

It did not take long for one of the Marin County "clunker" pioneers to come up with the idea of racing their new type of bicycle down the county's mountain roads. In 1976 Charlie Kelly helped organize a race down Pine Mountain, not far from Mount Tamalpais. The race immediately became known as the "Repack." The name came from the race's effects on the early "clunkers." After a 1,200-foot descent in 1.8 miles, Kelly explained, "our hubs overheated so much that the grease sizzled right out of them. Before we could ride again, we had to repack the bearings with grease." Soon, he said, "everyone called the hill 'Repack' and from that the race took its name." By 1984 the race's popularity, and mounting tensions between mountain bikers and others, prompted local authorities to ban the event. It was an augury of conflicts to come.[52]

Although Marin County, California, owns the title of mountain bicycling's birthplace, Colorado quickly became the sport's home. Crested Butte, home of Fat Tire Bike Week, the annual festival of mountain bike racing, exhibitions of new bikes and gear, and partying, has long claimed to be the nation's mountain bicycling capital, boasting more bikes per capita than any other town. Crested Butte is also the home of the Mountain Bike Hall of Fame and Museum, where technological and human relics of mountain biking are enshrined. Durango is Crested Butte's major rival for the title of mountain biking's capital. The town has lured many of mountain bike racing's top figures, including Ned Overend, a six-time national champion, and Ruthie Matthes and Juli Furtado, who have won women's titles. Durango's Fort Lewis College boasts a top-ranked collegiate mountain bike racing team that, though not supported by athletic scholarships, has won several National Collegiate Cycling Association championships. Although Crested Butte has its Fat Tire Bike Week, Durango has its own annual Iron Horse Bicycle Classic, pitting cyclists against the historic Durango-to-Silverton narrow-gauge train that has carried passengers between the two San Juan Mountain mining towns since 1882.[53]

At least ten thousand miles of dirt roads and trails crisscross U.S. Forest Service and Bureau of Land Management (BLM) lands in Colorado, and mountain bicyclists seemingly have staked their claim to all of them. As mountain biking's popularity grew in the 1980s and 1990s, so, too, did the popularity of off-road riding, especially on the challenging, narrow, rugged trails cyclists call "single tracks." In national parks and forests, rangeland, and open spaces in and on the edges of urban areas, the hum of knobby tires on dirt became a familiar, if not always welcome, sound.

As more cyclists took to the hills, conflicts soon developed between them and other trail users. Hikers and equestrians complained that the cyclists frightened horses and wildlife, littered, damaged the soil, were rude, and just plain made nuisances of themselves. Critics were especially incensed over cyclists riding in wilderness areas. Relying on claims that bicycle tires caused serious environmental damage, public land-management agencies in Colorado and throughout the country began in the 1980s to ban or severely restrict off-road bicycling. By the mid-1990s, however, as scientific studies showed that bicycle tires caused no more soil damage than hikers, and less than horse hooves, public agencies and environmental groups began to ease their opposition to mountain bikes. Bicycles remained excluded from wilderness areas, and are strictly regulated in national parks, but access to forest and BLM lands has increased, especially in more developed areas. Indeed, mountain biking has been encouraged in developed areas in order to minimize conflicts elsewhere. Several Colorado ski areas, including Vail, Winter Park, Purgatory, and Crested Butte, helped ease pressure and conflicts on the trails by opening their slopes and lifts to mountain bicyclists. Some new trails, however, were opened in less developed areas. Kokopelli's Trail, opened in 1989, winds 140 miles from the Grand Junction area to Moab, Utah, that state's major mountain bicycling center. The popular trail, named for a mythical Anasazi flute player, was the product of a cooperative effort by the BLM and an army of volunteers.[54]

Mountain biking organizations such as the National Off-Road Bicycle Association (which also organizes and sanctions mountain bike races) and the International Mountain Bicycling Association work to open and maintain off-road trails and to proselytize codes of trail ethics for cyclists, urging courtesy, self-control, and obedience of trail rules. Public land-management agencies also became involved in mountain biking etiquette and enforcement. In 1993 the U.S. Forest Service hired its first full-time mountain bike ranger to patrol the Arapahoe National Forest. Ranger Amy Bauer explained her job, noting that "although I have law enforcement powers, my intention is education—teaching novice mountain bikers about courtesy, to always yield to horseback riders or hikers and stay on established trails."[55]

The most bitter and enduring conflicts between mountain bicyclists and others took place not in the high country but on the edges of Colorado's urban areas. In Boulder, for example, the city council in 1983 banned bicycles from the city's greenbelt area, though angry protests from cyclists quickly forced the city to reopen twenty-three trails to bicycling. However, in 1987 Boulder banned bicycles from its mountain parks, citing soil erosion and mounting conflicts between cyclists and hikers as reasons. Elsewhere, trouble brewed between cyclists, hikers, and equestrians on the off-road trails of Jefferson County. About half of Colorado's population lives in the Denver metropolitan area. With tens of thousands of cyclists in the region, Jefferson County's mountain parks attracted off-road riding enthusiasts from Denver, Adams, Arapahoe, and Boulder Counties, as well as from fast-growing Jefferson County itself. By the early 1990s relations among trail users went from strained to openly hostile. Hikers complained of rude, aggressive, and dangerous cyclists. Cyclists complained of rude, uncompromising hikers who refused to share the trails. Referring to the bad blood, one cyclist declared, "[I]t's pathetic. That's what the outdoors are there for—to get away from all that. It's becoming a battleground." County officials said that though "the majority of mountain biking enthusiasts are courteous . . . there's always that certain percentage that doesn't announce when they're coming up. . . . They take the attitude that they own the trail." Efforts to educate that minority through signage had not worked because "a lot of people don't read the signs." By the end of 1996, Jefferson County was actively considering several options, including closing some trails to cyclists; opening trails on alternating days to cyclists, horse riders, and hikers; and constructing alternate trail sections for cyclists to bypass congested areas, especially at trailheads.[56]

ECONOMIC IMPACT OF CYCLING

Most mountain bicycles, and their riders, never see a high-country trail or a single track. The majority are used on city streets and bike paths. Recreational cyclists and commuters quickly adopted the mountain bicycle as the wheel of choice, finding it more comfortable and better suited than the narrow-tired traditional road bicycle to the hazards of potholes and broken bottles on the streets. Sales of mountain bicycles, in fact, were the driving force in the cycling boom of the 1980s and 1990s. Bicycle shops in the United States sold 30 million bicycles between 1980 and 1993. Of 8.7 million sold in 1993, nearly 8.4 million were mountain bicycles.[57]

Colorado reaped a generous economic boon from bicycling's popularity. In 1984 the bicycling industry in the state rang up $75 million in total sales and service. A decade later some 350 bicycle stores, fifty-seven manufacturers, marketing and publishing firms, and trade associations employed two thousand people and generated more than $700 million in sales. In addition, cycling was a source of indirect employment and profit, most notably in ski areas that offered their lifts and trails to cyclists in the warm-weather months. When Vail hosted the 1994 World Mountain Bike Championships, participants from forty-eight countries and forty thousand spectators pumped an estimated $15 million into the resort's economy. Small-town stores, restaurants, and motels near popular trailheads also profited from cycling's growth. In 1996 the town of Fruita, near the Utah border, inaugurated a Fat Tire Festival that attracted 350 cyclists. The town, which is near the eastern end of the Kokopelli Trail leading to Moab, hoped that cycling would become an important part of its economic recovery from the collapse of oil-shale development in the area. In addition, the Federal Intermodal Surface Transportation Act of 1992 gave Colorado about $7 million per year for building and maintaining bicycle paths.[58]

On the manufacturing side, Colorado-based companies made both production and custom bicycles, components and accessories, and clothing. Among them were Yeti Cycles, which manufactured high-end mountain bicycles in Durango from 1991 until 1999 when Yeti's parent company, Schwinn/GT, concluded that Durango's remote location put the operation too far away from the corporation's distribution centers. One of the oldest and best-known bicycle builders, Schwinn, was a transplant to Colorado. Founded in 1895, Schwinn made its headquarters in Chicago for nearly a century. A conservative, family-owned business, Schwinn had not kept pace with the rapid technological changes in bicycling in the 1980s and 1990s. By the early 1990s the company's share of the U.S. bicycle market fell to about 5 percent, and in 1992 Schwinn filed for bankruptcy protection. In 1993 Scott Sports Group (now Scott USA), a bicycle and accessory manufacturer, bought Schwinn and moved the company to Boulder. The reborn company, with one hundred employees, produces a full line of recreational and racing bicycles. The Schwinn operation merged with GT, one of the largest bicycle builders in the world, in 1998.[59]

Schwinn symbolized both continuity and change in a century and a quarter of cycling in Colorado. At the close of the twentieth century, bicycling remained largely a middle-class recreational sport. However, because the middle class had become the largest segment of society, cycling was no longer the elite sport it had been in the nineteenth century. That turn of events made the sport—like the social class that made it its own—only more socially, economically, and politically significant. Cycling remains primarily an urban sport, a characteristic underscored by the fact that most mountain bikes never leave pavement. To be sure, though, many cyclists yearn for open spaces, just as their forebears did at the turn of the century. Conflicts between cyclists and other users of the road today are remarkably similar to those of a hundred years ago. Indeed, tensions between mountain bicyclists and those who have a vision of a pristine countryside are not much different from the conflicts between cyclists on the Broadway–South Platte trail and the farmer who worried about them molesting his melons. In all of these battles, cyclists have more than held their own because, in the end, they represent a powerful middle-class constituency.

Cyclists of the Gilded Age and of the late twentieth century shared a dream expressed in verse by teenaged wheelman Frank Tupper in the 1890s:

I want to ride a gold wheel
Upon a golden shore
Where streets of gold are smoothly rolled
And punctures punk no more.[60]

THE RECREATIONAL SKIING INDUSTRY

Skiing in Colorado was born in the Rocky Mountain mining towns where long Norwegian snowshoes became important means of wintertime travel and communication. However, the men and women of the mining towns also learned to use their skis for fun. Cross-country outings and death-defying plunges down mountainsides became mainstays of recreation and social life in the camps. Without knowing it, the Reverend John Dyer (the skiing preacher), mail carrier Al Johnson, and ski racer Charles Baney also anticipated two different skiing traditions, the Nordic and the Alpine, which, like the sport itself, were imported from Europe and helped shape the development of skiing in Colorado. By the latter decades of the twentieth century, recreational skiing became a major industry controlled by corporate giants and second only to agriculture in its contribution to Colorado's economy.

Scandinavian immigrants brought the Nordic style of skiing, with its emphases on cross-country travel and competitive jumping, to America by the mid-nineteenth century. From the Norwegian redoubts of the upper Midwest, skiing spread west to California, carried there during the gold rush, and by the early 1860s to Colorado where it took root first as a utilitarian activity. However, to the Norse, skiing was much more than a means of getting from one place to another; it represented a social ideal harking back to the classical Greeks.

The Norwegian word *Idraet* expresses the ideal of sport as a means of physical and moral improvement. Skiing historian E. John B. Allen notes that by the mid-1830s the Idraet ideal "included the idea of striving to perfect the individual soul as well as the body." The moral and physical well-being of the individual, Allen notes, was to translate in societywide regeneration "by making all citizens dignified, courageous, skilled, healthy, and moral."[1]

In the upper Midwest, especially in Michigan, Minnesota, and Wisconsin, and in New England, local ski clubs dedicated to this Idraet ideal proliferated in the decades between 1880 and 1910. These clubs devoted themselves to promoting and preserving the *skiidraet,* the "skisport," as a physically and morally useful activity by organizing cross-country outings and competitions and, occasionally, ski-jumping contests. Until the turn of the century, many of these clubs limited membership to persons of Scandinavian descent, used Norwegian names, and sported uniforms to enhance their social cohesiveness. By the early twentieth century, however, ethnic exclusiveness gave way to pluralism as Scandinavian immigrants and their offspring fitted themselves into American society, and as interest in skiing spread beyond the Scandinavian community. The ski clubs were male-dominated organizations, though by the early twentieth century most welcomed women, if not as full members then as participants in club activities. Women, however, usually did not compete in club contests.

The formation of the National Ski Association (NSA) in 1905 underscored the spread of skiing in the early years of the twentieth century. Headquartered at Ishpeming, Michigan, the NSA's mission was to promote the Idraet ideal and, especially, to make and enforce uniform rules governing skisport competitions. Although many Idraet purists preferred cross-country skiing and racing, which highlighted the athlete's skill and stamina, the daring-do and quicker outcomes of ski-jumping competitions often proved more satisfying to American tastes, especially as spectator exhibitions.[2]

Ski clubs first appeared in Colorado in the 1880s. Although they promoted skiing as a healthful and enjoyable activity, they did not become as formal as the eastern clubs with their uniforms, complex rules, and Idraet idealism. In addition, they were much more transient. The ski clubs founded in the 1880s in the Crested Butte and

Gunnison areas disappeared by the 1890s. Skiing itself did not disappear from the Colorado Rockies, but the hard times in the mining industry in the late years of the nineteenth century caused a decline in the mining, and hence the skiing, population. For nearly a quarter century, skiing as an organized recreational activity lay virtually dormant in Colorado.

CARL HOWELSEN AND THE REVIVAL OF RECREATIONAL SKIING

The arrival in Colorado of a Norwegian ski jumper signaled a revival of recreational skiing. Carl Howelsen became the link between skiing's Nordic nineteenth-century beginnings and its twentieth-century development as a modern recreational industry.

Born in Oslo in 1879, Howelsen learned to ski at age four. By the time he left Norway in 1904 he had won every major cross-county and ski-jumping contest in the country. He came to the United States in 1904 and settled first in Chicago and worked at his craft as a stonemason. Skiing, however, was never far from his thoughts. One summer day he visited an amusement park and was intrigued at the sight of a small boat careening down a water chute into a pool. Could he slide down the chute on skis? Howelsen convinced the concessionaire to let him try. As his son related the story many years later, Howelsen "smeared the bottom of his skis with soap. He took off from the top of the chute, landing several yards out on the lake. He was going so fast that he skimmed along the surface on his skis for quite some distance before he began to sink."[3]

Howelsen's plunge down the amusement park water slide became a regular sight and one day caught the attention of the director of the Ringling Brothers and Barnum & Bailey Circus who asked him to perform his stunt under the big top. Howelsen became the circus's "Flying Norwegian," sailing down a wooden scaffold and flying off a jump at the bottom, sometimes leaping over two elephants. However, Howelsen's circus career ended abruptly when he fell from the top of the scaffold and injured his back.[4]

By 1911 Howelsen had moved to Colorado, working for a time as a mason in Denver (fig. 4-1). However, the mountains and their deep snow proved a powerful lure, drawing Howelsen to Hot Sulphur Springs, in Grand County. He found work as a stonemason, but

4-1. Ski jumper Carl Howelsen came to Colorado in 1911. He represents a link between skiing's nineteenth-century Nordic beginnings and the sport's development as a recreational industry in the twentieth century. (Back row, *left to right:* Hans Hanson, Carl Howelsen, Anders Haugen, Lars Haugen. Front row, *left to right:* Ivan Flood, Peter Prestrud.) Courtesy, Colorado Historical Society, F 8083.

devoted his free time to ski jumping. In the fall of 1911 he built a four-foot jump on Bungalow Hill and began to dazzle the townsfolk with his jumping feats. Within days Howelsen taught the area's children, and some of the adults, to ski and jump. By the end of December, the Norwegian newcomer convinced his neighbors to form a ski club, the Winter Sports Club of Hot Sulphur Springs. As its first project, the club decided to stage a winter sports carnival. After six weeks of preparation the carnival took place on February 14–15, 1912. Eight thousand people turned out to watch and participate in a variety of sledding, skating, and skiing events, including cross-country and, of course, jumping contests. Howelsen was the star of the carnival, winning the jumping event with a leap of seventy-nine feet. He also won a quarter-mile sprint, but Gunnar Dahle, from Williams Fork, de-

feated him in the five-mile cross-country race. Howelsen also dominated the Winter Sports Club's second annual carnival, in February
1913. The club tried to make that year's ski-jumping contest more
competitive by importing two professional jumpers from Minnesota.
However, both pros fell on their jumps and were eliminated. Howelsen
won easily with a jump of 119 feet, 3 inches, besting rival Gunnar
Dahle by more than twenty-three feet.[5]

Soon after the 1913 Hot Sulphur Springs carnival, Howelsen
moved back to Denver to find work as a bricklayer. A March 1913
blizzard created the setting for a chance encounter between Howelsen
and George Cranmer, who later became manager of Denver's park
system. In a sense, their meeting linked Howelsen to the development of Alpine, or downhill recreational, skiing in Colorado. Cranmer
recalled that "it had snowed for three or four days and there was four
feet on the ground." Walking from his Capitol Hill home toward
Broadway, on an errand to buy milk for his young child, Cranmer
paused in his struggle with the deep snowdrifts to watch a group of
men "sliding down the hill at the Capitol grounds. A friend loaned
me his skis and I took a couple of slides. Howelsen was there, and he
later ordered a pair of skis from Norway for me. You might say I was
bitten." By 1918, Cranmer was involved in ski-jumping and cross-
country outings, and he later played a role in the establishment of
Denver's Winter Park ski area.[6]

Howelsen's second sojourn in Denver was brief, for the attraction of steady work in the Queen City of the Plains was no match for
the lure of deep mountain snow. Marjorie Perry, herself a skiing legend known for her cross-country trips from Steamboat Springs to
Denver, convinced Howelsen that the Yampa Valley town could support a stonecutter. By the end of 1913, Howelsen moved to Steamboat
Springs, built a ski jump, and was dazzling the town's young people
with his leaps. Reports of a flying man soon brought a delegation of
parents to investigate. Rather than try to explain his sport, Howelsen
simply gave an on-the-spot demonstration with a seventy-foot jump.
The townsmen were satisfied that nothing supernatural was going
on, and, with their blessings, Howelsen was soon busy teaching Steamboat Springs' youngsters the art of ski jumping, including demanding
lessons in physical conditioning and maintaining equipment. One of

Howelsen's students recalled that he "insisted all the boys tie the skis to their feet." At first the boy's parents thought that plan was too dangerous, but "after they saw my skis come off a few times while I was still rather high in the air, they let me tie them on."[7]

Recalling his successful ski carnivals at Hot Sulphur Springs, Howelsen in 1914 organized Steamboat Springs' first winter festival featuring cross-country and novelty races and ski jumping. Not surprisingly, Howelsen won the jumping competition with a flight of 115 feet. The competition proved tougher in succeeding years. World champion Ragnar Omtvedt came to Steamboat Springs in 1915 and, on a new jump built on the hill later named for Howelsen, won with a leap of 145 feet. Omtvedt's jump, however, was fourteen feet short of his own world record. A local rancher is said to have asked the champion what encouragement he needed to break the record. Omtvedt answered, "Fifty dollars." After two more tries the champion managed only to tie his record, but the rancher was pleased enough with the effort to pay him.[8]

The next year Omtvedt easily broke his record with a jump of 192 feet. In 1917, however, Michigan's Henry Hall soared 203 feet, the first jump by anyone over 200 feet.[9]

Carl Howelsen left Colorado in 1922 and returned to Norway for his parents' fiftieth wedding anniversary. The trip was supposed to be only a visit, but while in Norway Howelsen married and never returned to the United States. He continued to ski and jump until two years before his death in 1955.

Ski Clubs

Ski jumping was well established as a recreational and spectator sport in Colorado by the time Howelsen departed for Norway. Ski clubs, including some based in Denver, sustained interest in the sport through the 1930s and helped pave the way for skiing's dual transformation from the Nordic style to the Alpine style and into a mass sport.

In 1912 a group of middle- and upper-class Denverites formed the Colorado Mountain Club. The club's agenda was both recreational and political, organizing winter sports outings and campaigning for conservation causes. The group played a role in the establishment of Rocky Mountain National Park, an area they favored for their cross-country skiing outings. Club members learned the basics of skiing from an Italian army officer who gave lessons on the grounds of the John Evans estate overlooking the elite Denver Country Club. In 1919 the club shifted its attention from cross-country to downhill skiing and jumping. At Genesee Mountain, Denver's first mountain park, the Colorado Mountain Club laid out a one-thousand-foot ski run and built a jump. That winter, "thousands of Denverites flocked up to Genesee to watch flying skiers sail off the strange chute."[10]

Meanwhile, across the Continental Divide at Dillon, Peter Prestrud, another Norwegian immigrant, organized local ski enthusiasts to build a world-class ski jump. Prestrud's jump soon caught the attention of the best jumpers in the country. In 1919 Anders Haugen, a South Dakotan transplanted from Telemark, Norway, traveled to Dillon to test the jump and promptly set a new world record with a flight of 213 feet. He topped that mark in 1920 with a leap of 214 feet. Four years later Haugen captained the first U.S. Winter Olympic team.[11]

Haugen's feats and skiing's quickly growing popularity in Colorado forced the national skiing establishment to take note. In 1920 National Ski Association president G. C. Torguson even predicted that "the Rockies will become the center of skiing in the United States."[12]

All across Colorado—from Denver to Dillon, to Gunnison, to Steamboat Springs—local clubs sustained and built enthusiasm for skiing. In the process, they also began shifting from cross-country skiing and jumping to downhill skiing.

Speeding downhill on skis was hardly a twentieth-century development, as the veterans of the Gunnison County Norwegian Snow-Shoe Club's races in the 1880s could testify. However, flying downhill on a beeline was far different from the Alpine style of skiing with its graceful turns. As one Summit County ski veteran put it, "Sure, you could turn, if you wanted to. But the skis wouldn't turn—no way!" Moreover, long, arduous climbs to the top severely tempered the attraction of downhill skiing for all but the hardiest adventurers.[13]

The problem of turning on skis was actually solved before guides, miners, and trappers began using long Norwegian snowshoes in Colorado. At Telemark, Norway, Sondrie Norheim developed a new heel binding that permitted him to make easy, controlled turns. British mountain climbers, who preferred fast descents after long climbs in the Swiss and Austrian Alps, soon adopted the Telemark technique. Early in the twentieth century, Austrian Hannes Schneider refined the Telemark technique with the "stem," or Arlberg, turn. Schneider found that by using a deeper crouch than the Norwegian method he could turn with greater control and at higher speeds. The Arlberg turn made fast, spectacular downhill slalom racing practical. By 1930 even the Federation Internationale de Ski (FIS), the skisport's world governing body, and a redoubt of the Idraet ideal, recognized downhill and slalom racing as legitimate competitive sports.[14]

Wealthy American tourists, including coaches and members of Dartmouth University's famed Outing Club, carried the Arlberg style of skiing across the Atlantic to America during the 1920s and made it the upper-class elite's preferred winter sport. The Arlberg's triumph among the East's skiing elite seemed complete in 1925 when the Dartmouth club held its first slalom race. By the end of the decade, high society in Denver had also adopted downhill skiing as its favorite winter pastime. The *Denver Post* noted in 1929 that "the latest wrinkle adopted by society is a pronounced interest in winter sports, and skiing is the favorite of them all." The *Post* also prophesied that Genesee would one day be a "miniature St. Moritz." Emblematic of the shift from Nordic to Alpine skiing, enthusiasts favored Bavarian and Austrian clothing styles and adopted German skiing terminology, including the robust greeting, "Ski Heil." That greeting, however, fell out of style by the 1940s as it sounded too much like the Nazi "Seig Heil."[15]

SKI TRAINS AND EARLY TOWS

The trick in downhill skiing is not so much getting down as getting up to the top of the mountain in the first place. During the 1920s and 1930s, ski enthusiasts in Colorado developed novel techniques to reach the mountains and their favorite runs.

The tracks of the Denver and Rio Grande Railroad (D&RG) served as many skiers' route to the slopes. When construction of the Moffat Tunnel was finished in 1927, Denver skiers began riding the train to the tunnel's West Portal where they found ideal skiing terrain

4-2. Skiers leaving the Rio Grande ski train at West Portal, near the future Winter Park ski resort. One couple's Bavarian ski outfits (lower left) suggest that this photo was taken before World War II, when German fashion and ski terminology were still in vogue. Before the era of modern highways and ski lifts, getting to a good ski site and up to the top of the hill were serious challenges. Trains solved part of the problem. Courtesy, Colorado Historical Society, F 23643.

(fig. 4-2). They also took over abandoned construction shacks and turned them into warming huts. West Portal was not a scheduled stop on the D&RG line, so leaving the train was itself something of an adventure. Skier Frank Ashley recalled that the train slowed as it approached West Portal, "so we'd throw the skis out and then jump." By the mid-1930s members of Denver's elite Arlberg Club were at work grooming trails near West Portal, which, in 1940, became the Winter Park ski area. By then the train carried so many passengers to the area that it had to stop to let them off. In addition, Denver's two daily newspapers, the *Rocky Mountain News* and the *Denver Post,* along with the Safeway and Montgomery Ward stores, sponsored train excur-

4-3. Riding Aspen's boat tow up the hill could be as exciting as skiing down.
The tow, operated in the 1930s and 1940s, had a tendency to flip over. Courtesy,
the Denver Public Library, Western History Department.

sions to the Hot Sulphur Springs and Steamboat Springs winter carnivals. Skiers from Gunnison and Salida rode the train to the top of
Marshall Pass.[16]

Ski trains only partly solved the problem of access to the slopes.
Unless the train made frequent back-and-forth trips, skiers still faced
the prospect of climbing back uphill after a run, or being satisfied
with only one run. Only the hardiest of ski maniacs relished the challenge of slogging thousands of feet uphill through hip-deep snow.
Skiers early on knew that the mechanical tow was the answer to their
uphill transportation needs.

As early as 1914 Carl Blaurock, Denver's dental gold manufacturer, and other members of the Colorado Mountain Club, fashioned
a rope tow, powered by a Model T Ford, on a slope at the Rilliet
ranch on Lookout Mountain. The era of the tow really arrived, however,
in the 1930s when ski clubs and local entrepreneurs using automobiles, freestanding engines, and scrounged mining tram equipment
began to build tows all over the state. In 1934 the Steamboat Springs

Winter Sports Club built a boat tow, a wooden sled with bench seats hauled up the slope on a cable (fig. 4-3). Aspen's Roaring Fork Winter Sports Club built another boat tow on Aspen Mountain in 1937. An old mine hoist pulled the eight-passenger sled up the mountain. The trip uphill could become exciting since the unstable contraption occasionally spilled its passengers into a twenty-foot ravine on the way up. Denver's May Company department store set up a rope tow on Berthoud Pass in 1937 to promote sales of ski equipment. In 1938 Thor Groswold, Denver's major ski manufacturer, and J. C. Blickensderfer, leaders of the Zipfelberger ski racing club, set up a portable tow at Porcupine Gulch on Loveland Pass. The tow, which they christened the "Little Sweden Freezer Company," consisted of a 4.5-horsepower engine mounted on a toboggan that pulled itself along one thousand feet of rope.[17]

More comfortable, if occasionally exciting, lifts appeared by the early 1940s. Winter Park had a Comstam T-bar tow operating by 1941. Chair lifts were also coming into use by then at Red Mountain, near Glenwood Springs, and at Cement Creek, north of Gunnison. The Cement Creek lift, "a marvel of seat-of-the-pants engineering," had eighty chairs and rose thirteen hundred vertical feet along three thousand feet of cable. Built with funds granted by the New Deal's Works Progress Administration, supplemented by local subscriptions, the tow used an old mine tram and a bull wheel salvaged from a Denver junkyard and parts from World War I trucks, all driven by a 400-horsepower engine. One of its builders noted that, "all things considered, it worked pretty well." However, Crested Butte's John Somrak recalled that "once in a while it would slip and start running backwards. Everyone had to bail out."[18]

Ramshackle affairs that they were, these first tows represented the earliest foundations of the commercial skiing industry in Colorado. Still, they served mainly club, local, and day skiers who depended on nearby towns for food, lodging, and other amenities. Nevertheless, skiing—and its commercial possibilities—grew rapidly in the 1930s, as evidenced by the estimated fifty thousand skier days spent at Berthoud Pass alone in the winter of 1938–1939. By the late 1930s enterprising ski enthusiasts began to explore the idea of building self-contained resorts.[19]

ASPEN, THE 1930S

Would-be developers in Colorado had a model of a luxury destination resort to emulate in the Union Pacific Railroad's Sun Valley development in Idaho. Opened in December 1936, Sun Valley quickly became a favored winter playground of America's rich and famous. Hollywood personalities, including Clark Gable, Gary Cooper, and Claudette Colbert, came to ski and be seen, and novelist Ernest Hemingway kept a house there. Sun Valley offered luxury accommodations, world-class slopes, and the world's first chair lift, modeled on a banana-loading hoist found in Honduras. Union Pacific engineers simply substituted chairs for the fruit hooks. There would be no climbing or uncomfortable, clumsy rope or boat tows for Sun Valley's guests.[20]

Aspen became the site of the first grand plans for a ski resort in Colorado to go beyond the dream stage. At the center of those plans were Thomas J. Flynn, William Fiske III, and Theodore S. Ryan. Flynn grew up in Aspen and, though he lived in Pasadena, California, cherished memories of wintertime sports and scenery in the Roaring Fork area. Fiske was the scion of a prominent eastern banking family and an avid winter outdoorsman. A skilled skier and bobsledder, Fiske won a gold medal in the 1928 Olympics. After college in England, Fiske went to work on Wall Street, but much preferred the excitement of sports to the drudgery of the office. Ted Ryan, another wealthy easterner, met Fiske at the 1936 Olympics in Germany, where the two commiserated over the lack of challenging, elite ski resorts in America. The following summer Fiske met Flynn at a party in California, and the two men talked about mining, real estate, and winter sports. Whether then or sometime later, Flynn convinced Fiske to go to Colorado to see Aspen's scenery and its skiing potential. In July 1936 Fiske and Los Angeles real estate developer Robert Rowan joined Flynn for a tour. The party motored up Aspen Mountain and, from a point above the Midnight Mine, gazed at the slopes and meadows of Mount Hayden. Fiske had seen enough. He said to Flynn, "Tom, you have it, this is the place."[21]

Flynn, Fiske, and Rowan soon formed the Highland-Bavarian Corporation and began recruiting new members to their team to develop Aspen into a major ski resort. Fiske turned to his friend Ted

Ryan to promote and run the company. He also recruited Swiss engineer and mountain climber Andre Roch and Gunter Langes, an Italian skier and mountaineer, to survey the area for suitable ski runs and consult in the resort development plan.[22]

By the time Roch and Langes arrived in Aspen, the Highland-Bavarian investors had already jump-started development. Construction began on the Highland Bavarian Lodge, on Castle Creek, in September 1936. When the lodge opened in December, it had accommodations for sixteen guests. Opening-day visitors included Denver Arlberg Club members Frank Ashley and William and Joseph Hodges. The skiers rode horse-drawn sleighs or climbed to the top of Little Annie Basin and the slopes of Mount Hayden and plunged downhill through unskied powder.[23]

The Highland Bavarian Lodge was a small beginning, but Fiske, Flynn, and Ryan had a grand vision of Aspen's skiing future. In November they told members of the local Lions Club that Aspen would become one of the world's greatest resorts. That news certainly sounded good to Aspenites who had been waiting four decades for the return of the kind of prosperity the town had known during the halcyon days of the silver boom in the 1890s. The *Aspen Times,* reporting the Highland-Bavarian plans, predicted that Aspen would become the "key city for all sporting activities and may again rise to the glories that were hers as the 'Crystal City of the Rockies' during the boom days of the early nineties."[24]

As construction of the Highland Bavarian Lodge proceeded, Andre Roch and Gunter Langes arrived and began their study of the terrain around Aspen. Roch at first was not impressed or optimistic. He found the town run down and depressing. Worse, the surrounding mountains seemed too steep, too heavily forested, and too exposed to sun and wind for viable commercial skiing development. Through the winter of 1936–1937 Roch and Langes divided their time between surveying the terrain and acting as guides for guests at the lodge. However, as Aspen historian Anne Gilbert notes, they "probably felt their trip had been a waste of their time."[25]

Then, in May 1937, with Billy Fiske in tow, they climbed Mount Hayden and skied back down to the nearly abandoned town of Ashcroft. Roch found the view "quite overwhelming," and the skiing even better. "The slopes leading down to Ashcroft," he later wrote, "can be compared with the best of the Parsenn [a mountain in the Swiss Alps]. Immense 'schusses' where your face freezes in the wind and clouds of powder rise behind you, making the skier seem like a rock shooting along the ground, are easily found. Hardly at the end of one schuss, we started into the next one, cheered by the fabulous skiing." Roch now believed that Aspen could be "a resort that would in no way be inferior to anything in the Alps." He later climbed and skied Castle Peak, which he described as more demanding than Mount Hayden, and even more rewarding. "The descent was again a series of basins and steps, one more rewarding than the next."[26]

Before he left Aspen in June 1937, Roch prepared an extensive report that included plans for fifteen ski runs on Mount Hayden, some as long as six miles, and a resort village to accommodate two thousand skiers. Aspen, he concluded, would be "a resort without any competition."[27]

The Highland-Bavarian investors did not wait for Roch's report to beginning promoting their new enterprise. Using film, advertising, and word of mouth, they lured members of America's skiing and social elite to their lodge. They scored an important coup in February–March 1937 when one of the most important figures in American skiing in the 1930s, Otto Schneibs, brought his Dartmouth Outing Club to town. Schneibs was impressed with Aspen, declaring that its climate and snow "surpassed anything I have seen in this country or Europe." Broadcaster Lowell Thomas also visited that first season. He and some friends had been vacationing at Sun Valley and decided to take a look at Aspen on their way home. Thomas became an Aspen regular, sometimes doing his radio program from the Hotel Jerome. Humorist Robert Benchley, a friend of Fiske and Ryan, also helped popularize the new resort in a pamphlet called "How to Aspen." Benchley, a contributor to the *New Yorker*, the eastern elite's guide to where to go and what to be seen doing, compared Aspen favorably to the rigors of a European skiing expedition. After all, to ski at Aspen one need not "get a passport, wrestle with the Atlantic, stop in Paris at the expense of your health, and come all the way back again." And, he added, "you can have just as good a time falling down there as you can on any of the European slopes. If, by any chance,

4-4. Andre Roch laid out Aspen's first ski runs on Mount Hayden in 1937. The Roch Run, on Aspen mountain, seems to go straight into town. Courtesy, Aspen Historical Society.

you want to stand up, you can go just as fast as you could down an Alp."[28]

Colorado's own skiing society also contributed to Aspen's popularity. Visits to the new resort by the Colorado Mountain Club and by ski equipment manufacturer Thor Groswold made Aspen a destination for Denver's elite.

Andre Roch understood that to be a successful ski resort the community itself would have to have a solid skiing culture. The tradition of mining-camp skiing had withered with the decline of the town's mining economy, and many Aspen locals did not know how to ski. In December 1936, Roch helped a group of Aspenites form the Roaring Fork Winter Sports Club (later renamed the Aspen Ski Club) and began giving ski lessons. In February 1937, the club staged its first race. Frank Willoughby, who later helped develop Ajax Mountain, and Doris Sheehan took top honors.[29]

Andre Roch convinced the club members that their ski-racing activities could be an important part of the overall plan to develop the

Aspen area as a major resort. Frank Willoughby recalled Roch's argument that a "difficult but excellent downhill race course" would "attract publicity for Aspen skiing." Thus, before he left Aspen, Roch laid out a trail on Aspen Mountain for the club to develop (fig. 4-4). During the summer of 1937 club members cleared the trail, which they named for Roch, and installed the famous boat tow. Later, with financial help from the town and the federal Works Progress Administration, the club added a warming shack and a ski jump on the mountain and built a clubhouse at the foot of the run on Monarch Street. (New Deal money also helped finance ski-area development at Winter Park, Ouray, and Gunnison.) As its namesake had predicted, the Roch Run added to Aspen's reputation and popularity as it became the site of local, regional, and, in 1941, national championship ski races.[30]

By the early 1940s, then, the stage seemed set for Aspen to become a premier ski resort. The Highland-Bavarian Corporation had won control of the Ashcroft town site, where it intended to build its main resort facilities, and had plans to construct a tramway lift to carry skiers four thousand feet up Mount Hayden. Talks were under way with the U.S. Forest Service for access to land on the mountain for ski runs. The State of Colorado, anxious to stimulate economic growth, had agreed to subsidize the project through the sale of $650,000 in bonds, about half the estimated cost of the tramway.[31]

World War II, however, ended the Highland-Bavarian Corporation's plans for Aspen. The war's first blow to Aspen fell long before American entry into the conflict. Billy Fiske, who in addition to his love of skiing was also an avid aviator, joined England's Royal Air Force (RAF) in August 1939, just days before German troops invaded Poland and sparked the war. A year later Fiske was shot down during the Battle of Britain, the first American killed in combat with the RAF.

Tom Flynn and Ted Ryan continued to work on their development plans after Fiske's death, but much of the fun and enthusiasm for the project seemed to have died with their friend. When the United States entered the war in December 1941, Ryan offered to turn the company's property over to the army to train ski troops. The Highland-Bavarian Corporation and its dream of a world-class resort faded away during the war and were never revived.

However, the company and the Aspen Ski Club had brought Aspen to the attention of much of America's and Europe's skiing and social elite. Other dreamers would pick up the pieces after the war. Even as it interrupted Aspen's dreams of skiing glory, World War II helped set the stage and introduced the players in Colorado skiing's next and greatest phase of development.

THE TENTH MOUNTAIN DIVISION

In November 1939 the Soviet Red Army invaded Finland. The "Winter War" raged through March 1940. That winter, probably in February, Charles Minot "Minnie" Dole, head of the National Ski Patrol Service, and Roger Langley, president of the National Ski Association, joined Boston's Hochbirge Ski Club on its yearly visit to Big Bromley Mountain, Vermont. The men talked of the Soviet-Finnish war. They admired the Finns' use of ski troops to harass and stymie the apparently more powerful Red Army. Dressed in white camouflage, the highly mobile Finnish troops used guerrilla tactics to attack Soviet forces on terrain of their choosing and retreat before the enemy could counterattack. Dole and Langley realized that the United States had no force comparable to the Finnish ski troops, an oversight they set out to correct.[32]

After more than a year of intense lobbying, General George C. Marshall ordered the army to begin training a unit of troops for skiing and mountaineering. In December 1941, three days before Japan attacked Pearl Harbor, the first members of the Eighty-Seventh Mountain Infantry Regiment began training at Fort Lewis, near Mount Rainier, in Washington.

While the first contingent of troops trained in Washington, the army searched for a suitable permanent base for the new unit. After examining and rejecting sites in Yellowstone National Park, Aspen, and Wheeler Junction, Colorado (where the Copper Mountain Resort is located today), the army settled on the town of Pando. Located in a broad valley along Highway 24, a few miles north of Leadville, the Pando site had plenty of room for a large base and good highway and railroad service, and the surrounding twelve-thousand-foot mountains offered superb skiing and mountaineering terrain. On nearby Cooper Hill, where recruits were to learn to ski, the army built the then-longest T-bar lift in the world.

When the not-quite-finished Camp Hale (named for Spanish-American War veteran General Irving Hale, a Colorado native) opened in November 1942, soldiers from South Dakota's Tenth Cavalry Reconnaissance Troop and the Thirty-First Dixie Division from Louisiana joined the troops of the Eighty-Seventh Mountain Infantry. The troops were reorganized into three units: the Eighty-Fifth, the Eighty-Sixth, and the Eighty-Seventh Mountain Infantry Regiments. By early 1943 Camp Hale was home to sixteen thousand soldiers. In July 1943 the army designated the three regiments as the Tenth Light Infantry Division, better known as the Tenth Mountain Division.

Ski historian Jack Benson notes that when the units from Washington, South Dakota, and Louisiana gathered at Camp Hale, "the average ski trooper . . . had never been on a pair of skis." That fact led to serious training and discipline problems, which became readily apparent in January 1943 when division commander Colonel Onslow Rolfe ordered all officers and men to begin ski instruction. Some officers refused to take lessons from lower-rank instructors and stayed away from the training course on Cooper Hill. One colonel insisted on tailoring his ski training to suit his personal needs. Because of an old injury to his left leg, the colonel ordered his instructor, a lieutenant, to teach only right turns. Recalcitrance among the officers spread to the troops, so poor training and lack of discipline became hallmarks of the division in its early days.[33]

Tactical maneuvers conducted in February 1943 exposed the division's problems for all to see. Army brass, and guest observer Minnie Dole, watched poorly trained and led troops struggle to conduct offensive operations in deep snow and subzero cold. By the time it was over, 30 percent of the participants suffered exhaustion and frostbite. One soldier, complaining of conditions at Camp Hale, declared that "anyone who transfers to combat from Camp Hale is a coward."[34]

Because the experiment in making skiers of soldiers had not worked well, the army decided to try to make soldiers of skiers and put Dole and the National Ski Patrol in charge of recruiting three thousand qualified men. Prospective recruits had to present three letters of recommendation to their local ski-patrol official who, if he judged the man competent, would then provide the documents necessary to route the enlistee to Camp Hale. No new recruit could join the Tenth without the approval of the ski patrol. The division's roster soon read like a list of Europe's and America's skiing elite and included the names of many men who became important to the post-war development of Colorado's ski industry. Friedl Pfeifer, winner in 1936 of Europe's premier Alpine event, the Arlberg Kandahar, came from Sun Valley. Dartmouth ski coach Walter Prager and students Percy Rideout, Larry Jump, and John Litchfield enlisted. Steve Knowlton came from the University of New Hampshire. Gordy Wrenn arrived from Steamboat Springs. U.S. national ski-jump champion Torger Tokle, a native of Norway, joined up. So did Peter Seibert and Robert Parker.[35]

Thus augmented, the men of the Tenth began the hard work of making themselves into an elite unit. In addition to standard army training, the troops trained in mountaineering and wilderness survival and worked on their skiing, with instructors empowered to enforce their orders on trainees of all ranks. Early-morning marches with eighty-pound packs, climbing fourteen-thousand-foot mountains, rappelling down cliffs, and traversing chasms on ropes became routine.

As arduous as the training was, most of the men preferred to stay in the mountains, away from Camp Hale and its infamous cloud of diesel and coal smoke that caused a respiratory ailment called the "Pando Hack." When they were not training, they often went off on their own climbing and skiing expeditions, or headed for Denver or Aspen. Steve Knowlton incurred the displeasure of the management of Denver's Brown Palace Hotel when he demonstrated his rappelling technique by jumping from an upper-floor balcony into the hotel's lobby. Aspen, eighty-two miles away, over Battle Mountain, was a favorite destination year-round for organized and small group skiing and hiking trips. Once in town, the soldiers could get a room at the Hotel Jerome for a dollar and anesthetize themselves with the Jerome Bar's infamous "Aspen Crud," a milk shake laced with whiskey. The ski troops also honed their skills on the Roch Run, and Torger Tokle set a new ski-jumping record there. Friedl Pfeifer was so taken with Aspen's skiing and beauty that he vowed to make the town his home after the war. He intended to pick up the pieces of Billy Fiske's dream.

4–5. Troops of the Tenth Mountain Division training in
Colorado. Members of the division returned to Colorado after World War II and played key roles in building
the modern recreational ski industry. Courtesy, the Denver Public Library, Western History Department.

Pfeifer told the town council, "I want to start a ski school here and I'll
give the local children free lessons, so that we can develop a real
skiing community. People will be interested in expanding commercial possibilities, and we'll get enough money to build more adequate
tows and lifts."[36]

In August 1943, part of the Tenth Mountain Division had the
chance to show their fighting ability when the army assigned the
Eighty-Seventh Regiment to participate in amphibious landings (the

one type of operation they had not trained for at Camp Hale) on Kiska Island in the Aleutians. Fighting against Japanese occupying forces at Attu Island the previous May was fierce, and heavy resistance was expected at Kiska as well. However, when the Eighty-Seventh went ashore on August 15, they did not know that the Japanese had abandoned the island. As they moved inland in a dense fog, units of the Eighty-Seventh mistook one another for the enemy and opened fire, causing casualties. Japanese booby traps also took their toll. In all, the Eighty-Seventh sustained twenty-three men killed and fifty-five injured at Kiska.[37]

In March and April 1944, the army gave the Tenth another chance to prove its combat readiness in maneuvers designated as the "D Series" (fig. 4-5). Intended as a demonstration of Alpine fighting methods, the D Series became a test of endurance and survival. A Rocky Mountain blizzard dumped eight feet of snow on the area and drove temperatures to as low as thirty degrees below zero. Frostbite and snow blindness were common, but the men and their units held together. In the end, the Eighty-Seventh Regiment had the best of the maneuvers, and at one point captured Camp Hale itself and made off with the division's payroll. By the time the D Series ended, the men of the Tenth Mountain Division believed that they were ready for anything.[38]

Although they had proved their combat readiness, the soldiers of the Tenth Mountain Division waited until November 1944 for operational orders. They went to Italy and spent the last six months of the war helping drive the last German forces from that country. Their mountain warfare training was invaluable in combat in the Alps, but only three platoons ever used their skis. Howard R. Koch recalled that he went on two ski patrols. "You'd get over the tree line in the Apennines, the Germans would see those ski tracks, and they wouldn't let you have any fun—Kaboom!" The Tenth experienced some of the hardest fighting of the war that winter and spring, including their famous assaults on German artillery positions on Riva Ridge and Mount Belvedere. In all, the Tenth Mountain Division suffered 992 killed and 4,154 wounded in Italy and on Kiska Island. Among the wounded were Friedl Pfeifer and Peter Seibert. Torger Tokle was one of the dead.[39]

After the war many of the men of the Tenth Mountain Division recalled their days in Colorado with great fondness. Some resolved to return, and when they did they played key roles in building Colorado's recreational ski industry. They built major ski areas, operated ski schools, and established equipment-manufacturing companies. Friedl Pfeifer became Aspen Mountain's first manager and later developed the Buttermilk ski area. Peter Seibert joined the ski school at Aspen and, later, in 1962, opened Vail. Robert Parker edited *Skiing* magazine and worked with Seibert at Vail. Larry Jump built Arapahoe Basin. And Gerry Cunningham went into the sports-equipment business. Nationwide, veterans of the Tenth founded twelve major resorts, managed another seventeen, and directed thirty-three ski schools. Four decades after the war, John Frew, president of Colorado Ski Country USA, a ski-industry promotional organization founded in 1963 by Steve Knowlton, noted that "there are very few examples in our country's history where a military division has had such an impact on the culture, economy and spirit of a region."[40]

ASPEN

Elizabeth Paepcke first visited Aspen in 1939. She had been entertaining friends at her ranch house, near Larkspur, when the pipes froze. Paepcke had heard of Aspen and its scenic beauty and used her frozen plumbing as an excuse to go and see the place for herself. She bundled her friends and their skis into a car, drove across the mountains, and checked into the Hotel Jerome. They found the hotel, like the rest of the town, tired but charming. The next morning the group shared a truck ride with miners up the mountain to the Midnight Mine and hiked the rest of the way to the top. Paepcke was stunned by the vista around her. Range upon range of mountains rose and fell "like storm driven waves." Veils of snow blew from the peaks through the bluest sky she had ever seen. She felt "as if the world had been created all over again." Many years later Elizabeth Paepcke recalled thinking to herself "what would happen when Walter got his hands on this place."[41]

Walter Paepcke was a successful Chicago businessman, the head of the Container Corporation of America. He accumulated a comfortable fortune by making better cardboard boxes. However, Paepcke

4-6. Walter Paepcke, a Chicago industrialist, envisioned transforming Aspen into an intellectual and cultural center, with skiing as its economic foundation. Tenth Mountain Division veteran Friedl Pfeifer supplied the skiing expertise and managed both the Aspen Ski Corporation and the Aspen Ski School when they began business in 1946. (*Left to right:* Friedl Pfeifer, Walter Paepcke, Herbert Bayer, and film star Gary Cooper.) Courtesy, Aspen Historical Society.

saw himself as more than just a businessman. Educated at Chicago's Latin School and at Yale, Paepcke believed that men of his class had an obligation to improve the cultural and intellectual fiber of society. The Paepckes brought into their social circle members of the intellectual elite, such as University of Chicago professor Mortimer Adler, whose Great Books seminar they had taken. By the late thirties, Paepcke was apparently nurturing the idea of creating a cultural community where artists and thinkers could gather, live, and create.

When Elizabeth Paepcke returned home to Chicago in 1939, she gave her husband an enthusiastic report on her sojourn to Aspen and urged him to go and see for himself. "Maybe in the summer," he replied. However, World War II began that summer, and wartime activities prevented a visit to Aspen until mid-1945. In the meantime, however, Paepcke made some inquiries about the town and had formed favorable impressions.[42]

The Paepckes finally traveled to Aspen in May 1945, arriving on Memorial Day. Walter quickly decided that here, indeed, was the place where he would build his cultural and intellectual mecca (fig. 4-6). Accessible yet isolated from the hubbub of daily life, and surrounded by uplifting scenery, Aspen seemed the perfect spot to create a community of the mind. To demonstrate his commitment, Paepcke began buying property in the town, including one Victorian home that he gave to Elizabeth. By the end of 1945 Paepcke chartered the Aspen Company to manage his real estate investments, and in 1946 he brought his friend Herbert Bayer, a noted designer, to supervise the town's restoration. Walter Paepcke made it clear that he envisioned not only the physical restoration but also the social transformation of Aspen. "We want writers and scientists and artists and businessmen and we want them to be citizens of Aspen, not seasonal visitors."[43]

Aspen greeted the Paepckes and their project with some degree of ambivalence. Many old-timers still hoped for a revival of the town's long-dormant mining industry. To them, mine tailings, not seminars, represented progress and prosperity. It would be hard to give up the dream of a return to the glory days of silver mining, especially when it was not clear to some where they fit into the new scheme. Nothing so symbolized the townspeople's ambivalence as the rejection by some of Paepcke's offer of free paint to spruce up homes, on the condition that the owners follow Herbert Bayer's advice on color schemes. Such paternalism must have been a bitter experience, indeed, to some proud Aspenites. Nonetheless, it was undeniable that things were happening, on a grand scale, and that money and life were once again flowing into town.[44]

Walter Paepcke was not especially interested in skiing, but he understood that his cultural city-on-a-hill needed a viable economic foundation. Skiing was the logical basis for the town's economic resurrection. Moreover, Paepcke the intellectual shared the conviction, deeply embedded in Western culture, that the health of the body contributes to the health of the mind. Skiing would thus contribute to the larger purposes of the cultural community. In a sense, then,

Paepcke would link the development of recreational Alpine skiing at Aspen to the traditional Nordic Idraet ideal.

Clearly, the Paepckes brought to Aspen a vision of the town's future that was different from the dreams of Ted Ryan, Billy Fiske, and Andre Roch. However, they also brought the organizing and administrative talents, and the financial resources, of corporate capitalism. In order to tie together their vision of a Rocky Mountain Athens, the profit motive, and Aspen's skiing potential, they needed to bring skiing experts into their circle.

Friedl Pfeifer provided the expertise and the leadership to link skiing to Paepcke's plans. Wounded in Italy, the Tenth Mountain Division veteran plotted his return to Aspen as he recuperated. After his release from an army hospital, Pfeifer took a job at Sun Valley, Idaho, but in August 1945 he returned to Aspen to begin fulfilling his wartime promise to build a ski resort and a skiing community.

Pfeifer's research into surface rights on the mountain and his fund-raising efforts soon caught Walter Paepcke's attention, and in September Paepcke invited Pfeifer to meet him at the Larkspur ranch. The meeting was congenial but produced no agreement. Pfeifer recalled that Paepcke recognized that skiing must be "a key to the town's vitality" and that it "would provide a piece to his plan." However, Paepcke did not then agree to finance Pfeifer's project. Pfeifer remained convinced that his dream of a skiing community was Aspen's true future. Much as he admired Paepcke, he was certain that "culture would never be bigger than skiing."[45]

Pfeifer pressed on, undeterred by Paepcke's apparent lack of interest in his plans. To attract the ski world's attention and bring top-notch professionals to town, he convinced the Aspen Ski Club to sponsor an annual race, the Roch Cup, named in honor of Andre Roch. Pfeifer also began surveying a route for a new chair lift, upgraded trails, and continued his fund-raising efforts. In December 1945, Tenth Mountain comrades Percy Rideout and John Litchfield joined him to establish the Friedl Pfeifer Ski School.

Although Pfeifer had no luck in attracting investors by the beginning of 1946, he had proved that he was serious and was not soon going away. Walter Paepcke must have realized that an important part of Aspen's future might slip from his control and so decided to throw in with Pfeifer. In January 1946, Pfeifer, Paepcke, and a group of investors, including Paepcke's brother-in-law Paul Nitze, Charles Minot Dole, Aspen mining and real estate heir D.R.C. Brown, and others, formed the Aspen Skiing Corporation, with Pfeifer supervising development of the mountain.[46]

With adequate financing in hand, the serious work of transforming the mountain got under way. Mine owners, including D. R. C. Brown, leased surface rights for lifts and runs, and the U.S. Forest Service quickly granted permits for construction on national forest land. Indeed, developers today would be astonished at the quick permit process in 1946. One tale has it that Pfeifer and the local forest ranger toured the mountain one day and the ranger supposedly delivered the permit the next. In fact, the process took a bit longer. Pfeifer applied for a use permit in July 1946 and received it in October. By mid-December 1946, lifts 1 and 2 were operational and were opened formally on January 11, 1947, in ceremonies led by Governor Lee Knous and Senator Edwin C. Johnson. Elizabeth Robinson, the daughter of Aspen's mayor, made the first official run down the mountain. Lift prices for the 1947 season were $3.75 per day and $140 for a season pass.[47]

Aspen in 1947 had in place many of the basics of a ski resort: a modern chair lift, a ski school, and a ski-patrol unit. Although the town's four hundred beds, the Sundeck Restaurant, and the Hotel Jerome's bar were hardly the sorts of amenities that Friedl Pfeifer envisioned, they were, for the moment, adequate. In fact, the first year was fairly lean. Pfeifer's ski school grossed only three thousand dollars that year, barely enough to cover expenses. Much work and promotion lay ahead if the *Aspen Times*'s prediction, on the opening of the new chair lift, that Aspen had "found a new, good, and profitable way of life" was to be realized.[48]

In October 1947 the ski corporation hired Dartmouth and 1936 Olympic skier Dick Durrance to manage the mountain and to attract more attention and paying customers to the fledgling resort. Durrance was spectacularly successful. He made motion pictures promoting Aspen's wonderful skiing terrain and sent them to ski clubs all over the country. Durrance also realized that to attract large numbers of skiers the mountain had to be tamed somewhat. As Friedl Pfeifer later recalled, "[W]e didn't have any trails except the Roch Run. Spar Gulch was skiable, but barely." With the help of volunteers from the ski club, Durrance laid out Ruthie's Run, wider and gentler than Roch Run and more suited to the skills of the intermediate skier.[49]

Durrance's most important promotional achievement came when he and an American delegation convinced the Federation Internationale de Ski to hold the 1950 World Ski Championships at Aspen. Professional racing was not new to Aspen. The town had hosted the 1941 nationals, and the ski club had inaugurated the Roch Cup in 1946. However, these races drew regional and national skiers. The FIS races would bring the world to Aspen. Once the FIS gave Aspen the nod, Durrance and a team of local volunteers readied new runs and arranged for accommodations for the fifteen hundred racers, coaches, and spectators who attended the February 1950 event. When it was over, Aspen had gained international recognition and could claim to stand, as the *Denver Post's Empire Magazine* put it, "among the great and hallowed ski spots of the world."[50]

The FIS championships were the second international gathering at Aspen in as many years. Walter Paepcke realized his dream of bringing the intellectual and cultural elite to Aspen in 1949 when he organized the Goethe Bicentennial Convocation and Music Festival. To celebrate the nineteenth-century German philosopher, poet, and artist, Paepcke brought to town such leading lights as Albert Schweitzer, Thornton Wilder, Arthur Rubinstein, Gregor Piatigorsky, José Ortega y Gasset, and the Minneapolis Symphony Orchestra. Lectures and discussions took place in living rooms and restaurants, but the focal point of the event was a $55,000 tent that Paepcke ordered for the music festival. It seated two thousand spectators. The Goethe Bicentennial's success encouraged Paepcke to create permanent institutions to make Aspen a cultural and intellectual haven. In December 1949 he established the Aspen Institute for Humanistic Studies to bring together intellectuals, artists, businesspeople, political figures, theologians, scientists, and so on, to discuss the issues of the day. The Goethe celebration also spawned the annual Aspen Music Festival, which began in 1951. Walter Paepcke had seemingly proved, as one local wag put it, that "the process of grafting culture onto an old mining town is entirely feasible." Feasible, yes; but though the institute and the music festival became fixed features of life in Aspen, skiing, not culture, became the town's mainstay.[51]

By the mid-1950s, Aspen's redevelopment and promotion was a great success, at least as measured by the lift lines. Even after the corporation added new lifts in 1954 and 1956, the crowds quickly surpassed their capacity. By 1960, skiers waited for an hour or more to ride up the mountain. Aspen in the fifties and sixties was ripe for growth.[52]

As he had in the 1940s, Friedl Pfeifer played a key role in launching Aspen's expansion in the 1950s. Aspen Mountain's growing popularity did not alter the basic physical fact that its slopes were challenging and best suited experienced intermediate and highly skilled skiers. Pfeifer, however, wanted to tap into the huge market of beginning and family skiers. In 1953 he sold his stock in the Aspen Skiing Corporation and bought three hundred acres of land at the foot of Buttermilk Mountain, west of town. He had tried to interest the corporation in developing the mountain, but when the company turned him down he set out to do it himself with the proceeds from the sale of his Aspen stock. Buttermilk opened for the 1958–1959 season with a single T-bar lift.

Buttermilk was no immediate threat to its larger neighbor that first season, hosting some sixteen thousand skiers compared to Aspen's ninety-three thousand. However, enough people rode Buttermilk's T-bar to show that Pfeifer was right about the potential market for new and family skiers. Before he could go any further, however, Pfeifer had to find new financial backing. Robert O. Anderson, president of the Atlantic Richfield Oil Company, agreed to join the venture and financed construction of two new chair lifts and a restaurant.

Competition between Aspen and Buttermilk was friendly, and the corporation even helped out with ticket sales and advertising. In 1963, after Pfeifer sold his share of Buttermilk, Aspen took control of its neighbor and expanded the area to include facilities at Buttermilk West and Tiehack.[53]

A third ski area, Aspen Highlands, also opened for the 1958–1959 season. A key player was investment banker Whipple "Whip" Van Ness Jones, who visited Aspen during the 1947–1948 ski season, returned for the Goethe festival, and moved his family there in 1951.

Jones did not intend to go into the ski resort business, but in the mid–1950s he purchased land at the base of what would become the Highlands ski area. In 1957 a group of investors invited Jones to join a proposed ski development on Sievers Mountain. The U.S. Forest Service at that time wanted new areas developed to relieve crowding on Aspen Mountain, but ruled out the Sievers Mountain site as too small and too steep. Instead, the Forest Service suggested that the group develop Highlands Peak overlooking Jones's property. In April 1958 Jones secured control over the area by taking a thirty-year lease on forty-two hundred acres of Forest Service land on the mountain.

Like Friedl Pfeifer when he began work at Buttermilk, Jones invited the Aspen Skiing Corporation to participate in his project, and again the corporation declined. Jones pressed ahead and opened Aspen Highlands for the 1958–1959 season. Peter Seibert, a Tenth Mountain Division veteran, signed on to manage the mountain, and Stein Erikson, the flamboyant Norwegian ski champion famous for his acrobatic back flips, came to run the Highlands ski school. That year thirty thousand skiers rode the area's two chair lifts, T-bar, and rope tow. Whip Jones ran Aspen Highlands until 1993 when the Aspen Ski Corporation took control of the area.[54]

By the 1964–1965 season, skier visits to the three Aspen ski areas reached nearly 330,000, and it was clear that even more lifts, runs, hotels, and restaurants were needed to meet the growing demand. The result was Snowmass, which represented important trends in the Colorado ski industry in the 1960s. Development of Aspen Mountain, Buttermilk, and Highlands began as entrepreneurial enterprises with corporate financiers joining in. By the 1960s the Aspen Skiing Corporation was the dominant enterprise. Snowmass was different in that it began as a corporate development, a partnership of the Aspen company, the California-based Janss Investment Corporation, a real estate developer, and the American Cement Corporation. Snowmass was also different from the other Aspen developments because it was built from the ground up as a totally planned resort community. Architect Fritz Benedict, another Tenth Mountain Division veteran, supervised all aspects of design and siting. When the resort opened in December 1967, it was complete with ski facilities, lodges, restaurants, and shops. Snowmass represented not only the instant planned community but also, as a corporation-directed recreational venue, a radical departure from the devotion to skiing, community idealism, and cultural pretensions of Friedl Pfeifer and Walter Paepcke. This development was sport purely for profit.[55]

When Friedl Pfeifer and the Aspen Skiing Corporation started work on Aspen Mountain in the late 1940s, building a ski resort meant putting up lifts, opening a ski school, and building a restaurant. By the mid-1960s, and thereafter, a ski resort had to be a completely integrated and managed recreation and entertainment environment. It seems inevitable, then, that Aspen would become not only emblematic of corporate recreation (it also owned Breckenridge; Fortress Mountain at Banff, Canada; and, later, Aspen Highlands) but also part of a larger entertainment conglomerate, as it did in 1978 when Twentieth Century Fox bought the corporation. Since then, Twentieth Century Fox and Aspen Skiing stocks have been passed from ownership group to ownership group, and with each trade management and its goals have become further and further removed from Aspen and the visions of its original developers.

Each winter an international elite flocks to Aspen, but it is not the intellectual and artistic elite Walter Paepcke hoped for. To be sure, some artists and intellectuals, most notably singer-environmentalist John Denver and gonzo journalist-iconoclast Hunter S. Thompson, have made Aspen their home. However, since the late 1960s, Aspen has been the place to be seen for the wealthy and the Hollywood set. The luxurious Ritz-Carlton Hotel today is as much "Aspen" as the Roch Run. Only in recent years have other resort towns, especially Crested Butte and Telluride, begun to lure some of Aspen's seasonal glitterati.

Aspen's emergence as a playground for the rich has had its costs. The comfortable informality of the town where Elizabeth Paepcke mixed easily with miners and ranchers in the Jerome Bar is long gone. Aspen today has a highly visible class system of wealthy residents, wealthy tourists, and everyone else. As one new arrival put it in 1965, "[T]he thing about Aspen is that you've got the working rich and the non-working rich, the working poor and the non-working poor." An economy geared to the wallets of wealthy tourists has meant that the prices of everything have risen sharply. The cost of living and soaring real estate values and tax assessments have driven away many old-timers and the town's corps of service workers. They live down the valley, as far away as Glenwood Springs, or over McClure Pass in Paonia, and commute to Aspen, Snowmass, Buttermilk, and High-lands to run the lifts, serve the meals and drinks, and make the beds. Carbondale used to be Aspen's working-class bedroom community, but today a local joke has it that "the billionaires pushed the million-aires out of Aspen, and so the millionaires are pushing everybody else out of Carbondale."[56]

Periodically, Aspen's residents war with one another over growth—they battled for three years over whether to permit con-struction of the Ritz-Carlton—and, ultimately, who should live there. Growth, and wealth, usually win. Sometimes, however, there are ges-tures to social leveling, as in a 1988 ordinance requiring future devel-opers to include employee housing in their plans.[57]

Hunter S. Thompson recalled in 1980 that "the thing that as-tounded me when I first saw Aspen was that we had so much room here, more room than I'd ever seen anywhere." However, Aspen's room was not unlimited. Its pristine mountain setting has been ur-banized. Town and county governments grapple with crowded streets and highways, air pollution, water and sanitation problems. By the 1980s and 1990s, the limits became visible. Rising costs, stiff compe-tition, and environmental concerns and regulations forced the can-cellation of the Little Annie area, on the back of Aspen Mountain, and the planned expansion of Snowmass.[58]

Thompson recognized the ideal and the reality of Aspen. "It was the best of all possible worlds. The skiers brought free enterprise and Walter Paepcke brought the aesthetics. It was the perfect mix. . . . But Paepcke's ideal was impossible to live up to." Aspen, and skiing itself, succumbed to the industrialization of skiing.[59]

SUMMIT COUNTY: ARAPAHOE BASIN, KEYSTONE, AND BRECKENRIDGE

One bright day in January 1946, Max Dercum and his friend, Tenth Mountain Division veteran and future University of Colorado engineering dean Max Peters, climbed to the top of Loveland Pass and skied into Arapahoe Basin, the huge natural bowl on the south side of the summit. Dercum had had his eye on the site since 1942 when Arapahoe National Forest ranger Wilfred "Slim" Davis had told him that "the best possible future ski area around was that alpine bowl up there." As they skied across the basin, Dercum and Peters came across some abandoned cabins—they almost missed them because they were covered with snow, but Peters fortuitously sailed off the roof of one of them—and Dercum correctly guessed that they were the site of a long-abandoned mining operation. In March 1946 he bought the property for back taxes.[60]

Mining had been the basis of the Loveland Pass area's economy since the 1860s. A group of prospectors in 1865 christened their collection of tents as the town of Montezuma. In later years other camps—Chihuahua, Sts. John, and Wild Irishman, to name a few—became neighbors on the mountains and valleys overlooking the basin. At more than ten thousand feet, the district was hard to get into and out of. A rough wagon road cut across the basin by the end of the 1870s, but comparative ease of access did not come until William H. Loveland improved the road in 1879. The district's boom days were in the 1880s and 1890s when the mines produced hundreds of tons of gold and silver ore. Some mines produced paying loads until the 1940s and 1950s, but the glory days were over by about 1910.

The arrival of Max and Edna Dercum in 1942 heralded Summit County's next boom. A devout skier, Max had been the star of Cornell University's ski team in the mid-1930s. He took a position with Pennsylvania State University in 1936, teaching forestry, but skiing remained his avocation. During a visit to Colorado in 1941, he bought an eighty-acre ranch site, complete with a ramshackle cabin and outbuildings, not far from Montezuma. The original cabin had been built in 1869 by a man named Elwood. Because pack trains going to and from Montezuma met the Denver and South Park Railroad nearby, Elwood's cabin soon became an important gathering place. In 1915, after the mining boom collapsed, the Thomas Black family homesteaded the site.[61]

It was here that Max and Edna hoped to fulfill their dream of a life on skis. Max took a job with the U.S. Forest Service as a fire lookout and, with Edna and their three-month-old son, headed for Colorado in June 1942. The Dercums dreamed that "sometime, somehow, and someway we would build a ski lodge, go skiing every day,

Max and Edna Dercum, Arapahoe Basin, 1946

4-7. Max and Edna Dercum at Arapahoe Basin, 1946. The Dercums played key roles in the Arapahoe Basin and Keystone ski areas, and built the famous Ski Tip Lodge. Courtesy, Max and Edna Dercum.

and live an uninvolved quiet life in the mountains" (fig. 4-7). World War II interrupted their plans, however. Late in 1942 the Dercums moved to Washington State, lured by the chance to make good money in the lumber industry. When they returned to Summit County in 1945 they did not settle on their ranch. Instead, they bought the Alhambra mine claim, up the road from the ranch, and moved into the accompanying cabin. They lived there while they worked on making the ranch, which became their Ski Tip Lodge, habitable.

Meanwhile, at Alhambra, Max used his bulldozer, which he had purchased in Washington for his lumbering venture, to cut a slalom run and a ski jump into the hillside near the cabin.[62]

A ski lodge without skiers would not make much money, so while they worked on the Ski Tip Lodge and enjoyed their private ski area at Alhambra, the Dercums also considered building a commercial ski area. That plan is what Max had in mind that day in January 1946 when he and Max Peters surveyed the basin. And that purpose is what he had in mind when he bought the tax-delinquent mining properties there.

However, Max Dercum was not the only man thinking about the commercial skiing potential of Arapahoe Basin. After the war the Denver Chamber of Commerce hired Larry Jump, a Tenth Mountain Division veteran, and Sandy Schauffler to survey potential ski areas close to the city. Forest ranger Slim Davis (another Tenth Mountain man) guided Jump and Schauffler to the great basin atop Loveland Pass. Jump and Schauffler quickly decided to develop a ski area in the basin and formed a partnership with Denver ski manufacturer Thor Groswold and ski racer Dick Durrance. They soon learned that Max Dercum had purchased a key piece of property in the basin. One morning in March 1946, Jump, Schauffler, and Groswold visited the Dercums at the Alhambra cabin. By the end of the day the men agreed to form the Arapahoe Basin Corporation, with Larry Jump as company president.[63]

As was usual in those days, obtaining Forest Service permits presented no difficulties, and by summer work was under way on trails and lifts. Larry Jump became the driving force and chief scrounger on the project. Certified to buy war-surplus material, Jump bought a steel tram from Camp Hale, generators for the lift, and trucks to haul equipment and, later, people. He hired Heron Engineers of Denver to turn the tram and generators into a chair lift. One element, the cable, was missing, however. Heron solved that problem by recycling cables from abandoned mines. Work on the lift was slow and stopped altogether when an early blizzard blew in. Jump was able to get a rope tow running in the upper meadow and so saved something of the 1946–1947 season. Skiers were loaded onto trucks and driven from the highway up to the tow. That year twelve hundred visitors paid one dollar each to ski at Arapahoe Basin. Amenities, to say the least, were lacking, but there was one essential: a privy with fur-lined seats for the customers' warmth and comfort.[64]

In the 1947–1948 season, with its chair lift now operating, Arapahoe Basin drew thirteen thousand customers and nineteen thousand the next year. By the 1961–1962 season seventy thousand skied the basin, and the area ranked fourth in the state, behind Aspen, Winter Park, and Loveland Basin. From the start, many "A-Basin" skiers developed a deep loyalty to the area and to its only lodge, the Dercums' Ski Tip Lodge, and the two businesses' futures were bound together for many years. "If Ski Tip had 20 guests," said Larry Jump, "that's all Arapahoe Basin would get all day." Edna Dercum recalled, in particular, two young English gentlemen, employees of Lloyds of London stationed in Chicago. Each Friday afternoon during the 1949 season they took a train from Chicago, arrived in Denver early Saturday, lodged at the Ski Tip, and skied all weekend. The next year one of the Englishmen was transferred to St. Louis. He drove his car all night Friday and met his friend at Union Station in Denver Saturday morning. The pair would arrive in time for a full weekend of skiing and then reverse the process, getting back to Chicago and St. Louis in time for work on Monday morning. Even after their return to England, the men kept in touch with the Dercums and always visited when business brought them back to the United States.[65]

With a loyal clientele and its proximity to the Denver area, Arapahoe Basin's attendance continued to grow, reaching 136,000 in 1969. By then, however, the area had been surpassed by Vail, Buttermilk, Snowmass, and nearby Breckenridge. By the late sixties, skiers had come to expect fast chair lifts, luxury lodges, fine dining, and first-class boutiques, amenities very much missing at Arapahoe. A lodge was built at the base area in 1961, but it went bankrupt in 1964. Another blow fell when the Eisenhower Tunnel bypassed Loveland Pass and aimed Interstate 70 at Breckenridge and Vail. When lift-ticket sales in 1972 fell to 89,000, the original partnership group sold the ski area to manager Joe Jankowsky for only $850,000. Jankowsky held on for six years, but by the time he sold out in 1978 Arapahoe Basin had fallen to fifteenth place in skier visits, and its market share stood at only 2.1 percent.[66]

When Jankowsky sold to the Ralston Purina Company, the era of private ownership ended and that of corporate management began at Arapahoe Basin. Ralston Purina improved base-area facilities and installed high-speed lifts to attract more customers. Skier visits during the Ralston Purina era have ranged from a low of 108,000 in 1980–1981 to 267,000 in 1985–1986, and market share has varied from 2 percent in 1980–1981 to 3.3 percent in 1981–1982. With a fairly stable market share, the area's growth reflected the growing popularity of skiing throughout Colorado in the 1980s and 1990s.[67]

Arapahoe Basin sustained growth and a stable market share with a skillful marketing strategy. Ralston Purina managers decided not to turn the area into a full-scale luxury resort on the order of Aspen and Vail. Instead, Arapahoe Basin's management worked to solidify and expand the area's niche among expert day skiers. Touting its early opening and late closing—sometimes as late as the Fourth of July—deep powder, and aggressive runs, the area advertised itself as "the Legend," an appeal, as Colorado ski historian Douglas Reynolds has noted, "to the day when skiing wasn't about multi-million dollar lifts, celebrities, or the Hard Rock Cafe and Planet Hollywood." It was a shrewd marketing strategy indeed for a corporation-managed ski area to model itself against the image of corporation-managed skiing.[68]

By the time Ralston Purina bought Arapahoe Basin in 1978, the corporation had already acquired a major foothold in Summit County skiing. Its Keystone resort, in fact, represented all that Ralston Purina marketed Arapahoe Basin as not being: a luxury destination resort.

As they had in the beginnings of Arapahoe Basin, Max and Edna Dercum played a key role in the creation of Keystone, the resort destined to become the heart of Ralston Purina's skiing empire in Summit County. Once their Ski Tip Lodge was habitable, the Dercums took up residence there and sold the Alhambra cabin, which was eventually leased to a group of Iowans who used it for their visits to Arapahoe Basin. Max worked at the ski school and did just about anything else that needed to be done. Edna managed the lodge and, from 1949 to 1952, did double duty as county clerk.[69]

Max was not satisfied. He dreamed of building a first-class resort and had his eye on Keystone Mountain (named by Pennsylvania miners in honor of their home state), which ski writer Charlie Meyers describes as "a rolling, unobtrusive hunk of national forest land certain to catch the attention of absolutely no one save the special few with keen eyes for ski terrain." Dercum spent his spare time walking and skiing all over the mountain, planning trails and lift lines. "The only way the trails can be laid out correctly," he told Edna, "is to know the entire mountain."[70]

By 1965 Dercum had plans and models of the project, lined up financial backers, and began talking with the Forest Service about a permit. Although one Forest Service official was enthusiastic about developing Keystone and suggested that it be given "first priority for the next area to be developed on the Arapahoe National Forest," the agency balked at Dercum's proposal, questioning especially his group's financial strength. Dercum was unrelenting in his lobbying and, finally, in February 1967 the Forest Service granted a conditional permit, giving him two years to come up with better financing.[71]

By late 1968, time had nearly run out on Dercum's permit, and he had not yet secured the required financial backing for the Keystone project. Then Max presented his plans to William Bergman, an attorney who was one of the Iowans using the Alhambra cabin. One version of their talk has it taking place in the Alhambra cabin, making it the birthplace of Keystone as well as Arapahoe Basin. Edna Dercum, however, recalled that Bergman and his wife "stopped in one evening for cocktails," suggesting that the meeting took place at Ski Tip. Whether they talked at Alhambra or Ski Tip, Bergman liked Dercum's plan and told Max that he knew "a company which can do it if anyone can." Back in Cedar Rapids, Bergman contacted the Ralston Purina Company. Bergman's timing was just right, as the pet food and cereal giant was looking for opportunities to diversify.[72]

Ralston Purina's agreement to back the Keystone project ensured its successful start-up. After another year and a half of planning and paperwork, the Forest Service issued final permits in May 1970. Max and Edna Dercum were, of course, delighted. Edna recalled, "Max realized that now, with the support of a large corporation, we would someday ski on *his* mountain." Unfortunately for the Dercums, things did not work out that way. Max became director of Keystone's ski school, but his financial interest in the operation, never more than a minority share, declined, and he never played a major role in management. Ralston Purina and its managers took over his dreams and his plans.[73]

Construction at Keystone proceeded quickly but carefully. Working under Forest Service scrutiny, the builders paid close attention to the area's environment and tried especially not to unnecessarily disrupt the mountain's topography. To reduce the need to bulldoze access roads, helicopters carried lift towers up the mountain. Lift lines and trails were laid out to follow the mountain's contours in what one Forest Service official called a "successful melding of slope and lift line with the natural environment."[74]

When Keystone opened in November 1970 it had two chair lifts, a Poma lift (an inexpensive lift system using a disk and pole to haul skiers uphill, invented by Larry Jump and first used at Arapahoe Basin during the 1953–1954 season), and restaurants at the base and the summit. Even with sparse snow that season, 79,000 visitors skied the mountain. With two additional lifts, attendance rose to 149,000 in the 1971–1972 season.[75]

Ralston Purina bought out Keystone's minority owners in 1973 and embarked on a major expansion and improvement program emphasizing resort facilities, including a hotel and conference center, condominiums, shopping, and a golf course. The corporation also installed an extensive snowmaking system that paid off in the drought seasons of 1976–1977 and 1980–1981, when Keystone was the only major ski area that did not experience a decline in skier visits. In the 1980–1981, season Keystone sold more than 600,000 lift tickets and commanded 11 percent of the state's ski market.[76]

Keystone's managers, like Aspen's, understood that resort visitors did not come just for the skiing. They came to be served. Thus, Keystone did not prosper because it had the most challenging and thrilling ski runs—it did not. Ski writer Charlie Meyers explains that "this rambling, rolled-back mountain indeed has almost universally easy skiing, and for most of the skiers who come here, that is enough. It is a place to be pampered, on the mountain as well as in the restaurants and lodges." Keystone's marketing director noted that successful post–World War II baby boomers, the backbone of the ski industry's clientele, had grown older, had money, and were "willing to pay for quality and service."[77]

Phenomenal growth in the entire Colorado ski industry, averaging 20.5 percent per year in the decade of the 1960s and 14.5 percent per year in the 1970s, helped fuel all of the major resorts' success, even as they increasingly focused their attention on the free-spending vacation skier. By the early 1980s the top seven resorts sold 67 percent of all lift tickets in the state. However, annual growth in the industry during the 1980s fell to 3.3 percent. That slowdown meant that competition among the luxury resorts for the skier's dollar had to intensify.[78]

Keystone in 1983 responded to expansions at other resorts with its own $15 million project on neighboring North Peak. Challenging new runs, three new lifts, a gondola, and a new base area doubled the resort's capacity. Lift tickets jumped from 700,000 in 1983–1984 to more than 900,000 the next season, and topped 1 million in 1986–1987.[79]

However, the newness wore off of Keystone's North Peak development quickly, and lift-ticket sales began to slip, falling to less than 900,000 in 1990–1991. Keystone responded with yet another round of improvements and expansion, adding the Outback area, high-speed quad lifts, another gondola, and a new restaurant on the top of North Peak, all costing $28 million. Once again, sales rebounded, topping 1 million skiers in 1991–1992 and staying above that mark since then. In all, Keystone spent $43 million in less than a decade to increase and hold on to its large share—9.8 percent in 1993–1994—of the Colorado ski market.[80]

Annual total lift-ticket sales in Colorado continued to grow in the early 1990s, but at even slower rates—1.4 percent per year—than in the 1980s. This declining rate of growth leads to the question of how long Keystone and the other major luxury resorts can compete by making multimillion-dollar improvements every few years.[81]

For Ralston Purina, part of the answer to that problem lay in the old mining town turned ski resort of Breckenridge. Located in the valley of the Blue River, south of Interstate 70 and Frisco, Breckenridge's peaks, part of the Ten Mile Range, rise from the valley like a wall. The miners who prospected them in the nineteenth century wasted no effort or imagination in naming them and assigned only numbers to identify them. Perhaps feeling unappreciated, the mountains yielded little precious ore, but the river and its tributary streams gave up paying quantities of gold to huge dredges until the 1930s. The results—rocks thrown out along the riverbank for miles on end—can be seen on the drive from Frisco. By 1960 only about three hundred people lived in the once-booming town.[82]

William Rounds, a Kansas businessman, and Whip Jones, who helped develop Aspen Highlands, decided in 1960 to build a ski area on Peak 8. Their plans hit a temporary snag when Vail's developers, who were about to begin construction, protested that Breckenridge was too close and would harm their interests. Rounds and Jones took their case to Washington, D.C. Political pressure produced the necessary Forest Service permits, and Peak 8 opened in December 1961 with a T-bar, a chair lift, and a restaurant. The area grew steadily, if unspectacularly, during its first decade. Skiers in 1961–1962 numbered 17,000. The addition of two more chair lifts drew 88,000 thousand in 1964–1965. Slow growth was explained, in part, by the mountain's lack of challenging runs. Experienced day skiers, who could just as easily go to Arapahoe Basin, began calling the area "Breckenflats." Expansion in 1969 onto Peak 9 with new lifts and expert runs, and the purchase of the area by the Aspen Ski Corporation in 1970, sparked a period of sustained growth at Breckenridge. Lift sales jumped to almost 198,000 in 1970–1971 and approached 725,000 in 1979–1980. Only the drought year of 1976–1977 saw a decline in lift sales.[83]

The addition of more and better lifts and base-area facilities helps account for Breckenridge's growth in the 1970s. Just as important, however, was the opening of the Eisenhower Tunnel on Interstate 70 in 1974. The tunnel put Breckenridge within a two-hour drive from Denver. Lift sales leaped from about 283,000 in 1973–1974 to almost 442,000 in 1974–1975, largely because of the area's greater accessibility from the state's major population center.[84]

During the 1980s, Breckenridge continued to expand and improve mountain and resort facilities, including new runs on Peak 10. As a result, lift sales topped 1 million in 1987–1988. In 1988 Aspen sold Breckenridge to Victoria, Inc., a Japanese-owned sporting goods company. Victoria and Breckenridge were never a good match, and in 1993 the Japanese corporation sold the area to Ralston Purina.[85]

The secret of Breckenridge's success, and its role in Ralston Purina's skiing empire, lay not only in the area's ski runs, lifts, and amenities. Just as important was the Breckenridge skier. A study of Breckenridge clientele in the mid-1970s found that 42 percent came from within Colorado. At about the same time, only about 7.5 percent of Aspen's skiers were Coloradans. One-third of Breckenridge skiers had household incomes of twenty-five thousand dollars or more, while 56 percent of Aspen's skiers had such incomes. These numbers and Breckenridge's proximity to Denver suggest the importance of day and weekend skiers to the area's success. They also suggest that many Breckenridge skiers, though not poor, had more modest incomes than those who frequented Aspen.[86]

These factors, in turn, are important in understanding Breckenridge's role in the Ralston Purina skiing empire and the empire's success. In the 1993–1994 season, Ralston Purina's three Summit County ski areas—Arapahoe Basin, Keystone, and Breckenridge—commanded an astonishing 23 percent of the Colorado ski market. Each area played a specific role in making the empire work. Keystone attracted up-scale, luxury-seeking guests. Arapahoe Basin continued to draw the expert day and weekend skier. And Breckenridge evolved into a hybrid, luring beginning to expert day and weekend skiers from within Colorado and a significant number of prosperous, if not always wealthy, vacation skiers. In a sense, then, Ralston Purina created a fully integrated ski empire in Summit County with attractions for all levels of skill and income.[87]

A few miles west on Interstate 70, a different kind of empire, but a similar story of entrepreneurship and corporate success, took root. Created by another band of ski enthusiasts, Vail grew into a colossus that, in the late 1990s, controlled half of the Colorado ski market, including Ralston Purina's Summit County holdings.

VAIL

In 1888 an English traveler named Theodore D. A. Cockerell camped on a pass crossing the Gore Range. Cockerell unearthed some ancient pottery shards and arrowheads and so named the place Pottery Pass. That name was long forgotten by the early 1940s when a little-used road over the same pass was named in honor of longtime state-highway engineer Charles Vail. This road was not the first to carry Vail's name, however. In 1939 he pushed a new road over the mountains west of the town of Salida. Unfortunately, Salida residents had wanted the road to follow another route, over Marshall Pass, and were angry that Vail had ignored their wishes. They became even angrier when the state named the new road for Vail, and they demonstrated their ire by quickly obliterating the letter *P* from all of the new Vail Pass signs. Governor Ralph Carr finally relented and rechristened the road as Monarch Pass. However, the highway department was not about to let Vail's name disappear from the map and settled on the little-used road over the Gore Range that some locals called Black Gore Pass. Folks in the area accepted the new name without fuss, and it remained fairly obscure until the 1960s.[88]

In a sense, the Vail ski resort, which made Charlie Vail's name and pass world famous, is a by-product of the Cold War. During the late 1940s and 1950s, as the United States stockpiled atomic weapons, prospectors spread out over Colorado's mountains and valleys in search of uranium. One such prospector was Earl V. Eaton, who grew up roaming the mountains of the Minturn area not far from where Vail would spring up. One day in 1954, when Eaton climbed the unnamed bump later called Vail Mountain, his Geiger counter's needle did not jump, but something registered in his mind. He saw something no one else had ever seen there: a future ski area.[89]

Eaton became acquainted with Peter Seibert, a Tenth Mountain Division veteran. In March 1957 Eaton led Seibert on a seven-hour climb up the same mountain. "The first time I stood on top," Seibert recalled, "I knew it was as good as any ski mountain I'd seen." The mountain's north slope had a variety of grades that would accommodate most skiers' skills. On the south side spectacular bowls, with the Mount of the Holy Cross as a backdrop, offered deep powder and thrilling plunges to suit the tastes of adventurous experts. The next two decades of Seibert's life lay before him on the slopes of Vail Mountain.[90]

Seibert came home from World War II badly maimed, with severe injuries to his face, arm, and right leg. Doctors told him that he might walk again one day, but skiing was out of the question. In 1946 Seibert was in Aspen. He defied the doctors' predictions and learned

4-8. Peter Seibert, a Tenth Mountain Division veteran, went to work for the Aspen Ski School after World War II. Seibert opened Vail in 1962. Courtesy, Colorado Historical Society, F 31948.

to ski again. In 1947 he had a job as a ski instructor and was racing again. He won the Roch Cup that year. He made the U.S. ski team in 1950, but a last-minute ankle injury kept him from competing in the FIS championship at Aspen. Seibert left Aspen and in 1953 graduated from a hotel-management program in Lausanne, Switzerland. Back in the United States, he managed the Loveland ski area from 1955 to 1957 and moved back to Aspen as assistant manager at Highlands in 1958–1959.[91]

Seibert's Tenth Mountain experience, his work at Aspen and Loveland, and his training at Lausanne were part of a career path that began to form in his mind as a boy in New Hampshire. "I had first started thinking of running a resort when I was 12 years old," he remembered. "There was nothing I wanted more in my life than to start a ski area." He began working on his dream in earnest in 1957 (fig. 4-8).[92]

Not long after their visit to the still-unnamed mountain, Seibert and Earl Eaton, along with two Denver men, attorney Robert Fowler and real estate man John Conway, formed the Transmontane Rod and Gun Club to acquire land at the base of the mountain. They used the rod and gun club name to throw potential competitors off their scent. Their first key purchase in 1957 was the 520-acre Hanson ranch that became the site of Vail Village.[93]

For the next two years Seibert and his partners developed their plans for the resort and looked for more investors. Finding backers was not easy, and even friends who contributed to the project were skeptical. One man asked Seibert whether Vail was going to be a hobby or a business. However, Seibert had no doubts. "Everybody else thought we were crazy, but we were convinced we could do any damned thing we decided to do."[94]

One thing that had to be decided was a name for the resort. One partner suggested using the Ute name, the Shining Mountains. Seibert rejected that one quickly. "When mountains shine," he said, "it means they're icy," not the best image for a skier's paradise. They decided to name the resort for the nearby pass.[95]

By mid-1959, Seibert and his partners were ready to take the next step and apply for the necessary U.S. Forest Service permit. On May 11 the rod and gun club asked for a permit to develop a year-round resort. Forest Service official Paul Hauk denied the application the next day. Hauk agreed that "Vail is feasible and has the required potential for another major development on the White River National Forest." However, he argued that there was "no real public need for the development" at the time and that the Forest Service had "an obligation to existing area permittees, especially at Aspen," to protect them from competition until their operations became profitable. Hauk was concerned especially with protecting Aspen Highlands, which, he said, would "need until 1965 to show a net profit." He would reconsider the Vail application then, "depending on forest and state-wide needs."[96]

After Hauk's supervisor rejected their initial appeal, Seibert and his partners enlisted help from members of Colorado's congressional delegation, some of whom questioned whether the Forest Service should guarantee the profits of one enterprise at the expense of another. Finally, in September 1959, the Forest Service gave in and issued Vail's permit, but required that the company raise enough money by December 1961 to build trails and lifts and finance the first year of operations, about $1.8 million in all.[97]

Seibert and partner George Caulkins, who came aboard in 1959, hit the road to peddle shares in the new Vail Corporation. New York's investment houses turned them down, so they started ringing doorbells in search of one hundred investors who would put up ten thousand dollars each. They sweetened the deal by promising lifetime ski passes. They offered development rights to base-area lots for one hundred dollars. They expected to raise the remaining eight hundred thousand dollars with a bank loan. By mid-1961 they had sold enough shares to new and existing partners to meet the Forest Service's financial requirements. The financial margin was slim, however, so the partners decided to hold on to the Forest Service grazing rights, which came with the land. If necessary, they could sell the rights. However, to keep them intact they had to use them, so the corporation bought fifty cows and hired a cowboy to tend them, just in case.[98]

With financing secured, work got under way at the end of 1961. Seibert intended to build his resort on a grand and unique scale. "Vail will offer runs of four miles in length on vast, open and wind-free slopes that lie entirely below timberline," he promised. "The combination of alpine terrain and sub-alpine weather conditions will be unique in this country." One year later Vail opened with three chair lifts, the country's first gondola, ten miles of trails, a small restaurant, and parking for 650 cars, all at a cost of $1.5 million. The Continental Oil Company built a motel and a gas station, complete with a rustic chalet-style moss rock fireplace, on the promise of a gasoline monopoly until sales reached six hundred thousand gallons per year. Another investment group built the lodge. The condominiums, chic boutiques, bistros, and theaters all came later.[99]

On opening day, December 15, 1962, the 650-car parking lot must have seemed like a wasteful extravagance. Although Robert

Parker, a Tenth Mountain Division buddy of Seibert's and former editor of *Skiing* magazine, had mounted a major publicity campaign that had "ski journalists and industry flacks . . . pounding the drums for Vail long before the first lift ticket was sold," there was one problem that no one could anticipate or control: the weather. There was no snow on the ground in the village and only a dusting on the mountain. Parker recalled that "there must have been skiers there," but his most vivid memory of the day was the sight of "some down country folks in cowboy boots riding the gondola out of curiosity." The snow finally came on Christmas Day, but business grew slowly. Asked years later if he had ever doubted Vail's success, Seibert could point to a specific day. "It was January 10, 1963. We collected exactly $60 for lift tickets. Twelve skiers were on the mountain."[100]

Nonetheless, the skiers did come, and by the end of the decade Vail was the largest and most successful ski resort in the country. The village covered ten square miles of the valley floor. It was too big and too complex to be managed as a single entity, so the corporation spun off Vail Associates to run the ski area and a resort association to manage housing development, and created a town government. Success also attracted the sort of major investors who had shied away in the beginning. The flood of money made possible a $20 million expansion and improvement program in 1972, but did not undermine Peter Seibert's control, yet.[101]

Disaster visited the mountain in 1976. On March 26 two gondola cars fell from a jammed cable, killing four skiers and injuring eight others. Vail soon faced $50 million in lawsuits, which, according to Seibert, was "a major reason the board decided to sell the company in the next few months." Although he was still chairman of the board, Seibert no longer controlled the company and could not block its sale. Harry W. Bass, Jr., head of the Goliad Oil and Gas Company of Dallas, was already Vail's largest stockholder at the time and now bought controlling interest in the company. Seibert had hoped for another possible buyer, Twentieth Century Fox, but the filmmaker had not yet reaped the financial boon of its 1970s blockbuster movie *Star Wars* and could not beat Bass's bid. "If *Star Wars* had been out," Seibert reflected, "things would have been different."[102]

Peter Seibert's days at Vail were numbered. As one observer put it, Seibert and Bass "had a personality clash that wouldn't let them be in the same state together at the same time." Shortly after Bass took control, Seibert resigned as chairman of the board and left Vail. He took a job as head of the Country Club of Colorado in Colorado Springs, but that was only a stopover. In 1978 he formed a new partnership and purchased the Snow Basin ski area near Ogden, Utah.[103]

Harry Bass remained in control at Vail until 1984 when his own children forced him out. The major accomplishment during his tenure was the opening of Beaver Creek in 1980 after a long and difficult battle with political and environmental opponents. The area's projected role in the ill-fated 1976 Winter Olympics helped jump-start development, but opposition gained strength after the Olympics fell through. Robert Parker, who remained at Vail after Seibert's departure and took the lead in developing Beaver Creek, is said to have outflanked the project's opponents by inviting them to participate in the planning. He then "conferenced them to death." In fact, Parker and Vail made significant concessions to the need for environmental planning. Governor Richard Lamm, who originally opposed the project, stood with former president Gerald Ford, Vail's highest-profile resident, at the December 1980 ribbon cutting at Beaver Creek. Lamm was practically effervescent in his praise, claiming, "Like Tiffany's is to jewelry stores, like Gucci is to luggage, like Cadillac is to automobiles, that's what Beaver Creek is going to be to ski areas in this country." Unfortunately, like its parent, Beaver Creek had no snow on opening day and closed the next day to await nature's pleasure.[104]

The Vail–Beaver Creek complex has dominated the Colorado ski industry since the 1980s. Indeed, Vail alone has ranked first in lift-ticket sales since 1966–1967. Vail and Beaver Creek together commanded 15 percent of the Colorado ski market in the 1980–1981 season, 17.8 percent in 1984–1985, and 18.2 percent in 1993–1994. Vail not only dominates the Colorado ski industry but also is North America's largest ski area.[105]

In 1985, sports and television magnate George Gillett bought Vail for about $130 million. He soon invested another $50 million in improvements, including developing China Bowl and expansion at Beaver Creek. By the late 1980s, Vail was worth an estimated $400 million.[106]

In 1989 Gillett vowed, "Vail is the last thing I will sell—ever. This is my family's home, and Vail will always be ours." In fact, Vail in 1996 began selling stock to the public for the first time. However, more important than the matter of who owns how much stock in Vail was the change in philosophy and purpose that Gillett, and before him Bass, brought to the resort. Peter Seibert wanted Vail's visitors to be comfortable, but the place was first and foremost to be a ski resort and a skiing experience. Gillett saw it as something more, or different. "We're not selling just skiing anymore, we're selling entertainment!" Gillett's management thus emphasized luxury and service. The skiing remained superb, to be sure, but it was more the lure than the purpose of Vail.[107]

Something else had changed, too. Vail in the 1960s and early 1970s was built not only by Peter Seibert and his partners but also by the people who came to work and live there. It was a community built on shared hopes and risks. Don Simonton, a Lutheran minister who moved to Vail in the late 1960s, summed it up: "I may tend to over romanticize the old days, but Vail was built by guys who were in the ski business because they loved skiing. They winged it. They had fun. It was a matter of friendship as much as a matter of business." However, when they left, or were forced out, "a corporate mentality took over. . . . Now they plan everything constantly. The executives come and go, interchangeable people. . . . They come in equipped with all the answers about us without knowing our history, our character." As a cowboy friend of Simonton put it, "Vail Associates is run by guys with M.B.A.s and BMWs who come here, play a few sets of tennis, divorce their wives and move on."[108]

For the investors and working people who built Vail, skiing was more than a sport; it was a way of life. For many of them, and their heirs, it still is. However, to the extent that there still is a ski culture, a way of life, at Vail, and at all the other great and small resorts, it is one subsumed by another culture, that of the corporate conglomerate.

George Gillett could not keep his vow never to sell Vail. By 1992 Gillett had overborrowed and was in financial trouble. Forced into bankruptcy, he sold out to New York financier Leon Black and his Apollo Advisers, Ltd. As a gesture to continuity, Black retained Gillett as a member of the board of directors of Vail Associates. (Gillett recovered financially and returned to the ski resort business in 1996 and 1997 when he acquired resorts in New Hampshire, California, Washington, and Wyoming.)[109]

Black built his fortune in the junk-bond and corporate take-over frenzy of the 1980s. By the mid-1990s his holdings included a large poultry producer, a shoe manufacturer, a grocery chain, and a luggage maker. After buying Vail, Black invested more than $70 million in mountain and real estate improvements, demonstrating that his days of corporate raiding were behind him and that he was committed to Vail as a long-term investment.

Indeed, Black's interest in Colorado skiing was more ambitious than owning merely Vail and Beaver Creek. The company added the Arrowhead ski area to its holdings in 1993. Then, in 1996, a breakfast-cereal price war cut into corporate earnings and forced Ralston Purina to put its Summit County empire on the market. In a $310 million deal, Black acquired Arapahoe Basin, Keystone, and Breckenridge and made Vail Associates the unrivaled skiing giant of Colorado and the United States. During the 1995–1996 season, the combined areas had more than 5 million visitors, about 47 percent of the total Colorado ski market. With the Summit County acquisitions, Vail Associates eclipsed the Maine-based American Skiing Company to become the largest ski-area operator in the nation.

Vail Associates vowed that all six areas under its control would retain their separate identities and characters. The deal received generally favorable reviews from skiers, Vail and Summit County residents, and business analysts. Some observers, notably the owners of Copper Mountain, the last independently operated ski area in Colorado, raised questions about the deal's antitrust implications. Others worried that the merger would lead to higher lift-ticket prices. What was certain, however, was that Colorado skiing had taken yet another giant step along the trail of industrial consolidation.[110]

SKIING, COLORADO, AND THE WEST

Skiing today is a billion-dollar industry in Colorado; its economic contribution to the state is exceeded only by agriculture. Deeply rooted in the state's life and work, skiing by the end of the twentieth century had evolved from a means of transportation to an elite club sport, and finally into a mass recreational industry. Along the way the sport shed the cultural and moral idealism associated with the Nordic tradition and the Idraet ideal. (To be sure, some skiers have tried to get back to the sport's roots by eschewing resorts and lift lines, and risking avalanches, in favor of cross-country skiing. A network of back-country trails and huts named in honor of the Tenth Mountain Division is especially popular among these skiers. In response to the growing popularity of cross-country skiing, however, some resorts are developing well-groomed trails of their own.) Skiing is entertainment, and it is business. For the wealthy and the celebrities who invade Aspen, Keystone, Vail, and, more recently, Crested Butte, Purgatory, and Telluride in southwestern Colorado each winter, skiing is not so much a pleasurable sport as it is a venue, a place to be seen.

Beyond the thrill of hurtling down a mountainside on a pair of narrow slats, there seems to be little to link today's high-tech, high-finance ski industry to its nineteenth-century roots. Regardless, the history of skiing reflects a number of important themes in the history and development of Colorado and the West.

Colorado's modern history begins with the era of the mining frontier. Skiing, of course, was an important part of life, work, and community in the early mining camps. The history of the mining industry and mining society illustrates the development of industrial capitalism in the West and anticipates the economic history of skiing. In mining, the first wave, or generation, of prospectors swarmed over the mountains in search of "color." The few who found paying diggings or, later, lodes of ore attracted others to their districts. Camps turned into towns, sometimes overnight, with banks, stores, and saloons to serve the miners' needs. Before long, the lone prospector gave way to the mining investor and the corporation. Individual enterprise gave way to corporate ownership and management.

Much the same has happened in recreational skiing in the twentieth century. The earliest ski areas were founded by ski clubs and by individuals such as Carl Howelsen for whom skiing was a way of life. Early Winter Park, Dillon, and Howelsen Hill at Steamboat Springs were not businesses so much as social gathering spots. By the 1930s entrepreneurs were beginning to think of skiing as a business and began the earliest efforts to build commercial ski areas and resorts, most notably at Aspen.

World War II and the Tenth Mountain Division brought a pool of talented ski entrepreneurs to Colorado. They, along with their forebears from the prewar era, were skiing's prospectors. They scouted out the best terrain and began the challenging job of turning a mountainside into a ski area. However, like the prospectors of the nineteenth century, they quickly learned that they could not do it all by themselves. Following a lode of ore deep into the earth was a complicated and expensive proposition. It took money and engineering and business know-how. The same was true of skiing. Friedl Pfeifer may have been Aspen's post–World War II prospector, but Walter Paepcke provided the money and the management that turned Pfeifer's dream into a going resort. Similarly, Peter Seibert, Max Dercum, and even Walter Paepcke gave way to Twentieth Century Fox, Ralston Purina, George Gillett's entertainment conglomerate, and Leon Black's financial empire.

Skiing, like mining, ranching, and the timber industry, is resource dependent. Without the West's scarcest resource, water—in the form of snow—there would be no ski industry. Throughout the nineteenth and twentieth centuries, western industries, farmers and ranchers, and cities and towns have fought over, tried to increase, and struggled to manage this indispensable and limited commodity. This strain has led to the development in the West of what historian Donald Worster calls a "hydraulic society," one whose politics, business, and culture are organized around the management of water. The Colorado and Arkansas River Compacts and an enormous and complex network of dams, reservoirs, hydroelectric generators, and canals are the political and infrastructural evidence of the hydraulic society. The West's irrigated agriculture is part of the economic evidence. And Los Angeles, Phoenix, and Denver are its social results. This hydraulic system has sustained the growth of western agriculture and cities throughout the twentieth century, though inevitably some users complain that they do not receive their fair share.[111]

Dependent as it is on precipitation, the ski industry has become another facet of the hydraulic society. Beginning late each fall and sometimes continuing through the winter, many ski areas pump water from streams and reservoirs to feed snowmaking systems. Snowmaking extends the ski season, at both ends, and helps ensure jobs and profits. Presumably, agricultural users do not need the water used for snowmaking during the ski months, and it returns to them in the spring and summer runoff. Sometimes snowmaking technology has enabled ski areas to overcome natural shortfalls. Keystone's successful thwarting of the 1976–1977 and 1980–1981 droughts is a case in point. Arapahoe Basin in 1996 announced plans to build a snowmaking plant that would permit limited skiing there virtually year-round. Technology and management have enabled the hydraulic society, and the ski industry, to divide, control, and even increase the West's water resources, so far. Ultimately, nature determines the success or failure of this elaborate hydraulic infrastructure. Without water, even the best snowmaking equipment is useless, a fact that a serious, prolonged drought may someday drive home.[112]

Federal money largely created the West's hydraulic infrastructure, and federal agencies largely manage it. The federal government has always been a major player in the West's settlement, organization, and economic development. After all, it is the largest landowner, a fact that prompts both deep ambivalence and deep passion among westerners. For a century and a half, some westerners have viewed federal ownership and management of the land and its resources as an obstacle to fast, efficient, and profitable exploitation. Others view federal management as the only effective barrier to environmental catastrophe. Although the federal government has followed policies grounded on the conservation, if not always the preservation, of land and resources, those policies have rarely proved to be serious obstacles to their economic use.

Like mining, ranching, and timber, the ski industry in Colorado has been the beneficiary of the federal government's policy of encouraging economic development of publicly owned resources. All of the major ski areas, and most of the smaller ones, are built on national forest land. Just as federal mining, timber, and land-management policies practically gave away use rights in exchange for both short- and long-term economic benefit to the country, ski developers, at least until the 1960s, enjoyed a cozy relationship with the U.S. Forest Service. Permits came quickly and with few serious restrictions. To be sure, that easy relationship changed by, and since, the 1970s. Environmental concerns especially have ended the era of quick and easy permits.

Unlike some western industries, most notably ranching, the ski business seems to have adapted well to the new regime. In some parts of the West, ranchers, accustomed to viewing leased federal lands as their private property, have resented, and sometimes resorted to violence to protest or block, more stringent federal regulation. However, the ski industry seems to recognize that tighter federal regulation brings reduced competition with it, a situation especially appreciated by the giant ski corporations that control two-thirds of the ski market in Colorado and for which stability and predictability are important elements in management and profits. And they continue to enjoy favorable terms in their relationship with the federal government. For example, Vail, worth an estimated $600 million in 1996, paid annual fees of only $3,057,635, or $199 per acre, for the 15,365 acres of national forest land the ski area uses.[113]

The ski industry has brought to Colorado's mountains not only economic transformation but cultural change as well, another link binding skiing to the history of Colorado and the West. In the nineteenth century, white Americans and their culture overwhelmed and displaced the West's indigenous Native American and Hispanic cultures. In the Colorado high country, the ski industry became the mechanism for another period of cultural conquest and transformation. In Summit County and Aspen, skiing utterly displaced the existing mining-town life and society. Locals could see the change coming, resented it, but were powerless to stop it. In the 1950s, a Frisco café refused service to a man wearing ski boots. "It took four or five years after Arapahoe started before some businessmen realized the potential of skiing in Summit County," one man noted. Even after some locals recognized that potential, the resentment persisted. "They were glad to take their money," the same man said, "but they didn't like skiers." Eventually, rising costs of living and swelling tax rates forced out many old-timers. Better-financed outsiders came in to take over their properties. Today, some of the old names and some of the old buildings survive, but only as relics of a dead culture.[114]

The cultural change brought about by skiing goes deeper than the displacement of one industrial society by another. As ski historian Annie Gilbert Coleman has suggested, ski developers have grafted their interpretation of skiing's European origins and culture onto the Colorado mountains, as is most evident in the industry's use of Nordic, Swiss, and Bavarian architectural styles in the construction of lodges, condominiums, restaurants, and boutiques. Those facilities, in turn, were named as chalets, *kellers,* and *haufs.* Sometimes the naming got silly. Perhaps embarrassed by its pedestrian, American-sounding name, the new Vail Village Inn in 1962 announced that it had employed a French chef named Pierre Kilbeaux to run the inn's kitchen. In fact, "Kilbeaux" was a Minturn man, Ed Kilby, renowned among locals for his chicken-fried steak.[115]

The fake European culture was only part of what historian Coleman calls the ethnic "whiteout" of skiing in Colorado. Advertisements for resorts, equipment, and fashions, she notes, "offered images and ideals that made up a recognizable ski culture associated with beauty, fashion, leisure, and athleticism." However, they also featured "blonde women and handsome white men." The skiing culture seemed uninterested in attracting nonwhite customers. And it seemed uninterested in employing people of color, except behind the scenes as service workers. In Vail during the 1960s only two Hispanics held skiing jobs. George Sisneros, who grew up in Minturn, recalled that "some people didn't think I should be there because I was just a local Mexican boy." One of the most visible appearances by Native Americans occurred in 1963 when Vail recruited a group of Ute dancers to perform a rain dance on the mountain.[116]

Skiing has very much mirrored the history of race and ethnicity in Colorado and the West, especially in the superimposition of Euro-American culture and the relegation of indigenous peoples to secondary, often invisible roles. A look today at a lift line, or at the customers at an Aspen restaurant, reveals few Native Americans, Hispanics, or African Americans. Part of their scarcity, of course, is economic, as these groups remain at the bottom of the economic ladder and have less disposable income available for what surely is an expensive recreation. However, their presence is also discouraged by the culture of skiing that has been self-consciously directed at white Americans and Europeans.[117]

This powerful industry inevitably became an important factor in Colorado's political life, just as the great mining corporations and their owners were a century ago. Like their mining forebears, the ski corporations became embroiled in hard-fought battles to shape Colorado's political, economic, social, and environmental future. The struggle over the 1976 Winter Olympics was one such conflict.

5

THE BATTLE OVER THE 1976 WINTER OLYMPICS

In the spring of 1961, following the disastrous Bay of Pigs invasion, the ill-advised scheme to land an anti-Castro brigade in Cuba, President John F. Kennedy fulminated about his and his advisers' failure to make the operation work. However, an aide to United Nations Ambassador Adlai Stevenson took a longer view, saying to Kennedy, "Mr. President, it could have been worse. It might have succeeded." Had the operation "succeeded," Castro, who was widely popular in Cuba at the time, would have launched a powerful counteroffensive, probably with the direct aid of the Soviet Union, which would have tied the United States to a long and bloody conflict in Cuba. Kennedy and the United States were probably fortunate that the invasion failed on the beaches.[1]

The Bay of Pigs fiasco seems far removed from the history of sports in Colorado, but this important episode in the history of the most dangerous years of the Cold War holds lessons for understanding one of the most important political struggles in Colorado's history, the battle over the 1976 Winter Olympics. The Bay of Pigs adventure was a dumb idea, poorly conceived and organized, and even more poorly executed. Moreover, the operation represented an arrogance of power and the certainty of the leaders of the world's greatest power that their will was correct and irresistible.

Bringing the Winter Olympics to Colorado was not an inherently dumb idea. Colorado's outstanding skiing terrain and facilities alone stand as an argument in favor of staging the games here. However, like the Bay of Pigs, the effort mounted between 1963 and 1972 to host the 1976 Winter Olympics in the state, though initially successful, foundered because of poor planning, arrogance, secretiveness, and a lack of understanding of the nature and strength of the opposition. When the dust settled after the November 1972 referendum that denied further public funding for the planned Olympics, it seemed as if Colorado was a new place, politically and culturally.

The men who tried to bring the Olympics to Colorado represented a class and a tradition. They were prominent, well-heeled, and widely respected business and political leaders for whom growth and economic development were gospel. Throughout Colorado's history such men and such ideas had held sway in the state. They equated their interests with the good of the state and all its people. Growth had always been viewed as an absolute positive. The Olympics organizers viewed their effort in that tradition. Bringing the Olympics to Colorado would mean jobs, profits, and good publicity. Obviously, they thought, everyone would support that notion.

However, by the early 1970s not everyone in Colorado supported growth for growth's sake. When at first a few voices, then more and more voices, challenged the gospel of growth in general and the Olympics in particular, the games' promoters tried to ignore the opposition and later reacted in a clumsy and arrogant manner that created only more opponents and eventually helped bring about their defeat.

It did not help, either, that from the beginning the plans for the 1976 Winter Olympics in Colorado were ineptly conceived and organized, and even more poorly carried out. In 1971, as the political conflict over the Olympics mounted, *Rocky Mountain News* reporter Richard O'Reilly noted that "one thing is certain. . . . The initial planning was careless to the point that if Colorado were forced to carry out those plans it couldn't show its best face to world television audiences." Colorado and its reputation fared better by not hosting the Olympics in 1976.[2]

Olympic leaders had the time and opportunity to prepare a workable plan. When the International Olympics Committee (IOC) awarded the 1976 Winter Games to Denver in May 1970, the decision capped a twenty-one-year effort. In April 1949, Governor Lee Knous invited the IOC to hold the 1956 Olympics in Aspen, "where the skiing is the finest in America," and at the Broadmoor Ice Palace in Colorado Springs, which he said boasted skating facilities "among the finest in the world." Governor Knous's bid, which was communicated to the IOC via a telegram to U.S. representative Avery Brundage, was, to say the least, premature; nonetheless, the idea of bringing the Olympics to Colorado took hold. Seven years later, in 1956, William Thayer Tutt, owner of the Broadmoor Ski Area, and Steve Knowlton, a Tenth Mountain Division veteran and founder of Colorado Ski Country USA, led a similar, though somewhat better conceived, bid for the 1960 Winter Games. Their proposal, which relied on private financing, would have held the games at Aspen and Broadmoor. The United States Olympic Committee (USOC), however, selected Squaw Valley, California, as the U.S. candidate to host the 1960 Olympics, and the event was held there.[3]

The campaign to bring the Olympics to Colorado began in earnest in 1963. After the failed 1956 bid, William Thayer Tutt continued pursuing his interest in a Colorado Olympics, but realized that the costs would require significant public financing. Others actively interested in the Olympics included Merrill Hastings, publisher of *Skiing* magazine and, later, *Colorado Magazine,* and Vail's Peter Seibert. These men, in turn, approached newly elected governor John A. Love, who took office early in 1963, with the idea of involving the State of Colorado in an Olympic campaign. Love, an avid winter sportsman, was receptive to the suggestion and in June 1963 in a speech at Steamboat Springs publicly endorsed bringing the Olympics to Colorado.[4]

Love originally hoped to hold the 1972 Olympics in Colorado and announced his intention to travel to Innsbruck, Austria, the following January to attend the 1964 Winter Games and there bid for the 1972 event. However, in talks with his circle of Olympic advisers the governor concluded that 1976 would be a preferable target, allowing more time for planning and preparation and tying the event to the U.S. bicentennial celebrations and Colorado's centennial. At Innsbruck, Tutt and University of Denver ski coach Willy Schaeffler, acting as Love's representatives, delivered a letter, bound in steer hide

branded with the five-ring Olympic symbol, to Avery Brundage, now
president of the IOC. In the letter Love stated Colorado's intention
to bid for the 1976 Winter Olympics. Although Colorado thus became a candidate for the Olympics, the public back home was not
aware of the fact.[5]

The Coloradans' reception at Innsbruck was warm enough to
convince Love and the others that the state had a realistic chance to
land the 1976 games. Governor Love thus appointed a Colorado Olympic Commission (COC) in December 1964 to begin the real work of
organizing and planning the state's bid. Originally financed from the
governor's discretionary funds and by a grant from the state's Division
of Commerce and Development, the commission began to receive
appropriations from the legislature in 1966. The commission's mandate was to study the economic feasibility of holding the games in
Colorado, select a host city, determine sites for events and facilities,
and supervise preparation of Colorado's bid to the USOC for designation as the U.S. candidate for the 1976 event. Members included
brewer Joseph Coors as chairman, William Thayer Tutt, Peter Seibert,
Merrill Hastings, and Donald S. Fowler, an executive with United
Airlines. Coors agreed to serve only on an interim basis and was
replaced a month later by Richard Olson, an executive with the
Sundstrand Corporation. Each committee member took responsibility for planning specific areas of the bid. Tutt handled hockey and
figure skating, Seibert took charge of skiing events, Hastings managed planning for press coverage and public relations, and Fowler
was responsible for transportation.[6]

As the COC worked to develop and promote its bid, it had to
recruit additional members and staff, almost invariably individuals
drawn from the business community who were selected on the basis
of their status, business and political contacts, or connections with the
USOC. Many were acquainted with one another through member-
ships in such institutions as the Denver Country Club, the Cherry
Hills Country Club, the Denver Chamber of Commerce, and the
Colorado Association of Commerce and Industry. The COC, in fact,
quickly became a who's who of Colorado business and finance.[7]

While their work progressed, the commission decided to keep
their decisions confidential in order to "minimize specific question-

ing of the commission or committees until we have an opportunity to further crystallize our plans." In other words, this major public project, likely to involve the expenditure of significant amounts of state, local, and federal tax dollars, was to be planned without significant public input or scrutiny by the press. This decision to operate in secret would haunt Olympic organizers and help bring their work to grief and failure.[8]

Criteria set by the IOC governed the commission's work. Especially important, and limiting, were requirements for a single host city and for event venues to be in close proximity with one another. The host city would have to be able to provide lodging and other amenities for thousands of athletes and trainers, Olympic officials and staff, the press, and spectators, as well as transportation and communications facilities. Although the major ski resort communities were interested in hosting some of the events, none had the necessary housing and infrastructure, and none were prepared to build it. That fact made Colorado's major population center, Denver, the inevitable choice to be the prospective host city. And that decision, in turn, meant that all of the events had to be sited in the Denver area and in the front-range mountains close to the city.

In May 1966 the COC made the decision to designate Denver as the proposed host city for the 1976 Winter Olympics. A month later, the commission informed Mayor Tom Currigan that his city had been chosen for the central role in the games. Although he had not participated formally in the decision, Currigan was delighted. The mayor, in turn, informed the people of Denver and Colorado of the choice on June 23, 1966, two months after the crucial decision was made by the COC.[9]

May 1966 was a busy time for COC members. In addition to selecting Denver as the host city, the commission sent members Merrill Hastings and Donald F. Magarrell, senior vice president of the Colorado National Bank, who had just replaced William Thayer Tutt as the COC's vice president, to the IOC's meeting in Rome where the site of the 1972 Winter Olympics was to be determined. The leading contenders that year were Alberta, Canada, and Sapporo, Japan. The outcome of this decision was of great interest to the Coloradans because of the tradition of not holding consecutive Olympics in the same hemisphere. Obviously, selection of the Japanese city would give a boost to Colorado and other Western Hemisphere candidates for 1976. In the course of the Rome meetings, Hastings acquired a copy of Alberta's bid book and made it available to the Japanese delegates. Hastings said later, "I didn't steal it; I just got it." It is unknown whether this bit of sports-industry espionage helped the Japanese bid, but the IOC did award the 1972 games to Sapporo, thus making a North American Olympics more likely in 1976.[10]

Following the announcement of the IOC's selection of Sapporo as the site of the 1972 event, the COC representatives delivered Governor Love's formal invitation to hold the 1976 Olympics in Colorado. Love's message noted that as "the home of Aspen, Vail, Steamboat Springs, and the famous Broadmoor Hotel, Colorado is the greatest winter sports center in America." It is notable, and ironic, that Love stressed Colorado's major ski areas in his invitation, since they did not figure in the Colorado Olympic plans.[11]

For the next year and a half, COC members concentrated on winning the USOC designation as the U.S. candidate for 1976. They lobbied USOC directors and made one of them, Clifford H. Buck, who was president of the National Amateur Athletic Association, a member of the COC; worked on financial and site plans; and reconstituted themselves as a new organization.

In October 1966, Hubert Dubedout, mayor of Grenoble, France, site of the 1968 Winter Olympics, visited Colorado. Asked for his advice, Dubedout said, "Start work early and be realistic where money is concerned."[12]

In November 1966 the COC hired the University of Denver's Denver Research Institute (DRI) to study the economics of staging the games in Colorado. The DRI's job was to examine construction needs and postgames use of facilities and to develop a kind of planning blueprint for preparing and staging the Olympics. The DRI report indicated that building facilities and staging the games would cost between $11 and $17 million, with revenues from television and ticket sales being between $6.4 and $8.9 million. The report assumed that the difference would be made up from state and federal appropriations.[13]

In April 1967, as the Denver Research Institute worked on its study, the COC essentially cloned itself into a new organization, the

Denver Organizing Committee for the 1976 Winter Olympics, Inc. (DOC). Nominally a new committee appointed by Mayor Currigan, it essentially replicated the leadership of the COC, which would continue to function as a liaison between the new group and the state government. The DOC's board of directors included as chairman Donald F. McMahon, an executive with the Colorado Interstate Gas Company who had been named executive director of the COC the previous March, Richard Olson, Donald Magarrell, Clifford Buck, Merrill Hastings, and Peter Seibert. Seibert resigned from the DOC later in the year, but his involvement in the Olympics did not end. In November, Denver City Council president Carl N. DeTemple, who would play a key role in the Olympic debate, joined the board.

In the same month, the Colorado legislature, acting without hearings or discussion, voted unanimously to endorse bringing the Olympics to Colorado and pledged its continuing support for the effort. The Denver City Council also passed a similar measure.

By late 1967 the DOC had strong political backing, a plan for event sites and facilities, a construction schedule, and an estimate of the costs and economic impacts of the games. However, as the organizing committee's official history notes, "this information was known only to DOC members" until it was presented to the USOC in December 1967.[14]

Although the people of Denver and Colorado did not know in any detail the plans that the DOC presented for the 1976 games, the USOC evidently liked what it heard. Using film, slides, and a forty-eight-page book prepared by a public relations firm, the DOC laid out its plans for the U.S. committee and explained that the event would cost only $14 million to stage, much less than the cost estimates of other bidding cities, while bringing as much as $100 million into Colorado's economy. On December 17, 1967, the USOC named Denver as the U.S. candidate to host the 1976 Winter Olympics.[15]

The plan for the Olympics that the DOC sold to the USOC in 1967 called for the use of new and existing facilities in Denver and in the front-range mountains west of the city. The downhill and men's giant slalom ski races were to be held on Mount Sniktau, an undeveloped site near Interstate 70, about forty-five minutes from Denver. The women's giant slalom and other slalom races were slated for the nearby Loveland Basin ski area. The Indian Hills area, supposedly only fifteen minutes west of Denver, would host the cross–country skiing, ski–jumping, bobsled, and luge events. The Indian Hills site, approved by the U.S. Ski Association, had excellent terrain for those events and "a natural bowl to allow development of a stadium complex."[16]

Ice-hockey and figure-skating events would be held at the Denver Coliseum and at the University of Denver Arena. A speed-skating stadium was to be built near South High School on a wedge of land owned by the City and County of Denver and the Denver Public Schools, bounded by University Boulevard and Interstate 25. Bears Stadium (renamed Mile High Stadium after completion of additions in 1968) would host the opening and closing ceremonies, and the city's new Currigan Exhibition Hall would serve as a press center. The campus of the University of Denver was to be transformed into an Olympic Village with athletes and other personnel housed in the school's dormitories.[17]

Bob Murri, owner of Loveland Basin, first heard on his car radio that his ski area was to be the site for some of the Olympic Alpine-skiing events. Olympic officials had visited Loveland Basin and looked around. He even fed them lunch. However, he had not been consulted in the design of the slalom courses and had not been notified that the DOC intended to use his facility. As late as April 1971, the manager of the Denver Coliseum said that no one had spoken with him about using that facility for the games. The plan to use the University of Denver was essentially a "handshake" deal with few specifics ironed out. Vance Dittman, a resident of Indian Hills, learned from the radio that the Nordic events would be staged near his home. Other Indian Hills residents became aware of the DOC plans when they encountered surveyors on their properties.[18]

For all their business talent, the leaders of the DOC had not found it necessary or desirable to consult with the people whose property, work, and lives would be directly affected by the Olympics. They still intended to "minimize specific questioning" of their plans.

Residents of Indians Hills and, later, Evergreen were the first to openly challenge the DOC's plans. Ironically, by failing to consult with them about how they intended to use their communities and their properties, the DOC managed to alienate a natural constituency. A *Sports Illustrated* writer, for example, characterized Evergreen as "an affluent suburb . . . with a population only slightly less rarefied than the 7,000 foot altitude." Many residents of these mountain communities were high-income business and professional people. However, those who first criticized and then opposed the Olympics worried that staging events in their backyards would have ruinous consequences for the environment and their own quality of life. They worried about cutting hundreds of acres of trees to build luge, bobsled, cross-country skiing, and ski-jumping sites. They wondered about the impacts of road and parking lot construction. What would hordes of tourists do to their towns?[19]

Beginning in 1968, mountain-town residents led by Vance Dittman, a retired University of Denver (DU) law professor, and Evergreen's Robert Behrens, also a DU law professor, waged a campaign to remove the Olympics from the front range. They did not oppose holding the Olympics in Colorado, at least not at first. Dittman in 1968 said, "[W]e share the wishes and hopes of the DOC that the 1976 Olympics will come to the Denver area. We realize the economic and other benefits to the state and to the city which will result from the presence of these events here, and we, as citizens of Colorado, have a stake in this too." However, their campaign eventually not only removed the Olympics from their communities but also opened the door for others who opposed having the games in Colorado at all.[20]

In June 1968 Dittman and twenty-six Indian Hills residents wrote to the DOC, protesting that holding the Nordic events there would violate property rights, harm their communities, and damage the environment. The events, they said, should be removed from the front range. In response the DOC said only that the sites would be reevaluated if Denver's bid to the IOC was successful.[21]

In fact, DOC and COC leaders saw the Indian Hills residents objections as petty annoyances and hoped they would just go away. Late in 1968, for example, COC chairman Richard Olson told members of the various organizing committees "not to get involved with controversies such as the Indian Hills situation." Another official, DOC legal counsel Richard Davis, recalled that, at the time, "it did not appear necessary for the committee to argue with citizen objections. Since the Governor and the Mayor were backing the Games, other input was irrelevant." Besides, he added, "the only protest was a couple of environmentalists," and "one did not get political results from these types anyway." DOC member F. George Robinson dismissed environmental concerns as "fear of hot dog stands, large crowds, and so forth."[22]

Whether or not the Indian Hills people had exaggerated fears about holding Olympic events in their midst, their concerns deserved serious consideration. Another group, the Evergreen-based Mountain Area Planning Council (MAPC), a citizens' advocacy group, did take their concerns seriously and in August 1968 agreed to work with them in assessing the potential impacts of the Olympics on the front range. Opposition to a front-range Olympics now had a more substantial organizational base and had spread beyond Indian Hills.[23]

DOC leaders evidently concluded that objections to the planned front-range events could be overcome by developing better front-range sites and plans. Late in 1968 the DOC decided to move the Nordic skiing, bobsled, and luge events from Indian Hills to the Evergreen-Kittredge area. They decided that Independence Mountain near Kittredge and the Evergreen golf course area were superior to the Indian Hills sites. The fact that much of the new choice lay on Denver Mountain Parks land also made it more attractive. However, as had been the case with the original Indian Hills site, the DOC did not consult with or even directly inform the people of Evergreen and Kittredge of its decision.[24]

Led by the MAPC, opposition to holding the Olympic events in the Evergreen area mounted through 1969. Again the DOC tried to ignore and then finesse criticism. Donald Magarrell, for example, dismissed the MAPC as a group that "resents all changes" and need not be taken seriously. In March and May 1969, the MAPC held public meetings in Evergreen and ran full-page ads in the town newspaper, the *Canyon Courier.* The increasingly visible MAPC opposition finally forced the DOC to respond with a campaign to build support in Evergreen and to discredit the MAPC's leadership. In August, at the DOC's urging, a pro-Olympic group, Evergreen Citizens for the 1976 Winter Olympics, was established with Public Service Company of Colorado executive Jack Rouse as chairman. The DOC also asked member Robert Olson to make inquiries with the University of Denver to try to find information discrediting MAPC president Robert Behrens, a DU faculty member.[25]

Despite the DOC's efforts, however, opposition in the Evergreen area mounted as other groups endorsed the MAPC. The Olympic leaders were no more impressed with most of the MAPC's allies than they were with the Evergreen group itself. For example, when the eight-thousand-member Colorado Grange passed a resolution against holding the Olympics on the front range, the DOC responded, "This group is not too important." One group's opposition, however, did catch the DOC's attention. In August 1969 the Upper Bear Creek Home Association passed a resolution opposing the front-range sites. "The ski jumps," the group said, "would destroy the natural beauty and cause a permanent scar to the landscape." They also worried about increased flood danger, water pollution, and after-use maintenance costs. This group worried at least one DOC staff member who noted that it represented "some very prominent citizens" whose opposition presented "a more formidable challenge to our plans than that posed by MAPC."[26]

Finally, late in the year, the DOC recognized that it had to deal directly with the MAPC and address the opposition to the Evergreen sites. In November 1969, DOC executive committee member Robert Pringle met with the MAPC. Pringle told the group that because the bid book and presentation for the IOC were complete, the DOC could not then officially change event sites. However, Pringle promised that the events would be removed from Evergreen if Denver won the 1976 games. A few months later, in April 1970, the full DOC adopted a resolution promising to reevaluate the Evergreen sites if Denver's bid to the IOC was successful and committed itself to accepting the decision of a review committee equally representing the DOC and the mountain communities. Although the DOC's formal position was not as definite on the removal of the events from Evergreen as that made by Pringle, it apparently satisfied the MAPC. The MAPC was further reassured by both Governor Love and Denver mayor William McNichols (Mayor Thomas Currigan resigned in 1968 to take a job with Continental Airlines), who told the group that the events would be removed from Evergreen. Having apparently achieved its goal, the MAPC agreed to keep the DOC's promises confidential until the IOC had acted in order not to jeopardize Denver's bid.[27]

As the DOC entered the final months of planning and lobbying for the IOC's designation, it prepared to submit to the international committee a plan for the games that it intended to change significantly, especially those events planned for the front range. In addition to the environmental and community objections to the front-range sites, climatological problems made them seem untenable. Further study of Mount Sniktau, for example, showed it to be windy and to have marginal snow conditions, explaining why it had never been developed as a ski area. Poor conditions made the mountain look undesirable for the Olympics and meant that it had little after-use potential. Said Forest Service ski expert Paul Hauk, "I think it's obvious that had Sniktau had something going for it there would have been a ski area there years ago."[28]

Snow conditions at Evergreen would also be problematic. When the Federation Internationale de Ski, ski racing's world governing body, inspected and approved the proposed cross-country ski course there in March 1968, a late winter storm had just dumped an usually large amount of snow on the area. However, weather history showed that the site had only a 4 percent chance of having the required ten inches of snow on the ground in February and only a 50 percent chance of having any snow at all. Good snow just could not stand up to the area's average February daytime high temperature of forty-six degrees.[29]

Despite the problems, community and environmental objections, and its own quiet commitments to change the front-range sites, the DOC persisted. Time did not then permit major changes in the bid, and the DOC wanted to submit a plan that met the IOC's demand for sites and venues close to one another. As Lieutenant Governor John Vanderhoof put it, "It's quite obvious there isn't a hell of a lot of snow and that it's hard to put on cross-country skiing without snow. The DOC had to meet all the IOC criteria and they were pressed for time so they lied a bit." Once the games were secured for Denver, the DOC apparently believed it could then change the plan, if necessary, and get the IOC to go along.[30]

While the DOC made its plans for events and sites and reacted to early opposition, it also worked to build support among Colorado's, and especially Denver's, social and business elite. The committee's first fund-raising event, a one-hundred-dollar-per-plate dinner for men only at the Cherry Hills Country Club in March 1968, featured newsman Lowell Thomas as speaker and netted thirty thousand dollars. Later that year the DOC held another fund-raiser, "primarily for businessmen," at the Denver Country Club. In the closed world of the Denver Organizing Committee, business leaders in particular came to be equated with the people of Colorado. For example, the group's official history recalled that in December 1969, "in seeking to inform the citizens of Denver and enlist their aid, the DOC presented a program . . . to the Denver Chamber of Commerce."[31]

The DOC claimed to speak for the people, but in fact it represented the movers and shakers of Colorado's business, political, and social elite. A survey of 139 DOC executive- and operating-committee members found at least sixty millionaires, sixty-nine corporate presidents or board chairs, sixteen bank presidents, thirty bank directors, sixteen members of the board of the Colorado Association of Commerce and Industry, and four presidents and four board members of the Denver Chamber of Commerce. As state representative Richard Lamm put it, "The people behind the Olympics are the same ones who stand to profit—the airlines, hotels, banks and ski resorts." They sincerely believed that the Olympics would be a boon for all of Colorado, just as members of their class had always believed that their best interests were the state's best interests.[32]

They were well suited to the foremost task they had set for themselves: winning Denver's designation as host of the 1976 Winter Olympics. That campaign required DOC members to travel to every continent to meet and persuade IOC members and leaders of the various international sports federations who would make the crucial decisions. When they were not traveling, they entertained a continuous stream of dignitaries visiting Colorado to inspect the proposed Olympic sites. They performed their task well, and in the spring of 1970 their labors bore fruit.

As the DOC's delegation prepared to leave Denver for the May 1970 IOC meeting in Amsterdam, where the decision on the host of

the 1976 Olympics was to be made, member Robert Pringle expressed confidence in the state's bid and in the outcome:

> I think that if the award is made on the basis of merit
> meaning the ability of a city to stage the Games in
> first class fashion and to hold a great event with facili-
> ties to please both the athletes and the spectators, as
> well as on the merits of weather, accessibility, accom-
> modations for visitors and transportation—then we
> need fear no competition.

Only some intangible factor—politics, personality, sentiment—"could
conceivably put the awarding of the Games on a basis other than merit."[33]

The bid book presented to the IOC differed from that given to
the USOC in 1967 only in that the Nordic skiing, bobsled, and luge
events had been moved from Indian Hills to Evergreen. It did not
mention, of course, that the DOC intended to review the Evergreen
sites and move them elsewhere. In the book, Governor Love declared
that "hosting the Winter Olympics has been a goal in Denver for
many years. . . . Denver has been watching, waiting, and grooming
itself for the time it would be ready to host the Winter Games. 1976 is
the year. Denver is strongly backed in its bid . . . by its people."[34]

Denver's bid book was "a magnificent piece of salesmanship,"
said Rocky Mountain News reporter Richard O'Reilly in 1971. It was
also a conscious misrepresentation of the DOC's plans and their ability to implement them. In addition to not mentioning plans to move
events away from Evergreen, it literally disguised problems with
Mount Sniktau by airbrushing "snow" onto bare spots on a photo of
the mountain. A photograph of Denver used a telephoto lens to com-
press the scene and make the mountains appear to lie on the very
edge of the city. However, DOC public affairs spokesman Norman
Brown acknowledged that the promised forty-five-minute drive from
Denver to Mount Sniktau would be possible only "by shutting off all
traffic on I-70 and running six lanes of buses up the mountain." Brown
also admitted that only thirty-five thousand hotel beds would be available for the event, not the one hundred thousand beds promised in
the bid book.[35]

The International Olympics Committee, of course, did not know
of the problems and misrepresentations in Denver's bid. Denver's pre-

sentation, including a fourteen-by-twenty-six-foot display, slides, movies, and models of Denver, proposed facilities, and mountain sites, sold the IOC on the city's bid. On May 12, 1970, the international body voted to award the 1976 Winter Games to Denver.[36]

May 12 was the DOC's best day. In the course of the next year and a half, the committee's misrepresentations, secretiveness, and arrogance and a new political climate in Colorado combined to provoke ever growing opposition to the Olympics, culminating in a public referendum to decide the event's fate. Former Denver mayor Thomas Currigan, a member of the DOC delegation in Amsterdam, aptly, if unwittingly, summarized the committee's attitude and the problem it had created for itself. Until May 12, he said, "the DOC was interested in just 75 people in the whole world. We had to pay most of our attention to the IOC—they could vote; Denverites couldn't." Despite the DOC's claims of broad popular support, no one had ever thought to put the matter before the electorate. By the time the people of Colorado were given the chance to vote on the matter, support for the Olympics had eroded beyond recovery.[37]

As the DOC turned from the task of winning IOC designation to actually staging the 1976 Winter Games, it could no longer operate behind closed doors. The Olympics became a public and controversial undertaking in Colorado. Even before May 1970, opposition to the front-range sites in Indian Hills and Evergreen proved that, like it or not, public opinion would intrude on the DOC's operations. However, the Denver committee had already proved itself temperamentally and institutionally unsuited to working in a public, democratic setting.

The IOC's award of the 1976 Winter Games to Denver made the people of Colorado and their political representatives sensitive not only of the proposed event but also of several difficult and volatile issues connected to it, including environmental and community impacts, costs to taxpayers, and broad political-philosophical questions about the desirability of unrestrained growth in the state. By the end of 1972 the DOC, and the Olympics, found themselves on the losing side of each of those issues.

Handling opposition to front-range sites, especially in Evergreen, was the DOC's first order of business, and the committee now found itself caught between its promises to the mountain-town residents and the plans it had sold to the IOC. The Evergreen people expected that now that the IOC had awarded the games to Denver, the DOC would review the front-range sites and relocate them. At a public meeting in Evergreen in June 1970, townspeople made it clear to DOC representatives that they opposed holding events in their area and wanted the sites removed. However, the DOC seemed to be in no hurry to get on with the review process. Not until November did the committee name Theodore Farwell, vice president of Snow Engineering, Inc., a ski-area consulting firm, to oversee the site-review process. Meantime, in August, mountain-community residents formed a new association, Protect Our Mountain Environment (POME), to organize their campaign to remove the games from the front range.[38]

While the site-review process progressed, the DOC kept the mountain-town residents and POME at arm's length, either ignoring their letters and calls or answering them with only vague statements. Although Governor Love assured opponents that the DOC "would honor its commitment to review the selection of Front Range sites," the Olympic planners aroused suspicions with statements that no promise could be made to change the sites "until all other possibilities had been explored," and that no changes could be made without IOC approval. DOC public relations director Norman Brown fueled distrust and ire in Evergreen when he declared that if the IOC would not allow site changes, "Evergreen is just going to have to eat it."[39]

In response to the DOC's apparent stonewalling, POME early in 1971 shifted tactics away from lobbying the committee to attempting to build support for its position in the state legislature and among international sports federations. In January, POME asked the state legislature to withhold funds from the DOC until it agreed to move sites away from the front range, citing environmental harm, lack of public participation in the planning process, and the fact that the DOC was not a state agency and, therefore, should not have state funding. In addition, POME orchestrated a letter-writing campaign by environmental groups to the international sports federations asking them to press the DOC to move the sites away from the front range. "We did all this," said Vance Dittman, "because of our complete inability to secure any communication with the DOC."[40]

By April 1971 the struggle between the DOC and the opponents of the front-range sites was out in the open, with Dittman and Farwell exchanging barbs in the newspapers. When Dittman asked, "[I]s an Olympic-caliber jump complex a real asset to the people of Denver when Denver is full of people who don't have a way to get to the mountains and then don't have a picnic table to sit at when they get there?" Farwell replied, "[I]t's an excellent way for Colorado to spend its money. Look what it cost us to play golf on the moon." In an effort to discount the significance of Evergreen's opposition, DOC member, and now USOC president, Clifford Buck said it was "unfortunate that a vocal minority can and does give the impression that it's speaking for more people than it is."[41]

Public opinion and environmental concerns did not figure strongly in the DOC's reevaluation of its original site plans, though it did name a Planning Board that was supposed to assist in "selecting sites and planning facilities compatible with the environment." When the DOC named Ted Farwell to oversee the review, he was told to consider proximity to Denver and technical criteria first, and environmental problems and community feelings only secondarily in his recommendations. Farwell himself made it clear that the wishes of mountain-community residents were not especially important. "The major reason that we are making the reevaluation of the Evergreen site," he said, "is for the competitors." On that basis alone, however, the front-range sites, with their probable lack of snow, adverse wind conditions, and terrain problems, had to be ruled out. One possible way to save the Evergreen cross-country site, by using artificial snow, met with vigorous objections from potential competitors and so was shelved.[42]

Farwell's search for alternative front-range sites proved fruitless. For a time he gave serious attention to sites near Sedalia and Buffalo Creek for the cross-country skiing events, but finally eliminated them. The DOC then resigned itself to moving the Nordic and Alpine skiing events to the western slope.[43]

As Farwell searched for new sites for the Nordic and Alpine events, a self-appointed group of Steamboat Springs businessmen who, as another resident of that town put it, "purported to speak in the name of the citizens of Steamboat," approached the DOC with the suggestion that the cross-country and biathlon skiing events be held there. The invitation to come to Steamboat Springs became more attractive when leaders and members of the Federation Internationale de Ski expressed their strong preference for holding the Nordic events there. In May 1971, with nowhere else to go, the DOC secretly decided to move the cross-country and biathlon events to Steamboat. There had, as yet, been no consultation with anyone there except the town's business leaders. The decision to move to Steamboat Springs was kept secret for seven months. The DOC also decided, in October 1972, to hold the ski-jumping events in Steamboat. By then, local opposition to holding Olympic events in Steamboat Springs had begun to develop, but opponents decided to await the outcome of the November 1972 statewide referendum on the games before mounting their own local campaign.[44]

There still remained the problem of deciding on permanent sites for the Alpine skiing, bobsled, and luge events. With the Mount Sniktau site ruled out by snow, terrain, and wind problems, and with no other suitable front-range sites available, the DOC had to look to established western-slope ski areas to host the Alpine events. Five ski areas—Vail, Keystone, Aspen, Copper Mountain, and Ski Country Enterprises (in Harrison Creek)—made bids for the events during a secret meeting of the DOC's Alpine Subcommittee. However, Peter Seibert and Richard Olson lobbied heavily for choosing Vail before the presentations, and it appears that the other bids were solicited in order to create the appearance of an "open" process in the decision. In February 1972 the DOC, acting over the objections of its Planning Board, voted to hold the Alpine skiing events at Vail's proposed new Beaver Creek area. The Planning Board, citing environmental problems, had ranked Vail last among the entrants.[45]

The decision to move the Alpine events to Vail was a significant boost to the resort's plans for developing the Beaver Creek area. At the time, the Beaver Creek site was under consideration by the Forest Service for designation as a wilderness area. Vail hoped that naming the area as an Olympic site would block the wilderness designation and expedite the permit process. That hope was well founded. The Forest Service decided to hold public hearings on the wilderness decision only if some group specifically demanded them. Since the decision to hold the Olympic events at Beaver Creek remained a secret, no one had any reason to ask for hearings, and the Forest Service duly exempted the area from wilderness designation. Regional forester William Lucas, a member of the DOC, made the final decision. Clearly, the decision to take the Olympics to Beaver Creek was closely held and guarded among the DOC, Vail Associates, and the Forest Service. No effort was ever made to consult with the residents of Vail and Eagle County.[46]

The selection of bobsled and luge sites, and construction of facilities, became one of the most openly controversial problems confronting the DOC, putting it at loggerheads with the sports' governing body, the International Bobsleigh and Tobogganing Federation (IBTF). After the decision to remove the events from Indian Hills, the DOC looked briefly at the Air Force Academy, near Colorado Springs, as a possible site, but finally voted, over strong public objections, to hold the events at Genesee Park, not far from Evergreen.[47]

Other problems were the high cost of the bobsled and luge facilities and their limited after-use potential. The only existing bobsled run in the United States, at Lake Placid, New York, cost the state one hundred thousand dollars per year to maintain for a small number of users. However, the IBTF insisted that the DOC build separate runs for the two-man and four-man bobsled competitions. The DOC, citing the high costs and negligible after-use, especially of the four-man run, proposed that all of the bobsled events be held at Lake Placid or, in the alternative, that the four-man event be dropped and that the two-man bobsled and luge events be held on a $4 million refrigerated combined run. The DOC's Ted Farwell noted that "if worst comes to worst, the Colorado Legislature is going to have to underwrite this." The IOC refused to move the events to New York and voted to drop the four-man event. However, the IBTF refused to accept the scaled-back events and, instead, canceled them entirely. Colorado's taxpayers, and Genesee Park, thus escaped the burden of those events.[48]

Other venue changes, including relocating the proposed speedskating arena to a site adjacent to Mile High Stadium, near downtown Denver, and the construction of a new arena, also near the stadium, for figure skating and hockey, were submitted. Of the two proposed facilities, only the latter was built. Denver voters in September 1972 approved spending $10 million to build the multiuse facility, which was eventually named in honor of Mayor William McNichols and became home to Denver's professional basketball and hockey teams.[49]

Another site problem that seemed to have been worked out by late 1972 was that of housing the thirty-five hundred reporters expected to descend on Denver to cover the Olympics. The DOC proposed building two press villages, two-thirds of the costs of which would come from federal housing funds. An earlier plan, submitted to the Denver Planning Board in 1969, drew fire from low-income and minority groups in Denver who objected to the use of federal Model Cities funds for press housing. Opponents also argued that the plan would dislocate too many low-income residents, provided for too little new housing, and had excluded low-income and minority representatives from the planning process. Ultimately, the federal Department of Housing and Urban Development rejected the first plan because its $29.6 million cost was too high. A revised plan, formulated with some input from the minority and low-income communities and still under review in the fall of 1972, scaled costs down to about $18 million. A total of 1,291 housing units—town houses, apartments, and motel-hotel rooms—would be built in the Five Points area and near the intersection of Colfax Avenue and Speer Boulevard, the eastern corner of the present-day Auraria Higher Education Complex.[50]

The DOC's carefully limited accommodation of low-income and minority groups in planning the press housing was exceptional. Throughout the initial planning, reevaluation, and final relocation of Olympic event sites, the committee and its representatives consistently placed community interests and objections and environmental problems at the bottom of their list of criteria for planning and problem solving. Instead, secretiveness and an elitist attitude toward Colorado's citizens, especially those who objected to the DOC's plans for their communities and their properties, typified the committee's approach to its work. They represented Colorado; they had won the Olympics for Colorado; and they would decide how to organize and stage the Olympics in Colorado. They agreed to move the front-range events away from Indian Hills and Evergreen not because the residents of those communities objected to the events but because meteorological reality forced them to. When they decided to hold those events in Steamboat Springs, they made the decisions among themselves, kept the conclusions to themselves as long as possible, and did not consult with the people of that community, just as they had not talked with the people of Indian Hills and Evergreen. In short, the whole experience of the front-range site decisions, and protests, taught the DOC nothing. And because they had learned nothing, moving the Nordic and Alpine events to Vail and Steamboat Springs did not end opposition to the Olympics.

Even if the front-range mountain towns' residents' opposition was not the most important factor in the DOC's decisions to remove the Nordic and Alpine events to Vail and Steamboat Springs, their increasingly vocal criticism contributed to a growing sense of ill-ease among Coloradans with the whole Olympic project and its planners. Especially important were questions about how much the taxpayers of Colorado and the United States would have to pay for the games.

By the time the International Olympic Committee awarded the 1976 Winter Games to Denver in May 1970, the DOC had spent $759,000 to plan and promote its bid. Of that money, 45 percent came from the State of Colorado, 19 percent from the City and County of Denver, and 36 percent from self-generated and private sources. From the outset, then, the Olympic project was largely a publicly financed, though not a publicly controlled, project.[51]

The DOC had no reason to doubt that the state would continue to finance its activities as it turned to the task of actually getting ready to stage the games. After all, the legislature had appropriated $150,000 for the DOC in March, and on May 13, 1970, the day after the IOC meeting, Governor Love promised continued state support. Since its first appropriation to the Colorado Olympic Commission in 1966, the legislature had exercised no real oversight of the Olympic enterprise. That fact, however, was about to change.[52]

When the legislature approved the DOC's request for $150,000 in March 1970, it was with the assurance that the funds would be sufficient for the 1970–1971 fiscal year. However, when the legislature's Joint Budget Committee (JBC) convened in January 1971 to begin preparing the state's annual budget, the members were presented with a request for an additional $179,000. In addition, the COC, which continued to function as the liaison and revenue funnel between the state and the DOC, asked for $424,000 for fiscal 1971–1972, more than $200,000 more than it had previously estimated it would need for that year.[53]

Now members of the JBC and other legislators began to ask questions. Back in 1967 the legislature had been told that the total cost of the Olympics would be about $14 million. In a letter to the COC on January 7, 1971, the JBC asked how much the Olympics would cost the state. In its reply the COC said that a precise figure was not possible, but estimated that the total cost of the games would be no more than $25 million. Pressed in later hearings, COC officials told the committee that Colorado's taxpayers would have to contribute between $10 and $15 million. The COC expected the balance to come from the federal government.[54]

The legislature decided to refer the question of further funding of the Olympics to a special committee that held public hearings in March 1971. Most of the thirty witnesses were opponents of the front-range event sites and asked that state funding be stopped until the sites were changed. However, the committee finally recommended that both the supplemental request for $179,000 and the 1971–1972 request for $424,000 be approved, largely on the grounds that the legislature in 1967 committed itself "to provide monies, and technical assistance for the development of the 1976 Games."[55]

When the Olympic appropriations moved to the floor of the Colorado House of Representatives, members Robert Jackson, from Pueblo, and Richard D. Lamm, from Denver, led an effort to end, or at least limit, the commitment of tax dollars to funding the games. Only a handful of their colleagues joined them, and their restrictive amendments failed by large margins. Moreover, the major Denver newspapers, both uncritical in their support of the DOC and the Olympics, vigorously condemned Lamm's and Jackson's effort. The *Denver Post* labeled them "uncompromising axgrinders" whose "sniping at the Denver Olympic Committee . . . is getting out of hand." Cutting funds for the Olympics, the *Post* editorialized, "would be a disastrous and stupid mistake." The *Rocky Mountain News,* for its part, accused Lamm and Jackson of trying to "sabotage" the Olympics through "the rawest kind of political pandering."[56]

Although the DOC and the Olympics weathered this first challenge in the legislature and clearly enjoyed strong support from the state's leading newspapers, opponents did not give up. The DOC's own inability to nail down the costs of the games continued to be a major source of suspicion and opposition. By early 1972 the DOC raised its estimate of total costs to $35 million, up $10 million in just a year. However, that increase was minor compared to the figure of $65.3 million that the DOC told the JBC the games would cost in March 1972. Committee chairman Don Friedman "literally forced the figure out of reluctant DOC officials." Asked if there were any other possible costs, the DOC officials answered no. Then, a few days later, Denver Mayor McNichols told federal officials that the games would cost $76.5 million. Finally, in April, the DOC said the games would cost between $81 and $93 million. At that point JBC chairman Friedman demanded that the entire DOC resign. "We must restore confidence in order to have a successful Olympics," he said. Even the normally supportive *Rocky Mountain News,* though not endorsing Friedman's demand, noted that "the DOC's performance to date has been patently uninspired and warrants a vote of no confidence."[57]

Escalating cost was not the only motive behind Lamm's and Jackson's opposition to state funding for the Olympics. Another issue, the problem of growth, also worried them, and it linked them to other opponents. To Lamm, Jackson, and many others, the Olympics represented an outdated booster mentality in Colorado that held that anything bringing people and money to the state was good and desirable. Governor Love, who made the Olympics part of his "Sell Colorado" campaign, had said that Colorado "wanted industrial parks, factories . . . all the economic progress we could get." However, by the early 1970s many Coloradans were worried about the consequences of unlimited development. During the 1960s the state's population had increased by 26 percent, nearly double the national rate of growth. Of that amount, 86 percent occurred in six counties along the front range (Denver, Adams, Arapahoe, El Paso, Boulder, and Jefferson), where the original Olympic sites would have had the greatest impact. However, the state's western-slope ski-resort counties had even more dramatic increases. Pitkin County, home of the Aspen ski complex, grew by almost 160 percent, and Eagle County, home of Vail, grew by

60 percent. By the beginning of the 1970s, Colorado was experiencing serious problems of urban sprawl and degradation of air, water, and land quality. By then, too, a new generation of environmental, social, and political activists was beginning to challenge the gospel of growth. Richard Lamm was one of them. "We're starting to realize that growth isn't necessarily good," he said. "We've got to stop the knee-jerk boosterism and mindless promotionalism."[58]

To Lamm and others, the Olympics embodied that mentality. Representative Jackson asked,

> [W]hy promote Colorado when the growth process in our state is something which we are unable to handle now? Our suburbs are already overlapping suburbs. Why are we out selling Colorado? We've got two million Coloradoans. To say that ten million Coloradoans would make a better Colorado is absurd. We made a mistake. Take the Games elsewhere.

Despite their newspaper's unswerving support of the Olympics, two *Denver Post* columnists weighed in with similar fears. Joanne Ditmer raised the spectre of urban sprawl spread over the mountains in a "solid line of phony Alpine motels and condominiums from Denver to Loveland ski basin." Tom Gavin equated tourism with population growth. "The trouble with tourists," he wrote in February 1972, "is that having looked around, many wish to return. . . . [I]t's as simple as can be, my opposition to the Olympics: people simply louse things up, and we already have a sufficiency of people lousing Colorado up."[59]

As opposition to the Olympics mounted, its bases were varied. Mountain-town residents worried about the games' impact on their homes, communities, and local environment. Some legislators, and a growing number of citizens, saw the events as a fiscal bottomless pit. Environmental and antigrowth activists saw the Olympics as a symptom of the destructive tradition of unencumbered growth.

Beginning in September 1971, an ad hoc group of mountain-town representatives, environmentalists, educators, and politicians began meeting to discuss the potential environmental and other consequences of the Olympics, and what they could do about it. The group included Representatives Lamm and Jackson, environmental

activist Estelle Brown, environmental and anti–Vietnam War activist
Sam Brown, University of Colorado law professor Donald Carmichael,
Vance Dittman from POME, and political activists John Parr and Meg
Lundstrom, veterans of Oklahoma senator Fred Harris's recent presi-
dential campaign. Early in January 1972 the group incorporated as
Citizens for Colorado's Future (CCF).[60]

CCF announced its birth by publishing a highly critical "Olympic Fact Sheet" in the *Denver Post*. The group followed up with an
informal public-opinion survey and petition mailed out to organizations such as the Sierra Club, the Colorado Open Space Council, the
Audubon Society, and the League of Women Voters. The response
surprised even the CCF. "In three weeks," Estelle Brown recalled,
"we collected over 25,000 signatures, which gave evidence of far more
latent opposition to the Games than we had anticipated."[61]

On the strength of its successful petition drive, the CCF leaders
decided to take their case against the Olympics directly to the International Olympic Committee's meeting in Sapporo, Japan, in January
1972. The group dispatched Estelle Brown, Sam Brown, and John
Parr to present its petitions to the IOC and to gain publicity for its
campaign. In Japan, IOC president Avery Brundage politely refused
to put the CCF delegation on the committee's agenda. Undeterred,
they simply invited themselves to the meeting where Estelle Brown
presented the IOC with an eighteen-inch stack of petitions; a thirty-
two-page booklet containing letters from state legislators, environmental groups, and property owners opposed to the Olympics; and a
fact sheet spelling out several of the DOC's misrepresentations. Brown
told the IOC that she hoped they would examine the documents and
"find the time to talk with us." Escorted from the room by police
officers, the CCF delegates found themselves surrounded by reporters. Most of the press were eager to get the CCF's story, though Brown
found reporters from Denver hostile.[62]

The IOC's executive committee soon agreed to give the CCF
representatives a private hearing. Afterward, the IOC stunned everyone by announcing that it had voted unanimously to withdraw its
invitation to Denver to host the 1976 Winter Olympics. The IOC
almost certainly did not base its surprising action solely on the case
made by the CCF. In addition to the IOC's awareness of growing

opposition in Colorado, other factors at work behind the decision probably included irritation with the DOC over the relocation of events, the eruption of student antiwar activism in Denver and Boulder, and, especially, Avery Brundage's hostility to the Winter Olympics. Brundage felt that the Winter Games were not in the tradition of the Olympics and was particularly affronted by the growing commercialism associated with the games and its stars. Brundage had even threatened to take away medals and ban offending skiers, including France's charismatic star Jean Claude Killy and "almost every competitor of note in the world." Only a counterthreat by the Federation Internationale de Ski to take all of its member skiers out of the Olympics and stage a rival event forced Brundage to back down.[63]

The IOC's stunning decision to take the games away from Denver produced a furious lobbying effort that stretched all the way from Sapporo to Washington, D.C. A flurry of phone calls resulted in a congressional resolution and a personal message from President Richard M. Nixon urging the IOC to reverse itself. The high-level pressure worked, and the next day the IOC restored the Olympics to Denver. Having escaped this near-death experience, the DOC emerged from the episode not chastened but, if possible, even more arrogant toward its critics. In an encounter with the CCF delegates, public relations director Norman Brown said, "Listen: You guys can't beat us. You can't fight the establishment. Could you have gotten a resolution through congress like that? Now, look, you've got to make an effort to sit down and talk with us when we all get back to Denver. . . . But you can't fight us; we're too strong." Less arrogant, but just as oblivious to reality, was Richard Olson who, in response to CCF environmental concerns, said to Estelle Brown, "We think we're environmentalists, too. . . . And why didn't you come to us earlier on this?"[64]

Back in Colorado, the CCF decided to do what the Olympic organizers had never believed it necessary to do: they would take the issue of the Olympics directly to the people. In March 1972 the CCF launched a petition drive to place an initiative on the 1972 election ballot to deny further state funding for the Olympics. DOC members, confident that the group would not be able to gather enough signatures to get on the ballot, quickly dismissed the campaign. One

DOC official, legal counsel Richard Davis, viewed the effort as symptomatic of what he apparently saw as the illegitimate social and political upheavals of the era. Opposition to the Olympics, Davis said, was "sheer political demagoguery . . . part and parcel of the general assault on accepted values which are characteristic of our times. The negativism of much of this criticism," he said, was "unworthy of serious response." Governor Love said the petition drive was both "too late and destructive." "Colorado," Love said confidently a few weeks later, "is in no danger of losing the 1976 Winter Olympic Games. I guess we've won it three times now and are entitled to keep it." Love did take the precaution of forming a new committee of business leaders, the Committee of '76, to promote the games.[65]

Although the DOC dismissed the campaign, the CCF, backed by volunteers from POME, environmental groups, and the League of Women Voters, went about the state gathering petitions. They needed 50,000 signatures to get their initiative on the November ballot. By July they had collected 76,000. Representative Lamm gleefully compared that number with Governor Love's Committee of '76. It was, he said, "a fitting number because the Governor has formed his own committee of bankers and land developers. Ours are just plain citizens." On July 6, 1972, the CCF submitted 77,392 signatures to the Colorado secretary of state, the largest number ever collected in support of a ballot initiative in Colorado. The CCF also succeeded in placing a similar initiative on the Denver ballot.[66]

Poorly funded, understaffed, and relying on brigades of highly motivated, mostly young volunteers, the CCF's campaign against the Olympics was a classic grassroots effort, though Representative Lamm became its most visible spokesperson. The effort focused on the issues of environmental impacts, population growth, and costs to the taxpayers. The CCF was especially effective in arguing that the economic benefits of the games would flow to a privileged few, though the taxpayers would pay most of the costs. For Lamm, especially, the cost was the most important issue. In a speech to the Colorado Press Association, Lamm even acknowledged that the "direct environmental abuse" from the games would be "minimal." However, he said, "the financial abuse . . . was originally and remains now as our principal question and objection." Lamm went on to show that the state could not possibly recover its investment in the Olympics. Using the DOC's own most optimistic estimate that 190,000 visitors would come to Colorado for the games, and assuming each spent about $200 a day, Lamm estimated that state tax revenues would be only about $1,140,000, less than Colorado had already spent on planning and organizing the event.[67]

As the campaign progressed, the list of groups supporting the CCF grew to include the Sierra Club, the Rocky Mountain Sportsmen's Federation, the Colorado Open Space Council, the Colorado Labor Council, the Colorado Grange, the League of Women Voter's, minority and low-income advocacy groups, and the mountain-town residents' groups, POME and the MAPC. Some groups worked directly with the CCF, while others, with differing specific issues and goals, kept some distance. However, the cumulative effect was to create the impression of a broad, diverse, and rapidly growing opposition to the Olympics.[68]

By September 1972, a poll showed that the CCF's issues were taking hold in the public mind. Although 61 percent believed the Olympics would benefit Colorado's economy, 60 percent also believed that staging the games would cost the state and the taxpayers too much money. In addition, 61 percent of those surveyed believed that Colorado was growing too fast.[69]

Another, perhaps unwitting, ally was IOC president Avery Brundage. In his final public address before retiring as head of the international committee, Brundage renewed his personal campaign against the Winter Olympics, calling on the athletic world to "give the Games a decent burial in Denver."[70]

As support for its campaign grew, the CCF also proved fortunate in it enemies. In July the DOC underwent a superficial reorganization and name change, calling itself the Denver Olympic Organizing Committee (DOOC). The membership and leadership of the organizing committee was largely unchanged, though William R. Goodwin, president of the Johns-Manville Corporation, replaced Mayor McNichols as chairman, and Carl DeTemple, a former Denver city councilman and lobbyist for the Colorado Association of Commerce and Industry, became the DOOC's general secretary in charge of day-to-day operations. The DOOC, preoccupied with the final selection of event sites and organizational matters, continued to try to ignore the CCF campaign and left the business of mounting a countercampaign mainly in the hands of the Committee of '76 and other supporters. Late in the summer of 1972, Governor Love reorganized the Committee of '76 into "Coloradans for the '76 Winter Games," specifically to operate as a political committee to oppose the CCF initiative.[71]

The pro-Olympic campaign emphasized the themes that the games' advocates and organizers had been relying on for almost a decade. The Olympics, they said, would be an economic boon to the state. The games would bring the world to Colorado, promote global peace and understanding, and be a unique learning experience for the state's young people. The new arenas and other facilities would become long-term assets for Colorado.

Denver's major newspapers, longtime supporters of the Olympics, weighed in with strong editorial positions against the initiative, going so far as to kill columns by their own writers suggesting problems with the games and the pro-Olympic campaign. The *Denver Post* was especially active in its support of the Olympics. *Post* executives served on the DOOC's Press Advisory Committee, and all articles in the paper were cleared with the DOOC. In the final days of the campaign, the *Denver Post* gave five times more space to pro-Olympic coverage than to the anti-Olympic side.[72]

Denver Mayor William McNichols also campaigned against the initiative and threw the resources of the City and County of Denver into the battle. The mayor had the city print shop publish pro-Olympic literature and even had pamphlets stuffed into city employees' pay envelopes. McNichols was confident that the Olympics would survive the CCF challenge and that the initiative would be voted down. In June the mayor declared that "at least sixty percent of the people strongly favor the Olympic effort and are confident that any referendum attempting to constrain the Olympic effort and participation will be soundly rejected by an overwhelming majority."[73]

What the pro-Olympic campaign did not do was answer the many questions and doubts about the DOOC, about the games' environmental impacts and, especially, their costs to the taxpayers. The campaign also made some serious tactical blunders. At an August 1972 celebrity dinner at Denver's Brown Palace Hotel, former Oklahoma University football coach Bud Wilkinson impugned the patriotism of Olympic opponents, saying that "it is inconceivable that there will be any Americans who will not take pride in getting to help the games." Such a gratuitous insult did nothing to soften the DOOC's reputation for elitism and arrogance. Later in the campaign, Olympic supporters circulated a *Denver Post* story describing some of the CCF's most active leaders as "a small but artful band of tenacious young political activists who have filtered into Colorado over the past two years seeking populist issues to exploit and promote." This caricature of CCF activists as outside agitators backfired on the DOOC, as Representative Lamm happily pointed out that Chairman William R. Goodwin himself had been in Colorado less than two years. CCF leader Meg Lundstrom, on the other hand, had been born in the state.[74]

The DOC-DOOC did try to soften its reputation for elitism, arrogance, and secretiveness. Following the narrow escape at Sapporo, the committee voted to open its meetings to the public and the press "as evidence of the new intent to make the public more a part of Olympic activity." Mayor McNichols also seemed to favor a more open process. "From here on you will see a different approach," he said after Sapporo. "A lot of people are eager to pitch in and help the Olympic effort. We intend to see that they are given the opportunity." However, behind the DOOC's doors the bunker mentality remained intact. When the CCF characterized parts of the 1967 bid book as untruthful, one official noted ruefully that "we never should have let the citizens of Colorado see that bid book."[75]

Throughout the summer of 1972 the DOOC and its supporters maintained an airy confidence that the initiative could not possibly pass, and even if it did it would not stop the games. McNichols declared that "the Olympics are to be here in '76. There's no question about that. If the amendment passes . . . we'll just have to look elsewhere for the state's four million [dollars]." Likewise, Carl DeTemple was sure that "voter rejection of state funding wouldn't sound a death knell to the Games. The Games are a sure thing." Olympic organizers had always assumed that the federal government would provide a major percentage of the funds needed to stage the games. In 1971 Governor Love had predicted that "there will be federal funds and in fairly substantial numbers." Surely, if Colorado refused to underwrite the Olympics, the national treasury would pick up the bill.[76]

In August 1972, however, the Senate Interior Committee, which would have to approve any federal funding of the Olympics, attached, at the suggestion of Colorado senator Gordon Allott, a provision to a bill appropriating $15.5 million for the games that made the federal money contingent on the outcome of the vote on the CCF's initiative. If the measure passed, the DOOC would not get the federal money. Reality now dawned on the DOOC leadership. If the initiative passed, there would be no Olympics. Carl DeTemple finally understood that "the fate of the 1976 Denver Olympic Games is now in the hands of Colorado voters. Twenty-four million dollars would have to be raised from private funds if the Games are voted down." DeTemple recognized that it would be "difficult, even ill-advised, to proceed in the face of such an obstacle."[77]

That understanding came too late for the DOOC to rescue itself and the Olympics. By the fall of 1972, public confidence in the organizers and the games had eroded beyond recovery. When Coloradans voted on November 7, 1972, the CCF initiative won with 60 percent of the vote. The proposed Denver charter amendment banning the use of city funds for the Olympics passed with 57 percent of the vote. There would be no state or city funding of the Olympics. There would be no federal funds for the Olympics. There would be no Olympics in Colorado in 1976. Later, the IOC went through the formality of removing the 1976 Olympics from Colorado and moved the event to Innsbruck, Austria.

After the vote Governor Love spoke of his feelings of "disappointment and shame" at the outcome. "But," he said, "I believe in the system of democracy. If the majority are against it let it be. Even if we could find some way to fund it, there's no way to force it down their throats."[78]

Each side offered its explanations of the election's outcome. More than a decade later, Richard Lamm described the Olympic supporters as "well-meaning business people who had the best interests of the state at heart, but they had an old agenda." That old agenda, of course, was the gospel of growth. Having just experienced a decade of rapid economic development and population growth, Coloradans seemed to want, if not a respite, at least a chance to think about the shape of future growth. The CCF's Meg Lundstrom echoed that view. "In Denver," she said, "the big issue was higher taxes," but "for the remainder of the Front Range, the fear was growth."[79]

John Parr, another CCF leader, pegged the result on the voters' "lack of confidence in the DOOC." "They lost their credibility a long time ago and tried to regain it with the same old unbelievable story they told in the first place." Parr even suggested that there might have been a Denver Olympics "if the DOOC had been candid with the people, had not conducted its affairs in secrecy." Then, he said, "our group would never have had to come along."[80]

Remarkably, Olympic supporters agreed with these assessments. One said, on election night, that "people in this state are saying they don't want more development and growth." Others pointed to the DOC-DOOC's arrogant and secretive methods of operating. Board member Norman Brown conceded that "the DOC and political leaders did not understand, or take seriously, the opposition. Not until September, or October did we understand its strength." Another board member, Neil Allen, pointed out that "when the Evergreen problem surfaced, the solution should have been simple enough—include these people in the process of solving the problem and nothing major would have come of it." However, Allen continued, "the DOOC was arrogant and aloof. Everyone outside the organization was treated like a clod." Campaign director Hank Kimbrough agreed. "In the beginning, when the opposition first arose," he said, "they wouldn't face up to the people. They were secretive; they wouldn't admit their errors."[81]

DOOC chairman William R. Goodwin gave the most intriguing postmortem. "This is a good state with good people," Goodwin said. "They are trying to tell us something and I think we should listen."[82] Just what were the people of Colorado saying in 1972 when they voted down the Olympics? Clearly, they did not trust the DOOC. In addition, they believed the environmental, community, and tax costs of the Olympics were too high.

The Olympic referendum seemed to touch off a political earthquake in Colorado, introducing a generation of leaders more attuned to environmental and other "liberal" issues. Some would dominate the state and influence national politics through the rest of the century. That year veteran U.S. Senator Gordon Allott lost his seat to Democratic environmentalist Floyd Haskell. Liberal Democrat Patricia Schroeder captured Denver's seat in Congress and held it until she retired in 1997. On the western slope, environmentalist Alan Merson defeated longtime congressman Wayne Aspinall in the Democratic primary. Two years later, in 1974, Richard Lamm defeated progrowth Republican John Vanderhoof for the governorship. Timothy Wirth, a Boulder Democrat, went to Congress, and Gary Hart defeated Republican senator Peter Dominick.

More important than the arrival or departure of specific political leaders was the Olympic controversy's role in injecting enduring issues into Colorado politics. Clearly, the era of unquestioned boosterism and growth was over in Colorado. The vote by no means ended growth, but it underscored a persistent ambivalence about it. All of the environmental evils that opponents said the Olympics would cause happened anyway. Referring to Denver in 1988, Richard Lamm noted, with no small amount of irony, that during the anti-Olympic campaign he had said, "if the Olympics came, we would become a sprawling, smoggy, polluted city. So we defeated the Olympics and what happened? We became a sprawling, smoggy, polluted city." Today an almost uninterrupted urban line extends from Fort Collins to Pueblo, and rapid population growth has stretched institutions, services, and infrastructures to the limits.[83]

When Lamm's successor as governor, Roy Romer, took office in 1987, Colorado's economy was mired in an economic recession. Governor Romer spent much of his first term traveling the country and the globe promoting economic development for Colorado and luring new employers to the state. By the mid-1990s, however, Romer had joined a new chorus of political leaders and environmentalists worried about the social, environmental, and fiscal consequences of unrestrained development.

Was, then, the supposed antigrowth sentiment behind the anti-Olympic vote a futile gesture? Not really. Expansion is the fundamental dynamic of a capitalist economy in good health. Before 1972 almost no one questioned the desirability of promoting any and all kinds of economic growth. After 1972 no one would ever again suggest that

the idea of at least thinking and talking about growth and its management was a silly or illegitimate suggestion. Leaders such as Richard
Lamm, who was tagged with the undeserved moniker of "Governor
Gloom" before he left office in 1987, argue that growth need not be
incompatible with environmental and social health, and few people
argue with that notion. However, that idea is a far cry from the old
gospel of growth that equated development with social health, and
the environment be damned.

Lamm and the other leaders of Citizens for Colorado's Future
could not have guessed that the struggle over the 1976 Winter Olympics was also the first in a long line of battles in Colorado, and around
the country, over the issue of public financing of athletics, especially
professional sports. In 1974 Denver voters narrowly approved the addition, at their expense, of twenty-five thousand seats at Mile High
Stadium. The Denver Broncos, the stadium's principal tenant, argued
that the franchise needed to sell more tickets in order to become
more competitive. More ticket revenue meant more money to hire
better players. In 1990 voters in the six-county Denver metropolitan
area voted to tax themselves to build a new stadium, part of the campaign to bring major league baseball to the city. The result was Coors
Field. Not long after the new baseball stadium opened in 1995, Broncos
owner Patrick Bowlen began a campaign to have a new football stadium built, mainly at public expense. At the same time, the owners of
the Denver Nuggets and the Colorado Avalanche demanded financial concessions from the City and County of Denver in order to
build a new basketball and hockey arena. Clearly, Colorado's vote
against financing the 1976 Winter Olympics did not settle the question of public funding of sports venues.

The Olympic experience in Colorado did send a clear message
to organizers of future games in other cities. In order to avoid the
politically volatile problem of public financing, organizing committees learned to sell commercial-sponsorship rights to the events. This
commercialization of the Olympics, the very thing that had turned
Avery Brundage against the Winter Games in the 1970s, became especially noticeable in the 1984 Summer Olympics in Los Angeles and
the 1996 "Coca-Cola" games in Atlanta. More disturbing were alle-
gations of bribery surrounding the awarding of the 2002 Winter Games

to Salt Lake City. Avery Brundage's ideal of the Olympics as "a revolt against Twentieth Century materialism" had been routed.[84]

Colorado may well have disqualified itself from ever hosting the Olympics. Whether that is to be lamented is debatable. However, the state has maintained a significant connection to the Olympics. Scores of athletes train at the regional Olympic training center in Colorado Springs. In 1995, thousands of competitors and spectators came to Colorado for the Olympic Festival, an exposition of some of the country's most promising young athletes. And in 1996 swimmer Amy Van Dyken won four gold medals in Atlanta, the most ever taken by an American woman.

6

COLLEGE FOOTBALL

Colorado 20, Nebraska 10.

Head coach Bill McCartney left the score illuminated on Folsom Stadium's scoreboard for the entire weekend following the University of Colorado (CU) Buffaloes' upset victory over the Cornhuskers in 1986. Since his arrival in Boulder in 1982, McCartney had made beating Nebraska, the perennial dominant power in the Big Eight Conference, his major goal. The win confirmed CU's reemergence, after a decade of mediocrity, as a major intercollegiate football power.

McCartney's teams won only seven games during his first three seasons as head coach, and plumbed the depths of futility with a 1-10-0 record in 1984. Sophomore receiver Ed Reinhardt's disabling brain injury, suffered in the 27-20 loss to Oregon that season, seemed to underscore the futility. The turnaround began in 1985 when the Buffs compiled a winning record and made their first bowl-game appearance since 1976. Although they lost the Freedom Bowl game to the University of Washington Huskies, 20-17, McCartney was able to showcase his program in one of his favorite recruiting territories, southern California. The next year featured the win over Nebraska, and an invitation to the Bluebonnet Bowl where CU lost to Baylor 21-9. The Buffaloes' 7-4 record in 1987 did not produce a bowl bid, but CU returned to the Freedom Bowl after an 8-4 season in 1988. Heavily favored to defeat Brigham Young University, CU led most of the game, but the Cougars, quarterbacked by Heisman Trophy winner Ty Detmer, came from behind to win 20-17.

The 1989 season had the stuff of legend. After quarterback Sal Aunese died from stomach cancer four weeks into the season, his teammates devoted the remainder of the season to his memory. Undefeated, they went on to Miami to play Notre Dame in the Orange Bowl for the national championship. The game was scoreless at halftime, but Notre Dame dominated the second half and won 21-6. Then, a year later, the 9-1-1 Buffaloes returned to the Orange Bowl for a rematch with Notre Dame. A penalty nullified a last-minute touchdown by Notre Dame's Raghib "Rocket" Ismail, and the Buffs left the field with a 10-9 victory and the national championship.

CU has not won another national championship, but McCartney and his successor, Rick Neuheisel, led their teams to winning records and bowl appearances in every season through 1996. The 1997 season, however, was a major disappointment. Prior to the season, the *Sporting News,* a national sports weekly, picked CU to finish number one in the nation. However, the Buffaloes won only five games, lost six, and failed to qualify for postseason play for the first time in a decade. Adding self-inflicted insult to injury, a few weeks after the season, the National Collegiate Athletic Association (NCAA) ruled that one CU player had been ineligible and forced the school to forfeit its five wins. Despite the setbacks of the 1997 season, fans and commentators still viewed CU as an important college football power.[1]

Although CU's emergence as a national football power attracted enormous public and media attention, Colorado's other major universities also achieved gridiron success in the 1980s and 1990s. Colorado State University's Rams, coached by Earle Bruce (1989–1992), defeated the University of Oregon in the 1990 Freedom Bowl, the school's first bowl game since the 1940s. Under Bruce's successor, Lewis "Sonny" Lubick, the Rams won the Western Athletic Conference championship in 1994 and 1995, and played in the Holiday Bowl, losing 54-21 to Kansas State in 1994 and falling to Michigan 24-14 in 1995. The Rams won the Western Athletic Conference title again in 1997, finished the season ranked eighteenth in the nation, and defeated the nineteenth-ranked Missouri Tigers, a Big Twelve team, 35-24 in the Holiday Bowl.

The Air Force Academy Falcons have coupled academic and football excellence year in and year out. Since 1959 the Falcons have played in thirteen postseason games, including their 55-41 victory over Texas Tech in the 1995 Copper Bowl. Air Force's dominance in interacademy competition is also a source of pride, as the Falcons have won the coveted Commander in Chief's Trophy ten times, more than either Army or Navy.

Colorado's second national collegiate football title of the 1990s was won not in the Orange Bowl but at Braly Municipal Stadium in Florence, Alabama, where, in 1996, the University of Northern Colorado Bears won the NCAA's Division II championship. In a play on the school's initials, newspaper headlines and fans trumpeted their team as the "Undisputed National Champions" (perhaps a dig at CU, which one poll after the 1990 season declared was only cochampion with Georgia Tech). The Bears repeated as Division II champions in 1997 with a convincing 51-0 pounding of the University of New Haven, but lost the title in 1998 in a 42-17 playoff quarterfinal loss to Northwest Missouri State.[2]

The successes of Colorado's college football teams in the 1990s were the result of good recruiting, talented coaching, institutional commitment, and fan support. However, these successes also reflected more than a century of development and change in collegiate athletics. The young men who play college football today are different from those who first played the game on rock-strewn or marshy fields more than one hundred years ago. Their reasons for playing, and the coaches and institutions they play for, are also different.

What began as an informal activity organized and run by students has evolved into a complex, multimillion-dollar enterprise conducted by and for the colleges and universities. By the latter half of the twentieth century, football at many schools defined the heart and soul of the university much more than academics. The student-athlete of a century ago has long since been replaced by the athlete-as-student.

A century ago, when CU's men challenged a rival squad at the School of Mines or at Colorado A&M, they played for personal satisfaction and the pride and honor of their schools. Today, the stakes are much higher. Big-time college football is an amateur sport in name only. The managers, coaches, and players (who are "paid" with scholarships) are professionals, and millions of dollars in income, jobs, and careers are at stake every season.

Universities are microcosms of society. Inevitably, they and their football programs mirror the stresses and changes occurring in American culture. This fact has been especially true as democracy and social opportunity have broadened across lines of class, race, and gender. Struggles over moral and religious values have also penetrated the locker room.

Origins of College Football

The first intercollegiate football game in the United States, played on November 6, 1869, matched squads from Rutgers and Princeton. Rutgers won 6-4. Although the players, who had arranged the contest themselves, called the game "football," it more closely resembled soccer. Rules agreed on for the event barred holding or tripping opponents, and points were scored by kicking a round ball through goal posts.

By 1869 some form of football had been a part of campus life for at least four decades. Beginning in 1827, the annual Bloody Monday game at Harvard pitted freshmen against sophomores in a rite of initiation into the college community. The Bloody Monday games were no-holds-barred contests in which the teams tried to score goals by any means. Afterward, the players sported black eyes, broken noses, and sprains with pride. By 1860 the mounting violence of Bloody Monday, and similar rituals at other schools, prompted efforts by faculty and governing bodies to ban the games. At Harvard, where students faced expulsion for defying the ban, the 1860 sophomore class staged a formal funeral for their beloved football. However, the game was too deeply entrenched in student life to disappear merely at the demand of university faculty and presidents, and the bans were most often observed in the breach.

Nonetheless, faculty hostility and the lack of widely accepted rules remained as obstacles to the development of intercollegiate play until the 1870s. In 1873, for example, Cornell's president, Andrew White, refused to permit his school's football squad to visit Michigan for a game, declaring that he would "not permit 30 men to travel four hundred miles merely to agitate a bag of wind." Hostility gave way to active support in the Gilded Age, however, as American colleges and universities experienced an era of rapid growth. Moreover, by the beginning of the twentieth century, faculty and administration support turned into control. As schools competed to enroll the sons and daughters of the wealthy elite and the burgeoning middle class, football became a measure of status and prestige and so was far too important to leave in the students' hands.[3]

By the 1870s two styles of play were most popular: English association, or soccer, rules; and the Boston Game, which permitted holding opponents and some running with the ball. In 1873 Princeton, Yale, and Rutgers agreed to play by association rules, but Harvard's footballers, who had adopted the Boston Game, refused to go along. In a letter to his counterpart at Yale, Harvard captain Henry Grant said, "We are perfectly aware of our position in regard to other colleges." He even allowed that his team had gone "so far as to practice and try the Yale game," but "we gave it up at once as hopeless."[4]

Harvard's holdout against association football was an important moment in the development of intercollegiate play. The search for worthy opponents in 1874 led Harvard to accept a challenge from Montreal's McGill University to play a two-game series, one according to Harvard's rules and one by McGill's. The Canadians' game was rugby, or a variation of it, which resembled the Boston style of play but was more complex and rougher. The Harvard players immediately decided that they preferred the visitors' game and adopted it as their own. Over the next two years other northeastern teams, even Yale, followed Harvard's lead. Finally, in 1876, the scholar-athletes representing Harvard, Yale, Columbia, and Princeton established the first American college football conference, the Intercollegiate Football Association (IFA). This student-run organization adopted the modified English Rugby Union rules featuring continuous play, use of any tactics to prevent opponents from advancing the ball, no forward passes, and scores by either running (one point) or kicking (four points). The association also decided to stage a championship game to be played each year on Thanksgiving Day.

The Yale team was the least happy with the new association's rules and had argued in favor of retaining the eleven-man soccer squad and allowing only kicked goals. However, Yale soon shed its conservatism, so much so that the school's longtime player and coach, Walter C. Camp, became known as the father of American football.

Camp attended Yale between 1876 and 1882, first as an undergraduate and later as a medical student. An avid athlete, he played most of the sports popular on campus but was especially taken with football and became the Yale team's captain. Camp also represented Yale on the association's rules committee. After graduation he took a job with a New Haven watchmaking company, a position that enabled him to maintain his connection with Yale football as manager and coach.

Although Camp's coaching made Yale a perennial football power, it was his innovative leadership in rule making that made him the architect of modern American football. In 1880 he convinced the rules committee to do away with the traditional rugby scrum as the method of putting the ball into play. In the scrum, offensive and defensive players formed a huddle around the ball and attempted to kick it free to a back who picked it up and ran or kicked it toward the goal line. Once the back was downed, a new scrum was formed. Camp's innovation separated the offensive and defensive teams on a line of scrimmage. The offense retained possession until it fumbled the ball or kicked it away. Teams quickly learned that they could keep their opponents from scoring by simply holding onto the ball indefinitely, even if they lost yardage on their plays. To solve that problem Camp later suggested requiring the offense to gain at least five yards in three plays or give up the ball. Because players and referees had to be able to measure yards gained, American football fields soon sported chalked lines at five-yard intervals. By 1912 the down-yardage rule had changed to require ten yards in four downs. Other Camp innovations included tackling below the waist and his point system for touchdowns, field goals, extra points, and safeties.

The development of a distinctive American style of football set in motion other changes in the game and its management. By the early twentieth century, much larger and more formal intercollegiate football institutions emerged, and they, along with professional coaches and managers, wrested control of the game from the students who played it. Football also mirrored the contending values of the era.

College football clubs began as open organizations. Any student with the desire to play could join, and, though superior talent and leadership naturally surfaced, every member had the opportunity to play. However, the days of congenial young men gathering casually to play football ended as teams ceased to be informal social groups. The specialized positional skills demanded by the new style of play, and the universities' growing interest in and identification with the fortunes of the team, made recruiting, training, and fielding the best possible talent, and winning games, the highest priorities. A new breed of professional coaches eclipsed the players as the central figures in college football. The schools, often using money donated by football-loving alumni, took over the job of equipping the teams and building and maintaining playing fields. Grandstands popped up around the gridirons, and college football became a moneymaking enterprise.

"Players like to win, but head coaches and especially paid coaches, had to win," a former Yale football team member recalled in 1904. By that year, professional coaches became the norm in college football. Harvard held out until 1905 when the university finally hired a coach at almost twice the average professor's salary. For players, the new regimen meant long hours of practice, discipline, and specialization. With jobs and careers on the line each season, coaches naturally wanted the best-possible talent for their squads and increasingly disdained volunteers from the student body. Schools competed to recruit the best players, and in the absence of effective rules governing recruiting, abuses became common. In 1896, West Virginia University's Fielding Yost transferred to Lafayette College in Pennsylvania just before that school's big game against the University of Pennsylvania. Yost led Lafayette to victory and then immediately transferred back to WVU. He eventually became head coach at Michigan where his recruiting shenanigans became legendary. Elsewhere, Walter Camp used a secret fund to pay tutors for his Yale players, and Amos Alonzo Stagg paid his University of Chicago players out of a Rockefeller-financed trust fund. In this environment, some professors began to wonder if football was not supplanting scholarship as the university's major purpose. The historian Frederick Jackson Turner complained of having to "play a game of hide and seek" with student-athletes.[5]

As early as the 1880s, faculties and presidents had recognized the need to impose their control over college sports, especially football. Acting in loco parentis—the principle that the school assumed the role of the parent—faculty justified this extension of authority because of potential conflicts with the participants' academic responsibilities and because sports had come to represent the school itself. As Princeton's president, Woodrow Wilson, noted, "[T]he side shows are so numerous, so diverting—so important if you will—that they have swallowed up the circus, and those who perform in the main tent must often whistle for their audience." Faculty committees promulgated rules governing travel, playing schedules, and player eligibility. They also took control of hiring trainers and coaches. Students, naturally, resented the intrusion into what they had always considered an independent area of student life. Experience, however, proved that athletic committees tended to be friendly to college sports and defended them from attacks by hostile faculty. Committee members were usually chosen carefully by school presidents, often in consultation with coaches and players. At many schools they eventually included student representatives, as well as alumni, whose presence indicated that group's growing influence, purchased with donations to the institution.[6]

Despite their growing influence, the athletic committees could not eliminate all of the problems surrounding intercollegiate football. A "clean" school might refuse to play against teams unwilling to adopt strict eligibility rules, but individual boycotts rarely intimidated an offending school. Only strong intercollegiate athletic institutions could hope to make and enforce meaningful rules.

The first enduring step in that direction came in 1895 with the formation of the Intercollegiate Conference of Faculty Representatives, composed of delegates from major midwestern universities, including Michigan, Illinois, Chicago, Purdue, Northwestern, and Minnesota. Later known as the Big Ten, the conference adopted rules requiring faculty supervision of athletics, player-eligibility standards, and banning financial subsidies for athletes. The ban against subsidies did not last long, and colleges and conferences began to support athletes openly by the turn of the century. Pennsylvania State University was probably the first school, in 1900, to offer open scholarships to its football recruits.

Although it was an important step toward intercollegiate governance of athletics, the Conference of Faculty Representatives hobbled itself by leaving enforcement of its rules in the hands of athletic committees and university administrations, most of whom would not sacrifice winning in order to adhere to amateur athletic ethics. Those that did found themselves under attack from hostile students, alumni, presidents, and governing boards. The legendary recruiting irregularities practiced by Michigan coach Fielding Yost illustrate the problem. In 1906 the conference adopted strict new rules in response to Yost's activities. When Michigan's faculty endorsed the new rules, the Board of Regents abolished the faculty committee and replaced it with a new athletic board under its direct control.

After the establishment of conferences, the next logical step was a national rule-making body for college sports. In 1905 delegates from sixty-two schools formed the Intercollegiate Athletic Association (IAA) to make recruiting and scholarship rules. The IAA became the National Collegiate Athletic Association (NCAA) in 1910. Like the conferences, the NCAA has never had the power, nor have American colleges and universities had the will, to fully eliminate recruiting and other abuses in college athletics.

The NCAA was created in large part to restore college football's public image, which, by 1905, had been sullied not only by the sport's recruiting free-for-all but also by the game's mounting violence. From the beginning of the Bloody Monday tradition at Harvard, football had always been a brutal game, but with the new style of play, and with the growing emphasis on winning, the sport became even more violent. Serious injuries became commonplace, and even death was a regular visitor to the gridiron.

To critics, and to supporters, football and its violence epitomized the culture of industrializing nineteenth-century America. *The Nation,* no friend of the game, noted that "the spirit of the American youth, as of the American man, is to win, to 'get there,' by fair means or foul; and the lack of moral scruple which pervades the struggles of the business world meets with temptations equally irresistible in the miniature contests of the football field." However, to Walter Camp, football's association with the ethos of the time was the game's greatest virtue. "American business," he claimed, "has found in American college football the epitomization of present day business methods." Football had "come to be recognized as the best school for instilling into the young man those attributes which business desires and demands," such as competitiveness, discipline, and respect for organization and authority. To some in the post–Civil War era, the rise of industrial capitalism, though an economic blessing, threatened to make a morally and physically weak, or effeminate, American man. Football could be an antidote, a rite and proof of manhood, a moral equivalent of the experience of warfare. In a letter from Harvard to his father, the president, Theodore Roosevelt, Jr., said, "I feel so large in my black sweater with the numerals on. Saturday's game was a hard one, as I knew it was bound to be. I was not seriously hurt at all. Just shaken up and bruised." He added, with proud nonchalance, "I broke my nose."[7]

Its manly, capitalist virtues notwithstanding, football's mounting brutality prompted some schools and state legislatures to threaten to ban the game, even in the face of its wide popularity and strong institutional identification. A crisis of sorts was reached after the especially brutal season of 1905. According to the *Chicago Tribune,* 18 high school and college players died that year, and 159 sustained serious injuries. In October, in the face of mounting institutional and editorial hostility to the game, President Theodore Roosevelt summoned coaches and other delegates from Harvard, Yale, and Princeton to a White House conference on the problem of football violence. Walter Camp, who worried more about weakening the game than about its violence, took control of the conference, which ended with a mild statement pledging to rid the game of unnecessary "roughness, holding, and foul play."[8]

The White House conference was not enough to still the controversy over football violence, but it did promote formation of the IAA in December 1905. Walter Camp's Intercollegiate Rules Committee, which represented several northeastern schools and the University of Chicago, refused to join the new body, but in 1906 agreed to work with it through a joint committee. That arrangement lasted until 1915, when Yale finally joined the NCAA.

Over succeeding years, the IAA and the NCAA tinkered with the rules of football until the game evolved as we know it today. However, the changes did little in the short term to eliminate football's violence. Thirty players, including eight collegians, died in 1909, and by 1946 more than five hundred players succumbed to football injuries. Nevertheless, the appearance of a national governing body quieted much of the hostility to the game.

By the 1920s, college football, the game and its institutions, was an important feature of the American cultural and sporting scene. In Colorado, the story of college football at the University of Colorado and Colorado State University (CSU) illustrate the major themes and problems in the game's history.

COLLEGE FOOTBALL IN COLORADO: THE STUDENT GAME

In 1880 a University of Colorado student, writing in the *University Portfolio,* complained about the lack of organized sports on campus. "Why don't you have a base ball or foot ball club?" he demanded. In the pragmatic spirit of the age, the writer observed that "to be a powerful man with no intellect is, to say the least no worse than to be a man whose learning so overbalanced his physical power that he reminds one of the boy with the big head. . . . The great workers of the age are men whose bodies can stand the strain of mental toil." A well-educated man also had to be physically fit.[9]

By the end of April 1880, the writer's fellow students had taken his admonition to heart, and the *Rocky Mountain News* reported that "the University boys of Boulder have organized a baseball club." University students also began playing football informally that fall. However, while students established an athletic club, organized football at CU was still almost a decade away. Meanwhile, students at other colleges in the state began intercollegiate football competition.[10]

Intercollegiate football in Colorado dates to at least April 1885, when teams from the University of Denver (DU) and Colorado College met in Colorado Springs. The Colorado College squad scored twelve points to defeat DU (score not given). A newspaper account of the game noted that "not a goal was made by either side, but all the points were made by touchdowns," suggesting that the rugby style of play had come to the West.[11]

By 1890, students at the Colorado School of Mines also formed a football team and in the fall of that year joined with teams from the

Denver Athletic Club (DAC) and the Colorado Springs Athletic Club to organize the Colorado Football Association. The University of Colorado's new team joined the association on November 1 and prepared for its first game, on November 15, against the powerful DAC squad.[12]

In the fall of 1889, William Horsford, a medical student, organized a new football squad at CU. Horsford had traveled in England and was familiar with association- or soccer-style football. Although the team quickly mastered the game, they had trouble finding opponents because the other teams in the area played rugby style. Finally, in October 1890, the athletic association voted to switch to rugby. Horsford stayed with the team, but another student, Tom Edmundson, became captain and quarterback.[13]

After only two weeks of practice the CU squad traveled to Denver to take on the Cherry and Black of the Denver Athletic Club. The Boulder collegians were "raw and undeveloped"; they had "no coaching, and as for team work all were most blissfully ignorant of the existence of such a thing." They lost 20-0, a score that one student later commented was "quite small" compared with others that first season. Unfortunately, five CU players, including captain Edmundson, were injured in the game, weakening the team for future contests. On November 22 the state champions, from the School of Mines, came to Boulder and thrashed the CU team 103-0. Recalling the game years later, CU fullback Conrad Bluhm thought the score "was not so bad" considering that their opponents were the "greatest team Golden ever had." On every play "it looked as if the Kaiser's army rushed through the holes" in CU's line. The game became so heated that at one point, when Bluhm was buried under a pile of Miners, CU president Horace Hale leaped into the fray and "started to clear up the adversaries single-handed." Hale was an ardent football fan who believed that the game would be good for the students and good for the university. However, the CU team seemingly had a long way to go before any positives would be realized. One week after the Mines disaster they lost to Colorado College 44-0. An account of the game did note that "for the first time the Varsity was able to advance the ball." CU ended its first season of intercollegiate football on December 13 with a rematch, in Golden, against the School of Mines. George

Darley, of Alamosa, picked up a Miner fumble and ran sixty-five yards for CU's first touchdown. It was a moral victory, of sorts, in an otherwise thorough 50-4 thrashing.[14]

The 1891 season, CU's second, was notable for two reasons. The team won its first victory, a 24-4 triumph over the Colorado Springs Athletic Association in the final game of the year. Second, they had their first coach, Dr. Frederick F. Kramer, an Episcopal minister who volunteered his services to the team. Kramer came to Boulder in 1891. "Having graduated from an eastern college, it was assumed that I knew something about up-to-date football," Kramer remembered. In fact, he had never played college football, though he had been a "scrub," or human tackling dummy, "pro bono collegio," as he put it.[15]

CU's 1892 squad won three games and lost two to achieve the university's first winning season. They twice defeated Denver University by identical scores of 46-0 and hammered the newly formed Colorado Aggies (now Colorado State University) team 70-6. CU football was now a respected power in the state and was a source of pride and spirit for students and faculty.[16]

The year 1893 marked an institutional change in intercollegiate football in Colorado. Students representing CU, Colorado College, Denver University, Colorado Agricultural College, and the School of Mines met in March at Denver's St. James Hotel to form a new all-collegiate association. However, the new Colorado Intercollegiate Athletic Association (CIAA) did not create a strictly amateur college game because CU and other member teams continued to play the semipro athletic clubs. Nor did the advent of a formal intercollegiate association bring about strict eligibility rules. For example, CU's 1893 team included law student George Wailes, a graduate of Amherst and a veteran of that school's football team. Wailes was a valued addition to the squad because he was familiar with all of the recent innovations in the game introduced in the East.[17]

CU's first full-time coach arrived in 1894. Team captain Harry Gamble recruited his friend Harry Heller, who had played at Baker University in Kansas. Team members and fans dug into their own pockets to pay Heller's salary. When he arrived in Boulder on October 1, Heller announced that "our games are not to be full of tricks, but straight snappy football." Under Heller the players began to give up some control over their athletic lives. He set out to put his team on a strict regimen, including a training table so that he could control the players' diet. One of the new coach's first problems was assembling a team. The university squad in those days was put together from the student body. As the *Silver and Gold* described the process, there were "days spent in entreating, begging, arguing," with potential players, some of whom were "made over-anxious by the harrowing accounts of games as faithfully reported by the Associated Press." When a CU player was knocked unconscious in a practice game against Denver's East High, the injury underscored Heller's recruiting problem. Barely a dozen men showed up for the team's next practice. The team's playing field on the grounds of the Boulder Athletic Club, located northeast of the downtown area, close to Lover's Hill near the present-day intersection of Twentieth Street and Alpine Avenue, probably also discouraged recruiting. Students mobilized to get the field ready, and by September 1894 it was declared "fit for use," which, according to university historian William E. Davis, "meant that a man might run from one side to the other without fear of being impaled on the old stumps."[18]

Coach Heller overcame his recruiting problems, and under his guidance the CU squad won the CIAA championship with a record of 8-1, losing only to the Denver Athletic Club. The most satisfying wins were the team's 20-0 and 18-0 victories over the arch rival School of Mines. The joy of CU's first triumphant season was dampened, however, by Heller's decision to give up coaching and return to full-time studies.[19]

The university team now looked to the Ivy League for a new leader. Captain William Caley wrote to his counterpart at Dartmouth asking for the names of possible coaches. The Dartmouth captain replied that his own teammate, Fred G. Folsom, was the only man not yet engaged. Folsom, he said, was "the best end ever graduated from Dartmouth," and had since been a coaching assistant there. He had a thorough understanding of the game, was a conscientious trainer, and knew "all the wrinkles of recent date." Folsom had intended to go to law school at Michigan, but when his CU recruiters assured him he could pursue a legal education at Boulder while coaching, he ac-

6-1. Fred Folsom, shown here in his ever present Dartmouth sweater, came to the University of Colorado as football coach in 1895. He remained at CU, with only brief interludes elsewhere, as coach, athletic director, and law professor until his death in 1944. Courtesy, Archives, University of Colorado at Boulder Libraries.

cepted the offer. Like his predecessor, Folsom's five-hundred-dollar salary was paid with money contributed by the team members and their fans.[20]

Folsom did not make an especially strong impression upon his arrival in Boulder. Athletic association manager Charles Southard found him "slight of build and sway-backed"; shaking hands with him was "like grasping a handful of bones." This unimpressive character was to spend most of a half century at CU, fifteen of them as football coach and the rest as an athletic administrator and a member of the law faculty (fig. 6-1).[21]

Folsom's first season at Boulder showed great promise as the team built on the previous year's championship. Using the "Boulder Tandem," an offensive formation in which the running back was guarded by blockers in front and pushed from behind by other team-mates, the CU team won its second championship, again losing only to the DAC. CU repeated as state collegiate champions in 1896 with their first undefeated and untied season.[22]

The 1897 season brought CU's fourth straight championship and a controversial institutional change in college football in Colorado. The Colorado Intercollegiate Athletic Association voted a new rule limiting players to four years of eligibility. CU objected to the new rule, and at season's end the students voted to withdraw from the CIAA in protest. Fortunately, the association never formally accepted CU's withdrawal, and by the 1898 season the disagreement was resolved.[23]

During the 1898 season, CU played its home games on a new field, which students quickly named in honor of former captain Harry Gamble, located on the southern edge of the campus on the site now occupied by the University Memorial Center. In November, CU played its first out-of-state foe, Nebraska, losing 20-10. The new eligibility rule deprived CU of a number of key players, including quarterback Harry Chase who had been slated to become captain that season, and the team fell to fourth place with a record of 4-4.

Folsom's squad rebounded to a 7-2 record in 1899, but the turn-around was soured by the coach's decision to quit. He had finished his law degree and meant to embark on a career in that profession.[24]

Harry Gamble, who had stayed with the team as "graduate manager," chose T. W. Mortimer to succeed Folsom. Mortimer had played football at Simpson College in Iowa and at the University of Chicago and had been a successful high school coach in that city. Mortimer's 1900 team achieved a 6-4 record, which, though not of championship caliber, was apparently good enough to earn him a second season.

Fred Folsom, however, found it hard to stay away from football. In his spare time during the 1900 season he worked for the Denver Wheel Club team and helped coach them to an 11-0 win over CU.

Moreover, he let it be known that he was ready to return to Boulder if CU wanted him, which they did. His teams won back-to-back championships in 1901 and 1902. After the 1902 season, however, Folsom again shocked CU by resigning. His alma mater, Dartmouth, had offered him its head coaching job and a position on the university's law school faculty. Folsom's attachment to Dartmouth had never flagged—he wore his "D" sweater year after year—and the prestigious job offer was too good to turn down.

Folsom's departure from Boulder marked not only a coaching change but also the end of an era. Harry Heller and Fred Folsom brought professional coaching to CU and made the university the dominant football power in Colorado. However, they worked for the team and the athletic association. The team, the students, and other fans raised and paid their salaries. College football at CU was still a student activity, but that situation began to change in 1903.

Meanwhile, in its first years at Colorado Agricultural College (CAC), intercollegiate football did not have the strong faculty support that the sport enjoyed at CU. One professor, L. D. Crain, lauded the sport for the lessons of discipline and team play it could teach. However, in November 1892, when Professor Crain wrote of the sport's virtues in the school paper, CAC had no team. Perhaps in response to the professor's call, students organized the school's first team and took the field on January 7, 1893, for a contest with the Longmont Academy. They lost 12-8, but avenged themselves in a later encounter. The CAC squad also defeated the Normal School at Greeley, but then fell 70-6 to CU. That spring the agricultural college also became a founding member of the Colorado Intercollegiate Athletic Association.[25]

However, Colorado Agricultural College's first foray into intercollegiate football was short-lived. The team played a four-game schedule in the fall of 1893, winning one of them, a 60-10 thrashing of Denver University. The football team enjoyed strong student support, evidenced by dances and other fund-raising activities, but members of the faculty, including the school president, were dead set against the sport. Like many contemporary critics of the game, President Alston Ellis was especially put off by college football's violence and professionalism. "I am strongly antagonistic to any so-called sport that smacks of professionalism and by its senseless brutality consigns many of its votaries to the invalid's chair," he declared. "A lively war skirmish is but little more dangerous to life and limb, than the game of football as now played," Ellis continued. Moreover, "the exercise of the football game is not needed by our students, for whom adequate physical exercise is assured by requirements of the different courses of study." With the college president and many faculty members opposed to football, CAC withdrew from the intercollegiate athletic association in 1894 and did not resume play against other schools until 1899. In the interval, football survived there as an intramural sport.[26]

President Ellis's successor was an enthusiastic supporter of student athletics, and in the fall of 1899, only a few months after Barton O. Aylesworth became the school's president, Colorado Agricultural College resumed intercollegiate football. Further evidence of revival was the construction, by student volunteers, of a new athletic field. Built on marshland along College Avenue, the field tended to flood in wet weather and was "a bed of rocks in all seasons." In 1901 alum-

6-2. Harry Hughes, Colorado Agricultural College's first full-time football coach, led the Aggies from 1911 until 1942. Courtesy, Colorado State University Photographic Archives.

nus Charles Durkee donated $650 to enclose the field with a board fence. Unfortunately, only three sides of "Durkee Field" could be enclosed since it was bounded on the west by railroad tracks. Non-paying spectators liked to gather on the tracks to watch the games, and the brawling that attended efforts to remove them often rivaled the action on the field. Further evidence of the intent to put sports at CAC on a paying basis came in 1907 with the addition of a two-hundred-seat grandstand.[27]

Colorado Agricultural College's first full-time professional football coach, Harry W. Hughes, arrived in Fort Collins in 1911 (fig. 6-2). Hughes played his college ball at Oklahoma and went on to a successful high school and college coaching career before coming to CAC. The new coach demanded self-discipline from his players and imposed a rigorous training program emphasizing the fundamentals of the game. He also introduced the team to innovative new tactics such as the unbalanced line and his "million dollar play," a highly successful version of the end around. By the time Harry Hughes came to Colorado, however, college football was no longer a primarily student-organized activity. The faculty had taken control.[28]

Faculty Control and the Evolution of Big-Time College Football

Fred Folsom's departure opened the door for the faculty to assert control over athletics at the University of Colorado. In May 1903 the Board of Regents adopted a formal athletic policy, which included the creation of a new Department of Physical Training. In June the university hired David Bertram Cropp as the new department's director. Cropp was the embodiment of the itinerant student-athlete causing so much concern in college football circles at the turn of the century. He enrolled in Iowa's Lenox College in 1893 and played there for four years. He then moved on to Cornell for a time and, in 1899, turned up at Wisconsin where he played fullback for two seasons. He returned to Cornell as coach in 1901 and went on to the University of South Dakota in 1902. In addition to leading physical education classes, Cropp's duties at Boulder also included coaching the football team. For the first time the football coach was a member of the faculty. Reporting on Cropp's appointment, the *Denver*

Times declared that "the placing of one man at the head of all the athletic interests of the university and giving him nothing else whatever to do, means a great advancement along athletic lines for the student." What it actually meant was that the university had taken control of college sports from the students.[29]

Within a few years, faculty control was mirrored in the institutional setting of intercollegiate sports. In January 1909, CU professor George Norlin, chairman of the university's Athletic Board, organized a meeting with representatives from the Colorado Agricultural College and Colorado College. The three schools agreed to form a new Colorado Faculty Athletic Conference in place of the old student-chartered Colorado Intercollegiate Athletic Association. The School of Mines joined the new conference later that year, and, in 1910, after Denver University and Utah joined, the group renamed itself the Rocky Mountain Faculty Athletic Conference. Utah State joined in 1914, followed by Montana State (1917), Brigham Young (1918), Wyoming (1921), Colorado Teachers College (1924), and Western State College (1924). Statewide, and then regional, "faculty control made possible the adoption of rules" governing eligibility and restricting financial aid to athletes, "which . . . would make the business of the professional or tramp athlete unprofitable, and which practically barred the student who wished to attend college primarily to gain athletic fame." Protecting college sports meant taking the last vestiges of control from the students.[30]

George Norlin was an articulate apostle of amateur idealism in college sports. A great fan of intercollegiate athletics, he was also aware of their potential for corruption. "Intercollegiate contests, when conducted in a spirit of mutual trust, of friendly rivalry, and of true sportsmanship, are good," he wrote in 1911, but "they are harmful when not so conducted." Norlin believed that winning for its own sake should not be the main goal. "So long as contests are held we shall win if we can, but we shall win honorably, regarding an unfair victory as far worse than a fair defeat." Norlin sustained and expanded his commitment to honorable amateurism throughout his long career as athletic board chairman and university president. In a 1929 address to the CU student body called "Going Straight in Athletics," President Norlin singled out recruiting as an evil to be avoided. He admonished everyone associated with the university to be "alert to make sure that any football team which represents the college . . . is really representative of the college, that it is built up out of a student body which has been attracted to the college by its character, it quality and its reputation as an institution of learning." Norlin pointed out that "mercenary armies have at times inspired men's fears and hopes, but they have never evoked a people's patriotism." Norlin also pointed out, prophetically, that excessive emphasis on athletics was a disservice to the student-athlete himself. There was "nothing more reprehensible, more dishonest, more unjust," than "placing such over-emphasis upon athletic success that the student is made to feel that nothing else is important." The great danger was that at the end of his brief athletic career the student-athlete would find that "the best years of his life have been largely wasted, and that he has been allowed to fall into habits of mental lethargy and inertia which are serious handicaps in the battle of life."[31]

To George Norlin, winning was important, but it was not the only, or even the most important, measure of a successful intercollegiate football program. That ideal was severely tested, and finally overthrown, in later years as college football became a business enterprise in which winning was not only the measure but also the foundation of success. More than a half century later, Norlin's sermon of "Going Straight in Athletics," his insistence on building teams out of the student body, and his demands that athletes be scholars first and that the university prepare them for life and careers beyond the football field seem quaint and naive.

CU's football teams produced five consecutive winning seasons between 1903 and 1907, even though they played for three different coaches (David Cropp, 1903–1904; Willis Keinholz, 1905; Frank Castleman, 1906–1907). However, they won the CIAA championship only once, in 1903, and so did not seem to be the football powerhouse of previous years.

Hope for a return to championship form came in 1908 in the person of Fred Folsom. The former coach had returned to CU two years earlier as a member of the law faculty. He helped out with the football team in 1907 and became head coach for the third time in 1908. Folsom's 1908 team won five games and lost two. His 1909,

1910, and 1911 squads were undefeated. No opponent scored on them in 1909, and CU yielded only three points in 1910 and five in 1911. The championship streak ended with 1912's 6-3 record, but a 5-1-1 campaign in 1913 earned another conference title, Folsom's last. The 1914 season (5-1) was his last in full command, and illness kept him off the field for much of 1915 when CU slipped to 1-6.

Although Fred Folsom resigned as CU's football coach after the 1915 season, he did not leave the university or the team. He headed the athletic board until 1927 and remained on the law faculty until his death in 1944.[32]

At Colorado Agricultural College, in 1912, the installation of the first sodded football field in the Rocky Mountain region underscored the school's commitment to building a successful football program. CU partisans had once complained about having to play on Durkee Field, "which had been freshly plowed, making fast play impossible with a team unaccustomed to the furrow." It was the Aggies team, however, that benefited most from the new surface, defeating CU in a 1912 contest that the CAC student newspaper, the *Collegian,* likened in import to Columbus's discovery of America. In a less hyperbolic assessment, Coach Folsom conceded that the CAC squad was "the fastest team Colorado has seen for five years. . . . [T]he best team won." The Aggies had come of age as a football force. Coach Harry Hughes's teams went on to win Rocky Mountain Conference championships in 1915 and 1916.[33]

Intercollegiate football went into a virtual hiatus during the World War I years. Many of both schools' best players traded football uniforms for army khaki. At least one star player, CU quarterback Eddie Evans, died in France. Although both schools played limited schedules, the teams and their fans had little to cheer about. CU's record for the 1916–1919 period was 11-13-2, and Colorado Agricultural College's team was winless in 1917 and 1918.[34]

Football prosperity returned quickly after the war. For CU, the years of drift during World War I ended in 1920 when the university anchored its football program to Myron Witham, a protégé of Fred Folsom. Witham, who was to coach at CU through 1931, played and coached under Folsom at Dartmouth during the 1903 and 1904 seasons. Once in Boulder, Witham instituted a number of innovations, including an athletic dorm and training table, a booster club to help finance team activities, tutoring for players, and a program of cultivating good relations with high schools (that is, recruiting). As CU historian William E. Davis notes, "these developments marked the first trends toward subsidization of athletes at the University."[35]

After three respectable, if unspectacular, seasons, Witham's program finally paid off in 1923 when his team was undefeated and untied. The winning ways continued in the 1924 season (8-1-1), and the CU squad earned a pleasant bonus: two postseason games in Hawaii, arranged and funded by boosters. They crushed a Navy team 43-0, but fell 13-0 to the University of Hawaii. Equally notable, however, was the opening of the university's new football stadium in 1924. Built in a ravine just east of the college gymnasium, the 26,740-seat Colorado Stadium was financed through a trust arrangement devised by Fred Folsom. The stadium was later renamed in honor of President George Norlin, and in 1944 its name was changed again to honor Fred Folsom. Norlin's name was appended to the university library.[36]

A solid 6-3 record in 1925 (when Witham briefly and unsuccessfully experimented with a T formation) was followed by losing seasons in 1926 and 1927. CU climbed back above .500 in 1928, but by then Witham was in trouble. His 1928–1931 teams produced winning records, but they were not of championship caliber. Worse, they failed to beat the school's arch rival, Utah. Early in January 1932 the Board of Regents decided against renewing Witham's contract.[37]

The firing came as a surprise to many. Although Witham had been under mounting criticism in the late 1920s, he remained popular with players, students, and alumni. When he was asked to comment on his dismissal, Witham said, "My friends don't need a statement, and the others don't deserve one." Witham's failure was not that he did not win. His record at CU, after all, was an impressive 63-26-7. His failure was that he did not WIN. His teams did not win the big games every year; they did not win the conference championship, if not every year, at least most years. By the 1930s winning was becoming the central purpose and preoccupation of intercollegiate football. The ideals of amateurism, building character, and promoting school spirit had assumed a kind of quaint nostalgia.[38]

CU President George Norlin could not or would not intervene on Witham's behalf, but he did understand that the coach's dismissal represented a disturbing trend in collegiate athletics, and he issued strong words to try to stem the tide. Witham's firing, he declared, did not represent a change of university policy on athletics. In replacing Witham, CU would not "follow the example of many institutions . . . which are hiring coaches at absurdly high salaries which are entirely out of proportion with salaries paid to other members of the faculty." Nor would the university go into the business of recruiting. "We shall not exploit young men in order to satisfy the clamor of the sporting fans," he said. Instead, CU would continue "to build our teams out of students who come here because they are attracted primarily by the educational opportunity furnished by the University." In sum, he insisted, "[W]e shall take no backward step." George Norlin was trying to hold back an inexorable tide. Witham's firing symbolized the primacy of winning, and it was a major step toward CU's entry into "big time" college football.[39]

Myron Witham's successor, William "Navy Bill" Saunders, a veteran Rocky Mountain Conference coach, led CU for three seasons and a record of 15-7-2. Saunders had a five-year contract but quit after the 1934 season to manage his family's business interests. The most notable developments during Saunders's tenure included the appearance of a star back, William C. "Kayo" Lam, who set rushing and all-purpose yardage records in 1935, and the decision the previous year to call CU teams the "Buffaloes." Both Lam and the new nickname had staying power. After graduating, Lam worked in the university's athletic department until 1970.[40]

Bernard F. Oakes, a hard-driving former marine with the unlikely nickname of "Bunny," coached the Buffaloes for five turbulent seasons. In many ways a prototype of the modern football coach, Oakes demanded total commitment from his players, and, as former CU sports publicist Fred Casotti has written, "his practices were long, meticulous and, [sic] almost cruel. Lights were installed at the practice field so the sessions could last longer." Clearly, Coach Oakes saw his team members as football players first and foremost and as students only secondarily.[41]

CU's greatest player of this era was future U.S. Supreme Court Justice Byron White (fig. 6-3). Born in Fort Collins in 1917, White

6-3. The University of Colorado's most famous football alumnus, Byron White, was an all-purpose player. The future United States Supreme Court justice won All-American honors in 1937 with big numbers running, passing, and kicking the ball. Courtesy, Archives, University of Colorado at Boulder Libraries.

grew up and played high school football in nearby Wellington, and burst onto the national college football scene in 1936. In that year's contest against Utah, White punted, ran back punts and kickoffs, ran from scrimmage, and passed the ball for all of CU's points in a 31-7 victory. In 1937, "Whizzer" White led the nation in rushing and scoring, completed twenty-two of forty-eight pass attempts, and ran up strong numbers in punting and punt returns to become CU's first All-American. After his collegiate career, White had a brief professional football career with Pittsburgh and Detroit. He abandoned his professional career for a Rhodes scholarship, the law, and, eventually, the Supreme Court. White's versatility anticipated that of a later CU player, Kordell Stewart, the quarterback of the early 1990s who distinguished himself in professional play at Pittsburgh as a quarterback, running back, and receiver. Stewart doubtless will not follow the rest of Justice White's career path, however, since NFL players today earn far more money than Supreme Court justices and, among many Americans, enjoy more respect.[42]

Record-setting performances on the field by Kayo Lam and Byron White were one measure of CU's advance toward college football's big time. Another was the university's participation in the formation of a new conference. In December 1936 the seven largest schools in the Rocky Mountain Conference (CU, CAC, Denver, Wyoming, Utah, Utah Aggies, and Brigham Young) broke away to form the Mountain States Conference, to be known as the Big Seven. The smaller schools could no longer compete with the large institutions either on the field or in filling the grandstands with paying crowds.[43]

The higher-profile conference and Byron White's performance in 1937 helped the Buffaloes earn their first bowl game, the Cotton Bowl. However, the excitement and glamour of the bowl appearance wore off for the Buffaloes long before the kickoff. Despite incessant rain in Fort Worth, Coach Oakes marched the team through two long practices daily. Outmatched by their more powerful opponent, Rice University, the Buffaloes lost 28-14. Bunny Oakes had never been popular with his players, but after the Cotton Bowl experience many team members were openly resentful.[44]

Oakes and the team weathered an unhappy 3-4-1 season together in 1938, but a rebellion erupted early in the 1939 season when three top players quit the team. In October, after the team lost its first three games, the *Boulder Camera* reported that team members had petitioned the athletic board to have Oakes fired. The board apparently sided with the players and asked the Board of Regents to dismiss the coach. The regents, however, sided with Oakes, and calm and harmony seemed to return to the football program, so much so that the Buffaloes went on to win the Big Seven title. However, rebellion erupted again in February 1940, when thirty-five of the team's forty members signed a petition threatening to quit if Oakes was not fired. The players criticized Oakes for his harsh coaching style, poor relations with the press and the faculty, and insistence on placing football ahead of academics. A faculty committee investigated the situation and finally recommended firing the coach. Defeated, Oakes negotiated a cash settlement of his contract and quickly left Boulder.[45]

Colorado Agricultural College enjoyed more stability and its own measure of football success during the interwar period. Coach Harry Hughes's teams won Rocky Mountain Conference championships in 1919, 1920, 1925, 1933, and 1934. The school also produced its own athletic star in the 1930s, Glenn Morris. Morris came to CAC in 1930 from the town of Simla, located on the plains northeast of Colorado Springs. He started at end all of his four seasons at Fort Collins and represented the school in the 1934 Shrine all-star game. Although he was a top-notch football player, Morris's real athletic love was track, especially the decathlon. He made the 1936 U.S. Olympic team and starred in the Berlin games, winning the decathlon and setting new records for the event. Morris also edged out the great Jesse Owens that year in voting for the James E. Sullivan Memorial Trophy given to the amateur athlete of the year.[46]

The 1934 championship was the last of Hughes's coaching career, and the 1935 season began a slump that lasted more than a decade. When Hughes came to Fort Collins in 1911 he was regarded as an innovator, but as the losses piled up in the latter 1930s fans began to wonder if his skills had failed. Some suggested that the school needed to recruit more aggressively, perhaps even bring in African American players, and offer direct financial subsidies to athletes. Hughes withstood the criticism through the 1941 season, but in April 1942 stepped aside as football coach to become athletic director.[47]

The United States had entered World War II by the time Harry Hughes gave up coaching. Aggie football suffered badly during the war years. A Hughes protégé, Julius "Hans" Wagner, took over the team in 1943, but a two-year suspension of football kept him from fielding a team, much less rebuilding the program. When play resumed in 1945 the Rams, the new nickname adopted for the school and its teams in 1944, went 2-6. Poor play continued in 1946. A humiliating 33-0 drubbing by Denver University in October was for many, including Wagner, the final straw. One student complained that the Ram offense had not deceived the Pioneers or any of the eighteen thousand people in the stands, "but apparently bewildered the already confused Rams." Wagner resigned three days later.[48]

In the wake of the "D.U. Disaster," the State Board of Agriculture, the governing body of Colorado A&M (the college was renamed in 1944), made a major commitment to improving the school's athletic program. The board increased grants-in-aid for athletes to 132, with 57 earmarked for football. To defray the costs of the expanded program, the board tripled the student athletic fee. Finally, the college hired Robert L. Davis, a veteran coach, to try to lead the Rams back to football respectability. Davis had eighteen years of coaching experience, was a talented recruiter, and had the public relations skills needed to restore fan support.[49]

Like Colorado A&M, CU also curtailed its football program during World War II. Buying out Bunny Oakes's contract left the athletic program financially strapped, so assistant coach Frank Potts, who also coached the track team, agreed to take over the football job for the 1940 season with no added salary. His team's 5-3-1 record earned him an offer to take the head coaching job permanently, but Potts declined. The university found its new coach, "Gentleman Jim" Yeager, at Iowa State. As much as Bunny Oakes foreshadowed the hard-driving postwar-era coach, Yeager was a throwback to the more innocent times of the early twentieth century, a man who, as Fred Casotti has described him, believed that "a football coach was hired to lead young men" and not merely to win at any price. Yeager's 1941–1943 squads compiled a 15-8-1 record. The 1942 season was the last for regular conference play during the war, and for the duration CU mostly played military teams from bases in Colorado and Wyoming. The wartime draft and the rotation of military personnel in and out of the school during the war made it next to impossible to keep a set of players around for long. The NCAA and the Mountain States Conference eased that problem somewhat in 1942 by permitting freshmen to play as a concession to wartime conditions. Football consistency became even more difficult after the 1943 season when Coach Yeager was called to active duty in the navy. Frank Potts once again took charge of the football team and remained at the helm for the next two seasons while the Buffaloes went 11-5.[50]

CU football fans greeted the return of peace, and of Coach Yeager, with a spirit of optimism. However, the disarray caused by the war could not be easily or quickly repaired. The combination of young players with whom the coach was not familiar, returning veteran players for whom football was no longer the most important thing in life, and Yeager's own easygoing style was not a formula for success. In the 1946 and 1947 seasons, Yeager's teams played only .500 football, compiling a record of 9-9-1. By the end of the 1947 season Yeager lost his enthusiasm for coaching, and in December the coach resigned to go into business in Boulder.[51]

The postwar period ushered in a new era in American higher education. Backed by the GI Bill, tens of thousands of veterans, men and women, flocked to college campuses determined to build better, more prosperous lives for themselves and their families. Colleges and universities, especially the public schools, would never again be the elite institutions they had traditionally been. Student bodies not only grew rapidly but also became more socially, ethnically, and racially diverse. Those changes were inevitably mirrored in intercollegiate sports. The development of the mass university was the final step in the transformation of college football from an elite student activity into an institutional enterprise. After World War II, more and more schools, including CU and Colorado A&M, set out to build programs that would elevate them into the rarefied ranks of big-time college football.

Big-Time College Football in Colorado

The University of Colorado took a major step toward joining the football big time several months before Coach Yeager's resignation. Indeed, the decision in March 1947 to leave the Mountain States Conference and join the Missouri Valley Athletic Conference—the Big Six—may have helped Yeager decide that his style of coaching was a relic of the past.

CU officials had attended the annual Big Six meeting in 1942, but decided then that the university would not try to join the conference. The war probably barred any major moves anyway. By early 1947, however, CU officials concluded that their entire athletic program had outgrown the level of competition in the Mountain States Conference and so asked for, and gained, admission to the Missouri Valley Conference, which now became known as the Big Seven. The Buffaloes' annual foes would now include national powerhouses Nebraska and Oklahoma, as well as Missouri, Kansas, Kansas State,

6-4. Dallas Ward's CU football teams won two-thirds of
their games, including the 1957 Orange Bowl. However,
he did not win a Big Eight championship and he did
not beat Oklahoma, so the university fired him in 1959.
Courtesy, Archives, University of Colorado at Boulder
Libraries.

and Iowa State. (The conference became the Big Eight in 1960 with
the admission of Oklahoma State.)

Most CU fans were overjoyed by the move. Athletic Director
Harry Carlson termed it "an advancement in our athletic status which
I have been looking forward to for many years." There were skeptics,
however, who believed the university had an inflated notion of its

athletic program's strength and had gotten in over its head. For years afterward, *Denver Post* cartoonist Bob Bowie savaged the university with the caricature "Big Time Cholly." Nonetheless, for better or worse, CU had joined the college football big time. As *Denver Post* sportswriter Jack Carberry put it nearly two years later, "Big Seven football is big-time—very, very big-time." By then, other observers wondered how the move would affect the amateur traditions to which Carlson remained steadfastly loyal. One speculated that "the days of snow-white athletic purity . . . may be numbered, with the Golden Buffaloes going into the open marts for football talent," since "the Herd has to compete in recruiting and aid to athletics if they wish to compete in Big Seven football." Indeed, soon after CU joined the Big Seven it increased athletic scholarships from forty to one hundred and designated sixty of them for football. George Norlin's spirit must have been very disturbed.[52]

CU hired Minnesota assistant Dallas Ward to lead the university to the football promised land (fig. 6-4). Ward was cut somewhat in the pattern of Bunny Oakes. He was all football, "a grim-visaged, stern tactician." Unlike Oakes, though, Dal Ward won and kept the affection and loyalty of his players during his eleven seasons at CU. As an assistant coach at Minnesota, Ward became a respected offensive strategist and an effective recruiter, an especially notable achievement in the highly competitive Big Ten. He used that experience to expand Colorado's recruiting efforts into the northern Plains and Midwest regions, including Chicago. Ward understood that money was the foundation of successful recruiting. In the spring of 1956, when his program teetered between major improvement or deterioration, Ward launched a public fund-raising campaign to finance more football scholarships. He kicked off the drive at an alumni association dinner at the Denver Athletic Club, telling the group that the university needed better football players and "stressed that it takes money to lure them to Boulder." Ward's audience pledged most of the initial goal of twenty thousand dollars on the spot.[53]

Ward's teams fared poorly in the 1948 and 1949 seasons, winning only six games and losing thirteen. Members of Ward's early recruiting classes, including Tom Brookshier, who became a prominent sportscaster, and future Apollo XIII astronaut Jack Swigert, whose statue now represents Colorado in the U.S. Capitol's Statuary Hall, began to make their presence felt in the 1950 season, and in 1951 the Buffaloes turned in a 7-3 record, the first of eight straight winning seasons (51-24-5). CU football enjoyed unprecedented popularity. The university added fifteen thousand seats to Folsom Stadium in 1956, but tickets could still be hard to come by, especially when Oklahoma came to town. When a Denver couple divorced, the woman demanded custody of one of their season tickets. The judge ruled in her favor, but lamented that he "should have impounded the tickets" and delayed his decision for three months, until after the Oklahoma game.[54]

Merely winning was no longer good enough; putting CU players' names on All-American and All–Big Seven lists and sending them to all-star games was not good enough. Although Ward was still respected and popular, by the mid-fifties he came under criticism for not beating Oklahoma, not winning the conference championship, and not taking CU to postseason games and galas. Some thought that Ward's single-wing offensive was outdated, even though, as the only such offense in the conference, it gave Big Seven foes fits week after week.[55]

Ward seemed to silence his critics in 1956 when the Buffaloes' 7-2-1 record, second in the conference, earned CU an appearance in the Orange Bowl. Oklahoma owned the Big Seven, and in order to maintain interest in the event, the Orange Bowl did not allow consecutive appearances. CU defeated Clemson 27-21 on New Year's Day, and Dal Ward's team carried their coach off the field on their shoulders. The fans, the press, even the state legislature roundly praised Ward. He seemed vindicated, and safe.[56]

Dal Ward's triumph in the Orange Bowl actually set him up for a fall. The victory made for expectations that his next two teams could not fulfill. A 12-7-1 record in 1957 and 1958 just was not good enough. In a closed-door meeting in January 1959, the Board of Regents voted 5-1 to fire Ward. The board acted on its own. It did not even consult Athletic Director Harry Carlson. There had been no clamor from alumni or students for Ward's dismissal—indeed, he remained popular among the fans—and the regents gave no reason for their action other than stating that it was "in the best interests of the university."[57]

The firing stunned Ward. He told the press that he had had no contact with any of the regents since the Orange Bowl when "they expressed complete satisfaction" with the football program. Ward was especially upset with the timing of the decision, long after the close of the season. "Nearly all college coaching changes are made before this date," he explained, "and this action is going to create a real hardship" for the members of his staff and their families because most coaching vacancies had already been filled.[58]

Reaction from students, alumni, and players was swift and angry. A group of alumni, joined by two members of the football team, petitioned the board to reverse their decision. This was the man, after all, who had "lifted Colorado football from the leaky roof circuit to major prominence." Ward's supporters were furious and confused to find, as the *Rocky Mountain News* reported, that nobody could "stand up to give one firm, definite and motivating reason for the dismissal."[59]

However, there was a firm, definite, and motivating reason for Ward's firing. "Don't let us kid ourselves," said *Denver Post* sportswriter Jack Carberry. "Ward did not win." To be sure, he won more than two-thirds of his games, but "he did not in his eleven years . . . bring a Big Eight Championship to Boulder. To put it more simply, his teams did not beat coach Bud Wilkinson's Oklahoma Sooners."[60]

Winning two of every three games was good, but not good enough. A big-time college coach had to WIN. Like Myron Witham before him, Dal Ward became the victim of an impossible standard. His firing was not honorable, but it was inevitable.

When Ward became coach in 1948, the job also included tenure in the physical education faculty. After the firing, Ward stayed on at CU, teaching volleyball and other sports. For a time in the 1960s he returned to the football team as an assistant coach. Before he retired in 1975 he was assistant athletic director. Years later the university built a new athletic training center at the north end of Folsom Stadium and put Dal Ward's name on it.

Colorado A&M's march toward the big time seemingly got a fast start under coach Robert Davis. Although Davis was a back-to-basics coach who emphasized fundamentals, he also introduced such innovations as scouting and filming opponents for game-day preparation.

6-5. Thurman "Fum" McGraw became Colorado A&M's first All-American in 1949. The Detroit Lions drafted him in 1950, and he was with the Lions during their 1952 and 1953 NFL championship seasons. After his NFL playing and coaching career, he returned to Fort Collins and eventually became CSU's athletic director. Courtesy, Colorado State University Photographic Archives.

He began to actively recruit and use African American athletes, a rarity at A&M under Harry Hughes. (Black football players were also rare at CU. The 1957 Orange Bowl team's starting offense had only one African American player, guard John Wooten.) During his nine years as coach, Davis's teams turned in seven winning seasons. Their 8-2 campaign in 1948 earned the Rams their first bowl appearance, a

New Year's Day meeting with undefeated Occidental College in the Raisin Bowl at Fresno, California, which they lost 21-20. Even with the Raisin Bowl loss, it had been a satisfying season for A&M, especially because it included a 29-25 victory over CU. The Rams defeated CU again in 1955, 10-0, and went on that season to win the Skyline Conference championship. (The Skyline Conference was the successor to the Mountain States Conference.)[61]

The Davis era brought to A&M the man whose name became synonymous with athletics there for most of four decades, Paonia's Thurman "Fum" McGraw (fig. 6-5). McGraw arrived in Fort Collins in 1946 after service in the Marine Corps. He excelled in football, playing on both offense and defense. He won all-conference honors during his junior and senior years and, in 1949, became A&M's first football All-American. The Detroit Lions drafted McGraw in 1950, and, with Doak Walker and Bobby Layne, he became a star of the Lions's 1952 and 1953 National Football League championship teams. McGraw had a bum shoulder, injured during his senior year at A&M, and whenever it popped out, Doak Walker recalled, "He'd yell, 'Doak, Doak, come here,' and I'd go roll it back in place." McGraw retired from the Lions in 1955 and return to A&M as an assistant wrestling and track coach, but he left again in 1958 to coach with the Pittsburgh Steelers. By the early 1960s, however, he decided that he did not want to raise his family in a large city and in 1962 returned to Fort Collins to become Colorado State University's assistant conference services director. (A&M became CSU in 1957.) The university was deeply in debt from a major dormitory construction program and wanted very much to fill the rooms during the summer. McGraw quickly lured forty-five hundred Tupperware salespeople to CSU. Fum became assistant athletic director in 1965 and oversaw the construction of Hughes Stadium and Moby Gym (so called because it resembles a whale), projects crucial to CSU's admission to the Western Athletic Conference. He left CSU in 1970 to scout professional football, but returned in 1976 as athletic director and held that job until he retired in 1987. Fum McGraw joined Byron White in the Colorado Sports Hall of Fame in 1971, and in 1997 the National Western Scholarship Fund honored him and his wife, Brownie, as its Citizens of the West.[62]

Coach Davis's successes in the early 1950s masked looming problems for A&M's football program. The lords of college football had one of their recurring fits of squeamishness about the changes they had wrought in the game. As CSU historian James E. Hansen II has put it, "concern over mounting costs and disgust over an unseemly professionalization of athletes led to corrective measures." In 1952 and 1953, the NCAA and the Skyline Conference enacted rules effectively requiring the return of one-platoon teams (that is, fewer players and fewer scholarships) and imposing new restraints on recruiting and eligibility. These rule changes only temporarily stemmed the tide in college football, but they had important short-term consequences in Fort Collins. As Hansen notes, "losing seasons, flagging attendance, and fiscal frustrations" were just around the corner, and "all exacted a damaging toll."[63]

Foreseeing problems he did not wish to deal with as a coach, Davis, at the end of his championship season in 1955, decided to quit while he was on top. He took the job of athletic director and replaced himself with assistant coach Don "Tuffy" Mullison. Plagued by shrinking budgets and rosters, Mullison managed to put together winning seasons in 1958 and 1959, but by the end of 1961, when disgruntled fans hanged the coach in effigy and pelted him with snowballs, CSU's football program had collapsed.[64]

A moment of crisis and decision at another institution forced CSU officials to consider whether or not the university would continue to try to have a major football program. In January 1961 the University of Denver announced that it was dropping intercollegiate football. Enraged DU students burned Chancellor Chester Alter in effigy, and some alumni canceled gifts to the university, but surprisingly most members of the athletic booster club and the alumni association agreed with the decision. DU simply could no longer justify or sustain annual losses of more than one hundred thousand dollars charged to the football program. The choice for DU, said one official, was to "Go big, go small, or go out." Going big time would have led only to greater financial commitments and losses, and going small would have been meaningless. Asked if DU might ever again field a football team, Vice Chancellor Robert McCollum said, "[I]f intercollegiate football were to return to its position during the 1920s and

1930s—a sport rather than a high pressure business—it's possible we'd take it up again."[65]

Fallout from the DU move was regionwide, triggering the disintegration of the Skyline Conference, which was especially serious for CSU. Despite cutbacks during the 1950s football continued to lose money, and, when DU dropped football, CSU president William E. Morgan told the *Rocky Mountain News* that the school was reassessing its entire athletic program due to "very considerable costs." Now the problem of supporting athletics, especially football, became even more difficult. Morgan and other CSU officials realized they had to significantly expand and upgrade the university's athletic program if it hoped to join a new conference. A new gymnasium or arena and a new football stadium topped the list of priorities.[66]

However, CSU had other, more pressing problems. Recent evaluations by the North Central Association of Colleges and Secondary Schools revealed embarrassing inadequacies in the university's library and liberal arts programs. To the dismay of football fans, President Morgan decided to put academics first and insisted that a new library and humanities and liberal arts buildings would have to come first. For the time being, the Rams and their fans would continue to spend their fall Saturdays at the antiquated field on College Avenue. Morgan's decision also meant that CSU would have to schedule its games as an independent because the newly formed Western Athletic Conference (1962) rejected the school's bid for membership.[67]

The early 1960s were also years of crisis for football at CU. The search for Dal Ward's successor lasted only seventeen days and ended with the hiring of twenty-eight-year-old Michigan State assistant Everett "Sonny" Grandelius. Grandelius seemed to embody the image of a jet-age coach: young, handsome, and charismatic. He promised a wide-open style of football with a pass-oriented offense. He promised to beat Oklahoma. And he delivered.

Most of Dal Ward's Orange Bowl team had graduated, and Grandelius took over a largely inexperienced squad. There were among the freshmen some talented players, most notably future All-American and Rhodes scholar Joe Romig, but the prospects for 1959 were not bright, as the 5-5 record that year bore out. In 1960

Grandelius's Buffaloes knocked off Oklahoma and finished 7-3. CU finished the 1961 season in championship form with a 9-1 record, undefeated in the Big Eight, and ranked seventh in the nation. And the Orange Bowl called. The Buffaloes fell to Louisiana State 25-7 on New Year's Day, but the loss took none of the luster off the season. Joe Romig won All-American honors for the second straight year, and Sonny Grandelius was named coach of the year in the Big Eight.[68]

Even as the accolades poured in, however, NCAA and university investigators were uncovering the dark reality behind Sonny's bright season. NCAA investigators began looking at the CU football program in August 1961, and in November a preliminary report cited evidence that twenty players had received illegal financial help. With Grandelius's knowledge, boosters had set up a slush fund to help players with living, travel, and other expenses. The players picked up their payments at a Boulder drugstore. The NCAA's preliminary findings prompted CU president Quigg Newton and the Board of Regents to order their own investigation. The probe, headed by future Colorado Supreme Court and Federal District Court judge Jim R. Carrigan, took three months and, in the end, confirmed the NCAA findings. On March 17, 1962, the Board of Regents voted to relieve Grandelius of his coaching duties and put him on paid leave until the end of his contract in March 1963.[69]

The university's actions in conducting its own investigation and firing Grandelius may have softened the blow from the NCAA, which punished CU by putting the school on probation for two years. The Buffaloes could not play televised games or appear in any postseason games during the probation. However, in May, the Big Eight Conference weighed in with its own sanctions, declaring nine lettermen named in the NCAA report ineligible for the 1962 season. Since they were seniors, the penalty ended their collegiate football careers.[70]

The Board of Regents fired Sonny Grandelius for undeniable violations of NCAA and conference rules. However, in doing so they refused to accept any responsibility for the corruption that forced their decision. In their resolution explaining the action, the board declared that they were "aware of the pressures of intercollegiate football," but claimed that those pressures "are more often exerted by over-zealous football enthusiasts than by the institutions themselves."

The regents' claim that "there has never been such pressure on Coach Grandelius from either the administration or the Regents" was either self-deceiving or incredibly disingenuous. Certainly, Grandelius got into trouble because he encouraged boosters or looked the other way while they slipped money to his players. And his accepting a gift of a new Cadillac suggests an overly cozy relationship with CU's "over-zealous football enthusiasts." But what did the regents expect after they fired Dal Ward? Ward's sin was not losing, but not winning enough. When Grandelius came to CU he had to have known that his employers, and not just CU fans, expected him to win it all. Grandelius did win it all, but in the process he showed CU and its fans the dark underside of successful big-time college football, the dark side of winning it all. The regents' posture of shocked sensibilities had no credibility.[71]

Finding a new head coach would be no easy task. College football's annual round of coaching musical chairs had already been played, and few good prospects remained on the market that spring. An in-house promotion seemed logical, at first glance, but Grandelius's staff was tainted with the odor of scandal. Finally, the search committee found their man within the university. He was Alumni Director William "Bud" Davis. Davis had been a member of Dal Ward's first team but, as a member of the scout squad, played only rarely. One time, Davis recalled, he told Coach Ward that he was not sure if he was best suited to play fullback or quarterback. Ward looked him over and told him, "Frankly, I don't think it makes a hell of a lot of difference." Although he did not make much of a mark as a player, Davis went on to coach championship high school teams in South Dakota and Colorado. However, he had no college coaching experience. Reactions to the appointment ranged from shock to outrage. Team captain Ken Blair threatened a player rebellion, telling school officials, "[Y]ou've got yourself a coach, now get yourself a team." Davis, who never lost his sharp sense of humor about his experience as head coach, said later that he might have been "the first coach in the history of intercollegiate football to be hung in effigy *before* he got the job."[72]

The task awaiting Davis would have been daunting for even the most experienced coach. No player rebellion occurred, but by the time the 1962 season began, graduation and sanctions had stripped the team of thirty-five players from the prior season. Only six seniors remained on the squad, and sportswriters called the Buffaloes the "vanishing herd." Davis lured Dal Ward onto his staff as defensive assistant, but even his presence could not make up for the lack of experienced talent on the field. The Buffaloes were 2-8 in 1962. They lost to Oklahoma 62-0 and fell 57-0 to Missouri in a four-week stretch in which they gave up two hundred points. Before the final game that season, against Air Force, Coach Davis, still in good, if grim, humor, rallied his team with the promise, "[I]f you beat the Air Force today, I'll resign after the game." As Davis recalled the game, "[T]hey went out and fought like hell" and beat the Falcons 34-10. Davis kept his word and resigned. He went on to a distinguished career as a university chancellor and president in Idaho, New Mexico, Oregon, and Louisiana.[73]

Two seasons of scandal, disintegration, and defeat left CU's football program barely breathing, and not everyone believed that the patient should be revived. Not long after Grandelius's dismissal, a student senate resolution called for abandoning intercollegiate football and returning to it only as a "strictly amateur" game. Nonetheless, there was really no doubt that the football program would be rebuilt. After all, as one faculty member noted, the NCAA investigation had been a kind of backhand compliment, an "almost inevitable accolade for athletic success." The regents, of course, "were horrified and decided upon a complete reorganization" of the football program. "Once again," the unhappy professor noted, "countless hours of administrative and faculty time were diverted from what a mossback might consider the essential functions of the university to deal with the question of how we are to entertain the public on Saturday afternoons."[74]

Eddie Crowder, one of Bud Wilkinson's assistants at Oklahoma, quickly surfaced as the only real candidate for CU's head coaching job. Crowder visited Boulder in December and signed a five-year contract on January 2, 1963, the day after Oklahoma played in the Orange Bowl. Reviving and rebuilding CU's shattered program would take time, as 2-8 records in 1963 and 1964 proved. However, Crowder was an effective recruiter and a fine coach, and in 1965 those talents began to show results in a 6-2-2 season. Rebuilding the football program was a challenging assignment, but Crowder also added the job of athletic director to his portfolio in 1965 after Harry Carlson retired. The university clearly had confidence in him. That confidence was borne out by the Buffaloes' 7-3 season in 1966, good enough for second place in the Big Eight.[75]

In 1967, one of CU's greatest all-time, all-around players, Bobby Anderson, took the field in the season opener against Baylor. He ran for 83 yards, threw for another 129, and scored three touchdowns. When his collegiate career ended in 1969, he had produced 5,017 total yards and 212 points as both a quarterback and a tailback. The university retired his number, 11, a distinction shared only with Byron White and Joe Romig.[76]

The 1967 season also marked the Buffaloes' return to postseason play. Crowder's team made a fast start, going 5-0, and earned number-three ranking in the nation at midseason. They finished 8-2, with losses to Oklahoma and Oklahoma State. The Bluebonnet Bowl invited CU to come to Houston to play Miami. On game day, Bobby Anderson overslept and missed the team bus to the stadium. However, he managed to flag down a cab and actually arrived at Rice Stadium ahead of his teammates and went on to lead them to a 31-21 win.[77]

Poor defensive play in the second half of 1968 led to a 4-6 finish, but Crowder had his team back in winning form in 1969 when they won seven and lost three. The 1969 season was also the first of four consecutive bowl years. The Buffaloes defeated Alabama 47-33 in the Liberty Bowl that year. CU fell to Tulane 17-3 in the 1970 Liberty Bowl, but defeated Houston 29-17 in the 1971 Bluebonnet Bowl. Houston had been favored to win that game, and the Buffaloes' upset win earned them third place in the final national rankings, behind Nebraska and Oklahoma— a Big Eight sweep. CU's four-year bowl run ended less happily in a 24-3 loss to Auburn in the 1972 Gator Bowl.[78]

The Gator Bowl loss seemed to carry over to the 1973 season. Fan discontent had surfaced in 1972 and boiled over in 1973. A "For Sale" sign appeared in Crowder's front yard one night, and fans held up "Goodbye Eddie" signs at the last game of that 5-6 season.[79]

It was a familiar situation at CU. Eddie Crowder had a winning record (65-49-2). During his eleven seasons Crowder's teams played in five bowl games and won three of them. His teams were littered with the names of future NFL stars, including Cliff Branch, Cullen Bryant, Mike Montler, Dave Logan, Jon Keyworth, and J. V. Cain. However, he never won the Big Eight championship, and he never took the Buffaloes to the Orange Bowl. Thus, Eddie Crowder became another victim of CU's, and big-time college football's, impossible standard. He won, but he did not win enough. Crowder resigned as head coach in December 1973, but kept his other job as athletic director, which meant that he would choose his own successor.

Crowder chose Bill Mallory, a protégé of Ohio State's Woody Hayes. Mallory had just finished an undefeated season at Miami University in Oxford, Ohio, capping the year with a bowl victory. In contrast to Crowder, who was "shrewd and smooth," Mallory was a "fire-breathing shouter who pounded tables and battered blackboards." Crowder, and CU fans, hoped he would bring a powerful, Big Ten–style of football to Colorado.[80]

Mallory's 1974 team earned a 5-6 record: disappointing but not unexpected for his first year. The Buffaloes' fortunes improved dramatically in 1975. Nine wins overshadowed losses to Oklahoma (21-20) and Nebraska (63-21) and earned CU a return to postseason play in the Bluebonnet Bowl against Texas. CU had a two-touchdown lead at halftime, but fullback Earl Campbell led the Longhorns to a second-half comeback and a 38-21 win. The 1976 season featured a home game victory over Oklahoma, an 8-3 finish, and an invitation to the Orange Bowl where Mallory and his Buffaloes faced his mentor, Woody Hayes and the Ohio State Buckeyes. Ohio State won 27-10.[81]

In his first three seasons at CU, Mallory's teams won two-thirds of their games, beat Oklahoma, and played in two bowl games. So, of course the fans were becoming disgruntled. After all, Mallory had not won those two bowl games. As pressure mounted on Mallory, the most important flaw in his management of the CU football program, recruiting, became apparent. Mallory had inherited solid young players from Crowder, and he turned them into top-notch teams. However, he was not as capable at recruiting as his predecessor. The 1977 team was all Mallory's, and they went 7-3-1. The 1978 squad finished 6-5.

Bad relations with boosters and the press further undermined the coach's position. CU fired Mallory on November 21, 1978, three days after the Buffs lost at home to Earle Bruce's Iowa State team. Mallory stayed out of coaching for a season and then went on to a long and successful career at Northern Illinois and Indiana.[82]

As the search for Mallory's replacement got under way, Athletic Director Crowder promised that he would find a big-name coach, and wealthy boosters such as oilman Jack Vickers and Continental Airlines chief Robert Six joined the hunt. Nebraska's Tom Osborne visited Boulder but had no real interest in the job. Six pursued UCLA coach Terry Donahue, but Donahue was happy in California. The names of Bud Wilkinson and Don Shula popped up, but quickly disappeared. Finally, Crowder found his man in Boston. New England Patriots coach Chuck Fairbanks expressed interest in the CU job, and, with Jack Vickers playing the role of mediator, the university and the NFL coach quickly closed the deal.[83]

Unfortunately, no one had bothered to inform Patriots owner Pat Sullivan about the arrangement. Sullivan angrily told Fairbanks, CU, and Monday Night Football announcer Howard Cosell that he would not release Fairbanks from his contract with the Patriots. There followed a nasty legal battle that cost CU and Fairbanks $410,000 in legal fees and payments to Sullivan to free Fairbanks to go to Boulder.[84]

As ugly as the circumstances were surrounding Chuck Fairbanks's hiring, it was the brightest moment of his three years at Boulder. Fairbanks took a football program that seemed to be in decline and drove it straight into disaster. Instead of trying to rebuild through aggressive recruiting, Fairbanks relied heavily on junior-college transfers to restock his teams. Short on solid talent, the Buffs won only seven games in Fairbanks's three seasons. A few weeks after the 1981 season, one of CU's few promising players, sophomore Derek Singleton, died of meningitis. It was a painful epitaph to the Fairbanks era. He resigned in June 1982 to become coach and part owner of the New Jersey Generals of the short-lived United States Football League.[85]

By the end of the 1961 season, Colorado State University's Rams had lost sixteen straight games. After being hung in effigy and pelted with snowballs after the final game, coach Don "Tuffy" Mullison was gone, abruptly fired by Athletic Director Bob Davis. CSU's football program was so ugly that it required either euthanasia or a major facelift. The university chose the latter course, though Vice President A. R. Chamberlain, the official most responsible for planning and administration at the school, warned that football could never be made to pay. However, as CSU historian James E. Hansen II notes, the school's alumni, who equated "institutional greatness with athletic prestige . . . refused to take no for an answer," and overcame Chamberlain's objections. CSU thus embarked on a major rebuilding program.[86]

The first priority was finding a new coach. The search led to University of Delaware assistant Milo "Mike" Lude. Lude was well aware of the "tremendous challenge" facing him at CSU, but was confident that "enthusiasm, intensity and eagerness are the things you can build upon." Indeed, enthusiasm became the hallmark of Lude's tenure, as the record of his visit to one faculty club shows. "Coach Lude was enthusiastic about the football team," the club's minutes note, "showing enthusiasm as he discussed the enthusiastic scouting procedure." The club itself "was enthusiastic about his enthusiasm."[87]

Enthusiasm alone, of course, would not build a successful program, and Lude vowed to make recruiting his top priority, and the university backed him by increasing the number of football scholarships. However, the new coach's attitude about college football players and, therefore, about recruiting made him seem like something of a throwback to earlier times in the sport. Lude declared that "if a boy is not interested in education, then I'm not interested in him. I want a boy to come to CSU because he believes he can get a good education here. The type of boy I'm looking for is one who wants an education badly, is an academic competitor and then, and only then, is the best football player I can get." Lude also promised that his scholar-athletes would play "wide open, crowd pleasing football."[88]

Mike Lude's enthusiasm and recruiting did not produce a winning season until 1966. Nevertheless, boosters and the State Board of Agriculture continued to support him. Evidence of that support came on the eve of the 1966 season when the board voted to build a new thirty-two-thousand-seat football stadium. The board promised that the $2.5 million stadium would be self-liquidating and thus would not require the use of tax dollars or increases in student fees. However, Vice President Chamberlain, who opposed the project, warned that the combined cost of the stadium and the university's existing athletic budget would produce a deficit of more than $500,000. Nevertheless, boosters were certain that the project would pay off, especially by securing admission for CSU into the Western Athletic Conference.[89]

The 1966 season and its aftermath seemed to justify the boosters' support for Mike Lude and the new stadium, as the Rams won seven games and lost only three. It was their first winning season since 1959. In addition, in September 1967 the Western Athletic Conference voted to admit CSU, beginning with the 1968 season.[90]

Unfortunately, Vice President Chamberlain's warnings also proved accurate. By the beginning of 1969, after the university's first year in the Western Athletic Conference, CSU's athletic program had run up a deficit of $565,000. The university set out to erase the deficit by cutting spending on sports other than football and basketball; shifting some costs, such as coaches' salaries, to the resident instruction budget; raising added funds from boosters; and, especially, by raising student fees. Student leaders objected to putting the athletic deficit onto the students' backs. Student government president Bruce Randall told the State Board of Agriculture that students would prefer that the university drop football rather than raise their fees. Randall also suggested that the athletic deficit was symptomatic of an overemphasis on sports that threatened the quality of CSU's academic programs. One university official dismissed the student leaders as "a small, anti-oriented minority" who were "against everything," but board member John Thimmig stated the real underlying issue for the university. Membership in the Western Athletic Conference and CSU's renewed commitment to big-time college football was, fundamentally, a business venture, and, as Thimmig put it, "I don't know of any business project that shows a profit the first year. We've already made up our minds that we are going to stay." Thus, despite student opposition, the board voted to impose the fee increase.[91]

In a sign of the growing militancy among American collegians in the late 1960s, student leaders at CSU attempted to organize a campaign to encourage students to withhold the eight-dollar fee increase. The protest movement failed, however, in the face of threats by the university administration to impose severe disciplinary measures. Revenue from the enhanced fees added $400,000 per year to the athletic budget and helped restore a delicate solvency, but funding the football program remained a recurring and contentious problem for the next three decades.[92]

The Rams' return to losing ways did not help the situation. After the promising 1966 effort, Mike Lude's teams turned in three consecutive losing seasons, capped by a humiliating 79-7 defeat by Arizona State. With a 29-51-1 record, Mike Lude no longer aroused any enthusiasm, and CSU released him at the end of the 1969 season.[93]

After Lude's departure, CSU looked to an established big-time college football program for its next leader. In December 1969 the university named Notre Dame assistant Jerry Wampfler as head coach. Wampfler's credentials seemed impeccable, having apprenticed under Bo Schembechler at Miami of Ohio, Woody Hayes at Ohio State, and Ara Parseghian at Notre Dame. Despite the Rams' 4-6 record in 1968, Wampfler inherited "a fairly talented" group of players "composed mainly of junior college transfers and sophomores."[94]

Unfortunately, despite his and his players' talents, Jerry Wampfler's three seasons at CSU only deepened the misery in the football program. The Rams won only eight games and lost twenty-five in the 1970–1972 seasons, including a dismal 1-10 record in 1972. One syndicated sports column listed CSU among the ten worst teams in the country. Nevertheless, after the 1972 season the State Board of Agriculture voted to retain Wampfler for the fourth, and final, year of his contract. Two months later, however, Wampfler resigned abruptly, complaining that the board should have extended his contract for at least an additional year so that he could "go out and recruit players who knew I was going to be here." The board's action, he believed, showed that they did not have unqualified confidence in him. Accordingly, he said that he found it difficult to put his heart into recruiting and could no longer "attempt to sell a young fellow on coming here." Wampfler also complained that Athletic Director Perry Moore had interfered with his and his assistants' coaching duties. Asked what effect his departure would have on CSU's football program, Wampfler took a final shot, saying, "[T]he athletic situation at CSU has spoken for itself in the past and I'm sure it will speak for itself in the future without me adding further comment on the dilemma."[95]

Although CSU had only one winning season in fourteen years, there was no shortage of applicants for the head coaching job, and Athletic Director Moore reported receiving as many as fifty calls about the position within two days of Wampfler's resignation. After a three-week search, the university hired Sarkis Arslanian. The new coach's most recent job had been at Utah's Weber State College, where in eight seasons he compiled a record of 50-26-2. Before that, Arslanian had been an assistant to John Ralston at Utah State. Ralston, who had become head coach of the Denver Broncos, gave Arslanian a strong endorsement.[96]

Arslanian lasted until 1981. His 1975 team turned in a winning season, the first since 1966. By the early 1980s, however, the football program had fallen apart again, in part because of a major cut in the football budget in 1977. The Rams were winless in 1981, and the university fired Arslanian midway through the season. As *Rocky Mountain News* sportswriter Teri Thompson put it, CSU fired Arslanian because he had not delivered "the kind of program it wanted, specifically, winning without spending a lot of money."[97]

CSU replaced Sarkis Arslanian with University of Texas defensive coordinator Leon Fuller. Fuller was familiar to the Rams because he had coached at Wyoming with Fred Akers before the pair moved on to Texas after the 1976 season. University officials were confident that they finally had the man who would build a successful program. Athletic Director Thurman "Fum" McGraw called Fuller "a very outstanding coach" and "definitely one of the top defensive coaches in the nation." Fuller was well aware that there was "a lot of work to be done," and was not especially worried about the tight football budget. In fact, he declared, "CSU has made a commitment to bettering things," though he admitted that he was not sure where the money for improvement would come from. No one could have expected a quick turnaround in CSU's football fortunes, but Fuller did not produce a winning team until 1986, his only winning year. The Rams fell to 1-11 in 1987 and 1-10 in 1988.[98]

CSU next turned to a man with big-time Big Ten experience, former Ohio State coach Earle Bruce. Bruce, who had the look and personality of a bulldog, began his college head-coaching career at Tampa in 1972, moved to Iowa State in 1973, and finally succeeded Woody Hayes at Ohio State in 1979 where he coached until 1987. In those sixteen seasons, Bruce led all three schools to bowl games, eleven in all. In hiring Earle Bruce, CSU landed a proven winner. Former CU coach Bill Mallory called Bruce "one of the top coaches in the country." He said, "I think CSU is very fortunate to get Earle," adding that "he can come in and take that program and make it work." However, in hiring Bruce, CSU chose to overlook a warning signal. Ohio State had fired Bruce before the final game of the 1987 season. Bruce sued for breach of contract and finally agreed to a $417,000 settlement. Both parties agreed not to discuss the case publicly.[99]

As he took up his coaching duties, Bruce said he did not think "the cupboard is bare," and that there was "a good nucleus to have a good football team." He was right. CSU's turnaround began with Bruce's first season when the Rams finished 5-5-1. The 1990 team won nine games and earned a berth in the Freedom Bowl where they defeated the Oregon Ducks, led by future Denver Broncos backup quarterback Bill Musgrave, 32-31. It had been forty-two years since the Rams had last played in a bowl game, but in only two years Bruce had taken one of the worst teams in the country and led it back to respectability. After the game, Bruce said, "[T]here's been a tremendous change in the attitude. Now we're looking for ways to win. Now by going to a bowl game, people can't recruit against us by saying we can't win a championship or go to a bowl game."[100]

Twenty-two Ram seniors, including fourteen starters, graduated after the 1990 season, and their loss showed in the 1991 team's 3-8 record. The 1992 squad was slightly improved, ending with five wins and seven losses.

CSU fired Earle Bruce in November 1992, but not because of the two losing seasons. Bruce remained popular among Ram fans and boosters, and his firing raised a firestorm of protest. CSU president Albert Yates and Athletic Director Corey Johnson received vulgar, racist, and threatening phone calls and messages from outraged Bruce supporters. However, Yates and Johnson explained that they had acted in order to protect the players' physical and educational well-being. At least ten current and former Ram players had signed written complaints alleging physical and emotional abuse by the coach. An investigation of Bruce's conduct revealed that he had punched several players in anger over poor practice performances, abused and intimidated players verbally with racist and demeaning language, required athletes to play with serious injuries, and refused to accommodate his players' academic needs.[101]

The Earle Bruce case illustrates how much college football had changed in a century. Student–athletes of the nineteenth century loved to play and liked to win. The athlete-students of the 1990s have to win, and their coaches, especially, have to win. Their employers, the colleges and universities, expect them to win, and many, though not all, coaches feel justified in doing whatever it takes to win, whether that means abusing NCAA rules or abusing their players. However, university administrations also do not want to be embarrassed by how their teams and coaches win. Coaches, working under the enormous pressure to win, sometimes either do not know or do not care if they cross the murky line between winning and embarrassment. Earle Bruce crossed that line, though he refused to acknowledge it. When told of the charges of abuse behind his firing, Bruce asked, "Did I hurt them?" As president Yates noted, "[T]he point is, did he demean them? It seems to me he went too far." Nevertheless, Yates and his predecessors at CSU, and every other would-be big-time football school, must share the responsibility for turning college football into a major business enterprise in which the bottom line is winning. In that setting, the athlete-student inevitably becomes just an expendable commodity.[102]

CSU replaced Earle Bruce with Sonny Lubick, defensive coordinator at the University of Miami. Lubick was familiar to Ram fans, having served as offensive coordinator at CSU under Leon Fuller from 1982 to 1984. Lubick quickly picked up the pieces of CSU's football program and in 1994 had the Rams back in winning form with the Western Athletic Conference championship and an appearance in the Holiday Bowl.

COLLEGE FOOTBALL AND CONTEMPORARY SOCIETY

After Chuck Fairbanks fled Boulder, another national search led CU to Bill McCartney, an assistant and the heir apparent to Bo Schembechler at Michigan. McCartney, with his Michigan credentials, edged out Drake coach Chuck Shelton, the early front-runner for the job. When he landed the job, McCartney said it would be "a bona fide challenge." When he left CU a dozen years later, the Buffs had won a national championship. McCartney led CU to its best moments in intercollegiate football. However, on the way, he and his Buffs, and the CSU Rams, also mirrored many of the stresses and conflicts irritating American society.[103]

When he became head coach in 1982, McCartney joined an athletic program that had been racked by debt. In 1980 a deficit of almost $1 million led to the elimination of six minor sports, including men's baseball, wrestling, gymnastics, and swimming and women's gymnastics and swimming. There was no consideration of serious cuts in the football budget. After all, football was not only the major cost in the athletic budget but also its largest source of revenue. Declining income, caused by the Buffs' slide into mediocrity, coupled with some profligate spending on staff and perks during the Fairbanks era, was part of the problem. However, university officials viewed the underlying problem as stemming, as Fred Casotti has put it, from "the required addition of women's programs, force-fed into being by governmental edicts."[104]

That "force-fed" edict was Title IX of the federal Educational Amendments of 1972, which mandates that "no person in the United States shall, on the basis of sex, be excluded from participation in, be denied the benefits of, or be subjected to discrimination under any education program or activity receiving federal financial assistance." In other words, because virtually every college and university in the United States receives some form of federal money, women could not be excluded from or discriminated against in any school program, including athletics. Figuring out what the law requires in athletic programs, however, has been a legal minefield. Does the law require absolute equality in such measures as funding and numbers of scholarships? Or can resources be allocated on the basis of the proportion of male and female students, or the proportion of men and women playing sports? Those issues, plus the determination of university officials to protect funding for major men's sports, especially football, has seriously impeded significant progress in applying the law.[105]

The enactment of Title IX was emblematic of the growing demand of American women in the latter twentieth century for genuine equality, and the battle to implement the law became symptomatic of the mounting militancy of women in their pursuit of equality. CU, CSU, and state officials have been aware of the problem and the pressure, and have taken some steps to accommodate the law. The state legislature in 1975 required equal dollar amounts for individual scholarships in most sports. For example, individual men's and women's basketball scholarships had to be equal, though the number of scholarships could differ. However, the legislature exempted football, as a men-only sport, from the requirement. That measure and other efforts by no means led to equality in athletic funding. CU paid women's athletic director Jane Wahl $19,000 in 1978, compared to Eddie Crowder's $40,500 salary. Similarly, while the women's athletic budget at CU grew from only $8,000 in 1974 to $450,000 in 1979, it still was only a small part of the total athletic budget of $3.8 million. When women's basketball coach Ceal Barry came to CU in 1983 her salary was about half that of the men's basketball coach. By 1994 Barry had built the women's team into a national powerhouse, while the men's team was a perennial loser. Barry attributed much of her team's success to significant increases in funding, some of which came from growing football revenues. The $618,000 Barry's program received was $133,000 less than the men's basketball budget, but her salary was equal to that of men's coach Joe Harrington in 1995. Overall, women's sports accounted for only 24 percent of the total athletic budget at CU in 1994, while men's athletics ate up 76 percent.[106]

A similar situation prevailed at CSU, where men's sports took 77 percent of the athletic budget versus 23 percent for women. CSU had taken some steps toward compliance with Title IX, though. In 1983 the school increased the number of athletic scholarships given to women and decreased the number for men. In 1989 budget problems forced CSU to drop men's baseball and women's golf and tennis, but the school continued to meet the NCAA Division I requirement of at least seven sports each for men and women. Then, in June 1992, in another budget-cutting move, CSU dropped women's softball. Members of the softball team, led by pitcher Jennifer Roberts, decided to sue the university to restore the program. During the summer of 1992, as the players' lawyers began to prepare their case, CSU added insult to injury by removing the softball team's trophy display from the athletic building. Roberts recalled that when she and her teammates returned to school that fall and found the display gone, they felt that "it was like we never existed. . . . We felt like we didn't mean anything." In February 1993, U.S. District Court Judge Zita Weinshienk ruled that CSU was in violation of Title IX and ordered the university to reinstate the softball program. The Tenth Circuit Court of Appeals upheld Weinshienk's ruling that July. CSU and Colorado attorney general Gale Norton appealed to the United States Supreme Court. Norton argued that the university had not intended to discriminate against women and pointed out that there remained eight women's varsity sports compared to seven men's teams. Norton also noted that the case had "profound implications" for every school participating in intercollegiate athletics. The ruling, she said, "places virtually all these institutions in violation of federal law," and might force them to eliminate football and other men's sports in order to provide equal athletic opportunities for women. The Supreme Court rejected Norton's appeal without comment.[107]

The women's softball case meant that CSU, CU, and every other school participating in intercollegiate sports would have to give much more serious attention than in the past to funding women's athletics. And there was a lot of catching up to do. As one newspaper report put it in 1994, "[S]ix of the 16 Colorado colleges offering intercollegiate sports readily admit their athletic programs violate Title IX, even though the law now is older than most of their students." Ironically, that mandate may put even more pressure on schools to build successful football programs, since football revenues, along with student fees, are the major source of athletic budget funds.[108]

Racism is American society's original sin. America's colleges and universities, and their athletic programs, have mirrored the nation's struggles with race and racism. Although the Civil War ended slavery, and even though Reconstruction supposedly guaranteed legal equality, by the early twentieth century a powerful body of law and custom forced the segregation of African Americans in the nation's public life. Jim Crow laws, more benign forms of racism, and economic reality effectively barred almost all African Americans from going to college. A small number attended exclusively black institutions such as Booker T. Washington's Tuskegee Institute in Alabama. Even fewer went to predominantly white schools. Obviously, opportunities for African Americans to play intercollegiate football were few and far between.

As is the case today, Colorado at the beginning of the twentieth century had a small African American population, but the spirit of Jim Crow was afoot nevertheless. In October 1905 Denver University's football team traveled to Fort Collins for a match with the Aggies. When they arrived they discovered that the Aggie squad included an African American player and refused to play if he was on the field. After some negotiation, the teams agreed to go ahead with the game as long as it was considered only a "practice game" that would not count in the Colorado Intercollegiate Athletic Association's standings. The *Colorado Statesman,* Denver's African American newspaper, noted the irony that DU had drawn the color line in this affair, as the school was affiliated with the Methodist Church, which had "always professed the utmost liberality in social matters."[109]

For more than a half century, African American players remained a rarity in college football. The presence of only one African American on CU's starting offense in the 1957 Orange Bowl game is a case in point. However, by that time the spirit of the civil rights movement had taken root in American society and was gaining force yearly. Beginning in the 1960s, African American enrollments in American colleges and universities grew, and so did their representation in college sports, especially as coaches felt freer to tap into an essentially undeveloped pool of athletic talent. By the 1980s and 1990s, the presence of black players was no longer exceptional, and black assistant coaches were becoming commonplace on the sidelines. Nonetheless, the growing presence of African Americans on college teams did not end problems of race and racism in collegiate athletics any more than enacting the civil rights laws of the 1960s eradicated racism in society as a whole.

In February 1989, *Sports Illustrated* published an article detailing a long series of arrests involving University of Colorado football players. "Since February 1986," the report said, "at least two dozen Buffalo players have been arrested, for everything from trespassing to serial rape." In a telephone interview, the article's author, Rick Reilly, said that the apparent crime wave made him ashamed to be a CU graduate.[110]

Reilly clearly blamed the problem of criminal behavior in the CU football program on the compulsion to do whatever it took to win. Following CU's pathetic 1–10 1983 season, one frustrated player, Loy Alexander, complained that the team had "enough altar boys." What CU needed, he said, were "some athletes." A half decade later, Reilly wrote, "Colorado has plenty of athletes. Altar boys, however, are in short supply." What Reilly did not mention in his article was made abundantly clear by the photographs accompanying the piece. Of the ten CU players shown who had had run-ins with the law, six were black, one was Asian, one was a Pacific Islander, and two were white. Unstated was the unfair stereotype not only that CU football players were prone to crime but also that minority, and especially African American players, had criminal tendencies. One university police officer stated those expectations explicitly. Tim DeLaria told Reilly that at the beginning of every season "a couple of detectives drop by the stadium and pick up a few programs. Saves you time. Instead of having a victim go through the mug book, you just take out our program and say, 'Is he in here?' "[111]

The offending players, whose ranks included stars Sal Aunese and Eric Bienemy, faced criminal penalties, usually probation or deferred sentences, and disciplinary action by Coach Bill McCartney ranging from suspension to removal from the team. Some thought that McCartney did not act fast enough or forcefully enough (and in one comment he showed an unfortunate lack of understanding of the dynamics of rape), but the coach did acknowledge that there were problems in his program.[112]

However, though McCartney held his players individually accountable for their acts, he also argued that race and racism played a role, especially in incidents involving fighting. McCartney recruited many of his African American players from inner-city neighborhoods in southern California and Texas. Some had little or no significant experience with white people and white society before they arrived on campus. For example, Chris Hudson, an All-American cornerback from Houston, Texas, noted in 1994, "I'd never been around a white person before, so I didn't know how to act or what to expect." Likewise, the African American athletes were as alien to CU and Boulder as the school and town were to them. In 1988 only 329 of CU's 22,900 students were black. As 1.4 percent of the student population, African Americans at CU were proportionately fewer than even the small percentage (3.7 percent) of their population statewide. (African American students accounted for only 1.3 percent of the student body at CSU.)[113]

African American students and football players naturally felt like outsiders in this environment and believed, often correctly, that the white campus and town communities regarded them with hostility and fear. Most often it was nothing overt. As fullback Anthony Weatherspoon described it, "[I]t's not said, it's basically just felt and it's known. It's something you're aware of, but it really doesn't get expressed in words a lot. You can just feel the uncomfortableness of the environment that you're in." (McCartney removed Weatherspoon from the team in 1988 after he tested positive for drugs.) Six years later, wide receiver Michael Westbrook spoke of walking into a room where "people would seem to be having a good time . . . and they'd look at me like, 'What are you doing here? Who are you?' You can't imagine how that can wear on you." Former defensive back Morris Copeland recalled that "you stand out as being black on this campus or in this community. You can't help but stand out. You're just like a grain of pepper in a shaker of salt. Everybody's looking at you."[114]

Seemingly mundane matters of daily life, unconnected with even covert racism, underscore the feeling of isolation among black students and athletes. CSU free safety Myron Terry said in 1997 that his woman friend could not get her hair styled in Fort Collins. "They don't know how to do it," he said. "She has to go to Denver for a haircut." Terry pointed out that he, too, could not get a haircut unless a teammate did the job for him. The problem was not that hair stylists and barbers in Fort Collins refused to serve them. They just could not find any who knew how to cut and style African American hair.[115]

Sometimes the racism was overt in the university community. Boulder police arrested Eric Bienemy and Kanavis McGhee in February 1986 after a bar fight. The brawl erupted after another patron bumped into Bienemy and called him "nigger." Sal Aunese spent fourteen days in jail after a fight with a drunken student who, as the police report noted, had repeatedly taunted and cursed him. CU admissions officer Steve Washington defended Bienemy and Aunese and other students who had been embroiled in race-based conflicts, saying that in his opinion they were cases of "blaming the victim." "If you're called a name, a nigger," Washington said, "you're going to react and have a right to react." Coach McCartney agreed, at least in part. "When people make racial slurs, certainly it's in the culture of a lot of minorities to defend yourself in circumstances like that," he said. However, McCartney also said that he needed to do "a good job of educating our guys on how to exercise restraint in those situations."[116]

After the *Sports Illustrated* article appeared, McCartney explicitly blamed racism at CU and in Boulder for many of his players' problems. "The problem exists outside the team and in the community," he told an interviewer. The community treated black football players like "foreigners" and incited their anger, which got them into trouble. Part of the solution, he said, lay in promoting a greater black presence. "We need more black students. We need black faculty. We need black role models. . . . We need more blacks in the police department. . . . We need more black coaches (and) head coaches [*sic*]."[117]

McCartney's appeal for more African American head coaches proved especially ironic. When McCartney resigned at the end of the 1994 season, assistant head coach Bob Simmons quickly became a leading contender to succeed him as head coach. In fact, McCartney recommended Simmons, along with offensive coordinator Elliott Uzelac, for the job. However, Athletic Director Bill Marolt chose quarterback coach Rick Neuheisel over the more experienced Simmons. Neuheisel is white, and Simmons is black. African Americans in Colorado and around the nation were outraged. Civil rights leader Jesse Jackson even joined the fray, demanding that the university explain why it passed over Simmons and why African Americans were underrepresented among CU coaches and administrators. Jackson talked of asking for a Justice Department investigation and even threatened to intervene in CU's recruiting campaign by contacting parents of prospective black players. Jackson complained that CU had used Simmons's position as assistant head coach as part of its recruiting message for black players. "They would display his position that he was the No. 2 guy, with the assumption that No. 2 meant he could become No. 1. They not only used him on the field as a coach, they also used his likeness and image as an appeal factor to get athletes to come there."[118]

Although Bill McCartney refrained from criticizing the decision to hire Neuheisel, he clearly agreed with Jackson's larger complaint about the underrepresentation of African Americans at the top levels of college football coaching and administration. McCartney said, bluntly, that there were few black head coaches "because white people won't hire them. Why else would it be?" The fact that half of the players were black though only four blacks held head coaching jobs, he said, "doesn't add up." McCartney specifically praised Jackson for "taking a concerned and caring role" in the problem.[119]

McCartney and Jackson did not alter the outcome of this episode, and only time will tell if the glass ceiling for black coaches will be shattered. CU did promise to actively recruit African American head coaches in the future. In the meantime, Bob Simmons did get a head coaching job, at Oklahoma State.

Black football players will remain a distinct and visible minority at CU, CSU, and most other colleges and universities. Their ongoing isolation and frustration is a measure of America's continuing struggle with race and racism. Unfortunately, many African American athletes have learned that the best way to avoid trouble is to stick to themselves and avoid contact with the white community.

Bill McCartney is a deeply religious man. He was raised a Roman Catholic, but in 1974 one of his players at Michigan introduced him to evangelical fundamentalism. "It was the most exciting moment of my life," McCartney recalled in his autobiography, and he thereafter made his born-again faith the centerpiece of his life. When he interviewed for the CU head coaching job, he warned university officials "that with me, it was God first, family second, and football

6-6. Bill McCartney coached the University of Colorado football team from 1982 through 1994. His 1990 team won the national championship. A deeply religious man, McCartney was a strong advocate of racial justice and of conservative Christian moral values. Courtesy, University of Colorado at Boulder Athletic Department.

third." As CU's head football coach, McCartney became a highly visible public figure, and his religious convictions naturally became an important part of his persona (fig. 6-6). That fact, in turn, embroiled him, his football program, and the university in some of the most sensitive and controversial issues of the day.[120]

In 1985 McCartney and his religious faith came into conflict with constitutional law. After the American Civil Liberties Union (ACLU) filed complaints and threatened lawsuits, the university required McCartney to stop leading his team in locker room prayers. Individual players remained free to pray, or not pray, as they wished, but the coach, as a public employee, could not impose his personal religious values and practices on the team. At the time, McCartney said that he had "no problem whatever" with the university's decision. In his memoirs, though, McCartney showed some resentment. "Sharing the gospel is more important to me than coaching football, and the American Civil Liberties Union had forced the university to come down on me about praying with my players or sharing my faith with them. As a result," he wrote, "I was beginning to feel stifled."[121]

Three years later McCartney had an opportunity to break away from the stifling requirements of coaching at a public institution. By early 1988 three consecutive winning seasons made him an attractive prospect for other schools struggling to rebuild football programs. The school then most in dire need of rebuilding was Southern Methodist University (SMU). The NCAA had imposed its so-called death penalty on SMU because of serious recruiting violations. The school could not compete for two years, had its scholarship program reduced, and would face scheduling limitations when it did return to competition. SMU approached McCartney, and after visiting the school he accepted the job there, though he did not sign a contract. SMU officials went so far as to schedule a news conference to introduce McCartney as the university's new coach. SMU, McCartney admits, "had every right to believe I was coming."[122]

McCartney pursued the SMU job because of the obvious challenge of rebuilding their football program. He had proved his ability to bring a program back from the dead at CU. Most important to McCartney, however, was the fact that SMU was a private school with an affiliation with the Methodist Church. He would be free to practice and proselytize his faith as he pleased, inside and outside the locker room. "What I was seeking was freedom," he recalled, "freedom to say whatever I wanted, whenever I wanted, without worrying" about an ACLU lawsuit. Finally, SMU officials assured him that they wanted "excellence with integrity," which he knew he could deliver.[123]

By the time McCartney arrived back in Colorado from his visit in Dallas, news of his defection from CU had gotten out, and a phalanx of reporters met him at the airport. Although he did not confirm his intentions, the reporters clearly understood that he was leaving CU. Back in Boulder, McCartney told his staff of his decision to leave and then met with CU president Gordon Gee. Gee was determined to change McCartney's mind and went after him by appealing to one of the coach's most important values: loyalty. Gee reminded McCartney that CU had stood by him and extended his contract in the middle of the 1984 season when his team won only one game. He also pointed out that McCartney had extracted a promise from Gee that he, too, would stay at CU and that he had turned down an offer to become president of one of the most prestigious schools in the country because of that promise. McCartney explained that the SMU job was something "the Lord has led me to do." Gee countered that he did not "believe that Almighty God wants guys to neglect commitments and break contracts."[124]

McCartney agreed to think the matter over, and, after consulting the Bible and a Boulder clergyman who told him that leaving CU would violate Scripture, he decided to stay on with the Buffaloes. SMU officials and fans were, of course, furious, but the CU community was greatly relieved. "Coach Mac" would stay on the CU sideline and lead the Buffs to greater glory. McCartney and CU reaffirmed their commitment to one another in 1990 with a fifteen-year contract. Gordon Gee left CU in 1991 to become the president of Ohio State University.[125]

Despite the Buffaloes' development into a national championship–caliber program and the long-term commitment with CU, McCartney continued to be uncomfortable in his dual role as coach and apostle of fundamentalist Christianity. His life and career began to move away from football in 1990 when he founded Promise Keepers, an organization devoted to encouraging men to be more responsible husbands, fathers, and citizens by following the precepts of fundamentalist Christianity.

Along with his work with Promise Keepers, McCartney became more and more outspoken on hot-button social issues, especially reproductive and gay rights. He quickly became a hero to other

Christian, conservative, and right-wing activists and groups, as well as a lightning rod for criticism. His association with conservative and right-wing social and political activists sometimes caused conflicts between his religious and political activities and his job as CU head coach, even though some problems were not of his own making. At a July 1992 Promise Keepers rally at Folsom Field, a vendor sold T-shirts showing a cross superimposed over CU's trademarked buffalo. The shirts' manufacturer claimed that a man representing himself as the CU football team chaplain had said that McCartney's office had authorized the shirts. McCartney and Promise Keepers officials denied knowing anything about the shirts prior to their appearance. At about the same time, a Colorado Springs religious publisher printed copies of the New Testament bearing the CU logo. The publisher initially claimed that McCartney's office had authorized the use of the logo but later recanted. In these cases, zealots had exploited McCartney's association with CU without his knowledge. However, the same cannot be said of McCartney's lending both his name and his position to Colorado for Family Values, a Christian-right group headquartered in Colorado Springs that spearheaded the drive for an antigay-rights amendment to the state constitution in 1992. McCartney allowed the group to use his name and his title as CU head coach in a list of members of its advisory board. By the end of the 1994 season, Bill McCartney believed that the pull of his religious faith was stronger than the lure of the football field, and so decided to step away from coaching to devote his time and energy to his family and Promise Keepers.[126]

Money Walks

Bill McCartney left CU for reasons of faith and conscience. His successor, Rick Neuheisel, departed after four years for more mundane reasons. Neuheisel's teams won thirty-three games and lost fourteen during his stay at Boulder (including the five 1997 wins later forfeited because of a player-eligibility violation). Three of his teams' wins were bowl victories. However, twenty of the thirty-three wins came during his first two seasons with squads still heavily loaded with Bill McCartney's recruits. Neuheisel's third and fourth seasons were less impressive with thirteen wins and ten losses on the field and an official record of only eight wins and fifteen losses due to the 1997 forfeitures.

Nevertheless, Neuheisel seemed to have succeeded in preserving the winning heritage he inherited from McCartney, as evidenced by 1998's 8-3 regular-season record and the Buffaloes' 51-43 victory over the University of Oregon in the Aloha Bowl. Neuheisel's name often surfaced when high-profile coaching jobs, including NFL head coaching positions, opened. After the Aloha Bowl win, however, Neuheisel stated that he loved CU and intended to stay "for the long run," mentioning Penn State's durable coach, Joe Paterno, as a role model.[127]

Two weeks later, Neuheisel was gone. The University of Washington offered him a seven-year contract worth up to $10.5 million, making him one of the highest-paid coaches in the country. Neuheisel claimed that his decision was not motivated by money, though he conceded that Washington "made me a heck of a deal." CU fans and officials were, understandably, disappointed and angry, especially since Neuheisel left in the middle of the recruiting season. Athletic Director Dick Tharp noted bitterly that the next coach would have to show that he understood the meaning of "commitment." Anger at Neuheisel reverberated across the sports pages, too. *Rocky Mountain News* columnist Bob Kravitz suggested that Colorado was better off without Neuheisel who, he said, had taken Bill McCartney's "Top 10 machine and turned it into a program that couldn't beat Kansas." Perhaps, Kravitz continued, "Neuheisel knew the same truth that was clear long ago to his harshest critics: He was taking one the country's preeminent programs down the road to ruin. Better to get out now, one step ahead of the posse."[128]

However, university officials and sportswriters should have been among the least surprised and angry that Rick Neuheisel jilted CU in favor of a more lucrative job. After all, it was the universities, along with the press and broadcast media, that had taken the lead over the previous half century in transforming college football from a student-oriented, amateur game into a multimillion-dollar professional sports business. In leaving CU, Neuheisel may not have demonstrated much loyalty to the school and to his players, but his decision to follow the money reflected the ethics of the modern college sports business.

Four years earlier, Rick Neuheisel's hiring provoked a national controversy over college football's failure to promote African American coaches to top positions. At the time CU promised to actively recruit African Americans for future head coaching openings. However, the university evidently forgot that commitment in 1998. Although Oklahoma State head coach Bob Simmons's name popped up in the press as a candidate, the school did not give him or any other minority coach serious consideration. CU's search for Neuheisel's successor led, first, to the Denver Broncos' offensive coordinator, Gary Kubiak, who decided, just hours before his hiring was to be announced, to stay with the Broncos. The university then turned to Northwestern University coach Gary Barnett, a former assistant at Colorado under Bill McCartney.

That college football became big business and a backdrop for conflicts of race, gender, religion, and social values is neither novel nor surprising. From its beginnings in the nineteenth century, when young middle- and upper-class men demonstrated their status and manliness on the gridiron, to the present, when the game is a complex, high-cost, and high-stakes enterprise, college football has mirrored the values and tensions of American culture. From its inception the game has been a powerful source of identity, a potent emotional tie binding individuals, even those who participate only from the grandstands, to their college or university.

Professional football evolved from different social foundations, but like the college game, it, too, has been a mirror of American society, reflecting its values and conflicts. And, in Colorado, especially, it has become a powerful icon of personal and community identity.

7

BRONCOMANIA

Salute That!

During the 1997 National Football League season, Denver Bronco running backs and receivers gave one another salutes whenever the team scored a touchdown. They called it the "Mile High Salute." Over the course of the season, some opponents returned the salute in a mocking, derisive manner. However, by the end of the playoff series, in January 1998, the slogan "Salute That!" became the Broncos' and their followers' proud retort. After a 12-4 regular season, a record good enough only for a somewhat disappointing wild-card berth, the team stormed through the playoffs, defeating the Jacksonville Jaguars and the Pittsburgh Steelers to win the American Football Conference championship. And, on January 25, 1998, they won Super Bowl XXXII, defeating the defending-champion Green Bay Packers 31-24. The Broncos became only the second wild-card team ever to win the Super Bowl (the other was their arch rival, the Oakland Raiders).

The 1998 Super Bowl was the Denver Broncos' fifth appearance in professional sports' greatest spectacle, an event that had practically become a national holiday and a global event watched on television by hundreds of millions of people around the world. The outcomes of Denver's previous four Super Bowl games ranged from disappointing to humiliating, not only for the team but also for all of Denver and Colorado. Although they had earned the right to play in football's most important game four previous times, the Broncos and, by extension, Denver seemed forever stigmatized as losers, as second-rate.

Quarterback John Elway, possibly the best ever in the game, led the Broncos in three of the four Super Bowl losses and felt the sting of failure more than anyone. Going into the 1998 game, much of the country pulled for him, and even his opponents wished him well. Nonetheless, the oddsmakers pronounced Green Bay the favorites to win.

Elway did not have an especially good game in Super Bowl XXXII, completing only twelve of twenty-two passes for 123 yards. In fact, Denver's superb running back, Terrell Davis, dominated the game, with 157 yards rushing and a Super Bowl record three touchdowns, even though a migraine headache forced him to miss the entire second quarter. Davis's performance earned him the game's most-valuable-player honors. However, after the game, team owner Pat Bowlen handed Elway the Vince Lombardi trophy and declared, "This one's for John." Elway's teammates carried him from the field on their shoulders. It was the crowning moment of his spectacular fifteen-year career.[1]

The Denver Broncos' victory in Super Bowl XXXII was more than John Elway's personal triumph, however. And it was more than a football team's victory. To hundreds of thousands of fans in Denver and Colorado, winning the Super Bowl also meant achieving a long-desired, but long-denied, sense of legitimacy and respectability.

The Broncos' story in many ways parallels the history of Denver and Colorado in the second half of the twentieth century. It also illustrates many of the developments and problems in major league professional sports.

BEGINNINGS

The Denver Broncos' record of four wins, nine losses, and one tie in 1960 was not the ugliest thing about the team's first season. It was the socks. Vertically striped socks in mustard yellow and barnyard brown, matching the team's equally ugly brown pants and yellow jerseys. The Broncos had only one set of uniforms, and they wore them both at home games and on the road. But the socks were so ugly that some players ignored American Football League rules and refused to wear them. The socks, and poor play, made the Broncos a laughingstock in the team's first years. Finally, just before the 1962 season, the team ceremonially cremated the socks. One specimen survived and today is displayed in football's Hall of Fame. The laughing stopped a few years later.

The socks were an apt symbol of the team and their host city. Both aspired to the big time in 1960, but neither was ready to get there. The Broncos and Denver grew up together.

Denver in 1960 was an insular city, its economy based on serving and financing Colorado's and surrounding states' agricultural, mining, and other natural-resources industries. Although many citizens of Denver, and the emerging suburban communities, nurtured pretensions to cosmopolitan sophistication, the city's culture was still rooted in western regional traditions. One still was more likely to find men and women wearing cowboy boots than Italian loafers, even on Denver's Seventeenth Street, the city's financial district.

By the late 1990s, Denver had become an international city, a figurative and literal crossroads for America's and the world's business, peoples, and cultures. Agriculture and natural resources, especially energy, remained important to the city's economy, but high-technology industries, including computers, communications, and aerospace, had moved to the forefront.

The Summit of the Eight, a gathering of the heads of state of the world's major economic powers, held in Denver in June 1997, symbolized the city's emergence as an important world center. Today, the person wearing Italian loafers on Seventeenth Street might well be the prime minister of Italy.

The history of the Denver Broncos is in many ways representative of Denver's transformation from a hinterland capital to an international metropolis. Originally a patchwork organization whose local owners had roots deep in Colorado's history, the Broncos evolved, with their namesake city, into a sophisticated, powerful organization whose influence, and following, spread far beyond Colorado.

The Broncos' rise from ragtag operation to respected professional sports powerhouse also revealed, among the team's fans, the stresses and anxieties of a city and its people headed for greatness, but not sure how or when they would get there and worried that the rest of the world would not recognize and accept them when they arrived.

The announcement, in August 1959, that Denver was about to get a professional football team did not prompt dancing in the streets. In fact, a brief article in the *Rocky Mountain News* about the formation of the new American Football League did not identify the owners of the Denver franchise until the last paragraph. It was not an auspicious beginning. The new franchise was among the weakest in the new league, both financially and on the field. During its first decade the team changed hands twice, had five head coaches, and nearly left town twice. However, by the end of the 1960s the Denver Broncos were well on their way to solvency and respectability. In addition, they were becoming a powerful source of civic pride and personal identity among Coloradans.[2]

Denver had proven itself a good sports town by 1960. The Broncos' principal owner, Robert Howsam, bought the Denver Bears baseball team in 1948 and built it into a potent minor league force. Denver also supported semipro basketball. Professional football, though, had not taken root.

The first football seen in Denver arrived in a bull wagon in 1867. A group of schoolboys turned their pockets out and pooled six dollars to send away for the ball. However, the boys evidently lost interest in the sphere, for as George W. Clelland, one of its owners, recalled in 1890, the last time he saw it, "it lay flattened out like a discarded fireman's hat that had been stepped on by an elephant, in a woodshed on the alley in the rear of what is now Daniels and Fisher's great female pocketbook employing emporium."[3]

Semipro club football appeared in Denver and elsewhere in Colorado by the early 1890s. Sporting Cherry and Black uniforms, the Denver Athletic Club's team dominated Colorado football until 1905. The DAC squad took the field for the first time on November 15, 1890, and thrashed the fledgling University of Colorado team 34–0. The Cherry and Black began to face a new local rival in 1895 when the Denver Wheel Club formed a football team. Both teams recruited players and coaches from Ivy League colleges, as well as local high school and college talent. By the mid–1890s the club teams had become semiprofessional, with paid coaches and players. In 1899 the

DAC hired coach Frank Cavanaugh, who played college ball at Harvard and coached at Dartmouth, for a salary of six hundred dollars a year. Denver Wheel Club stars earned as much as fifty dollars per game and in 1900 were coached by Fred Folsom, who was between coaching stints at the University of Colorado. However, because the DAC and the Wheel Club had been founded as amateur sporting clubs, the growing professionalism of their football teams did not sit well with all members. The Denver Wheel Club quit football after the 1899 season, and the DAC abandoned the sport at the end of the 1905 season when coach David Cropp, who had been CU's coach in 1903 and 1904, resigned in protest, as the *Denver Post* characterized it, "over the payment of money to several so-called amateur players."[4]

After club football faded away, football fans in the Denver area contented themselves with college games. CU's Buffaloes played in the 1937 Cotton Bowl and the 1957 Orange Bowl and, after a slump, returned to Miami after the 1961 season. Denver University's decision in 1961 to drop football made the Buffs the only college football show in the Denver area, but fans could make the short drives to Fort Collins and Colorado Springs to cheer the Rams and the Air Force Academy Falcons. Besides those opportunities, the Broncos began playing in 1960.

The Denver Broncos' story begins in Texas. Lamar Hunt, oilman H. L. Hunt's son, had tried for several years to bring a National Football League team to Dallas, but the league rebuffed his efforts. Finally, in 1959, Hunt decided to end his frustration by creating his own new football league. Hunt first took his idea to fellow Texan Bud Adams, who had been trying to land an NFL franchise for his town, Houston. Adams agreed to join the venture, and Hunt next contacted Denver's Robert Howsam, who had also been making inquiries about buying an NFL team. Hotelier Barron Hilton signed up for a franchise in Los Angeles. This core group formed the new American Football League. When the new league was announced, on August 14, 1959, it included six franchises, in Dallas, Houston, Denver, Los Angeles, New York, and Minneapolis–St. Paul. Buffalo and Boston soon joined the loop, but Minneapolis–St. Paul dropped out, in part because of stadium problems and in part because the NFL weighed in with a promise to expand into the Twin Cities. The new league replaced the

Minnesota franchise with one in Oakland, California. A television contract with the ABC network, though small in comparison to the NFL's broadcast deal, provided the new league with a crucial financial base, and Denver's Bob Howsam insisted that the TV revenue be shared equally among the owners. To manage the league, the owners hired as commissioner former South Dakota governor Joe Foss.

Bob Howsam had more experience in professional sports than the other American Football League owners. With his father, Lee, and brother, Earl, and other partners, Howsam had built his Denver Bears into perennial contenders in the Western League and the American Association. And he owned his own stadium. Despite the Bears' success, though, crowds at Bears Stadium began to shrink in the mid-1950s (one of Howsam's partners, Gerald Phipps, blamed television), and Howsam began looking for ways to fill the seats again. In 1958 Branch Rickey, one of baseball's great men, approached Howsam with the idea of starting a new baseball league to compete with the majors. Howsam agreed to join the new Continental League and, on Rickey's advice, built a new eighty-one-hundred-seat grandstand, at a cost of five hundred thousand dollars, at the south end of Bears Stadium. Unfortunately, the new baseball league did not materialize, and Howsam was left in debt and with more empty seats to fill. Lamar Hunt's invitation to join his new football league was a chance to bring fans into Bears Stadium year-round.[5]

Bob Howsam was a baseball man, and he knew that he must find a strong football manager to run his new team. He found his man in Canada. Forty-five-year-old Dean Griffing, an All–Big Six center and graduate of Kansas State, had spent his entire professional football career as a player, coach, and general manager in the Canadian Football League. His Saskatchewan Roughriders won the Western Division in 1936. Griffing later worked in Toronto and Calgary, but returned to Saskatchewan in 1952. Griffing went into semiretirement in 1958, taking the job of executive secretary of the Optimist Bowl in Tucson. Two years later Bob Howsam called.

In Canada, Griffing had earned a reputation for fielding competitive teams on small budgets, a talent that appealed to the cash-short Howsam. Indeed, his tightfistedness was legendary. It was claimed, though never proved, that he salvaged tape from locker room floors.

It was Griffing who bought the hideous yellow and brown uniforms with the striped socks. He got a good deal on them from the defunct Copper Bowl. During his tenure as general manager of the Broncos, Griffing went into the stands to retrieve field-goal balls. When one upset fan tried to hold on to his prize, Griffing wrestled it away. To calm the ensuing furor, he explained that in Canada it was the custom to return balls kicked into the stands, and he gave the disgruntled fan a ball autographed by the team.[6]

Griffing hired Frank Filchock, who had coached for him at Saskatchewan, as the Broncos' first head coach. A native of Grindstone Gulch, Pennsylvania, Filchock played his college football at Indiana and had pro tours quarterbacking the New York Giants and the Washington Redskins. In 1939, he and Redskin teammate Andy Farkas set an NFL record with a ninety-nine-yard touchdown pass against Pittsburgh. In 1946, when he was with the Giants, Filchock was implicated in a scheme to fix the NFL title game against the Chicago Bears. Although he was cleared of any direct involvement in the attempted fix, Commissioner Bert Bell later suspended him for failing to tell the league what he knew about the plan. Rather than sit out his suspension, Filchock moved to Canada, where he finished his playing career and began coaching.[7]

Coach Filchock handled all of the offensive coaching duties, while his two assistant coaches took care of the defense. Dale Dodrill, a graduate of Colorado State University and veteran of the Pittsburgh Steelers, coached the defensive line, and Jim Cason, a defensive back for the San Francisco Forty-Niners and the Los Angeles Rams, supervised the backfield.[8]

Griffing and Filchock's first, and highly daunting, task was to assemble a team. Neither man knew much about 1959's crop of college talent, and what little they knew they gleaned from magazines. In hiring Griffing as general manager, Bob Howsam had hoped that he would be able to stock the team with good talent from the Canadian league. "I had this theory," he recalled, "that there were a lot of players in Canadian football who could help us and I thought Griffing would give us an in with them." However, that plan did not work out. The Broncos signed one solid, if aging, Canadian player, quarterback Frank Tripucka, but most of the rest of the team were NFL rejects and

7-1. Denver Bronco quarterback Frank Tripucka throws a pass to receiver Lionel Taylor in a 1960 game against the Boston Patriots. Some Broncos refused to wear the vertically striped socks. Courtesy, the *Denver Post*.

over-the-hill veterans. Howsam later especially regretted not recruiting more African American players, men "who signed with other AFL teams and became stars." It was a curious oversight since Howsam had recruited African American and Hispanic players for his Denver Bears baseball teams since the early 1950s.[9]

The Broncos did land a few quality players, most notably Frank Tripucka. The "Tripper" quarterbacked national championship teams at Notre Dame in the late 1940s, including an undefeated season in 1948. After college, Tripucka played for the Detroit Lions and Chicago Cardinals until 1953 when he went to the Canadian league. He had retired as a player when Dean Griffing hired him to coach Denver's quarterbacks in training camp. When he arrived at the Broncos' camp in Golden, it quickly became obvious that Tripucka had more talent than any of the quarterbacks on the roster. Griffing and Filchock convinced him to sign as the Broncos' starting quarterback. Frank Tripucka played for just more than three seasons and was the backbone of the

Bronco offense, such as it was. Coach Filchock had no playbook for his offense, so Tripucka often diagrammed plays in the dirt. In 1960 he joined Jack Kemp and Johnny Unitas as the first pro quarterbacks to pass for more than three thousand yards in a season.[10]

Other standouts on the 1960 squad included receiver Lionel Taylor, whose ninety-two catches netted the AFL receiving title (fig. 7-1); running back and place kicker Gene Mingo; and defensive back Austin "Goose" Gonsoulin. Taylor had been cut as a defensive back by the Chicago Bears and landed a tryout with the Broncos. During an after-practice touch-football game, Taylor demonstrated a previously undetected talent, spectacular one-handed catches, and was promptly converted to a receiver. Gene Mingo had played service ball in the navy, where Griffing had seen him play. Griffing brought Mingo to Denver to try out as a defensive back but converted him to a running back. One day at practice, Filchock saw Mingo laughing at a place kicker and invited him to try kicking if he thought he could do better. Mingo became the Broncos' place kicker as well as a running back. He finished the 1960 season with 123 overall points, the most scored by any player in the league. On the defensive side, the Broncos found in Goose Gonsoulin a player who "can do everything well and for a rookie has amazing reactions in pass coverage," as proved by his eleven interceptions in 1960.[11]

The Broncos held their first summer-training camp at the School of Mines in Golden. Players were housed, or warehoused, barracks-style in a loft in the school gymnasium. The early days of camp resembled a Hollywood "cattle call," with prospects brought in, quickly auditioned, and most of them just as quickly dismissed. In all, more than three hundred men passed through that summer. The chances of sticking were slim. Goose Gonsoulin arrived in a group of ninety hopefuls and was the only one to make the team.[12]

With only a handful of quality players, hopes for the 1960 season were understandably low, an expectation confirmed by five preseason losses. However, on Friday night, September 9, 1960, at Boston University stadium, the Denver Broncos defeated the Boston Patriots 13-10 in the American Football League's first regular-season game. The next week they beat the Bills at Buffalo, 27-21. A 28-24 loss to the New York Titans ended the Broncos' three-week opening road trip. They came home to beat Oakland 31-14. Losses to the Los Angeles Chargers and the Dallas Texans, and another victory over Boston, gave the Broncos a respectable record of four wins and three losses at midseason. However, they did not win again that year, managing only a 38-38 tie with the Buffalo Bills in front of 7,800 home fans. The 1960 season established a pattern of fast starts and late-season collapses that plagued the Broncos for years to come.

Fan interest in 1960 rose and fell with the win-loss record. A crowd of 18,372 turned out for the home opener, and 19,141 showed up the following week, but only 5,861 attended the final home game. In all, only 91,333 home fans watched the Broncos play at home in 1960. The days of dyed orange-in-the-wool loyalty and sold-out stadiums lay many years in the future.[13]

Gate receipts and the Broncos' share in the AFL television money were not enough to sustain Bob Howsam's investment in the team. In addition to players' and coaches' salaries, equipment, transportation, and lodging for the team, Howsam still carried a large mortgage on Bears Stadium. His Rocky Mountain Empire Sports, Inc., finished the 1960 season with losses of more than two hundred thousand dollars, which he attributed to poor attendance and the costs of operating the stadium. "A big factor," he recalled, was that "we were the only team in the league that had its own stadium and had to put money into it. In retrospect, it might have been better to have just leased the Denver University stadium." In an observation that today seems quaint, Howsam also noted that "we never gave a thought that the city should or would take our stadium and improve it for us. We tried to do it ourselves, and it cost us dearly."[14]

Howsam's financial troubles forced him to put the Broncos and the Bears on the market in 1961. He found a buyer in San Antonio, Texas, who wanted to move the teams to that city. However, Cal Kunz, a vegetable wholesaler and a member of the board of directors of Rocky Mountain Empire Sports, set out to keep the teams in Denver. Kunz went to fellow board member Gerald Phipps to enlist his support. Phipps, a lifelong baseball fan, told Kunz, "I don't care really about football but I'm not about to let baseball leave Denver." By the end of May 1961, Kunz and Phipps assembled a group of Denver-area business leaders, including Earl Howsam, to buy the company.

Kunz became chief operating officer, while Gerald Phipps, and his brother Allan, with 48 percent of the company's stock, were the largest stockholders. After he sold his Denver teams, Bob Howsam stayed in baseball and became a major league general manager, and eventually led the St. Louis Cardinals and the Cincinnati Reds to World Series victories.[15]

The new management did not have time to make any dramatic changes before the 1961 training camp and season got under way. Griffing and Filchock brought in a few new players, including colorful Ed "Wahoo" McDaniel, a linebacker who supplemented his football income by wrestling in the off-season.

The 1961 Broncos won only three games and lost seven straight in the second half of the season. Cal Kunz fired Frank Filchock in December and replaced him with Jack Faulkner, a former marine and a protégé of coaching great Sid Gilman. By midsummer, Dean Griffing was also gone, and Faulkner added the job of general manager to his portfolio.

Faulkner was determined to shake things up in Denver. He brought in more assistant coaches, and one of them, Ray Malavasi, began setting up a computerized scouting operation. Faulkner also developed a playbook and began using game plans, things unheard of in Filchock's regime. And he got rid of the ugly socks and uniforms. In a public relations master stroke, Faulkner staged a public bonfire to burn the socks, a gesture designed to "convince everybody that a new day in Denver football" had arrived. Faulkner ordered new uniforms in orange, blue, and white. When they arrived, however, the new uniforms were not exactly what Faulkner had had in mind. "I was a Cleveland Browns fan," he recalled, "and I wanted those same burnt orange uniforms like they wore. But the manufacturers sent us bright orange instead." Nevertheless, the new apparel was a great improvement. Faulkner's color scheme, with orange predominating, became closely identified with the Broncos and was not tampered with in any significant way for thirty-five years.[16]

Faulkner had no better luck than his predecessor in bringing new talent to the team in 1962, but he did seem to get more out of what he had. That season, in fact, proved the best of the entire decade of the 1960s, and beyond. The Broncos' best performance of the decade came in week seven, against Houston. The 20-10 score was not spectacular, but Frank Tripucka threw for 301 yards, Gene Mingo kicked two field goals, and the defense held the Oilers to only 67 yards on the ground. After the Houston win, however, they won only one more game and finished the season 7-7. Nevertheless, the AFL honored Faulkner as its coach of the year. However, the second-half slide in 1962 began eleven years of futility for the Denver Broncos; they did not win half their games again until 1973. In spite of 1962's respectable record, Bronco opponents held them in contempt. One opposing player called Denver "the next best thing to an open date."[17]

The most glaring and persistent problem that developed during Jack Faulkner's tenure as head coach was at quarterback. Frank Tripucka was an island of stability for the Broncos during their first three seasons, providing leadership on and off the field. However, Tripucka retired after the second game of the 1963 season, and his departure began a quarterbacking merry-go-round that lasted through the rest of the 1960s. Of the forty-five quarterbacks who appeared on the Broncos' roster in the 1960s, thirty-one came and went after Tripucka.[18]

Coach Faulkner brought in Minnesota Viking veteran John McCormick to replace Tripucka. McCormick took charge quickly and led the Broncos to solid wins over Boston and San Diego. However, in his third game, against Houston, McCormick injured his knee and was out for the season. His two wins were the Broncos' only victories in 1963. Faulkner had drafted Louisiana Tech's Mickey Slaughter (one of the few draft picks to sign with the team in the early years) as Frank Tripucka's heir apparent, but McCormick's injury forced him into the starting job sooner than anyone expected. The next week the Patriots put Slaughter in the hospital. By the last game of the season, Faulkner was down to one quarterback, Don Breaux, who had signed with the Broncos only two days before Slaughter's injury.[19]

In 1964 Faulkner tried to beef up the quarterback corps with what may have been the strangest trade in the history of the game. Denver gave the Houston Oilers defensive tackle Bud McFadin and a draft pick in exchange for a two-year *loan* of quarterback Jacky Lee. With Lee in camp, Faulkner released John McCormick and Don

Breaux. Lee and Mickey Slaughter alternated as starting quarterbacks throughout the season, and in one game rotated in and out seven times. The Broncos finished 1964 with two wins, eleven losses, and a tie.[20]

Jack Faulkner was gone long before the 1964 season ended. Cal Kunz fired him after game four, a 39-10 loss to the Patriots. Assistant coach Mac Speedie, a former outstanding receiver for the Cleveland Browns, took over for the rest of the season and stayed on as head coach in 1965.

Speedie's tenure as head coach seemed to start well in 1964. In his first game the Broncos upset the Kansas City Chiefs 33-27. Speedie believed strongly in building fan support, and during the game he became so excited that he began leading cheers on the sidelines. He also opened team practices to the public. However, the Broncos won only one more game after the Kansas City win and finished 1964 with two wins, eleven losses, and a tie.

The best news the Broncos, and the American Football League, had in 1964 was the National Broadcasting Company's agreement to televise AFL games. The $36 million deal provided a much needed financial boost for the league.

In Cal Kunz's mind, however, the deal with NBC did not come soon enough. By 1965 the Broncos had lost $2 million, and Kunz concluded that there was no future for football in Denver. Thus, while Mac Speedie struggled with preparations for the 1965 season, Gerald and Allan Phipps struggled to win control of the team and to keep it in Denver. Kunz quietly organized a voting trust representing 52 percent of the stock in Rocky Mountain Empire Sports and set out to sell the team. The Cox Broadcasting Company offered to buy the company with the intention of moving the Broncos to Atlanta. However, Cox insisted on buying 100 percent of the stock, and the Phipps brothers refused to sell their 48 percent. In the end, Kunz and his supporters agreed to sell their stock to the Phipps brothers for $1.5 million.[21]

Buying the Broncos was an enormous risk for the Phipps brothers. After all, the team's cumulative record was an unimpressive 18-49-3, and they appeared to be going nowhere but down; the franchise was heavily in debt; and the new owners assumed the added burden of operating Bears Stadium. Asked why he decided to buy the Broncos, Gerald Phipps said, facetiously, "Sometimes I think I'm just a stupid idiot." There was much more to it than that.[22]

The Phipps brothers were scions of one of Denver's most prominent and powerful families. Their father, Lawrence, represented Colorado in the United States Senate in the 1920s. The Phipps family had a long and deep commitment to Denver and its development. To Gerald Phipps, keeping the Broncos was a matter of community pride and good business. Denver would not have suffered had it never had a football team, he believed, "but once you have an operation of that kind, if you lose it, then I think the community gets a black eye which would take a long, long time to recover from. I felt my business, the construction business, would be the very first to feel the effects of the black eye on the community that would result from the loss" of the Broncos. In Phipps's mind, Denver's prestige and its economic future were tied to the Broncos. "We are trying to attract industry to this community," he said, and "nothing would hurt us more than headlines around the country saying Denver had lost its football team. I would be cutting my own throat if I did something that would set back the community."[23]

By the time the Phipps brothers took over the Broncos there were already symptoms of the intense loyalty among Bronco fans that became known as Broncomania. By mid-decade, fans in Bears Stadium's south stands already had a reputation for fanaticism and raucous behavior. Visiting teams, who had to enter and leave the field from their locker room below the stands, learned to be alert for barrages of snowballs and bottles. However, when the Phipps brothers bought the Broncos they touched a deep nerve in the community.

The intimate bond between the Broncos and their fans in Denver and around Colorado was forged in the spring of 1965. Gerald Phipps set a goal of selling twenty thousand season tickets in 1965, the number he believed necessary to break even for the year. Fans and business leaders in Denver quickly took up the challenge. *Denver Post* publisher Palmer Hoyt let his employees pay for tickets through a payroll deduction, and twenty other businesses soon followed suit. An Aurora bank offered no-interest loans to finance ticket purchases, and other area banks soon matched the offer. The twenty-thousand-ticket goal was met by April 1965, less than two months after the Phipps brothers bought the team. Eventually, fans bought 22,905 season tickets, an increase of 14,903 over 1964 sales. Bronco fans went on to set a Western Division attendance record in 1965 with almost 220,000 turning out for the seven home games.[24]

Ticket sales and attendance in 1965 had been helped by the acquisition of one of the AFL's leading stars, flamboyant running back Carlton "Cookie" Gilchrist, who came to the Broncos in a trade with Buffalo. Gilchrist had been the league's most valuable player in 1962 when he became the first AFL back to run for more than one thousand yards. In January 1965, before the trade to Denver, Gilchrist helped organize a boycott by African American players of the AFL All-Star Game in New Orleans, where they had encountered Jim Crow discrimination in hotels, restaurants, and bars. Gilchrist was not thrilled with the trade and told the *Denver Post*, "I would rather retire than play in Denver." However, when the Broncos sweetened his thirty-five-thousand-dollar contract by throwing in a new Cadillac as a signing bonus, Gilchrist joined the team. Gilchrist's 954 yards in 1965 were the best part of the Broncos' season. They finished only two games better than in 1964, with four wins and ten losses. When the team boarded their flight to Kansas City for the last game, the temperamental Gilchrist declared that the aircraft was too rickety, a symptom of the Bronco management's penury, and stalked off the plane. After he cooled down, Gilchrist remembered a provision in his contract providing for a five-thousand-dollar bonus if he gained 900 yards. He was within reach of that mark, but would not make it if he did not play in Kansas City. Gilchrist jumped on a commercial flight to Kansas City and rejoined the team. Speedie and Phipps were unhappy with Gilchrist, but allowed him to play and earn his bonus.[25]

When Gilchrist showed up for training camp in 1966 he had in tow his friend Willie Ross, a running back who had been released by Buffalo. Gilchrist demanded that Speedie give Ross a tryout. The coach emphatically rejected the demand, and Gilchrist walked out of camp, intending to sit out the year. A few weeks into the 1966 season, however, the Broncos traded Gilchrist to an expansion team, the Miami Dolphins.[26]

Mac Speedie was gone by the time the Broncos shipped Cookie Gilchrist to Miami. They lost the opener in Houston 45-7, a game in which they failed to gain a first down. Speedie resigned after losing 24-10 to Boston the following week. Assistant coach Ray Malavasi took over for the rest of the season, which ended with another 4-10 record.

The Broncos' quarterback circus continued unabated from 1964 through 1966, contributing much to the team's failure. Speedie rotated back and forth between Jacky Lee and Mickey Slaughter during 1964, and added John McCormick to the parade in 1965. Lee's "lease" expired, and he returned to Houston in 1966. Slaughter was gone after the first game in 1966, and the Broncos added Tobin Rote, Max Choboian, and Scotty Glacken to the roster. Season ticket sales fell below nineteen thousand in 1966, and the fans aimed their animus at the quarterbacks. John McCormick recalled that fan hostility drove Mickey Slaughter from football in 1966. Slaughter needed only three more games to qualify for his pension, but "the fans were so rough on Mickey that he just didn't want to put his uniform on again."[27]

However, such misery was not universal in the Bronco organization in the mid-1960s. Robert "Red" Miller, who coached the offensive line from 1963 to 1965, later summed up the Faulkner-Speedie era. "We had fun," he recalled. "We weren't any good, but we had fun."[28]

The best news for the Broncos in 1966 again came from off the field. Since the AFL's founding in 1960, the National Football League had struggled to drive the upstart competitor out of business. However, the AFL had survived and, with the infusion of money from the NBC television contract, had begun to sign better players, men who otherwise would have gone to the NFL. In 1964 the New York Jets signed top draft prospect Joe Namath for $420,000. The bidding war for players forced the two football leagues to come to terms, and in 1966 they agreed to a phased merger. Each league became a conference in the NFL. The new league would conduct a unified draft and play an interconference championship game. Interleague preseason play began in 1967, and regular-season interleague games started in 1970.[29]

The NFL merger actually created a new financial problem for the Broncos. The agreement required each team to have a stadium with at least fifty thousand seats. Either Bears Stadium would have to be enlarged or a new stadium built. In March 1966 the state legislature created a four-county metropolitan stadium district to organize a bond-issue election to be held in 1967. If passed, the bonds would raise $20 million to build a new stadium. Polls showed strong support for the bond issue, but the campaign was poorly organized, and when the votes were counted in March 1967, the proposal was defeated.[30]

Having saved the Broncos for Denver in 1965, the Phipps brothers now faced the possibility of having to move them. Birmingham, Alabama, was rumored to be the most likely site. However, the Denver business community and Bronco fans weighed in to keep the team, founding DOERS, the Denver Organization to Erect the Right Kind of Stadium. Recognizing that a new stadium was out of reach, DO-ERS set out to expand Bears Stadium. Their fund-raising campaign collected the nearly $2 million needed to retire the Phippses' debt on the facility. Major donations of up to one hundred thousand dollars came from corporations, including Mountain Bell, the Public Service Company of Colorado, Coors, and Samsonite. A local radio station held a twenty-four-hour pledge marathon that raised twenty-five thousand dollars. Kindergarten classes collected pennies. With the mortgages cleared, Gerald Phipps signed the stadium over to the City and County of Denver. The city then issued self-liquidating revenue bonds to finance a sixteen-thousand-seat expansion. When the facility was renamed Mile High Stadium in 1968, it sported fifty-one thousand seats. The DOERS campaign forged a more tangible bond between the Broncos and the community, from the corporate elite to the fan in the street. There would be no more talk of the Broncos leaving Denver, at least not for three decades.[31]

THE LOU SABAN YEARS

The stadium bond-issue and expansion campaigns were part of Lou Saban's baptism as the Broncos' new head coach. Saban, who led the Buffalo Bills to AFL championships in 1964 and 1965, signed a ten-year contract with the Broncos in December 1966. As both head coach and general manager, he faced a daunting task, and with great understatement said his new job was "the most stimulating assignment I have undertaken during the years I have been associated with football."[32]

Saban quickly began a housecleaning. In March he supervised the Broncos' move into a new headquarters at Fifty-Eighth Avenue and Interstate 25. (The old facility, located near the stadium, at Twentieth Avenue and Decatur Street, consisted of a quonset hut and a sixty-yard practice field. Denver sportswriter Dick Connor speculated that the short practice field accounted for the Broncos' inability to sustain long offensive drives.) Saban staffed the new facility with an entirely new coaching staff and swept out many of the team's mainstays, including Lionel Taylor and Goose Gonsoulin. The merger with the NFL ensured that the Broncos for the first time would be able to sign their number-one draft pick. Saban chose Syracuse running back Floyd Little. Little wanted to play for the New York Jets, but the draft left him no real choice but to sign with Denver. To strengthen the offensive backfield further, Saban brought Cookie Gilchrist back from Miami. In addition, he tried to bring new blood and stability to the quarterback corps by trading first-round draft picks in 1968 and 1969 to San Diego for back-up Steve Tensi.[33]

The 1967 campaign started well. On August 5, 1967, the Broncos defeated the Detroit Lions 13-7 in a preseason game, becoming the first AFL team to beat an NFL team. Prior to the contest, Detroit defensive lineman Alex Karras vowed, "I'll walk back to Detroit if they beat us." The future Monday Night Football announcer not only suffered the humiliation of being beaten by the lowly Broncos but also was tossed from the game in the second quarter, but not before Cookie Gilchrist slammed him into a goal post and challenged him to a fight. The Broncos startled the NFL again the following week by defeating the Minnesota Vikings 14-9. In the first regular-season game, at home against Boston, the Broncos won 26-21 in front of 35,488 fans. Cookie Gilchrist suffered a career-ending knee injury in the game, but the rest of the team looked as if Saban had worked a miracle.[34]

Reality, however, set in in the second week when the Broncos traveled to Oakland. The Raiders humiliated Saban's team with a 51-0 pounding. The Broncos had minus-five total yards of offense in the game. Afterward, Saban said simply, "We stunk." Denver won only two more games and finished with three wins and eleven losses.[35]

The year 1967 was tough for the Broncos and for Denver. The ill-fated stadium bond issue; the danger of the team leaving, averted by the DOERS campaign; and the Broncos' continued poor play made both the city and the team look small-time. One syndicated columnist wrote that NFL owners did not want to bring their teams to Denver, and not because the Broncos had beaten two of them at the beginning of the season. Similarly, he wrote of a UCLA draft prospect who was visibly relieved not to have been drafted by the Broncos. Why, he wondered, had Denver "come to symbolize Siberia?" After all, Denver was a nice town, with broad streets, clean air, and "a healthy attitude on nudity." However, if the people of Denver did not start acting like citizens of a big-time city (that is, by passing bond issues for stadiums) and if the Broncos did not start winning, he warned, nightclub comedians would "start babbling that first prize in their contest is one week in Denver and second prize is two weeks."[36]

Denver did not build a new football stadium, but it did expand Mile High Stadium to fifty-one thousand seats and later to more than seventy-five thousand. However, the Broncos did not start winning more games than they lost until 1973. In both 1968 and 1969, Lou Saban's Broncos won only five games. The most memorable, and meaningful, victory was the 1969 win over the Super Bowl champion Jets, a game in which tackle Dave Costa, one of Saban's many trade acquisitions, hit Joe Namath so hard that the New York quarterback had to leave the game. It was a sign that Denver was beginning to put together a respectable defense.

Instability at quarterback remained the Broncos' most serious problem in the late 1960s. Steve Tensi started eleven games in 1967 and played in the other three, but he did not have a good year, completing only 40 percent of his passes for sixteen touchdowns, while giving up seventeen interceptions. Saban benched Tensi for the first three games of the 1968 season in favor of Jim Leclair, the 1967 backup, and John McCormick. Leclair and McCormick were both gone by the fourth game, and Saban then tried Marlin "the Magician" Briscoe at quarterback. Saban had drafted Briscoe, a running back from Omaha, in the fourteenth round that year, but tried him at quarterback in training camp. Briscoe showed that he could do the job and started in the fourth week of the season. Tensi returned to the starting lineup the following week, but Briscoe played in ten more games, starting the final four after Tensi broke his collarbone. Briscoe was the first African American quarterback to have significant playing time in either the AFL or the NFL.[37]

The Broncos tried to keep Briscoe on the roster in 1969, promising to use him primarily at quarterback, but would not meet his salary demands. Briscoe left Denver and, in 1970, became the AFC's leading pass receiver with the Buffalo Bills. Many years later, Briscoe recalled with pride his season as the NFL's first black quarterback. "I think that I proved to the world that a black man could think and throw the football," he said, adding that "I disproved the negative myths about a black man playing the position."[38]

Saban started Steve Tensi in 1969, backing him up with veteran Pete Liske, who had played with the Jets and the Bills in the mid-1960s before going to the Canadian league. Liske was talented enough to lead the Calgary Stampeders to the Canadian league's Grey Cup championship in 1968 before coming to Denver.

Injuries plagued Steve Tensi throughout his career in Denver, which ended midway through the 1970 season. Even worse, though, was his treatment at the hands of Denver fans who blamed him for the entire team's poor performance. He received obscene phone calls, found garbage dumped on his lawn, his children were harassed at school, and he was the butt of vicious jokes attacking his intelligence. When Tensi quit, he said, "[F]ootball is not fun anymore." Denver fans had bagged another quarterback, and they would soon help drive away the head coach, in the process showing the underside of their increasingly ferocious attachment to the team—the phenomenon becoming known as Broncomania—and proving that they were not ready for prime time.[39]

Steve Tensi's retirement prompted a quarterback housecleaning as Coach Saban released backups Pete Liske and Al Pastrana before the 1971 season, replacing them with Steve Ramsey, from New Orleans, and Green Bay's Don Horn. Saban also traded for New York Jets place kicker Jim Turner and drafted defensive end Lyle Alzado, who heralded from Yankton College, South Dakota, via the streets of New York's Spanish Harlem. Alzado quickly joined the starting lineup, and Turner improved the Broncos' kicking game, but it was not enough. The two new quarterbacks proved no better than the long line of predecessors, and so the offense remained mediocre.

The Broncos opened the 1971 season at home against the Miami Dolphins. After trailing most of the game, Miami managed to tie the score late in the fourth quarter. The Broncos regained the ball with more than a minute left to play, but Saban decided to run out the clock and settle for a tie. The fifty-one thousand fans at Mile High Stadium were furious that Saban had not tried to score and let him know it with jeers and snowballs. Afterward, Saban explained that "we didn't want to throw from our own territory, especially when we had to work out of the muck. Half a loaf," he said, "was better than none."[40]

Saban had doomed himself as the Broncos' head coach. Two weeks later, when he next walked onto the field at Mile High, Saban found it littered with half loaves of bread. Fan restiveness at his failure to produce a winning team had suddenly turned to full-fledged hate. By November, verbal abuse from the stands and critical newspaper ads escalated to eggs thrown at his home and garbage strewn on his lawn. Schoolmates' taunts prompted Saban to take his children out of school. (Nearly two decades later Saban said that he still was not sure he knew all that his family went through during his last weeks in Denver.) Finally, after the ninth week of the season, with his team having won only two games, Lou Saban quit.[41]

Despite the poor record, the Broncos were a better team than when Saban arrived. The organization, including scouting, was stronger; the team trained and played in better facilities; and several players who would figure in the team's "sudden" success in the late 1970s had joined the roster. A *Denver Post* columnist noted that the Broncos under Saban had become "the hottest sports property in Colorado, always excepting, of course, the dog tracks, which have the lure of gambling going for them." Nonetheless, it was not enough. They did not win. Team owner Gerald Phipps summed up Saban's tenure in Denver by noting that "when he came in 1966 the organization was in pretty bad shape. We looked to Lou to bring us respectability in all phases of the game. He has done an absolutely superb job of it. To me, it's nothing but tragedy it has not been reflected in more victories."[42]

Saban turned up in 1972 as head coach of the Buffalo Bills and stayed there until 1976, leading them and their star running back, O. J.

Simpson, to the playoffs twice. After Buffalo, Saban bounced around in college football; tried his hand at baseball, briefly, as president of the New York Yankees, and even coached high school football. As he approached the end of his career, Saban seemed to have set aside any bitterness about his Denver years and the ups and downs of the succeeding decades. To him, just being able to coach was what mattered. "When you're out there on the sidelines," he said, "it doesn't matter where the hell you've been or why you left. At the moment, you're right there coaching football. You are where you are, and all that other crap just doesn't matter."[43]

THE JOHN RALSTON YEARS

The Denver Broncos' search for a winning coach now led to the West Coast and Stanford University, where John Ralston had just won his second straight Rose Bowl. Four days after his Cardinal team upset Michigan, Ralston became the Broncos' head coach. Team owner Gerald Phipps had been especially impressed with the grit Stanford had shown in coming from behind to win. "Ralston's team was behind with every reason to fold," Phipps noted, "but they showed motivation, discipline, spirit, and guts in rallying to win." That determination convinced Phipps that "Ralston was the man for us."[44]

When he arrived in Denver, Ralston, a disciple of Dale Carnegie's teachings on the power of positive thinking, explained that "my basic philosophy is if you hang in there tough enough, long enough, work hard enough, dedicate yourself with a positive approach, anything can be accomplished." And he set his sights high. "The goal here," he declared, "is to win the Super Bowl, and believe me . . . it will be done."[45]

Ralston quickly put his imprint on the team. Through trades and the draft he acquired wide receiver Haven Moses, center Bobby Maples, and guard Paul Howard, all players destined to be mainstays in the Broncos' development into a championship-caliber team in the 1970s. Ralston's most important early acquisition, however, was quarterback Charley Johnson.

A twelve-year veteran—ten years in St. Louis and two years in Houston—Charley Johnson was smart and tough. He had a Ph.D. in chemical engineering. Prone to injury, he spent almost every off-

season with one limb or another wrapped in a cast. Nonetheless, he
always did what he had to do to be ready to play. Once, when Ralston
was about to bench him because of a locked knee, Johnson told the
coach, "[N]ever mind that. I can get that loosened up." He then directed the team doctor where to inject anesthetic behind his kneecap.
Other players in the locker room could not watch.[46]

Johnson made his first start for Denver in game six of the 1972
season, against the Oakland Raiders. The Broncos had not beaten the
Raiders since 1962, but Johnson threw for 361 yards to lead his team
to a 30-23 victory. Johnson finished the 1972 season the third-ranked
quarterback in the NFL, with 1,783 yards and fourteen touchdowns.
For the first time in a decade, since Frank Tripucka retired, the Broncos had a top-notch quarterback. Although the Broncos won only
four more games in 1972, they seemed to be a different and better
team. After the victory over Oakland, a *Denver Post* columnist wrote,
"Ralston's positive thinking approach is starting to pay big dividends.
These young Broncos sincerely believe in it and more importantly in
themselves."[47]

Ralston continued to restock the team with promising young
talent during the 1973 off-season. His draft acquisitions included running back Otis Armstrong, defensive end Barney Chavous, and linebacker Tom Jackson. Ralston also specified his goals for the upcoming season. A card on his desk read, "Win 10 games, lose 4, Go to and
Win the Super Bowl."[48]

The 1973 edition of the Broncos did not go to the Super Bowl,
or even win ten games. However, their record of seven wins, five
losses, and two ties did give the franchise its first winning season and
brought the Broncos serious national attention. When they met the
Oakland Raiders on October 22, in their first Monday-night game,
an exciting, nationally televised contest that ended in a 23-23 tie,
announcer Howard Cosell observed that the team, and their fans, had
"been thirsting for national recognition and they got it tonight. And
they've given a performance that lives up to the opportunity." Cosell
also noted that Denver mayor William McNichols had proclaimed
the event Orange Day and that viewers would "see every Denver
Bronco fan here wearing some article in orange." Cosell failed to
note, however, that some south-stands fans had chosen to solemnize

the occasion by wearing formal evening attire. The National Football League and other teams' players recognized the Broncos' winning record by naming Ralston the AFC's coach of the year for 1973 and by electing Floyd Little, Haven Moses, Riley Odoms, and Paul Smith to the Pro Bowl.[49]

The Broncos' organization had an outstanding off-season in 1974, adding Ohio State's spectacular linebacker Randy Gradishar and tackle Claudie Minor to the team. In September, Denver voters approved a $25 million bond issue to expand Mile High Stadium to seventy-five thousand seats.

Another winning season in 1974 (seven wins, six losses, and one tie) earned Coach Ralston a five-year extension on his contract. Curiously, however, when owner Gerald Phipps announced the move, few of the players seemed pleased. Although Ralston had proved himself a sound judge of football talent and had led the team to consecutive winning seasons, many players harbored doubts about his coaching style and his ability to lead them to a championship.[50]

Many players, especially older veterans, resented the higher standards of discipline Ralston imposed on the team. His training camps, which he held in hot Pomona, California, were tougher than the camps many men were accustomed to. Ralston's discipline went beyond the practice field. For example, he did not permit players to drink alcohol on team planes.

Some players disliked Ralston's college-style enthusiasm for the game. As professional athletes, they found the coach's "rah-rah" approach undignified. Ralston's enthusiasm, however, could be infectious. Denver sportscaster Larry Zimmer tells of Ralston trotting onto the field with his squad before the kickoff of a game against the Oakland Raiders. In the huddle he told the players that he envied them and wished that he could put on a helmet and run down the field with them. At that, player Fran Lynch took off his helmet, handed it to Ralston, and began to run to the sideline. The Broncos' huddle dissolved in laughter, a sight that caused some consternation on the Oakland sideline.[51]

During the 1975 and 1976 seasons, Ralston added more standout players to the squad, including cornerback Louis Wright, running back Rick Upchurch, defensive tackle Rubin Carter, defensive back Steve Foley, and guard Tom Glassic. However, Floyd Little and Charley Johnson retired after the 1975 season. Johnson's retirement left the quarterback position in the hands of backup Steve Ramsey and rookie Craig Penrose.

Without Charley Johnson, the Broncos' offense slipped from capable to mediocre in 1976 as quarterback Steve Ramsey completed only 47 percent of his passes. Otis Armstrong's 1,008 rushing yards was the only offensive highlight. Nonetheless, with a continually improving defense, the Broncos had their best season ever in 1976, winning nine games and losing only five.

However, many players' confidence in Coach Ralston ran out by season's end. An important turning point for Ralston and his players came when the Broncos lost 17-7 in Houston. Offensive coordinator Max Coley fell ill before the game, and without him the offense sputtered, gaining only seventeen yards in the second half. "We were very unprepared," said Otis Armstrong. Ralston, Armstrong complained, had never taken a major role in running the offense and, with Coley gone, "he didn't know what to do." Back home in Denver, Lyle Alzado, out of action with an injury, watched the game on television until, angry and frustrated with what he saw as Ralston's failure to lead the team, he threw his crutch through the screen. Alzado and other Broncos were determined from that day to get rid of their coach.[52]

Ralston's hold on his job began to slip one week after the season ended when owner Gerald Phipps stripped him of his role as general manager of the club and gave the job to player personnel director Fred Gehrke. In announcing the action, Phipps did not refer to player unrest, but said that "having Ralston act as coach for six months and general manager for six hasn't worked. We've looked at other teams and the ones who are successful are those where the coach and general manager responsibilities have been divided." Phipps explicitly asked Ralston to stay on as head coach, saying that "a separation of duties will enable him to devote his total time and efforts toward continuing the improvement of our football team." Phipps thus was telling Ralston to focus his efforts exclusively on coaching, the very job that many of his players believed he could not do.[53]

While Ralston pondered whether to stay on as head coach, a group of twenty-two Bronco players took matters into their own hands and brought their rebellion into public view. On December 21, 1976, the group summoned reporters to a press conference at a Denver hotel with the intention of declaring their lack of confidence in the coach. Prior to the press conference, however, they agreed to meet with Gerald Phipps and Fred Gehrke, who convinced them to soften their statement. At the press conference, spokesman Billy Thompson read a statement declaring the players' confidence in Bronco owners and management, but made no mention of Ralston. Later, members of the group leaked a copy of their original statement, which expressed their true sentiments: "We don't believe that it is possible to win a championship under the guidance of John Ralston. He has lost the respect of the players, and we don't believe that he is capable of coaching us to a championship."[54]

Ralston tried to rise to the players' challenge, announcing the next day that he would stay on as head coach. Admitting that he was surprised by the player rebellion, he nevertheless claimed that it had no bearing on his decision. He conceded, however, that "obviously, we have some problem areas, but I don't consider them insurmountable." Ralston then challenged each of the dissident players "to come in and say that they wanted to be traded or to say that they've made a mistake. Then we'll go from there."[55]

Gerald Phipps seemed to back Ralston's tough stance. "In all of the years I've been associated with the Broncos and in the even more years that I've been in business, I've never run into anything which disturbed me as much as that action by some of our players," he said, adding that he had "never seen anything handled so miserably." Phipps pointedly told the dissidents that "we are running the organization, not the players," and that it now was up to them "to prove, not just to the organization but to the people of Denver, that they can contribute in a positive way to the Broncos."[56]

Although Phipps had sided with him in the showdown with the dissident players, Ralston's position within the Bronco organization was weakened. Only a few players supported him, and he no longer had authority over team affairs off the field. Ralston's lack of real power became increasingly apparent over succeeding weeks as he came into conflict with general manager Gehrke over control of scouting, the college draft, and the offensive coaching staff. Finally, at the end of January 1977, Ralston resigned as head coach.[57]

John Ralston never again coached in the National Football League. He became a vice president of the San Francisco Forty-Niners, coached the Oakland franchise in the short-lived United States Football League, and eventually returned to college coaching. He retired from San Jose State University after the 1996 season.

Ralston left the Broncos a much stronger, more talented team than when he arrived in 1972. In truth, he assembled the team, minus a first-rate quarterback, that was to give Denver its first divisional and conference championship. However, the team he brought together repudiated his leadership and denied him any hope of achieving his goal of taking them to the Super Bowl.

Now the Bronco players, having helped oust Ralston on the grounds that he could not lead them to a championship, had to prove that they could become a championship team without him. Only a couple of ingredients were missing: a coach who could push them to play up to their potential, and an offense, especially a quarterback, that could score points.

BRONCOMANIA: RED MILLER AND SUPER BOWL XII

By 1977 the National Football League's annual championship game, the Super Bowl, had become something much bigger than a football game. It was a major national, even international, event driven by media out to sell advertising space and time, and commercial sponsors out to sell beer, cars, clothing, even computers. It was a unique advertising opportunity, and, since hundreds of millions of people around the globe watched or listened to the game, a minute of commercial airtime sold for several hundred thousand dollars. When Apple launched its new Macintosh computer, it produced a unique commercial intended to air only once, during the Super Bowl.

Winning the right to appear in the Super Bowl meant standing atop the professional football world. In the days between the conference championships and the game, players, coaches, and owners became objects of intense media attention. Coaches and star players became fonts of wisdom and virtue. Less important and marginally talented team members became icons of the American dream, proof that with determination any kid could make it to the top.

Fans experienced a kind of reflected glory. To be the loyal fan of a Super Bowl team was to be part of something grand, successful, and important, which translated into civic pride. To be a city with a Super Bowl team was to be an important city.

The Denver Broncos won the American Football Conference title in 1977 and the right to appear in Super Bowl XII, in the Superdome in New Orleans. By the time the final gun sounded in the conference championship game, in which the Broncos defeated arch rival Oakland, the whole country knew about Broncomania. The 1977 Broncos became instant media darlings. They were overnight sensations, a miracle team who had enjoyed a Cinderella season.

Of course, none of that was entirely true. The team that won the AFC title in 1977 was largely the same bunch who had been racked by dissension only a few months before. They were largely the same team built by Lou Saban and John Ralston. Nonetheless, the players and the fans felt something different. That new feeling owed mainly to one man: Robert "Red" Miller.

Red Miller's nickname was apt, and not just because of his shock of flaming red hair. An open and friendly man, he could also be fiery, even pugnacious. Sportswriter Lou Sahadi said of him, "[H]e is as subtle as a punch in the mouth."[58]

Football had been Miller's ticket to college and away from his family's life in the coal mines and factories of southwestern Illinois. After graduating from Western Illinois, Miller coached high school football in Illinois and Ohio. His first college job was at Carthage College. Later, he returned to Western Illinois as an assistant to Lou Saban. In 1960 Saban took Miller and another assistant, Joe Collier, with him to the Boston Patriots. All three men moved on to the Buffalo Bills in 1962. Miller left Saban for a job in Denver from 1963 through 1965, then went to St. Louis through 1970. He spent two years with Baltimore and then joined Chuck Fairbanks as offensive coordinator of the Patriots.[59]

Fred Gerhke and Gerald Phipps originally hoped to bring Miller to Denver as offensive coordinator, but Miller rejected the offer. When

John Ralston resigned, the Bronco management offered him the head coaching job. At his introductory press conference Miller said, bluntly, "I want to win. Period."[60]

Miller knew that he had taken over a talented team, just a key player or two short of being championship caliber. Miller quickly made the crucial move in that direction by trading quarterback Steve Ramsey to the New York Giants for that team's unhappy quarterback, Craig Morton.

Morton, a thirteen-year veteran, spent most of his career with the Dallas Cowboys. The Cowboys drafted Morton in 1965 and, after four years as Don Meredith's understudy, made him the team's starting quarterback in 1969. He led them to the Super Bowl in 1970, losing the game to the Colts, 16-13. In 1971, Cowboy head coach Tom Landry benched Morton in favor of Roger Staubach, and for the next three and one-half seasons he played only when Staubach was injured. Finally, in the middle of the 1974 season, Morton asked to be traded, and the Cowboys sent him to the Giants. The next two and one-half years were miserable, as Morton caught most of the blame for the poor performance of the talent-deficient Giants. However, the move to Denver rejuvenated Morton, giving him the chance to start again with a team loaded with talent. His arrival in Denver marked the beginning of a period of comparative stability at the quarterback position that was to endure—with brief interludes of upheaval—for at least two decades.[61]

Miller and Morton were the catalysts around which the Broncos jelled into a championship team. The head coach quickly won his players' respect and trust. One day in training camp Miller lined up against offensive tackle Claudie Minor to demonstrate a blocking technique. Miller collided head-on with the big tackle and opened a bloody gash over his own left eye. The distressed Minor begged Miller to have the cut treated, but the coach refused to leave the field until he was satisfied that Minor had mastered the technique. A coach who would butt heads with his players surely would also butt heads for them.[62]

The Broncos got off to a fast and powerful start in 1977, winning their first six games. Especially satisfying was their 30-7 victory over Oakland, highlighted by a faked field goal that ended with a touchdown pass from holder Norris Weese to place kicker Jim Turner. As the season progressed, Morton emerged as the leader of a more confident and productive offensive. He became particularly comfortable and adept at throwing to wide receiver Haven Moses, and the two were soon nicknamed the "M & M Connection."

Defensive coordinator Joe Collier's potent squad, now called the Orange Crush (much to the good fortune of a soft drink bottling company), remained the backbone of the Bronco attack. At the defense's core was the linebacking corps of Tom Jackson, Randy Gradishar, Bob Swenson, and Joe Rizzo. Their speed and instinct for finding the ball made them the bane of virtually every quarterback, runner, and receiver they faced.

When the regular season ended, the Broncos had lost only twice, in a rematch with the Raiders and to Craig Morton's former team, the Dallas Cowboys. They had won the AFC Western Division title and would play for the first time in the NFL playoffs.

In the first round of the playoffs, the Broncos defeated the Pittsburgh Steelers, 34-21, in an offensive and defensive show that featured pass interceptions by Tom Jackson on consecutive Steeler possessions. That win earned them a slot in the AFC title game, on New Year's Day 1978, against the defending Super Bowl champions, the Oakland Raiders. One Raider player vowed, "[A]fter we beat the Broncos, I'm going to get a can of orange pop, open it, and turn it upside down . . . slowly."[63]

Craig Morton spent most of the week before the game in a hospital bed, nursing a deeply bruised thigh muscle. The seriousness of Morton's injury was a closely held secret at Bronco headquarters, and by the weekend Miller and the team still did not know if he could play. On game day, Morton told Red Miller that he would try to play, but the coach had to tie the quarterback's shoes. Morton's throbbing thigh was too painful to take the stress of bending over.[64]

Morton did play. His offensive line protected him well, and he led the team to a 20-17 victory, which included a seventy-four-yard touchdown pass to Haven Moses.

The Broncos were champions of the AFC. They would travel to New Orleans to face the Dallas Cowboys in Super Bowl XII on January 15, 1978. Red Miller was named coach of the year in the NFL, and Craig Morton was honored as the league's comeback player.

Broncomania had been building throughout the season, and now it erupted in full force. After the AFC championship game, while the team celebrated in the locker room, fans stormed out of the stands at Mile High Stadium and tore down the goal posts. One section of goal post ended up decorating the bar at the Aeroplane Club and Café on West Alameda Avenue, carted there by two fans in a Volkswagen. Over the next two weeks Denver, and the rest of Colorado, almost literally turned orange. Merchants could not keep orange T-shirts, sweatshirts, jackets—anything orange—on the shelves. Ardent fans dyed their hair—and sometimes their pets—orange. Homes, businesses, and buses sported fresh coats of orange paint. Drinking Orange Crush soda pop became practically a civic duty, if thirsty fans could find any. Sales of the beverage doubled over the previous January. Business analysts guessed that sales of orange artifacts pumped $35 million, perhaps more, into Denver's economy.[65]

The Broncos and their fans also celebrated in song. A Denver attorney penned a tribute called "The Modern Battle of New Orleans," a takeoff of singer Johnny Horton's 1959 ballad about the War of 1812. The 1978 send-up predicted a Bronco victory in the forthcoming battle against Dallas. Meanwhile, Bronco fullback Jon Keyworth, who scored a touchdown against Oakland in the championship game, admonished teammates and fans in song to keep making miracles happen.[66]

What sportswriter Woodrow Paige later called "Orange Madness" was an infectious and generally harmless civic celebration of the Broncos' success. Before the team could leave for New Orleans, the city held a parade for them. More than one hundred thousand people lined the route. It took the caravan two and one-half hours to thread its way through the mob. Even people who had shown little or no interest in the team found themselves caught up in the frenzy, sporting orange clothing, and discussing the virtues of the running game versus the passing attack. A Denver psychiatrist diagnosed Broncomania, for most people, as "a healthy outlet for a whole variety of emotions that need to be channeled in some direction." He pointed out that "commitment, investment, fervor, and interest are always better than apathy, distance, and wanting to be involved." For Bronco fans, strong identification with the team "symbolizes what we would like to be in terms of power and success." In Broncomania, then, fans found individual and collective identity, validation, and empowerment. Unqualified support of the team made them and their city important.[67]

However, Broncomania also had substrata of personal and civic resentment and insecurity. Some people felt that Denver and its football team were not accorded the respect they deserved before, and even after, the Broncos won the AFC championship. Said one fan, "Denver hasn't received the recognition it deserved. People back East always thought this was a one-horse town. They have the feeling that this town is still the heart of cowboy country. But it's not. It's changed." Another fan declared that "any time you have national coverage you like to stand up and shout, 'Hey, we're a great city—eat your heart out, New York.' " Denver, to these fans, was a great city, and the Broncos proved it. However, they also were hurt that the rest of the world did not seem to fully accept the fact.[68]

Even Red Miller expressed resentment that the Broncos did not receive their due. As he prepared for the Super Bowl, Miller reflected on the season and observed that "nobody ever gave us any credit. After each victory, none of the rival coaches would compliment us. They'd come up after a game and say, 'Boy, we played a bad game today,' or 'Wow, we sure got a lot of work ahead of us.' It's funny in a way. All along you're doing the job, winning games week after week—and nobody seems to recognize it." That lack of respect was all too apparent once the team arrived in New Orleans. Miller recalled that, though the Dallas Cowboys had accommodations "in a plush downtown hotel . . . they put us in a dump clear out in the boonies. The chef quit on our first night in town, there were huge cockroaches in the rooms, [and] the elevator kept getting stuck."[69]

While the Broncos prepared for the game, tens of thousands of their fans poured into New Orleans intent on partying as intensely as possible right up until game time. The city's hospitality and souvenir industries expected a big week from the Broncos' fans, and they got it. They were, after all, "fresh money," as one bartender put it, unlike the more jaded Dallas fans who had been to the big game before.[70]

Finally, after two weeks of celebration, hoopla, and hype stretching from Denver to New Orleans, there was the game itself. The Broncos lost, 27–10. The Cowboys' defense harassed quarterback Craig Morton mercilessly. Morton threw four interceptions and, finally, in the third quarter gave way to backup Norris Weese. The Orange Crush defense also went flat, giving up two long touchdown passes and a scoring run.

As the game clock ran off the final minutes of the game, Bronco fans inside the Superdome began to chant, "We love our Broncos! We love our Broncos!" In the CBS broadcast booth, the announcers stopped talking long enough to let the international television audience listen to the chant. The fiercely loyal Bronco fans, they said, were the real story of Super Bowl XII. When the team arrived back in Denver, Miller told a crowd of fans at the airport, "[A]ll I can promise you is that we'll get better."[71]

Over the next three seasons the Broncos played well, but not better. They won the AFC West again in 1978, with a 10-6 record, but lost to the Pittsburgh Steelers in the first round of the playoffs. An identical regular season record in 1979 earned the Broncos a wild-card berth in the playoffs, though the San Diego Chargers won the division. Denver again lost in the first round of the playoffs, falling to Houston 13-7. In 1980 the team finished the season with eight wins and eight losses and failed to qualify for the playoffs.

Injuries to key players, including linebackers Bob Swenson and Joe Rizzo, were part of the problem in 1980, but Coach Miller's effort to replace Craig Morton with a younger quarterback also contributed to the slide. In 1979 Miller had given the starting job to Norris Weese, but Morton returned to the job midway through the season. Before the 1980 season, Miller sent backup Craig Penrose to the New York Jets in return for that team's backup quarterback, Matt Robinson. Robinson started the first four games of the season, throwing one touchdown pass and eight interceptions and losing three games. The durable and popular Morton returned to the starting lineup in game five, but could not salvage the season.[72]

Red Miller was still popular and well respected among the fans, the media, and his players after the 1980 season. Nevertheless, he never again took the field as head coach of the Denver Broncos.

TRIUMPH AND DISAPPOINTMENT: REEVES, ELWAY, AND BOWLEN

Late in February 1981, Gerald Phipps stunned Denver and the Bronco organization by selling the team to Vancouver, British Columbia, businessman Edgar F. Kaiser, Jr. Phipps indicated that he wanted to spend more of his time attending to his personal life, especially to his ailing wife. Kaiser, a grandson of the legendary industrialist Henry J. Kaiser, reportedly paid as much as $40 million for the franchise. The new owner added the Broncos to a business portfolio that included a Denver-based oil company. In a sense, then, the Broncos became linked to Colorado's booming energy industry and to the Canadian money that financed much of that boom.[73]

When he was introduced to the local media, Kaiser said, modestly, "I'm a new kid on the block and I have a lot to learn," and indicated that he planned no immediate or wholesale changes. However, as general manager Fred Gerhke said at the time of the sale, Kaiser appeared to be "a guy who will want to dive in and have a say about the way this football team is run."[74]

Gerhke was right. Only two weeks after taking over, Kaiser fired him and head coach Red Miller. Kaiser, who was only thirty-eight years old, wanted to bring in a younger management team. He was also not happy with the condition of the Broncos' organization, especially its failure to turn a profit in recent seasons, high players' salaries (reportedly among the highest in the league), Miller's perceived failure to put together a high-powered offense, and chaos in the front office. Kaiser may have believed, too, that Miller would not accept his new relationship, and diminished authority over the team, in the new regime. As one observer put it, Miller "might have come on too strong when talking to Kaiser."[75]

Red Miller remained in Denver and worked for a time for an energy company and, later, as a stockbroker. More than a year after his dismissal, sports columnist Bob Collins noted that Miller "still winces when he has to say the word Broncos." However, to his credit, Miller evidently passed on an opportunity to even the score by joining the staff of the Oakland Raiders. Miller returned to football, briefly, as head coach of the Denver Gold of the United States Football League. He was soon feuding openly with the Golds' owner, Ron Blanding, who fired him in May 1983, before the end of the team's first season.[76]

Edgar Kaiser hired Dallas Cowboy offensive coordinator Dan Reeves as his new head coach. Iron jawed, fiery tempered, and fiercely competitive, the thirty-eight-year-old Reeves became the youngest head coach in the league. Sometime after he got the job, Reeves spoke with Red Miller and told him that his success as head coach had opened the door to advancement for Reeves and other assistant coaches. NFL owners, Reeves recalled, "had been going after college coaches, but because of Red, they were going back to hiring assistants" like himself.[77]

Raised in Americus, Georgia (his thick Georgia-Texas accent bemused, and sometimes befuddled, the Denver media for years), Reeves played his college football at South Carolina and in 1965 joined the Cowboys as a running back. He had spent his entire professional football career, as both a player and a coach, with Dallas. In Super Bowl V, in 1971, against the Baltimore Colts, Reeves missed a pass from Craig Morton. A Baltimore player intercepted the ball, setting up the Colts' winning field goal. Morton caught most of the blame for the errant play, but Reeves always took responsibility himself. "Baltimore beat us," he wrote many years later, and "they did it on a field goal set up on an interception off my hands." Cowboy coach Tom Landry used Reeves as a player-coach from 1970 through 1972. Reeves left football for one season, but rejoined the Cowboys as an assistant coach in 1974. He became Landry's offensive coordinator in 1977.[78]

When he took over in Denver, Reeves kept his former Cowboy teammate as his starting quarterback for the first season. However, with a view to the future, he also moved to strengthen the quarterbacking corps by releasing Matt Robinson and trading for the San Francisco Forty-Niners' talented backup, Steve DeBerg.

The new head coach's first two seasons in Denver were a mixed bag. The 1981 team won ten games and lost six, but did not qualify for the playoffs. A two-month-long strike by NFL players shortened the 1982 season to only nine games, and the Broncos won only two of them in the first losing season since 1975.

During the 1983 off-season, Edgar Kaiser and Dan Reeves set the Denver Broncos' future for many years to come with a single trade. They acquired rookie quarterback John Elway.

John Elway seemed to have been born with a football in his hand. His grandfather Harry quarterbacked a semipro team in Altoona, Pennsylvania, and his father, Jack, had a long career as a high school and college coach. A talented baseball player, too, the Kansas City Royals drafted John out of high school. However, Elway chose college, and football, at Stanford. When he graduated, he held five NCAA and ten Pacific Ten Conference records and came in second to Herschel Walker in voting for the 1983 Heisman Trophy.[79]

Elway was the most talented player in the 1983 college draft and the certain number-one pick. The Baltimore Colts had the right to the first choice and intended to draft Elway. However, Elway made it clear that he would not play for the team's erratic owner, Robert Irsay. If Baltimore drafted him, he vowed, he would opt to play baseball for the New York Yankees and their erratic owner, George Steinbrenner, who now held the rights to Elway's baseball services.

The Colts' management finally concluded that Elway's threat was genuine and, deciding that something was better than nothing, began to take trade offers. The Broncos were overjoyed when the Colts accepted their offer of first-round draftee Chris Hinton, an offensive guard, along with backup quarterback Mark Herrman and a future first-round draft pick for Elway.

Elway immediately came under intense, withering media scrutiny. During training camp, for example, the *Denver Post* ran a daily column, "The Elway Watch," to keep fans updated on the young man's every move, including his diet.

Coach Reeves compounded the pressure on Elway by deciding to give him the starting job over veteran Steve DeBerg (who had moved into it following Craig Morton's retirement two years before). Elway had performed well in training camp and in preseason games, and Reeves believed that "in almost every statistic, he and Steve DeBerg were pretty even." Perhaps Reeves simply could not resist the temptation of using Elway's enormous talent as soon as possible. However, as Reeves later conceded, it was a mistake—Elway was not ready.[80]

In the first game of the season, against Pittsburgh, a ferocious Steeler pass rush kept Elway confused and off balance. He threw eight times for one completion and an interception. The next week in, of all places, Baltimore, enraged fans, who believed Elway had insulted them by refusing to play for the Colts, created such a din of boos and catcalls that no one on the field could hear anything. The noise made Baltimore's blitzing defense all the more effective. Reeves had to take Elway out of both games, and DeBerg came on to engineer wins.[81]

Elway started again the following week, in Mile High Stadium, against Philadelphia and threw his first NFL touchdown pass in a 13-10 loss. In week four the Los Angeles Raiders pounded the Broncos, 22-7. With that loss Reeves gave the starting job back to Steve DeBerg. DeBerg had a strong run, including four consecutive wins, until game ten, in Seattle, when a shoulder separation put him back on the bench. Elway was much improved, if still inexperienced, in his second round as the starter. He played well in a 22-20 loss to the Raiders in Los Angeles and, in an especially satisfying outing, led the Broncos to a rematch victory over the Colts at Mile High Stadium.[82]

The Broncos' 9-7 record in 1983 earned them a wild-card spot in that year's playoffs. However, the Seattle Seahawks ended their postseason quickly with a 31-7 thumping.

Following the 1983 season, Reeves put to rest any controversy over who would be the team's quarterback by trading Steve DeBerg to the Tampa Bay Buccaneers. Ready or not, John Elway now had the job permanently.

The Reeves-Elway relationship was strained from the beginning and sometimes erupted into open conflict during their decade together in Denver. However, they also combined to give the Broncos, their fans, and the NFL some of the greatest moments in football history, and led their team to three Super Bowl appearances.

The Broncos' second Super Bowl came after the 1986 season, and after the most thrilling AFC championship game ever. Following an 11-5 season, the Broncos defeated the New England Patriots in the first round of the playoffs to qualify for the championship game against the Cleveland Browns. More than seventy-nine thousand howling, barking, dog-biscuit-chewing Cleveland fans, who loved to call themselves the "Dawgs," jammed that city's Municipal Stadium on January 11, 1987, confident that they would cheer the Browns to victory. Denver led through most of the game, but late in the fourth quarter Cleveland quarterback Bernie Kosar threw the go-ahead touchdown pass to receiver Brian Brennan. On the ensuing kickoff, Bronco kick returner Ken Bell fell on the ball on Denver's two-yard line. Five minutes and forty-three seconds remained on the game clock, and Cleveland began making plans for the Super Bowl.

As the offense huddled in the Denver end zone, guard Keith Bishop told his teammates, "[W]e got these guys right where we want 'em." Many in the huddle laughed. Elway smiled and said, "[I]f you work hard, good things will happen." Fifteen plays later, Elway threaded a five-yard touchdown pass to receiver Mark Jackson. Place kicker Rich Karlis's extra-point kick sailed through the goal posts, and the score was tied with thirty-seven seconds left. Although over-time loomed, the Cleveland players and fans sensed that Elway, who by 1987 had established a reputation for engineering dramatic, come-from-behind wins, had wrested the game away from them. The Browns had the first overtime possession, but moved the ball only eight yards. Following Cleveland's punt, the Broncos ran nine plays, moving the ball sixty yards to the Cleveland fifteen-yard line. Rich Karlis nailed the winning field goal from there.[83]

Broncomania seemed to be alive and well nine years after the Broncos' first Super Bowl appearance. As many as twenty thousand fans greeted the team at the airport when they returned from Cleveland. Homeowners again painted their houses orange. Hospitals swaddled newborns in orange blankets, and Denver's B.M.H. synagogue ordered orange yarmulkes for its male members.[84]

Like Super Bowl XII, Super Bowl XXI ended in disappointment. The Broncos fell to the New York Giants, 39–20. Unlike the 1978 experience, however, just being in the Super Bowl this time was less of a consolation to Bronco fans and their city. As one fan in the stands at the Rose Bowl in Pasadena, California, put it, "Denver doesn't get no respect—ever. And this isn't gonna help." Nevertheless, one hundred thousand fans turned out for a Bronco homecoming parade.[85]

The 1987 season was a strange and strained time in the NFL, but for the Broncos it mirrored the 1986 experience. The Broncos compiled a record of ten wins, four losses, and one tie in the season shortened by a players' strike during which teams operated with replacement players. Denver went on to the playoffs and defeated Cleve-

land in the AFC championship game, played this time at Mile High
Stadium. Broncomania this time displayed some new wrinkles. In a
bid to win tickets to the Cleveland game, one Denver woman, wearing only a smile and a coat of blue paint, rode a horse along Denver's
Sixteenth Street Mall. One man offered to trade his "non-cooking and
non-shopping wife" for a pair of Super Bowl tickets. And when President Ronald Reagan appeared in Ohio wearing a Cleveland Browns
sweatshirt, Denver representative Patricia Schroeder sent him a pair of
Bronco boxer shorts with a note saying "real men wear Bronco shorts."[86]

On the Broncos' first offensive play in Super Bowl XXII, John
Elway threw a fifty-six-yard touchdown pass to wide receiver Ricky
Nattiel, and it seemed as if Denver was on its way to an easy victory
over the Washington Redskins. However, Washington rallied and scored
five unanswered touchdowns in the second quarter. The Broncos never
recovered and suffered one of the worst defeats in Super Bowl history, losing 42-10. Some fans reacted to the loss as a personal and civic
embarrassment. Said one man, "[T]he embarrassment is harder to
take than just losing the game." For better or for worse, the Broncos
and their fortunes remained a powerful collective experience. And
worse was still to come.[87]

The front page of the January 29, 1990, *Rocky Mountain News*
said it all: a photograph of a dejected John Elway below headlines
reading "NIGHTMARE" and "55-10 drubbing worst in Super Bowl
history." After sitting out the 1989 game, the Broncos returned for
their third Super Bowl appearance in four years. This time the opponent was the powerful San Francisco Forty-Niners, led by their spectacular quarterback, Joe Montana. In losing the game, the Broncos
joined the Minnesota Vikings as the only teams that had been to and
lost four Super Bowls. The thrashing was so thorough that the team
asked Denver city officials and fans to call off a planned welcoming
rally at the airport. Said John Elway to a teammate, "[T]hey'll never,
ever forgive me for this."[88]

A Metropolitan State College psychology professor viewed the
game as a reflection of Denver's and Colorado's economic state and
continued sense of cultural inferiority. Harvey Milkman said:

> The odyssey of the Broncos mirrors the plight of the
> Denver or Colorado resident. All dressed up and no

place to go. It really parallels the expectation of a
state that was built up and expected to be on top of
economic growth and development, and has really
fallen short in that endeavor. We feel a sense of un-
derdog, struggle, not being able to actualize our
dreams. That is symbolized in what the Broncos have
been doing.[89]

What is notable in this statement and in expressions of embarrassment at the Broncos' losses is the idea that the team and, by extension, Denver and Colorado somehow were second-rate. The Broncos had played in four of the twenty-four Super Bowl games and
three of the immediate past four. The team was, in fact, a powerful and
respected force in the National Football League both on and off the
field. Yet, because they had not won a Super Bowl, they—and Denver—somehow seemed second-rate.

Denver and Colorado in 1990 were far different places from the
insular city and state of 1960, the year of the Broncos' founding. The
population of the five metropolitan Denver counties had grown from
fewer than 1 million to almost 2 million. In 1990 the entire American
economy was flirting with recession. In Colorado, the energy boom
of the 1970s and 1980s had leveled off and began to fade. However, an
economic transition was also well under way, as the economy shifted
toward high-technology industries, especially computers and related
products, and communications. This economic change, along with
earthquakes in California, accounted for the more than doubling of
the Denver area's population. That population growth also helps explain not only the fans' reactions to the team's latest Super Bowl losses
but also, more fundamentally, their evolving relationship with the
team.[90]

The Denver area's population was not only larger but also more
diverse. With relatively smaller numbers of native and long-term residents, proportionately fewer people harbored the deep and enduring attachment to the Broncos that characterized Broncomania in the
1970s. Plenty of people were "actualizing" their dreams, but a Bronco
Super Bowl victory for many was not one of them. One businessman,
who makes his living selling Bronco merchandise, has observed,
shrewdly, that there are two types of Bronco fans: "People Who Wear

Orange" and "People Who Don't Wear Orange." The difference between them, he explained, is that the People Who Don't Wear Orange
tend to be interested, week to week, in the games, while the People
Who Wear Orange still make being a Bronco fan a central part of
their lives. They "come to the stadium real early; they come out to the
Saturday practices; they go to the stores when players make personal
appearances; they really get into it." There is another difference. The
People Who Don't Wear Orange tend to be the new Coloradans.
They are highly educated, professional, and middle and upper class.
For them, the Broncos and their fortunes are only one of a myriad of
interests and concerns. Ironically, as the 1990s wore on, winning these
fans', and many nonfans', support became increasingly important to
the Bronco management.[91]

This point does not mean that tens of thousands of people do
not live, breathe, and bleed orange and blue. At every home game,
people still paint their faces orange and strut around the stadium in
orange barrels and bunny suits. Living rooms all around Denver, the
rest of Colorado, and surrounding states become the sites of weekly
game-day parties. Broncomania still exists, but it is a more subdued
phenomenon.

The story of the Denver Broncos in the late 1980s was one of
triumph and disappointment. Presiding over this era, and since, was a
new owner, Patrick Bowlen. Edgar Kaiser had already sold a 40 percent interest in the franchise to two area businessmen, John Adams
and Tim Borden, when, in March 1984, he approached Bowlen with
an offer to sell him the remaining, controlling, interest. Bowlen, who
had a lifelong interest in owning a football team, had asked Kaiser to
"call me first if you ever plan on selling." When the call came, the new
owner recalled, "it took me about five seconds to decide what to do."
The reported $70 million deal made the Broncos the most valuable
franchise in the NFL. Bowlen and other family members bought out
the minority shareholders in 1985.[92]

Pat Bowlen was born in Prairie du Chien, Wisconsin, but is a
Canadian citizen whose home, until he bought the Broncos, was in
Edmonton, Alberta. Bowlen and his father had built their family fortune in the oil-drilling and land-development businesses. However,
sports was Pat's real passion. He played football, briefly, as a student at

the University of Oklahoma, where he earned business administration and law degrees. "I didn't have the size or talent to play football at Oklahoma," he recalled, "but I had the heart and desire. I really wanted to play football." Later, Bowlen took up the triathlon, a grueling sport that combines long-distance running, long-distance bicycling, and swimming. At age forty, he was ranked third in the world in his age category.[93]

In his first press conference, Bowlen assured Bronco staff and fans that he did not intend to shake things up and that his purchase of the team was more than a simple business move for him. Denver, he said, would be his full-time home, and he intended "to be here forever, if there is such a thing." Bowlen also demonstrated his sensitivity to the deep connection between the team and its fans. "I think I have a good idea of what the Broncos mean to the people of Colorado. I look at the team as sort of a public trust." Bowlen also indicated that he was willing to spend the money needed to get top-quality players. "To me," he said, "winning is more important than making money."[94]

Bowlen intended to be an active owner, but acknowledged that as "a rank rookie" he had much to learn. To that end, he quickly secured Dan Reeves's agreement to stay on at least through the 1984 season. Reeves, in fact, remained as Bowlen's head coach for nine years, and for most of those years the owner was content to allow Reeves to control the team. "I know enough about Dan Reeves that I would be very, very upset if he left," Bowlen said in 1984. "I would hope he would give me an opportunity to see what kind of owner I am." Two and one-half years later, as the Broncos prepared for their first championship season since 1977, Bowlen's enthusiasm for Dan Reeves was undiminished. "I'm going to consider myself a failure here," he told an interviewer, "if I'm unable to keep Dan Reeves for the length of his career."[95]

Three Super Bowl appearances testify to the success of the Reeves-Bowlen tandem, at least through the 1989 season. However, after the humiliating defeat in Super Bowl XXIV, Reeves came under mounting press and fan criticism for an offensive system many viewed as too conservative and predictable, for not fully using John Elway's talents, and for poor draft choices. Ultimately, however, it was Pat Bowlen's personal growth as owner that spelled the end of Reeves's tenure in Denver. By 1992 Bowlen believed that he had learned enough to assume a larger and more direct role in running the Broncos' football operations. That belief brought him into conflict with Reeves, who insisted that he had to have complete control. Bowlen sent a clear signal before the 1992 season when he did not extend Reeves's contract, which was in its final year. The Broncos won eight and lost eight that year, and immediately after the season Bowlen announced that Reeves would not return as head coach. In announcing his decision, Bowlen both acknowledged his debt to Reeves and made clear his reason for letting him go. "When I came into football, I didn't know whether it was pumped or stuffed," he said. "Now, I do. I had a very strong head coach and he ran the football operations and did a hell of a job. But the two of us can't live in the same house anymore."[96]

Dan Reeves's twelve years in Denver was one of the longest tenures in NFL history. Only nine other coaches stayed longer with teams. His teams won 60 percent of their games (110-73-1). He coached in thirteen playoff games and won seven. He lost three Super Bowls.[97]

Reeves quickly landed another head coaching job, with the New York Giants. After four unhappy seasons there, he moved on to the Atlanta Falcons in 1997. In a sense, his life and career had come full circle. Atlanta is only about 125 miles from his hometown of Americus, Georgia. The Falcons were a perennial doormat in the NFL, posting only three wins and thirteen losses in 1996, but Reeves quickly built them into a powerhouse. In his second season as head coach, Reeves's Falcons won fourteen games and lost only two in the regular season, the same record compiled by the Broncos that year, earning him NFL coach of the year honors. The Falcons went on to win the NFC championship and the right to play the Broncos in Super Bowl XXXIII in January 1999.[98]

Pat Bowlen wanted to replace Reeves with former offensive coordinator Mike Shanahan. Shanahan had already worked three times for the Broncos, as wide receivers' coach (1984) and as offensive coordinator (1985–1987 and 1989–1991). Between his tours as Denver's offensive coordinator, he spent the 1988 season and the first four games of 1989 as head coach of the Los Angeles Raiders. The Raiders' autocratic owner, Al Davis, not only did not give Shanahan control over player-personnel decisions but also did not allow him to choose all the members of his coaching staff. Shanahan's experience with the Raiders was, to say the least, unhappy, and everyone in the Broncos' organization was glad to get him back in 1989. However, Shanahan's relationship with Dan Reeves soured during the 1991 season. Reeves suspected that Shanahan and quarterback John Elway made decisions about offensive game plans without including or informing him. Reeves also suspected that Shanahan was sharing privileged information from coaches' meetings with Elway, who was his close friend.[99]

Bowlen and Shanahan failed to come to terms on issues of money, length of a contract, and control of personnel decisions. Instead, Bowlen gave the head coaching job to defensive coordinator Wade Phillips, who was happy to accept the owner's terms.[100]

A congenial bear of a man with a self-effacing sense of humor, Phillips brought impressive credentials to his new job. The son of a legendary coach, O. A. "Bum" Phillips, who had led the Houston Oilers and the New Orleans Saints, Wade Phillips had been an NFL assistant since 1976 with Houston, New Orleans, and Philadelphia. He joined the Broncos as defensive coordinator in 1989, and his defense, on the way to that year's AFC championship, gave up the fewest points in the league.[101]

Players, media, and fans almost unanimously welcomed the choice of Phillips as head coach. To many, it seemed as if the nice guy, the regular guy, finally got the grand prize. At Maxfield and Friends, a downtown Denver sports bar, patrons actually tabled their drinks to applaud the announcement. John Elway, who had to have been disappointed that his friend Mike Shanahan would not take over the team, nevertheless said that he believed "the best man got the job." Elway predicted that there would "be a lot closer relationship between the players and head coach," something he looked forward to. And, said Elway, Phillips would be "a players' coach. The players have a great deal of respect for him." A *Rocky Mountain News* sports columnist echoed Elway's comments, characterizing Phillips as the sort of coach "whose players will bust their guts for him."[102]

Phillips's 1993 team compiled a regular-season record of nine wins and seven losses: not a spectacular improvement over the previous year's record of eight and eight, but good enough to earn a wild-card spot in the playoffs. The Raiders eliminated the Broncos from the playoffs in the first round, clobbering them 42–24.

Bronco players and their owner exuded optimism and confidence as the team prepared for the 1994 season. John Elway said the team would be Super Bowl contenders that year, and owner Pat Bowlen predicted a perfect sixteen-win season. Coach Phillips joined the chorus, saying that the Bronco offense would be unstoppable.[103]

Unfortunately, the offense did not live up to its billing, while poor play by the defense became an even more glaring problem. The 1994 squad lost its first four games and finished the season with only seven wins. Especially worrisome was the team's poor performance at home. Since the 1970s, NFL teams had considered Mile High Stadium one of the toughest fields in the league. The Broncos had owned the best home-game record since 1977, but won only four games at home in 1994. By season's end, the enthusiasm that had greeted Wade Phillips's appointment as head coach two years before was gone. At the final home game in 1994, a loss to New Orleans, nearly eleven thousand ticket holders did not come to the stadium. Fans carrying signs reading "Wade Must Go" jeered the coach as he left the field.[104]

Pat Bowlen fired Wade Phillips and his entire coaching staff at the end of the 1994 season. The press discussed a number of reasons for Phillips's demise. The defense had been porous; the offense did not produce enough points; Phillips's easygoing relationship with the players had backfired; and the team lacked discipline. Bowlen put his reasons in simple terms: he had lost confidence in Phillips's ability to lead the Broncos to a championship. "This football team was certainly more talented than what we showed this year," Bowlen said.[105]

Phillips found work quickly as defensive coordinator of the Buffalo Bills. After three years in that position, he became the Bills' head coach.

Now Bowlen set out to hire the coach he had wanted in the first place, Mike Shanahan. Shanahan's current employer, the San Francisco Forty-Niners, wanted very much to keep him on their payroll and offered him a huge salary increase and promised that he would succeed head coach George Seifert when he left the job. This time, however, Bowlen met all of Shanahan's demands for salary, tenure, and complete control of player personnel. The seven-year contract the men signed in January 1995 included an unusual feature: barring Bowlen from firing Shanahan during the first three years.[106]

Shanahan set to work shopping the free-agent market to strengthen the team offensively and, especially, defensively. He also installed the so-called West Coast offense, which he had mastered at San Francisco, a complex scheme based on fast, closely timed passes. The results in Shanahan's first season were disappointing, as the Broncos finished with an eight-and-eight win-loss record. The highlight of the season for the team, the fans, and, especially, Mike Shanahan was a 27-0 shutout of the Raiders in October.

The 1996 season was the Broncos' best since 1984. Unfortunately, it ended in even worse fashion. Unbeaten at home, they compiled the best record in the NFL with thirteen wins and three losses and secured home-field advantage throughout the playoffs. Although some fans and sportswriters were concerned when they lost two of the three remaining regular-season games, more were ready to anoint them as the inevitable AFC, and probably Super Bowl, champions. Confidence ran high, among the team and its followers, as the Broncos prepared to meet the Jacksonville Jaguars on January 4, 1997.

The Jaguars were an expansion team stocked, for the most part, with castoffs from other NFL teams left unprotected in the expansion draft the year before. The Jacksonville team had won plaudits for making the playoffs in their second season, something no other team had ever accomplished, but they were considered at best a bump on the Broncos' road to a championship. On game day the betting line favored Denver by fourteen points.

The Broncos seemed to take command of the game early, scoring two touchdowns in the first quarter. Missed extra-point efforts left Denver with a 12-0 lead. However, Jacksonville would not concede defeat and, with quarterback Mark Brunell and running back Natrone Means leading the way, battled back. As the Jaguars counterattacked, the Broncos seemed to flounder both defensively and offensively. When the final gun sounded, Jacksonville had defeated the Broncos 30-27.

What had happened? Some sportswriters argued that the Broncos, having won the AFC West and securing home-field advantage by

December 1, 1996, had become complacent. "The edge the Broncos had from September to December dulled like a 50-cent steak knife," wrote *Rocky Mountain News* columnist Mark Wolf. Some, including the Jaguars' players, credited *Denver Post* sportswriter Woodrow Paige's insulting column about Jacksonville, the team, and the city, in which he dismissed the Jaguars, in near scatological language, as insignificant, for inspiring the underdogs to victory.[107]

What did the defeat mean for the Broncos and for Denver? Some writers and fans noted that the 1996 season had been John Elway's best, and possibly last, chance to win a Super Bowl. Would the Broncos ever again have such an opportunity with Elway in the lineup? Was Denver once again a laughingstock? The loss seemed to bring back all the old insecurities that Denver and Colorado tied to the Broncos. "Denver can now hear the country laughing behind its backs, chortling at the one NFL team that always invents a way [to] take a pratfall with millions of Americans watching," claimed *Denver Post* columnist Mark Kiszla.[108]

However, the laughing ended just a year later when the Broncos won what *Sports Illustrated* called "the greatest Super Bowl ever" (fig. 7-2). Defensive back Tyrone Braxton knew what the win meant for the Broncos and for Denver. "It means everything," he said, "not only for this team but for the past Broncos teams, all the way back to 1960. We're not a city of losers anymore."[109]

FAREWELL TO MILE HIGH STADIUM

When the Broncos suffered the humiliating playoff loss to Jacksonville in 1997, the *Denver Post*'s Mark Kiszla also saw a greater consequence for the Broncos and their future in the loss than not going to the Super Bowl. The Broncos, Kiszla wrote, had "only themselves to blame for stinking up old, rusty Mile High Stadium. Now, they might have to live in it long into the next century." The team's Super Bowl win a year later, however, made that prospect less likely. When the Broncos arrived back in Denver after the game, members of a crowd at the airport chanted, "Stadium, Stadium."[110]

By the mid-1990s, Pat Bowlen had decided that Mile High Stadium was too old and no longer a profitable-enough venue for NFL football. The Broncos' owner wanted a new stadium.

7-2. John Elway holds the Vince Lombardi Trophy after the Denver Broncos' victory over the Green Bay Packers in Super Bowl XXXII, 1998. Copyright 1998, Ryan McKee/Rich Clarkson and Associates.

When Bowlen bought the Broncos in 1984, he said that winning was more important to him than making money. Made, perhaps, in the flush of the moment, it was, nevertheless, a sincere statement. By the 1990s, however, the business environment of professional football had changed so dramatically that winning and making money could not be separated, even ideally.

Television revenue is the foundation of major league sports. Until the 1990s, television money, shared equally by the franchises, was sufficient to operate an NFL team, keep it competitive, and turn a profit. Good coaching, shrewd draft choices and trades, and team "chemistry" set the losers apart from the winners. However, the economics of NFL football changed dramatically in 1993 when antitrust suits brought by the players' union forced owners to accept free agency. In exchange for the owners' recognition of free agency, the players agreed to team salary caps, but contract and accounting sleights of hand, such as signing bonuses and deferred payments, made the salary caps almost meaningless. Players' salaries had already more than doubled since Bowlen took over the Broncos, but free agency triggered a rapid, upward spiral in salaries that sent owners scrambling for new sources of money to sign free agents who could now command multimillion-dollar contracts. That change made secondary sources of income, especially from stadiums—leases on luxury boxes, concessions, parking, and advertising—crucial in determining the competitive edge and the financial bottom line. In an analysis of professional sports economics in the 1990s, *Financial World* magazine stated the case simply and bluntly: "[N]o team that can't maximize its venue revenues . . . can expect to see its value grow significantly. The pecking order in professional sports today is determined primarily by venue revenues."[111]

Among all National Football League franchises, only the Detroit Lions and the Denver Broncos earned no money from stadium operations. Under the terms of a lease negotiated in 1977, when Gerald Phipps still ran the team, and amended in 1987, when Bowlen owned the Broncos, the City of Denver takes all revenue from parking, concessions, and advertising and pays operating and maintenance expenses. Bowlen's lease on Mile High Stadium was to expire at the end of 2018. The Broncos' only stadium income came from the sale of novelties. Bowlen had disposed of one source of stadium revenue in 1987 when he sold sixty newly built luxury skyboxes, installed by the team, in order to raise money to pay debts to former minority owners whom he and his family had bought out. Annual rent on the skyboxes was about $3 million. In contrast to the Broncos' situation, most NFL teams earned between $2 million and $15 million per year in stadium income, and one, the Dallas Cowboys, took in almost $40 million.[112]

Pat Bowlen set out not just to change his lease on Mile High Stadium but also to convince the people of the Denver metropolitan area to tax themselves to build a new stadium. Bowlen's bid for a new stadium was hardly unique in the NFL, or in professional sports in general. Franchise owners, in fact, had become adept in pressuring local and state governments and taxpayers to finance new stadiums and arenas. Beginning in the 1950s, baseball, basketball, and football teams pulled up stakes and moved to new cities in pursuit of bigger, better, and more profitable venues and markets. New York lost the Dodgers and the Giants to Los Angeles and San Francisco. The Minneapolis Lakers become the L.A. Lakers. The Los Angeles Chargers moved to San Diego, and Lamar Hunt's Dallas Texans became the Kansas City Chiefs.

In 1982 the Raiders' owner, Al Davis, took his team from Oakland to Los Angeles, primarily because that city offered him a better stadium deal. The other NFL owners tried to block the move, saying that he had to have their permission, which they were not about to grant. Davis, however, won an antitrust suit against the league that freed him, and all the other owners, to move their teams virtually at will. Davis eventually returned the Raiders to Oakland when that city bested L.A.'s deal with him.

Few other teams have followed Davis's example. The St. Louis Cardinals became the Phoenix Cardinals. The Baltimore Colts stole away from their longtime host city, literally under cover of night, and set up shop in Indianapolis. And, after a half century in Cleveland, the Browns accepted a lucrative offer to go to Baltimore, where they became the Ravens.

The mere threat, or perceived threat, of losing a major league team can send local and state officials scrambling to provide more money and better facilities for their cities' teams. Indiana University professor Mark Rosentraub describes the relationship between sports franchises and government as a system of welfare for the rich in which taxpayers subsidize the income and profits of wealthy owners and players. Rosentraub describes the process of wresting more money from the public as a kind of melodrama in five acts. In the first act, the team owner complains of being victimized by an unfair financial system in professional sports. Rising player salaries and other mounting costs make it more and more difficult to field a competitive team. However reluctantly, the owner suggests that the team might have to move if no solution to the income problem is found. The good news, however, is that a new stadium or arena will solve the whole problem. In the second act, the owner tells the fans that the effort to build a new facility and a better team is really for their benefit. After all, they deserve a championship team. In act three, the campaign for a new venue is portrayed as a needed economic and public relations boost for the entire city or region. The new stadium or arena will make the area look like a progressive, big-league city and attract new business and investment. In the fourth act, community political, business, and social leaders line up in support of the project. In the fifth and final act, the institutions of government and/or the voters agree to finance the project.[113]

The Broncos' campaign for a new stadium both followed and departed from this scenario in several ways. Bowlen argued that he had to have more income in order to sign the most talented free agents so that the Broncos could compete with dominant teams such as Dallas. He claimed that a new stadium would add to Denver's major league image and enhance the Broncos' economic impact in the region. "The facts are," he said, "that the people of Colorado need a new football stadium." He added that "the Broncos are willing to put in their fair share." Thus, according to Bowlen, the campaign for a new stadium was really for the community, and the Broncos were just doing their part.[114]

Bowlen never made an explicit threat to move the Broncos to another city if a new stadium was not built. Indeed, he declared that he would not move the team if the stadium campaign failed. Bowlen stated his belief that "sports teams, especially of the vintage that the

Broncos are, have a moral responsibility to their communities." The closest Bowlen came to threatening to leave Denver were oblique comments about the impossibility of the Broncos remaining financially viable over the long term if the team had to stay in Mile High Stadium. In October 1996, Bowlen did say that he might be forced to sell the team to an owner who would move it. In addition, some viewed the introduction of a new uniform in early 1997 as ominous. The new, highly stylized uniforms had less orange, more blue, and no "D" on the helmets to link them to Denver.[115]

A more explicit threat about the Broncos remaining in Denver came from NFL Commissioner Paul Tagliabue who, in March 1997, declared that without a new stadium the Broncos were destined to leave Denver. "How quickly does the economics of the Broncos franchise turn to the point where they can't compete [for] players?" he asked rhetorically. "I can't put a specific year on it," he said, "but it's going to happen. And you can't stay forever in a situation that's not viable."[116]

Public officials and new-stadium advocates did not react well to Tagliabue's graceless intervention in the discussion. Some were quick to challenge the commissioner and the league to weigh in financially if they really believed a new stadium was vital to the Broncos' future in Denver. Bronco owner Bowlen refrained from commenting on Tagliabue's statement.[117]

After an intensive lobbying effort, the Colorado legislature in May 1996 passed legislation to permit the voters in the six-county Denver metropolitan area to decide whether to pay a one-tenth of 1 percent sales tax to underwrite a new football stadium. If approved by the voters, money from the sales tax would be used to retire a maximum of $180 million in revenue bonds to be sold to raise cash for construction. The Broncos would pay for the balance of the estimated $260 million needed to build the stadium. A commission appointed by Governor Roy Romer and chaired by former Northglenn mayor, and former Bronco, Odell Barry would select a site for the stadium.[118]

The projected date for the referendum was November 1997. However, delays in the site-selection process and in organizing for the election forced its postponement. Meanwhile, cost estimates for the project rose to at least $350 million. By late 1997 team owner Pat Bowlen demanded that the state legislature amend the stadium referendum law to increase the public's share in financing the stadium. As the Broncos' 1997 playoff campaign progressed, Bowlen renewed his claim that without a new stadium he would be forced to sell the team to a new owner who almost certainly would take it to another city. Stadium opponents dismissed Bowlen's demands, and his threat to sell the team, as "ridiculous" and as "posturing," but could not muster the votes to block a new stadium bill, especially after the Broncos' playoff and Super Bowl successes (polls after the Super Bowl for the first time showed majorities in favor of the new stadium). In April 1998 the legislature voted to increase the public share of the new stadium's cost to $266 million with the team responsible for the balance. Metropolitan Denver voters would decide the issue in November 1998.[119]

Although the Broncos' campaign for a new stadium included the themes of community image and economic growth, Bowlen based his case most squarely on the claim that half-century-old Mile High Stadium had outlived it usefulness. Bowlen argued that the stadium was a "decaying structure" that would not "last very much longer unless the city is prepared to spend an awful lot of money." The facility, he claimed, was becoming unsafe, and he predicted that eventually it would be "condemned by the city's own building inspectors." Building a new stadium was simply good, smart business. Bowlen acknowledged that Denver could prop up Mile High Stadium by spending $9 million or $10 million per year, but for the same money "you can get a stadium pretty close to something that was like Joe Robbie Stadium," a new, state-of-the-art facility in Miami.[120]

Contrary to the Broncos' claims, an engineering study of Mile High Stadium in 1994 found the facility structurally sound, but in need of mainly cosmetic repairs. The study estimated that operating and maintaining the stadium until 2024, six years beyond the Broncos' lease, would cost $264 million. Since the estimated price tag for a new stadium was $260 million, the study seemed, at first glance, to support the team's case that a new structure could be built for the same money maintaining Mile High Stadium would cost. However, the report noted that $150 million of the projected $264 million would be for normal maintenance and operations, while $114 million would be needed for major repairs and improvements. Although a new structure could be presumed to be more efficient, many of the normal operating costs anticipated in the projected $150 million for Mile High Stadium would also be incurred at a new stadium. Unless the Broncos' lease arrangements at the new facility required the team to pay those costs, they would have to be added to the public's share. In that case, the actual cost to taxpayers for building and operating the stadium might be more than $300 million.[121]

Selling the stadium project to the public would be a daunting task for the Broncos. More than a year before the prospective referendum, a *Rocky Mountain News* poll found that 63 percent of Denver-area voters opposed the proposed sales tax, while 62 percent agreed with the proposition that owners, players, and fans should bear the costs of building new sports facilities. Some opponents zeroed in on the perception that a new stadium would amount to a massive public subsidy for the already wealthy in an era when government at all levels was under pressure to cut taxes and budgets. *Rocky Mountain News* columnist Gene Amole observed that many taxpayers "rarely have enough money to attend the games themselves. We hear about limiting welfare for the poor. How about limiting welfare for the rich, too?" In a similar vein, Denver City Council member Dennis Gallagher found it "ironic to devote $180 million in tax revenue to millionaires of society while we lift a sneering lip to the welfare mother in the food line."[122]

Even a member of the Metropolitan Football Stadium District board worried about that perception. Boulder County's representative, former federal judge Jim Carrigan, who supported building a new stadium, or renovating Mile High Stadium, said in July 1997 that the proposed sales tax to finance the new structure was a "classic case of corporate welfare." Carrigan added that, in his view, it was "fundamentally immoral to force the poor to pay for a rich man's toys." Instead of imposing a sales tax, Carrigan favored imposing a seat tax on the new stadium's users. Requiring a consumer "to pay a sales tax when she buys a hammer or clothes for her children so that somebody doesn't have to pay a seat tax is wrong," he said, and warned that "voters will reject this if the tax is not fair."[123]

Odell Barry, chairman of the separate stadium site-selection committee, dismissed Judge Carrigan's concerns. "I have a hard time listening to that nonsense. I don't buy into those comments," the former Bronco said. Implying that government subsidies were indispensable for economic growth, Barry asked, "[W]hat would we have without the so-called corporate welfare? We wouldn't have gas stations or factories."[124]

Although professional sports receives massive subsidies from government, studies have shown that sports franchises and facilities have only minimal economic impact on a city or region. Construction of a new stadium would have a significant, but short-term, impact on the construction industry. However, long-term employment would be small, since most stadium jobs would be low-paying seasonal and part-time. Nowhere in the United States do sports franchises account for so much as 1 percent of local employment or payrolls. Indirect economic benefits, in the form of spending in restaurants and hotels, and for merchandise, are also small. In fact, sports tend to siphon consumers' discretionary spending away from other entertainment and recreation attractions. The greatest positive impacts on consumer spending tend to occur when franchises locate in locales without major entertainment and recreational resources. That scenario, of course, would not be the case in Denver. Indeed, consumer spending for Bronco games and related activities would probably change little. The major difference would be who pocketed the money.[125]

Of course, supporters of a new football stadium pointed to a different, local model to make the case that the proposed facility would have a positive economic impact. Construction of Coors Field, a new major league baseball stadium, boosted a major redevelopment, already under way, of Denver's dilapidated lower downtown area. Land values skyrocketed, historic old buildings found new uses as restaurants, brew pubs, residences, shops, and galleries. The neighborhood came back to life, with year-round residents and activity. The Broncos believed that their proposed new stadium could have a similar effect on the area where it would be located.

In 1995 Pat Bowlen observed that Denver had "grown up from a relatively small Midwestern city to a much more sophisticated city than it was even when I came in 1984." Therein lay the Broncos' problem, for though the team still enjoyed enormous popular support, though it remained a potent symbol of civic identity and pride, the population of the Denver area and Colorado was larger, more diverse, and more sophisticated. Indeed, *Denver Post* columnist Mark Kiszla dismissed hardcore Bronco fans as "nitwits who bleed orange," a caricature unthinkable ten years before. Clearly, the future of the stadium proposal, the future of the Broncos, and the future of Broncomania lay in the hands of the People Who Don't Wear Orange.[126]

About 57 percent of the voters, including People Who Don't Wear Orange, were in a generous mood when they finally went to the polls on November 3, 1998. The prostadium campaign, aided by a strong economy, and a Bronco team that remained undefeated halfway through the season, overwhelmed stadium opponents. The feeble, poorly organized, and underfinanced opposition had only $23,000 to spend compared to the $1.4 million ($650,000 contributed by Pat Bowlen) spent in support of the stadium initiative.[127]

Bowlen, the Broncos, and their fans had more to celebrate. After much speculation about his possible retirement, John Elway decided to return for the 1998 season in hopes of repeating the Broncos' Super Bowl championship. The team won thirteen straight games, prompting hopes of an undefeated season, before losing consecutive games to the New York Giants and the Miami Dolphins, and finished with fourteen wins and only those two losses. Running back Terrell Davis amassed 2,007 yards rushing, joining Eric Dickerson, Barry Sanders, and O. J. Simpson in gaining more than 2,000 yards in a season. Davis's feat made him the NFL's most valuable player for the year. John Elway joined Miami's Dan Marino as the only quarterbacks to pass for more than 50,000 yards in their careers.[128]

Even more satisfying, however, were playoff victories over the Miami Dolphins and the New York Jets, which earned the Broncos the chance to win a second consecutive Super Bowl. The fact that the Broncos' opponents in Super Bowl XXXIII would be Dan Reeves and the Atlanta Falcons gave the game an added, ironic twist. The press inevitably focused on the story of Reeves's past with the Broncos, including his firing. Reeves fueled the story by renewing claims that Mike Shanahan, as a Bronco assistant, had conspired with John Elway to undermine his authority as Denver's head coach. Another interesting story, little noted in the buildup to the game, was the presence on the Atlanta roster of forty-five-year-old backup quarterback Steve DeBerg, the man John Elway displaced in Denver.[129]

When the Broncos and the Falcons finally met at Miami's Pro Player Stadium on January 31, 1999, John Elway helped break Dan Reeves's heart for the fourth time in a Super Bowl. The Falcons took the opening kickoff and drove down the field efficiently, capping the drive with a field goal. They never led the game again. The Broncos won 34-19, behind John Elway's strong passing performance (eighteen completions in twenty-nine attempts for 336 yards), which made him the game's most valuable player.[130]

Broncomania was still visible in 1999, but comparatively subdued this time around. To be sure, area newspapers and television stations promoted the Super Bowl story extensively, and fans' cars sported Bronco flags and bumper stickers, but two measures of fan frenzy in 1999 were noticeably smaller than in 1998. One was the relative scarcity of souvenir stands around the Denver area. In 1998 it seemed as if every major intersection and parking lot sprouted a stand selling commemorative sweatshirts, pennants, and other trinkets. In 1999, though, the population of souvenir vendors seemed to decline significantly. Even more revealing was the size of the crowd on the parade route and at Civic Center plaza for the official homecoming celebration. In 1998 some 600,000 people jammed the celebration, but in 1999 the crowd was estimated at "only" 375,000. One thing, though, had not changed. As had happened in 1998, mobs of thugs, mostly young and usually inebriated, used the Broncos' Super Bowl victory as an excuse to riot in downtown Denver, breaking windows and looting stores, setting bonfires in the streets, overturning cars, and embarrassing the decent, civilized people of Denver.[131]

That unfortunate exception notwithstanding, Broncomania remained a significant feature of Denver's and Colorado's civic identity. That the crowds were smaller and the hoopla more restrained may be a result of fans getting used to winning championships. Still, the day after Super Bowl XXXIII, fans, players, and coaches talked about a "three-peat," a prospect many hoped might convince John Elway to put off retirement for yet another year. Indeed, Elway told the crowd at Civic Center plaza that a "three-peat does sound interesting."[132] However, in May 1999 Elway announced his retirement. More than any individual, John Elway, recognized on sight around the world, had become the face not only of professional sports in Colorado, but of Colorado itself.

Even without Elway, the Broncos are, and likely will long remain, the center of gravity of professional sports in Denver, but they are not the only game in town. Major league baseball, basketball, and a Stanley Cup champion hockey team all claim their parts of the Denver and regional professional sports market, and each tells its own important stories about sports and about Colorado.

"Fellas, We Got No Shot"
Amateur and Professional Basketball in Colorado

In his memoirs, published in 1941, University of Kansas professor James Naismith, a frequent visitor to Colorado, recalled an excursion to the Royal Gorge bridge, which spans the Arkansas River near Cañon City. At the south end of the bridge, Naismith and his party found the deserted camp once occupied by the bridge's construction crew. "There was little to tell of the number of men and boys who had spent many months playing and working on this spot," Naismith recalled, but he was delighted to find there two basketball backstops. "The goals had been removed, and they stood alone against the dark pines, a mute reminder of the activity that had once been a part of the camp life."[1]

Naismith reflected that "no man can derive more pleasure from money or power than I do from seeing a pair of basketball goals in some out of the way place." Indeed, basketball was Naismith's game; he invented it, and he brought it to Colorado. In the century since James Naismith came to Colorado, basketball has grown from a popular recreational activity to an organized amateur and collegiate game, to a multimillion-dollar corporate enterprise. Along the way, the game has mirrored important changes in American society, culture, and business.[2]

Beginnings

A native of Ontario, Canada, James Naismith was a deeply religious man. As he reached adulthood, Naismith found himself caught up in a powerful new evangelical movement, Muscular Christianity. A response to the rapid industrialization and urbanization transforming Western Europe and North America in the late nineteenth century, Muscular Christianity presented itself as an antidote to the debilitating physical and moral consequences of that change. Harking back to the classical Greeks, Muscular Christians argued that a healthy and vigorous body could help the individual become spiritually and morally strong. By the 1890s the Young Men's Christian Association (YMCA) was the institutional core of Muscular Christianity, with nearly a quarter of a million, mostly middle-class, members.[3]

In 1890, after graduation from Montreal's McGill University, Naismith enrolled in the YMCA's Training School, in Springfield, Massachusetts. Among his fellow students was future football coaching great Amos Alonzo Stagg. The school's faculty included Luther Halsey Gulick, perhaps the most important spokesman for Muscular Christianity and physical education for children.

In 1891 Naismith took a seminar with Gulick and drew the assignment to devise a new game that could be played indoors. YMCA instructors found that attendance and enthusiasm dropped off markedly in the winter months as participants grew bored with the standard athletic fare of the cold weather months: repetitive gymnastics and calisthenics. Some new sport—fast, varied, and challenging— was needed.

Naismith first tried to adapt outdoor games, such as football, rugby, soccer, even baseball, but quickly realized that they did not translate well to the confines and hard floor of the gymnasium. With these failures, Naismith refined the criteria for a new game. It would be a team ball game, permitting a large number of players; the game's object would be to move the ball through a goal; it would be fast paced, but not rough or violent. As he thought through these criteria, Naismith remembered a childhood game called "Duck on the Rock," which combined elements of target throwing and tag. He recalled that the best players threw their stones toward the target in an arc, suggesting to him the goal in his new game should be set on a horizontal plane. Elevating the goal above the players' heads would keep teams from preventing goals by simply blocking the target. Since the game was to be played in a gymnasium, he would place a goal at each

8-1. James Naismith, shown here with his wife in the 1930s, invented basketball in 1891 at the YMCA's Training School in Springfield, Massachusetts, where he was a student. After graduation, Naismith came to Denver to attend medical school and work at the YMCA. Courtesy, YMCA of the USA Archives, University of Minnesota Libraries.

end, one for each team. With these elements, Naismith's new game took shape in his mind.

Naismith asked the school custodian for two boxes, about eighteen inches square, to use as goals. The custodian had no boxes, but offered two old peach baskets instead. Naismith nailed the baskets to the lower rail of the gym's balcony and, on December 21, 1891, brought in a class of young men (fig. 8-1). Suspicious that they were about to be guinea pigs in yet another boring experiment, the men listened as Naismith read a list of thirteen rules that he had penned the night before. A goal would be scored "when the ball is thrown or batted from the grounds and stays there" (the idea of removing the bottoms from the baskets occurred only after players grew weary of climbing into the balcony after each score to retrieve the ball). The ball could be advanced in any direction, but only by passing it or batting it with an open hand. Thus, players not only could not hit the ball with their fists but also, more important, could not run with it. Instead, they had to pass the ball from the spot at which they caught it. Fouls consisted of "shouldering, holding, pushing, tripping, or striking" other players and were penalized with temporary disqualification, or ejection from the game in severe cases. A ball passed or knocked out of bounds would be thrown back into play by the person who touched it first. The game would consist of two fifteen-minute periods, with victory going to the team scoring the most points. In addition to these rules, Naismith also decreed that the game would begin with a center jump for the ball by one player from each team. The center jump was also to be used to restart play after a goal.[4]

The new game was an immediate hit with Naismith's students and spread quickly through the YMCA system and beyond to playgrounds, schools, and colleges across the country. As basketball gained in popularity, it also evolved into the game modern fans would recognize. Dribbling, which effectively permits players to run with the ball, became standard by 1900. Foul shots, the shot clock, and elimination of the center jump after each goal evolved over the succeeding decades. In Naismith's first game at Springfield, eighteen players formed two teams of nine each. Gradually, however, experience showed that five players per team was best. At first the YMCA and Luther Gulick tried to act as a central rule-making authority for the game, but Gulick soon handed the task over to the more experienced Amateur Athletic Union (AAU). By 1909 another group, the National Collegiate Athletic Association (NCAA), claimed authority over the collegiate game. However, James Naismith presided over basketball and its rules as a kind of godfather until his death in 1939.

Naismith stayed on at Springfield as an instructor until 1895 when he decided to pursue a new career. His work in physical education had grown into a broader interest in medicine, and Naismith thus determined to become a physician. However, with a wife and young child in tow, he would also have to work while attending medical school. Two opportunities in Denver solved Naismith's problems. He won admission to the Gross Medical School (which later merged with the University of Colorado), and the Denver YMCA hired him as its physical education director. Naismith earned his medical degree in 1898 and in that year moved on to the University of Kansas, first as chaplain and later as a professor of physical education. Naismith's classmate at Springfield, Amos Alonzo Stagg, recommended him for the Kansas chaplaincy, describing him as the "inventor of basket-ball [*sic*], medical doctor, Presbyterian minister, teetotaler, all-around athlete, non-smoker, and owner of [a] vocabulary without cuss words."[5]

During his stay in Denver, Naismith organized YMCA-sponsored basketball teams and tournaments and watched his game take root in local high schools and colleges. He recalled having to be organizer, referee, and coach all at once. "As the high schools did not have a gymnasium, the games of their league were played in the 'Y' gym," located in the Florence Building at Eighteenth and Champa Streets. "There were few officials at that time, and as a result I did much of this work. Many of the high-school players were also students in my YMCA classes, and usually after a game the boys would ask me for information about their technique or play." In his memoirs, Naismith claimed that Denver's high school basketball league was the first such association he knew of.[6]

Denver's young women took to basketball as quickly as the city's young men. In February 1896, Naismith attended an exhibition of calisthenics and basketball at Wolfe Hall, a private school for girls. Before the game Naismith "read a short paper showing the great advance made in athletics by women, and how opinions as to what is 'womanly' have altered during the past few years." Naismith, noted the *Rocky Mountain News,* "evidently believes in the new woman, for he says the ideal woman is possessed of a sound mind, in a sound body, and is able to take care of herself."[7]

By the early twentieth century, YMCA and other amateur teams could be found in Boulder, Greeley, Colorado Springs, and Pueblo, as well as in Denver. Competition among the cities was spirited and sometimes even rowdy. One of a team captain's most important jobs was making sure that the locker room windows were unlocked in case players and referees needed to make a hasty escape from aroused fans and opponents after a game.[8]

The Denver YMCA's Victors seem to have been Colorado's first championship-caliber team. The Victors played between 1900 and 1904 and included "Big Harry" Gebhardt, whom a teammate described as "a human giant, weighing well over 200 pounds and standing six and a half feet without his shoes." In 1904 the Victors traveled to the World's Fair in St. Louis and there defeated a Chicago team that claimed to be national champions.[9]

By the 1920s, high school teams moved to the fore in Colorado basketball. The Windsor Wizards represented Colorado in the National High School Tournament in Chicago in 1923 and 1924, winning the national title in 1924. Five years later a team from tiny Joes, Colorado, reached the semifinals in the national tournament.[10]

College basketball came into its own in Colorado in the 1940s. The University of Colorado team won the National Invitational Tournament (NIT), at New York's Madison Square Garden, in 1940. In 1949 Coach Larry Varnell's Regis College squad reached the finals of the National Association of Intercollegiate Basketball (NAIB) tournament before losing to Hamline, but came back to Denver to win the National Catholic Invitational Tournament.[11]

No viable professional league emerged before the mid-twentieth century to challenge high school, collegiate, and amateur basketball. Although tournaments such as the NIT and the NAIB drew large crowds and much press attention, the Amateur Athletic Union's annual tournament became the center of gravity of basketball in the United States.

The Amateur Athletic Union Tournament

Beginning in 1897, the AAU tournament brought together the finest basketball teams in the country, usually sponsored by businesses or local athletic clubs, to compete for a championship that for decades was widely considered to be the national championship. Not until the 1960s did collegiate and professional titles eclipse the AAU prize.

By the 1920s, teams from the Missouri Valley region dominated the AAU competition, and in the years from 1921 through 1934 teams from Missouri, Oklahoma, and Kansas won all but one of the tournaments. Because of that region's domination of the tournament, Kansas City played host to the event in those years. However, by the mid-1930s declining attendance created the opportunity to lure the tournament away from Kansas City. In 1935 a campaign led by the *Denver Post* and William N. Haraway, a regional executive of the Piggly Wiggly–Safeway stores, brought the AAU tournament to Denver where it remained, with the exception of one year, through 1968.[12]

Haraway and Piggly Wiggly–Safeway sponsored Colorado's best basketball team, the Piggly Wigglys (also referred to as the Safeways, the Grocers, and the Pigs). Anchoring the team were "Jumping Jack" McCracken, who had played high school and college ball in Oklahoma and Missouri under coaching great Henry Iba, and Bob "Ace" Gruenig, a high school and AAU veteran from Chicago whom Haraway had lured away from the Lifshultz Fast Freight team.[13]

In March 1935 some thirty-three thousand fans—enough to make the event profitable—turned out in hopes of watching the Piggly Wiggly team win the tournament. However, the Pigs lost their quarterfinal match to the Southern Kansas Stage Lines team from Kansas City. Denver waited until 1937 for the first of its three AAU championships, which came in a win over Oklahoma's Phillips 66 team. The grocery chain dropped its sponsorship of the team after the 1938 tournament, but several other businesses—including the Public Service Company of Colorado, the Brown Palace Hotel, a car dealer, and an insurance company—stepped in. The team, renamed the Denver Nuggets (the first of several appearances of that name), went on to win the 1939 tournament with Jumping Jack McCracken as player-coach, again defeating Phillips 66. Colorado's third AAU championship came in 1942 when the team, now sponsored by the American Legion and playing as the Denver Legion, once more defeated the Phillips 66 team.[14]

The period from 1937 through 1948 was the best for Denver's AAU basketball teams. The Pigs/Nuggets/Legion reached the finals eight times. Ace Gruenig and Jumping Jack McCracken made the AAU's All-America list several times (fig. 8-2). The team's second-place finish in 1948 earned it a spot in that year's Olympic qualifying tournament in New York City. Another loss to Phillips in that

8-2. The 1943 Denver Nuggets included "Jumping Jack" McCracken (back row, left) and Bob "Ace" Gruenig (back row, second from left), who starred in AAU basketball tournaments beginning in 1935. Courtesy, Colorado Historical Society, F 37687.

tournament meant that only one Denver player, Vince Boryla, a Notre Dame veteran who came to Denver in 1947, made the Olympic team.[15]

Colorado teams never again dominated the AAU tournament as they had in the late 1930s and the 1940s. The Poudre Valley Creamery team, staffed with Colorado A&M players, made a Cinderella appearance in the 1951 semifinals, and the Luckett-Nix Clippers, a team of CU seniors, made the finals in 1955, losing to the Peoria Caterpillars. The Denver-Chicago Truckers reached the finals in 1958, 1961, and 1962. The 1961 Truckers were notable because they included the first African Americans on a Denver AAU team, Marquette University's Walter Mangham and Michigan State's Horace Walker. In addition, Maceo Brodnax, Sr., a veteran of a Denver Negro league baseball team, the White Elephants, managed Colorado's last AAU finals team.[16]

Interest in amateur basketball and the AAU tournament faded in the 1960s as competition for Colorado sports fans' attention and money became too strong to sustain amateur basketball. The Denver Broncos had established themselves as regional sports favorites, and college football and basketball also drew large crowds. However, it was the development of major league professional basketball that spelled the amateur game's doom. In March 1968, when the AAU held its last tournament in Colorado, the Denver Rockets, of the American Basketball Association, were playing their first season. By the end of that 1967–1968 season, more than 168,000 fans attended Rockets games. After the 1968 tournament, when only 10,000 fans attended, the AAU left Denver for Macon, Georgia.[17]

Professional Basketball Comes to Colorado—Briefly

The roots of organized professional basketball lie in the ethnic communities of the industrial Northeast. Progressive-era reformers, including settlement-house workers, adapted the values of Muscular Christianity to the problems of the burgeoning industrial city. Organized sports became a tool for improving the moral tone of low-income neighborhoods, and local basketball teams such as the South Philadelphia Hebrew All-Stars grew into objects of community pride and an important part of neighborhood social life. A spirited game pitting rival teams, playing for part of the gate, often preceded a neighborhood dance or some other gathering. Some teams added to their income by barnstorming the region. Occasionally, a barnstorming team ventured into other parts of the country. New York's original Celtics, for example, toured the South and the Midwest. In New York City the Harlem Renaissance and the Harlem Globetrotters established an African American presence in the game.[18]

Professional-league play was a hit and, mostly, miss proposition until the 1930s and 1940s. The first league appeared in the Philadelphia–Trenton area in the late 1890s. Strictly a local loop, it folded quickly, setting a pattern that plagued most other leagues in the early decades of the twentieth century. Finally, in 1937, a new National Basketball League (NBL) appeared. Anchored in industrial towns and cities of the Midwest, the NBL was an outgrowth of factory and community teams such as those sponsored by the Goodyear and

Firestone rubber companies. In its first decade the NBL struggled just to survive. Most of its teams played in small to medium-size cities such as Dayton, Syracuse, and Oshkosh (the Chicago Bruins were an exception), and, with a limited fan base, they could not offer salaries high enough to attract top college talent. As it did with all sports, World War II further restricted the available talent pool. However, the war ultimately helped professional basketball grow into a viable enterprise. Defense-plant and service teams introduced basketball to hundreds of thousands of new fans and players, and their games drew large, appreciative crowds. After the war, the NBL enjoyed greater success, moving into new towns and, especially, signing top-rated college players.[19]

Denver was one of the new towns added to the NBL in the postwar years. Following the 1947–1948 season, Ike Duffy, owner of the Anderson, Indiana, Packers, invited the Denver Nuggets to join the NBL. Nugget manager Hal Davis quickly accepted, though the league had to waive its franchise fee for the cash-poor team. Davis hired Ralph Bishop, who played at the University of Washington and on the 1936 Olympic team, as coach. Players on the 1948–1949 team included Jimmy Darden, from the University of Wyoming; Leonard Alterman, from the University of Denver; Guy Mitchell, from Pittsburgh State College in Kansas; Bob Doll from CU; and Arizona's Morris "Mo" Udall, a law school graduate and future member of the United States Congress, who also served as the team's unofficial lawyer. At midseason, Davis, hoping to strengthen the team, both on the court and with fans, added Ace Gruenig to the lineup.[20]

Davis tried to finance the Nuggets by selling stock in the franchise, but found no buyers. Without a large bank account, the team had to operate, and live, off receipts, leaving little money for salaries. Coach Bishop held down a second job to support himself. When Bishop could not get time off to travel with the team, Gruenig took over the coaching chores. Most of the players agreed to accept stock in the team in lieu of paychecks. When Gruenig joined the team at midseason, the player-stockholders agreed to pay him three thousand dollars in cash, making him the only Nugget to take home more than token earnings that year.[21]

The professional Nuggets played their first home game on November 15, 1948, at the City Auditorium. A crowd of 1,240 watched them lose 60–50 to the Oshkosh All-Stars, led by Alex Hannum, who later coached another Denver basketball team. Because plays, symphonies, and AAU basketball caused scheduling difficulties for Nugget games, the team looked for another home court. Hal Davis learned that the federal government had decided to scrap some aviation hangars at the Farragut Naval Training Base in Idaho, where Davis had served during World War II. Davis knew that the University of Denver wanted to build a new field house and suggested that one of the hangars would serve that purpose well. With the help of Colorado U.S. senator Edwin Johnson, one of the structures was dismantled, shipped to Colorado, and reassembled on the DU campus. The building was up and a basketball arena installed in time for the Nuggets to play there during the 1948–1949 season.[22]

Little else went well for the Nuggets that season. Although the team flew on an airplane provided by Continental Airlines for only fifteen hundred dollars for the season, lodging was a major problem. Davis recalled that "we went from town to town with our cut of the gate receipts from the previous night paying the next day's expenses." Sometimes that was not enough, and the team skipped out on hotel bills. On a trip to Davenport, Iowa, the local sheriff sat on the Nugget bench to make sure he collected the team's earnings to pay a hotel bill from a previous visit.[23]

The Nuggets worked and played hard, but they were as poor in talent as they were financially. Indeed, Hal Davis conceded that "the fact that we lost kept a lot of fans away." The team finished the season at the bottom of the NBL's Western Division with a record of only eighteen wins and forty-four losses.[24]

By the time the Nuggets began playing as professionals, the NBL's survival, and basketball's growing popularity, had prompted the appearance of a rival league. In June 1946 a group of arena owners led by Ned Irish, founder of college basketball's National Invitational Tournament, organized the Basketball Association of America (BAA). In contrast to the NBL, whose teams and players had strong ties to their communities, the BAA and its teams began strictly as a moneymaking venture. Ten of the eleven team owners also owned hockey teams and wanted to use basketball to fill their arenas more afternoons and evenings. Furthermore, the BAA teams were in major cities, including New York, Washington, Detroit, Philadelphia, Boston, St. Louis, and Cleveland, where they could draw on large fan bases.[25]

Although the BAA was better financed and commanded a larger fan base, its teams had difficulty signing the most talented college players, most of whom opted for the NBL. Thus, though the BAA had the fans, the NBL had the players, and both leagues were hemorrhaging money. Finally, after the 1948–1949 season, negotiations between the leagues produced a merger of seven NBL teams, including the Nuggets, and ten BAA teams to form the National Basketball Association (NBA).

Unfortunately, the merger did not improve the Nuggets' basketball or financial fortunes. Ned Irish, the ruler of Madison Square Garden, insisted that the NBL teams be segregated in the new league's Western Division and the schedule arranged so that they played the ten former BAA teams only once. That arrangement guaranteed that the Nuggets and other former NBL teams did not get to share fully in the gate receipts at the big-city arenas. The Nuggets finished the 1949–1950 season with only eleven wins against fifty-one losses, and broke. In the off-season, the NBA demanded that each franchise post a fifty-thousand-dollar performance bond. The Denver franchise did not have the money and was forced to quit the league. An irate Hal Davis claimed that Denver had been forced out of the NBA "because of our geographical location." He complained that "we were thrown out by strong arm tactics. . . . We had hopes of bringing high class and honest basketball to Denver, but found it impossible to do that under those phony operators."[26]

The Denver team tried to carry on the next season, playing as the Frontier Refiners in the short-lived National Professional Basketball League. The Refiners, led by player-coach Jimmy Darden, won their first twelve games, but the team continued to struggle financially. Finally, during a road trip in January 1951, the team folded.[27]

Colorado did not see professional basketball again for sixteen years.

THE AMERICAN BASKETBALL ASSOCIATION AND THE DENVER ROCKETS

In 1967 Dennis Murphy was the mayor of Buena Park, California, a suburb of Los Angeles. He was also an ardent sports fan and an inveterate promoter who eventually played a role in founding a half-dozen professional sports leagues. Murphy and a group of friends had been working for two years to bring an American Football League franchise to nearby Anaheim. However, the merger of the American and the National Football Leagues thwarted the plan. Undaunted, Murphy soon came up with the idea of starting a new basketball league, and in February 1967 he and a group of associates announced the formation of the American Basketball Association (ABA). George Mikan, who had been one of the NBA's first major stars, signed on as league commissioner. Although its organizers intended the new league to be a rival for the NBA, they did not challenge the senior league head-on, choosing, instead, to place ABA teams in non-NBA cities, including Indianapolis, Pittsburgh, Louisville, Dallas, Houston, Minneapolis, New Orleans, Teaneck, Anaheim, and Kansas City. James Trindle, a California engineer, led a group of investors who purchased the Kansas City franchise. However, problems in finding a home court in Kansas City prompted Commissioner Mikan to suggest moving the franchise to Denver. Mikan also suggested that Trindle hire Vince Boryla as general manager. Boryla, who had won a local following as a member of the 1947 AAU Nuggets and as a member of the 1948–1949 University of Denver squad, had retired to Denver after ending his playing and coaching career with the New York Knicks.[28]

Boryla quickly set out to recruit players for the new team that, with the owners' approval, he had named the Larks, for Colorado's state bird, the Lark Bunting. Within weeks, however, Boryla halted recruiting and was feuding openly with Trindle over the team's financial condition. In June, Trindle fired Boryla after he told a Denver audience that he would not "go out and sell a bag of beans." Boryla was right about the ownership group's poor financial condition, and when Commissioner Mikan demanded that the franchise post a performance bond of one hundred thousand dollars, Trindle set out to find additional, preferably local, backing. Jack Ashton, an official of the Denver Chamber of Commerce, read press accounts of the fledgling team's financial woes and decided to try to help. Ashton put Trindle in touch with Bill Ringsby, owner of a large Denver-based trucking company. Ringsby and his son Don agreed to buy a two-thirds interest in the franchise, which they immediately rechristened as the Denver Rockets. Ringsby believed that owning a basketball team would be good for his trucking business, so the team and his trucks carried the same orange and black logo showing an encircled basketball with the words *Denver, Rockets,* and *Ringsby System.*[29]

The new owners hired Oklahoma Baptist University's Bob Bass to coach the Rockets. Bass filled the roster with a group of NBA, AAU, and minor league veterans. University of Denver and AAU standout Byron Beck anchored the team at center. Beck spent his entire nine-year ABA career with Denver. Larry Jones, a minor league veteran, led the Rockets in scoring the first season and became the first ABA player to score fifty points in a game. Forward Wayne Hightower lent the credibility of NBA experience to the team.[30]

The Denver Rockets played their first home game on October 15, 1967, and defeated the Anaheim Amigos 110–105 before a crowd of more than twenty-seven hundred in the Denver Auditorium. They went on to a record of forty-five wins and thirty-three losses, good enough for third place in the ABA's Western Division and a spot in the playoffs. The New Orleans Buccaneers, led by the tandem of Larry Brown and Doug Moe, knocked the Rockets out of the first round.

The Rockets first season was successful off the court, too. Attendance at home games averaged forty-one hundred, second only to the Indiana Pacers, and the Rockets led the ABA in season-ticket sales. Despite their success and comparative financial strength, the Rockets—like most ABA teams—did not lead lives of athletic luxury. The team traveled in a 1941 vintage DC-3 aircraft, called the *Vomit Comet,* piloted by a German air force veteran nicknamed the "Red Baron." With tight budgets, early ABA teams often could not take all of their staff with them, and home teams were expected to provide trainers for the visitors. Larry Brown recalled one trip to Denver when the trainer taped his ankle so tightly that it bled. After cutting the tape off himself, Brown asked the trainer "what he did in real life," because he could not believe that the man was a professional. The man hesitated for a moment, but then admitted, "I'm a poultry farmer."[31]

The Rockets' second season mirrored the 1967–1968 campaign. Forty-four wins and thirty-four losses earned them another playoff appearance. This time, the Oakland Oaks, led by Rick Barry and the itinerant duo of Larry Brown and Doug Moe, eliminated the Rockets in the first round.

The ABA set itself apart from the NBA with a flashier style of basketball aimed at attracting and pleasing large audiences, not basketball purists. The league's red, white, and blue ball symbolized its style of play and its goals. A New York broadcaster said that the ball "made the game much easier to watch for the novice fan," and players recalled its "mesmerizing" effect. Gene Littles, a future Denver coach, remembered that "it was a special feeling to take a long shot and watch those colors rotate in the air and then see the ball with all those colors nestle into the net. It made your heart beat just a little faster when you hit a 25-footer with the ABA ball." When no red, white, and blue ball could be found for the Rockets' first exhibition game in 1967, Bob Bass recalled, "some genius got the idea of taking a brown ball and spray-painting it." Unfortunately, the painted finish made the ball so slick that the teams committed forty-four turnovers in the game's first half.[32]

By the 1960s, African American players such as Wilt Chamberlain and Bill Russell had become superstars in the NBA. However, the senior league had struggled with the question of bringing African Americans into major league professional basketball. The league did not recruit its first black players until 1951 and increased their numbers slowly thereafter.

In contrast, the ABA pursued black athletes aggressively from the beginning. By the time the ABA appeared in 1967, black athletes were widely accepted in professional sports. The league's birth in the immediate wake of the most active and successful period of America's civil rights struggle encouraged further efforts to bring black players into the limelight. In addition, it was the African American players who brought to the league the more aggressive, flamboyant "playground" style of play that became its hallmark. As one history of basketball notes, "The ABA helped to shift the balance of power in professional basketball to African-Americans by basing its existence on them and not pretending otherwise."[33]

The Denver Rockets made history in 1969 by hiring John McClendon to succeed Bob Bass as coach (Bass resigned after a contract

dispute with the Ringsbys over vacation time). McClendon was the
ABA's first African American coach. The new coach had been highly
successful in the AAU. In addition to his coaching talent, however,
McClendon had also become a friend to one of the country's top-
rated college players, Spencer Haywood.[34]

The ABA made a priority of signing Haywood, who had just
completed his sophomore year at the University of Detroit, in order
to show the NBA that the league could compete for the best college
talent (fig. 8-3). McClendon had helped Haywood win a spot on the
1968 U.S. Olympic team, and his relationship with the player gave the
Rockets one advantage in the effort to sign him. The franchise's relative financial strength was another advantage, so the league assigned
Haywood's ABA rights to the Rockets. Both the NBA and the NCAA

SPENCER HAYWOOD

ROCKETS

AMERICAN BASKETBALL ASSOCIATION

SPENCER HAYWOOD
Denver Rockets 6-9 225

8-3. When the Denver Rockets signed University of Detroit star Spencer
Haywood in 1969, the move proved that the American Basketball Association
could compete with the NBA for the best talent. Note the multicolored (red,
white, and blue) ABA basketball. Courtesy, Denver Nuggets.

sued, unsuccessfully, to block Haywood's move to the Rockets on the specious grounds that the ABA team had signed him unfairly before his college eligibility had expired. The Rockets and the ABA answered press and public criticism of the Haywood signing by arguing that his was a "hardship case." Haywood, they explained, had to leave college in order to support his mother and sisters.[35]

Even with Spencer Haywood on the court, the Rockets got off to a poor start in the 1969–1970 season, winning only nine of their first twenty-eight games. In December, Joe Belmont replaced John McClendon as coach. Belmont was employed in the Rockets' marketing office when he was tapped for the job. He had been an All-American at Duke University and had played AAU ball with the D-C Truckers, but his only coaching experience was with Duke's freshmen team. Despite his lack of coaching experience, the Rockets won forty-two games under Belmont and finished with a total of fifty-one wins and thirty-three losses to win the Western Division. Spencer Haywood proved that he was ready for pro basketball by leading the league with an average of thirty points per game, earning him rookie of the year and most valuable player honors. The Rockets lasted into the second round of the playoffs before the Los Angeles Stars eliminated them.[36]

Spencer Haywood played only one season with the Rockets. Unhappy with his contract, Haywood bolted to the NBA's Seattle Supersonics. His departure, along with that of Larry Jones, began a half-decade period of decline and upheaval in the Rockets organization. The Rockets won only thirty games in the 1970–1971 season. Along the way, the team fired Joe Belmont and assistant coach Stan Albeck took over for the balance of the season. The only hopeful note that year was the arrival of guard Ralph Simpson, who turned pro after his second year at Michigan State. Simpson became a major star, but did not help the Rockets much in his first season.[37]

In an effort to reverse the team's fortunes, the Ringsbys hired Alex Hannum away from the San Diego Rockets of the NBA. Hannum's new bosses had good reason to expect big things from him. After all, he had coached two NBA teams (St. Louis and Philadelphia), an ABA team (Oakland), and an AAU team (Wichita) to league championships. Hannum demanded, and got, complete control over the franchise as president, general manager, and head coach. He quickly changed the team's colors and logo to a blue and gold scheme with a smiley-faced ball-dribbling rocket named "Rocky."[38]

Hannum's first season was disappointing. Ralph Simpson averaged more than twenty-seven points per game in 1971–1972, but he could not carry the team alone. The Rockets finished with only thirty-four wins and fifty losses. Despite the losing record, they qualified for the playoffs and took the Indiana Pacers to seven games in the first round before being eliminated. By season's end, the Ringsbys had given up on being basketball owners and sold the Rockets to an out-of-town partnership, Frank M. Goldberg and A. G. "Bud" Fisher of San Diego.[39]

The ownership change and Hannum's coaching seemed to pay off the next season as the Rockets won forty-seven of their eighty-four games. Once again, however, the Indiana Pacers knocked them out of the playoffs in the first round. In the 1973–1974 season, Hannum's Rockets reverted to losing form and finished with forty-seven losses and only thirty-seven wins. The Rockets' owners fired Hannum at the end of the season.

Part of the problem was Hannum's inability to deal with many of his players. One member of the team, Dave Robisch, remembered Hannum as "a very hardline guy" who, by the 1970s, found that "he wasn't dealing with the same kind of players he had in the past." Hannum, Robisch said, "was an old-school coach and that era was gone." Robisch's comments suggest that the modern ABA player was a freelance athlete, unaccustomed to, and resentful of, a disciplinary coaching style. Hannum did not entirely disagree and acknowledged, "I had trouble communicating with some guys." However, he also noted a problem among some of the Rockets that was to loom large in professional sports, and in American society, in the future. Drugs, he said, "were starting to become a factor." Hannum recalled "hearing guys say that cocaine was the greatest thing, if you could just afford it. It was a very discouraging situation and I was glad to get out in 1974." Drugs became an open and destructive problem for the Denver team soon enough, but in the meantime Hannum's departure opened the way for a new and more successful era of management, coaching, and play.[40]

Rocket owners Frank Goldberg and Bud Fisher hired former NBA deputy commissioner Carl Scheer to run the franchise. Scheer had also been president and general manager of the Carolina Cougars, where he had twice been honored as ABA executive of the year. In Denver, Scheer quickly hired his Cougar coaches, Larry Brown as head coach and Doug Moe as assistant. The Scheer-Brown-Moe triumvirate established a management and coaching dynasty that has presided over Denver's most successful basketball years since 1974.[41]

As the Rockets' performance declined in the early 1970s, so did the team's popularity. Average home-game crowds fell from a high of about 6,300 in 1969–1970 to only 4,100 in 1973–1974. Scheer wanted to rebuild support for the team quickly and embarked on an aggressive marketing campaign. His first step was to change the team's name. Reaching back into Denver's AAU and early NBA history, he picked the name "Nuggets." A new logo in red, white, and blue included a pick-wielding miner called "Maxey."[42]

Scheer and Brown also moved to strengthen the Nuggets on the court. To the core of Byron Beck, Dave Robisch, and Ralph Simpson they added guard Mack Calvin, who had played for them with the Carolina Cougars, and University of North Carolina defensive forward Bobby Jones. Brown coached a fast-paced "running-and-pressing" style of basketball that emphasized aggressive defense and opportunistic shooting.[43]

The new management and coaching styles worked a quick turnaround for the Nuggets in 1974–1975. Attendance soared to almost 282,000 enthusiastic fans who watched the Nuggets on their way to sixty-five wins and only nineteen losses, a winning performance that is still unmatched by succeeding Denver teams. The Nuggets dispatched the Utah Stars in the first round of the playoffs before falling to the Indiana Pacers in the Western Division series. Larry Brown won the first of two consecutive ABA coach of the year honors. During the off-season in 1975, Carl Scheer organized an investment group of local businessmen to buy control of the Nuggets from Goldberg and Fisher. The Nuggets once again had local owners.[44]

The Nuggets won sixty games in 1975–1976, five fewer than the previous season, but they were a stronger team and went further. In the off-season, Scheer had signed the two best college players in the

8-4. David Thompson was one of the most coveted college players in 1976. Thompson chose to sign with the
Denver Nuggets instead of the NBA's Atlanta Hawks,
helping convince the NBA to merge with the Nuggets
and three other ABA teams. Courtesy, Mark Junge.

nation, center Marvin "The Human Eraser" Webster and guard David
Thompson (fig. 8-4). Thompson was the top prize, and signing him
took some stealthy maneuvering. The Virginia Squires drafted Thompson, as did the NBA's Atlanta Hawks. The financially troubled
Squires, however, did not have the money to sign Thompson and

agreed to trade their rights to Denver if the Nuggets could sign him. The Nuggets' effort to court Thompson included bringing him to Denver for one of the 1976 playoff games, where a sellout crowd and a huge "Welcome" sign greeted him. Thompson also visited Atlanta, but was unimpressed with the crowd of only 3,000 at the game. Scheer was delighted with the contrast, as the Nuggets "came off as far more major league than the Hawks." Thompson agreed that "it didn't matter that Denver was in the ABA, because the Nuggets were very big league." The Nuggets made playing in Denver even more attractive by signing Thompson's closest friend, five-foot-seven-inch guard Monte Towe. Thompson's $450,000 contract with the Nuggets made him the highest-paid player in the ABA.[45]

More important, in the long run, than Thompson's signing was the arrival of center Dan Issel (fig. 8-5). Issel had played his entire college and professional career in Kentucky, and he wanted to stay there. His Kentucky Colonels won the ABA championship in 1975, but the team and owner John Y. Brown were in bad shape financially. To raise cash, Brown sold Issel's contract to the even more financially troubled Baltimore Claws (formerly the Memphis Sounds). Issel was unhappy, but had little choice but to report to Baltimore. Within a few days, however, Brown discovered that the Baltimore owners could not pay for Issel. Brown then brokered a three-way deal that sent Issel to Denver, Issel's purchase price to Brown's bank account, and Nugget veteran Dave Robisch to exile in Baltimore where the Claws folded before the 1975–1976 season began. (Robisch went to the San Diego Sails, which also folded in 1975, and then to the Indiana Pacers.)[46]

With David Thompson and Dan Issel on board (Marvin Webster was sidelined with hepatitis), the Nuggets ran up the best record in the ABA for the second straight year. At midseason, the league held its annual All-Star Game in Denver. The event pitted the league-leading Nuggets against the best players from the remaining seven teams. The Nuggets won the game with a score of 144-138, but the real show came at halftime. Scheer wanted to fill every seat in newly opened McNichols Arena and showcase Denver and the Nuggets. He hired country-western singers Glenn Campbell and Charlie Rich to perform a pregame concert, but most of the fifteen thousand fans

8-5. Dan Issel has personified the Denver Nuggets for almost a quarter of a century. He joined the team as a player in 1976 and retired in 1985. He returned as head coach for two and one-half seasons beginning in 1992, and became general manager in 1998. Courtesy, Mark Junge.

on hand came to see the slam-dunk contest. High-flyers from around the league entered, but the contest was really between David Thompson and the New York Nets' Julius "Dr. J" Erving, who won with a fifteen-foot leap from the foul line (film later showed that he had stepped on the line).[47]

With perhaps the strongest team in the ABA, and the league's best record, the Nuggets entered the 1976 playoffs with a great deal of confidence. They defeated Kentucky in a seven-game semifinal series, but then fell to the Nets in the ABA's final championship game.[48]

THE NUGGETS IN THE NBA

The acquisition of David Thompson, the slam-dunk contest, and other efforts to raise the Nuggets' profile had a purpose larger than just selling tickets. Carl Scheer wanted to prove that the Nuggets could compete in the NBA.

By 1976 only seven teams remained in the ABA, and four of them were in bad shape financially. It was clear that the league could not last much longer. Nevertheless, nine years of competition with the ABA had strained the NBA. The loss of players such as David Thompson and Julius Erving and, especially, escalating player salaries caused by the leagues' rivalry made the NBA open to an accommodation with the ABA. League representatives had been negotiating a possible merger for several years, and even came close to a deal in 1971. In 1975 the Nuggets and the New York Nets applied directly for admission to the NBA as expansion teams. The major obstacle to a merger came from the Players Association, which worried about the probable loss of jobs and restraints on salaries that a single league would mean. The players, led by Oscar Robertson, filed an antitrust suit claiming that a merger would establish an illegal monopoly. In February 1976, however, the players and owners reached a settlement that met the players' demands on such issues as free agency and draft eligibility. Months of hard-nosed negotiations followed. At one point, the Milwaukee Bucks' owner and NBA negotiator William Alverson told ABA representatives that he had "no mandate from my NBA colleagues to make any deal with you SOBs." The NBA, Alverson continued, was not "a charitable organization. If it's not good for Milwaukee or for the NBA, then screw you! . . . There's really only one team than means anything to us and that's Denver. The rest of the ABA couldn't draw flies in Milwaukee." Finally, however, in June 1976, an ABA delegation, including Denver's Carl Scheer, concluded an agreement to bring four of the remaining ABA teams—the Nuggets, the Indiana Pacers, the San Antonio Spurs, and the New York Nets—into the NBA. The four teams agreed to pay an admission fee of $3.2 million and to buy out the other three ABA franchises.[49]

The Nuggets led the NBA in attendance in their first two years in the league and advanced to the Western Division playoffs in the first three seasons. However, trouble lurked behind the scenes. Although Larry Brown's teams had won 65 percent of their regular-season games and finished first in their division every year, he had not won a league championship. By the 1978–1979 season, Brown and Carl Scheer quarreled over player-personnel moves, and Brown had become frustrated over his relations with some members of the team. David Thompson was particularly worrisome. Although he still averaged twenty-four points per game, Thompson had been showing up late, sometimes missing practices, team flights, and even a game. Brown and the Nuggets did not know yet that Thompson had begun using cocaine. In 1982, after the Nuggets became aware of Thompson's addiction, they traded him to the Seattle Supersonics in exchange for defensive forward Bill Hanzlik, who had averaged only 5.5 points per game. Thompson's drug abuse ruined his career and eventually landed him in jail. To his credit, he overcame his addiction and in 1992 returned to Denver to see his number retired. By early 1979, Larry Brown was emotionally exhausted and in February resigned as head coach.[50]

Assistant coach Donnie Walsh, a Brown protégé, took over and coached the Nuggets until December 1980. Walsh had given up a career in law (he turned down an offer to join Richard Nixon's New York law firm) to become an assistant coach at the University of South Carolina, where he stayed until 1977 when he joined Brown in Denver. The Nuggets won only thirty games in Walsh's one full season, 1979–1980, and were 60-82 overall during his tenure. The most important achievement for the Nuggets in this period was the acquisition of Alex English, a deadly shooter who averaged 25.9 points per game in his eleven years with the team.[51]

The Nuggets replaced Walsh with assistant coach Doug Moe. Moe had come to Denver in 1974 with his friend Larry Brown, but left in 1977 when a head-coaching opportunity came with the San Antonio Spurs. Moe feuded with Spurs owner Angelo Drossos from the beginning, and when Drossos finally fired him in 1980 Moe's wife, Jane, celebrated with champagne.[52]

Doug Moe was sui generis among NBA coaches. In a profession of tense, buttoned-down men, Moe appeared as a relaxed slob who refused to wear a jacket and tie until the league forced him. He had a biting, usually self-depreciating sense of humor. He called his favorite players "stiffs" and "no-hopers," and referred to himself as the "king of the dipshits." Moe did not care that the whole world knew of his fear of flying, so long as his keen intellect remained secret. He was direct and brutally honest. Asked in 1987 about his team's chances in a playoff series against the Los Angeles Lakers, Moe answered, "Fellas, we got no shot."[53]

Moe installed a fast-motion passing game that emphasized running and intuitive passing instead of designed plays. It was a scheme that depended upon players more interested in team success than personal statistics. Moe believed that "the faster you get the ball up the floor, the quicker you move it, the easier it is to score—if you're unselfish." With team anchors Dan Issel and Alex English, augmented by forward Kiki Vandeweghe and, later, by defensive standouts Calvin Natt, Lafayette "Fat" Lever, and Wayne Cooper (who came to Denver from Portland in a trade for Vandeweghe), Moe made the Nuggets "the NBA's champions of overachievement" in the 1980s (fig. 8-6). The NBA eventually recognized Moe's "overachievement" by naming him coach of the year in 1987.[54]

After a two-year absence from postseason play, Moe had the Nuggets back in the playoffs in 1982, and they returned every year through 1990, though they never advanced beyond the Western Division finals. Although Moe did not produce a championship team, his was the most successful era in the Nuggets' history.

However, the 1980s also saw changes in the Nuggets' ownership and management that, first, delivered the team to out-of-town owners, stirred up public-policy issues that would become endemic to professional sports in the 1990s, made the team part of an entertainment conglomerate, and then, unfortunately, plunged it into a long period of mediocrity.

Despite the team's renewed success on the floor, Carl Scheer's ownership group struggled financially and in 1982 sold the franchise to Texan B. J. "Red" McCombs. Scheer stayed on as general manager until after the 1983–1984 season, but was forced out when McCombs hired Vince Boryla to run the club as president. Boryla kept Moe on, but insisted on a stronger defensive game and so engineered the trade of Vandeweghe for Natt, Lever, and Cooper.[55]

While McCombs and Boryla worked to strengthen the franchise, the Nuggets continued to play well, if erratically, under Moe.

8-6. During Doug Moe's tenure as head coach (1980–1990), the Nuggets were "the NBA's champions of overachievement." Moe's casual, sometimes profane, personality offended some in the Nuggets' and the NBA's office suites, and some of his players, but endeared him to most fans. Courtesy, Mark Junge.

They won only thirty-eight games in 1983–1984, the only season in Moe's tenure when they won fewer than half their games. The next year, however, was one of their best, with fifty-two wins and only thirty losses. The team advanced to the 1985 Western Conference finals before falling one game to four to the Lakers.

Center Dan Issel, who had anchored the Nuggets for a decade, retired in 1985. His last season with Moe and the Nuggets was difficult. He no longer led the team as the starting center and watched more and more from the bench as younger men, Wayne Cooper and Danny Schayes, took his place. In April 1985, Issel's number-44 jersey joined Byron Beck's as the second retired Nugget number.[56]

An even more important change came at season's end when owner Red McCombs sold the Nuggets to fellow Texan Sidney Schlenker, a Houston investor. McCombs was not happy to sell the team, but could not turn down a deal that gave him a twenty-fold profit on his investment. The new owner promised to leave running the team to Boryla and Moe and focus his efforts on the business side. For the most part, Schlenker kept that promise, though Boryla left the organization under cloudy circumstances in 1987.[57]

In a move that anticipated a major theme in professional sports in the 1990s, Schlenker set out to wring more money out of the Nuggets' playing venue, McNichols Arena. Within a few months of buying the team, Schlenker and the City of Denver, which owned the arena, were locked in a dispute over management and improvements at McNichols. Early in 1986 Schlenker and the city agreed to a new fifteen-year lease that put the management of the arena in Schlenker's hands. In exchange, Schlenker agreed to pay for $7.5 million in improvements, including three restaurants, a VIP lounge, and a high-tech scoreboard. Schlenker predicted that the renovated arena would rival the Rocky Mountains as a tourist attraction. Proud Denverites, he said, would tell their guests, "You haven't seen Denver until you see McNichols."[58]

By the time Schlenker's restaurants and other renovations were completed, their cost rose to more than $12 million, money borrowed at the ruinously high interest rates prevailing in the mid-1980s. Denver diners stayed away from the McNichols restaurants, and other gambits to bring in crowds, including indoor football and soccer teams, also failed. In midsummer 1989, Schlenker gave up and sold the Nuggets.[59]

The prospective new owners were Chicago businessmen Peter C. B. Bynoe and Bertram Lee, and their purchase of the Nuggets was hailed as a historic moment in professional sports and for American society. Bynoe and Lee were to be the first African American majority owners of a major league sports franchise. The Reverend J. Langston Boyd, a leader in Denver's African American community, declared, "I will no longer be loyal to the Lakers or proud of the Pistons but a 100% Nuggets supporter from here on out." An Aurora, Colorado, businessman said that the sale meant "a great deal to me and to the black community and society. It means that we can begin to put behind us the myth that blacks don't have the ability or the wherewithal to pull together this kind of capital."[60]

Unfortunately, Bynoe and Lee did have trouble financing the purchase, and by October 1989 it appeared that the deal would fall through. However, NBA Commissioner David Stern, anxious to preserve at least partial minority ownership, intervened and arranged for COMSAT Video Enterprises to buy 67.5 percent of the Nuggets, leaving Bynoe and Lee with 32.5 percent. Under the terms of the deal, Bynoe and Lee became managing general partners, with Bynoe in charge of day-to-day operations while COMSAT president Robert Wussler kept an eye on things from his office in Washington, D.C.[61]

Chaos infected the Nuggets' front office before the sale was completed. As part of the abortive sale to Bynoe and Lee, Sidney Schlenker agreed to name former Utah Jazz executive David Checketts as president of the club. Pete Babcock, whom Schlenker had made president in 1987, was demoted to general manager. However, when the original sale fell through in October, Checketts quit and Babcock became president again. That arrangement lasted only until the season began, when Babcock once again was shunted into the general manager's office and replaced by former Portland Trailblazers vice president Jan Spoelstra. In November, Spoelstra and Babcock signed a seven-year, $17.5 million contract with starting center Blair Rasmussen, much to the displeasure of Bynoe, Wussler, and coach Doug Moe, who believed the contract gave Rasmussen far more than he was worth. Spoelstra resigned on February 2, 1990. Bynoe, who had no real basketball management experience, decided to run the team himself with Babcock as a powerless general manager. Fed up with this front office merry-go-round, Babcock quit less than two weeks later to become general manager of the Atlanta Hawks (where he later exacted some revenge). Late in March, Bynoe decided that he needed an experienced basketball man in the office and hired Carl Scheer as president. Scheer promised to restore stability and "a little credibility to the organization." A month later, however, Allen Bristow—one of Doug Moe's assistant coaches, whom Bynoe had promoted to player-personnel director—left to become vice president and, later, head coach of the Charlotte Hornets. (Nugget veterans Bill Hanzlik and T. R. Dunn became his assistants.) Bynoe still needed a general manager. Georgetown University coach John Thompson turned down the job in June. Finally, in July, Seattle Supersonics vice president Bernie Bickerstaff took the job. Bickerstaff managed, and eventually coached, the Nuggets until 1997.[62]

The upheavals in the Nuggets' management suite inevitably spilled into the locker room. The new owners intended to dismantle the team and rebuild through draft choices. With Doug Moe's support, they let free agent Alex English, who had been feuding with the coach, go to Dallas, and traded Fat Lever and Danny Schayes for draft choices, one of which was used to acquire LSU's Chris Jackson, whom Moe characterized as the most talented player to come along since Michael Jordan.[63]

Moe went along with the wholesale changes in the Nuggets' lineup, in part because he agreed that the team had aged and in part to protect his position with the new owners, who were locked in a battle to control the team. However, Moe finally fell victim to that struggle. He had Peter Bynoe's support, but he had been in Robert Wussler's crosshairs from the moment the COMSAT executive joined the ownership group. Wussler simply did not like Doug Moe. Although he knew nothing about basketball and coaching, Wussler did know that Moe did not measure up to his image of a basketball coach. Moe was, in Wussler's opinion, "inappropriate."[64]

Wussler first tried to maneuver Moe out by arranging broadcasting auditions for him. When that gambit failed, Wussler forced general manager Bernie Bickerstaff to fire Moe. On September 6, 1990, Moe held a press conference to announce his own firing. As they had in San Antonio, Moe and his wife, "Big Jane," toasted his dismissal with champagne. Fans and reporters were outraged. Some said they would not renew their season tickets. Even Alex English's agent, no friend of Moe, said that he "got a raw deal" from the Nuggets'

owners, whom he characterized as "a bunch of weasels." Team president Carl Scheer, who had played such a crucial role in building the
Nuggets into a successful franchise in the 1970s, best appreciated Moe's
importance to the team. "When you talk about the Nuggets and you
talk about professional basketball in Denver," Scheer said, "you have
to start with Doug Moe." Scheer himself was fired nine months later,
another victim of the struggle between Bynoe and Wussler.[65]

Moe's successor, Paul Westhead, seemed to be the ideal replacement. Westhead dressed stylishly and could quote Shakespeare, and
thus fit Wussler's image of a corporate-style coach. He came to the
Nuggets from Loyola Marymount University, where he had coached
since 1985. His teams there won better than 68 percent of their games
and in 1990 advanced to the Final Eight in the NCAA Championship
Tournament. Westhead also had significant NBA head-coaching experience, having led the Los Angeles Lakers from 1979 to 1982 and
the Chicago Bulls in 1982–1983. Westhead's 1979–1980 Lakers won
the NBA title. In addition to his winning record, Westhead brought
to the Nuggets a coaching system that favored a fast-break offense
and high-pressure defense, which promised to build on the style of
play that Moe had coached. Westhead promised suspicious Nugget
fans that they "haven't seen anything yet," and that his edition of the
Nuggets would "knock your socks off."[66]

Westhead's hiring brought only a temporary pause to the chaos
in the Nuggets' organization. Westhead inherited a young and talent-
poor team, a situation that Peter Bynoe tried to blame on the team's
previous management. Even the addition in 1991 of seven-foot-two-
inch Zairean Dikembe Mutombo, a talented rookie center from
Georgetown University, did not help. In Westhead's two seasons, the
Nuggets turned in the worst records yet in franchise history, winning
only twenty games in 1990–1991 and only twenty-four games in 1991–
1992. General manager Bernie Bickerstaff fired Westhead at season's
end in 1992.[67]

Westhead's dismissal came in the midst of another shakeup in
the Nuggets' management that, if nothing else, ended the division
and conflict in ownership that plagued the organization since 1989. In
January 1992, COMSAT replaced Robert Wussler with a younger
executive, Charlie Lyons. Then, in August 1992, COMSAT bought

Peter Bynoe's remaining share of the team (Bertram Lee had been ousted from the ownership group in April 1991 after failing to fulfill his financial obligation to the partnership).With ownership completely in COMSAT's hands, Charlie Lyons vowed that he would leave day-to-day management to Bickerstaff and team president Tim Leiweke, who had replaced Carl Scheer in 1991. COMSAT in 1996 created Ascent Entertainment Group, Inc., as the Nuggets' owning company. Ascent also owned the Colorado Avalanche ice hockey club.[68]

While COMSAT moved to consolidate its ownership of the Nuggets, Bernie Bickerstaff looked for a new coach. Early speculation centered on Houston Rockets coach Don Chaney and Charlotte Hornets vice president Gene Littles. However, Bickerstaff surprised and delighted Nugget fans by hiring Dan Issel. Issel had no coaching experience, but remained one of Colorado's most popular and respected sports figures. His hiring was a clear attempt to restore some faith and credibility in the franchise by linking it to the era of success in the 1980s.[69]

Issel's 1992–1993 team, augmented by draft picks LaPhonso Ellis and Bryant Stith, improved to a record of thirty-six wins and forty-six losses, but missed the playoffs for the third year. Nevertheless, Issel's Nuggets seemed to have a new confidence and intensity.

Issel's second season, 1993–1994, seemed almost magical. The "kids," as Issel called his players, won forty-two of their eighty-two regular-season games, enough to earn the eighth and last spot in the playoffs. In the first round of the playoffs the young Nuggets faced the potent Seattle Supersonics, the team favored to win the NBA championship. In the first game, Seattle inflicted a humiliating 106-82 defeat. The next day, Issel made his players watch a replay of the entire game. They responded by losing the second game, 97-87, but it was a hard-fought game that was closer than the ten-point margin suggested. The third and fourth games were in Denver, where sellout crowds turned out to cheer the suddenly popular Nuggets. Before game three, Bronco quarterback John Elway, wearing a Nugget jersey, challenged the crowd to "rip the roof off" McNichols Arena. At the final buzzer the Nuggets had a convincing 110-93 win. The next morning, Dikembe Mutombo told reporters that he had dreamed about beating the Sonics in game four. Mutombo's dream came true, as he and his teammates evened the series in game four with a 94-85 overtime win. Back in Seattle, the two teams again battled into overtime. At the end, Dikembe Mutombo lay on the floor, cradling the game ball and crying tears of joy for the Nuggets' 98-94 victory. It was the first time that an eighth-ranked team had defeated a number-one-ranked team in the NBA playoffs. Sportswriters compared the upset to the New York Jets' victory over the Baltimore Colts in Super Bowl III.[70]

The Nuggets continued to play well in the Western Conference semifinals against the Utah Jazz, but finally lost the decisive seventh game of the series. Measured against the stunning upset of Seattle, the loss to Utah did not seem to matter. After the dreadful experience of the early 1990s, the Nuggets would once more have to be reckoned with as a respectable force in the NBA. Or so it seemed.

When the team regrouped for the 1994–1995 season, the drive, intensity, and discipline that had characterized them just a few months before seemed to have withered, and with it Dan Issel's enthusiasm for coaching. By mid-January 1995 the Nuggets had lost more games than they won. A humiliating 114-88 loss to Utah was the last straw for Issel. At the next practice, Dikembe Mutombo found Issel quiet and standoffish. The normally congenial Issel "didn't say hello. He was just quiet. We were just looking at him in a [sic] distance (saying), 'Big Fella is mad. Big Fella is mad.' " Issel quit three days later, saying that he no longer wanted to deal with the pressures of coaching.[71]

Whether it was a cause or a consequence, Issel's departure coincided with the Nuggets' slide back into mediocrity. Assistant coach Gene Littles took over, on an interim basis, but won only three of the next sixteen games. Bernie Bickerstaff thus decided to add the duties of head coach to his portfolio. The Nuggets won twenty games under his direction and finished the season with forty-one wins and forty-one losses. The San Antonio Spurs eliminated them from the playoffs in three straight games.

The Nuggets' record slipped to thirty-five wins and forty-seven losses in 1995–1996. Bickerstaff, as team president and head coach, came under increasingly strident criticism, especially for his player-personnel moves. Most controversial was the decision not to re-sign free agent Dikembe Mutombo. Bickerstaff was dissatisfied with Mutombo's play, but could have re-signed him and then traded him to another team for players or draft picks. Instead, Bickerstaff let the signing deadline pass, Mutombo went to the Atlanta Hawks, where general manager Pete Babcock was happy to have him, and the Nuggets got nothing. Outraged sports columnists demanded that Bickerstaff be fired for this "colossal blunder," but one disgruntled Nugget staff member said that "Bernie's punishment should be that he is forced to coach this team next year and suffer."[72]

Bickerstaff did return as coach for the 1996–1997 season, but did not stay long. In November, with only four wins in thirteen games, he handed the coaching job to assistant Dick Motta who had thirty years of experience coaching in the NBA. His 1978 Washington Bullets won the NBA championship. Nonetheless, the Nuggets won only seventeen of the remaining sixty-nine games. By season's end, Bickerstaff left the Nuggets to become head coach of Motta's former team, the Bullets.[73]

With Bickerstaff gone, the Nuggets hired Allan Bristow to run the team as vice president of basketball operations. Bristow had been Doug Moe's assistant coach from 1984 to 1990, and served briefly as player-personnel director after Moe's firing, before moving on to Charlotte to be the Hornets' manager and, from 1991 through 1996, head coach. Bristow hired his Hornets' assistant, Bill Hanzlik, to be the Nuggets' new head coach. Hanzlik, of course, had been one of Doug Moe's "no-hopers" in the 1980s.[74]

In turning to Allan Bristow and Bill Hanzlik, the Nuggets' owner, Ascent Entertainment, tried to restore the tradition of success and respectability in the team's history that dated to the eras and leadership of Carl Scheer, Larry Brown, and, especially, Doug Moe. However, the team Bristow and Hanzlik inherited from Bernie Bickerstaff was demoralized and short of talent. And they became worse. Under Bristow and Hanzlik, the Nuggets had their worst season ever, and one of the worst in NBA history, in 1997–1998, winning only eleven games and losing seventy-one. Only the 1972–1973 Philadelphia '76ers had a worse record with only nine wins. Bristow, who lost or traded several starters from the previous year, and failed to replace them with even equivalent talent, was fired in February 1998. As the Nuggets' losses mounted during the season, Hanzlik lost control of the team. In April, rookie Bobby Jackson, miffed because he had been dropped from the starting lineup, refused to go into a game when Hanzlik told him to. By season's end, team captains LaPhonso Ellis and Bryant Stith, probably the most talented players on the squad, made it clear that they did not want to play another year for Hanzlik. The coach, who had pleaded, rhetorically, for someone to "find some ground and bury me," was out immediately after the season.[75]

In an effort to restore some credibility to the franchise, the Nuggets again turned to Dan Issel, who rejoined the franchise as vice president and general manager. By putting Issel in charge, Ascent clearly turned again to an icon of past Nugget successes. Issel in turn hired Nugget player-personnel director Mike D'Antoni as head coach. D'Antoni had no NBA or college head-coaching experience, but had been successful in the Italian Professional Basketball league, where his Milan and Benetton teams won almost 70 percent of their games (178-78) over seven years. His Benetton Treviso team won the Italian league championship in 1997. Issel also acquired two popular and talented players to strengthen the team both on the floor and among fans. Forward Antonio McDyess, traded to the Phoenix Suns in 1997, returned to Denver, along with former George Washington High School and University of Colorado star Chauncey Billups.[76] The 1998–1999 Nuggets were only slightly better than the previous year's team, winning only fourteen games and losing thirty-six in a season mercifully shortened by a labor dispute between NBA players and owners.

Despite the frustrations of the 1990s, the Nuggets' owner, Ascent Entertainment, seemed to have a strong commitment to the team and to Colorado, symbolized by the decision to build a new arena. After many months of difficult negotiations, Ascent and the City and County of Denver agreed to a deal releasing Ascent from its lease at McNichols Arena, and from payment of the city's seat tax. In exchange, the company agreed to build and manage a new arena, keep the Nuggets in Denver for twenty-five years, and pay Denver $1 to $2 million per year in compensation for the terminated lease at McNichols.[77]

Ascent's ownership of the Nuggets, and of the Colorado Avalanche hockey team, reflected an important trend in professional sports. Traditionally, individuals, often with strong ties to their communities, owned sports franchises, but by the 1990s more and more teams came under the control of large-scale corporations. Communications corporations were especially aggressive in acquiring major league teams. Ascent, for example, based its growth on television and motion-picture production and satellite broadcasting. Its new arena complex in Denver was designed to function not only as a venue for the basketball and hockey teams but also as a movie and television production center. Charlie Lyons, Ascent's chief executive officer, viewed the Nuggets simply as a part of the corporation's larger purpose. "We own the Nuggets," he said in 1995, "because we're an entertainment company. We distribute entertainment. We package entertainment. We create entertainment." Other important sports conglomerates included the Disney empire, which owned the Anaheim Angels baseball team and the Mighty Ducks (named after a Disney movie) of the National Hockey League, and financier Wayne Huizenga's sports, media, and auto-sales combine included the 1997 World Series winners, the Florida Marlins, and the Florida Panthers hockey team. Cable television mogul Ted Turner owned the Atlanta Braves and the Atlanta Hawks. Major brewing companies also bought sports teams. Anheuser-Busch owned the St. Louis Cardinals, Molson Breweries owned the Montreal Canadiens, and LaBatt Brewing had the Toronto Blue Jays.[78]

The integration of professional sports into corporate conglomerates had positive and potentially negative consequences. Corporate ownership could bring greater financial strength and, if executives are smart enough to rely on experienced sports people, more managerial stability. However, as one scholar has noted, professional sports teams "have always been rooted in places." Fans and local public officials could well wonder if their teams meant as much to stockholders and boards of directors as they meant to them and their communities. Would corporate owners sell or, worse, move their teams if the bottom line was inadequate? Or would deeper corporate pockets mean more willingness to build for the future and weather tough times? Colorado's experience with Ascent Entertainment cut both ways. The corporation's decision to build a new arena and to keep the Nuggets in Denver for twenty-five years suggested a strong commitment. However, Colorado sports fans also knew that Ascent had uprooted its hockey franchise and moved it from Quebec to Denver.[79]

WOMEN'S PROFESSIONAL BASKETBALL

By the late 1990s, the Nuggets were not the only professional basketball show in Denver. In October 1996 the Colorado Xplosion, Denver's entry in the new American Basketball League (ABL), began playing in the old Coliseum. Founded in 1995, the ABL hoped to become the first successful women's professional sports league.

Previous efforts to create such a league had failed. The Women's Professional Basketball League lasted three seasons, from 1978 to 1981, and the Women's American Basketball Association survived only one season, 1984. Since the mid-1980s, however, girls' and women's sports had grown enormously in popularity. Basketball was the leading youth participation sport for girls, and attendance at women's collegiate games had quadrupled. Many colleges and universities, including Stanford, Seton Hall, North Carolina, and Colorado, had developed successful women's basketball programs. Ceal Barry's CU team won consecutive Big Eight championships in 1992–1993 and 1993–1994, and by 1996 had made six trips to the NCAA championship series, attracting large crowds all the way. In 1996 a larger crowd attended the NCAA women's championship game than had seen the men's championship, attesting to the popularity of the women's game.[80]

However, postcollegiate opportunities were few for women players. A small number played professionally, and for low pay, in Europe. The appearance of the ABL and a second league, the Women's National Basketball Association (sponsored by NBA owners hoping to fill arena seats during the off-season), provided some opportunity for women to play professionally in the United States. Players in the eight-team league had an average salary of about seventy thousand dollars, a pittance compared to even the lowest NBA salary. However, for some, money was not the entire motivation. Xplosion player Shelley Sheetz, a local favorite and a veteran of Ceal Barry's CU program, explained that "our motto has kind of become, 'Little girls need big girls to look up to.' This is about being able to play in your own country, to play in front of your friends and family, and we're going to do whatever it takes."[81]

The Xplosion's first season, 1996–1997, appeared to be a success, on the boards and in the stands. Head coach Sheryl Estes, who came from Wayland Baptist University (in Plainview, Texas), where her teams advanced to the NAIA Championship Tournament six out of seven years, from 1990 to 1996, led the Xplosion to a record of twenty-five wins and fifteen losses to win the Western Conference title. The Richmond Rage knocked the Xplosion out of the ABL semifinals, and the league's first championship ultimately went to the Columbus Quest. Attendance at Xplosion home games averaged 4,105, well above the level of 3,000 that the league believed necessary to break even in its first year.[82]

The team's second season, however, was less successful. The Xplosion qualified for the playoffs, even though they had a losing record of twenty-one wins and twenty-four losses. Coach Sheryl Estes resigned in February 1998 after the Long Beach Stingrays, an expansion team, ousted the Xplosion from the playoffs in a humiliating 91-62 rout. Mainstay Shelley Sheetz also quit the team. Wichita State University coach Linda Hargrove replaced Estes as head coach.[83]

The departures of Sheryl Estes and Shelley Sheetz were the beginning of even worse troubles for the Xplosion and the ABL. By late December 1998, the team stood at the bottom of the league's Western Conference with a record of five wins and eight losses. Worse, attendance dropped sharply from the previous two seasons, averaging only 2,484 per game. Finally, on December 22, 1998, the American Basketball League folded. League and team officials blamed the collapse on their inability to interest television networks in the women's game. The ABL's collapse left women's professional basketball in the control of the NBA, which continued to sponsor the Women's National Basketball Association.[84]

The failure of the Xplosion and the ABL is symptomatic of a persistent problem in American sports: the difficulty of sustaining women's team sports, especially at the professional level. Certainly, the terrain of women's athletics is larger and more open than even a quarter century ago. Homophobia and other cultural biases are not the powerful barriers they once were to girls and women participating in sports. At the collegiate level, Title IX has required colleges to provide a fairer share of athletic budgets for women. It would also be an overstatement to say that the American public, and the sports broadcasting industry, will not support women's sports. Professional women athletes have found great success in such sports as golf, tennis, figure skating, and skiing. Nancy Lopez (golf), Martina Hingis (tennis), Tara Lipinski (figure skating), and Picabo Street (skiing) have loyal followings, earn substantial incomes, and get significant television exposure. However, the sports in which women are succeeding professionally are comparatively small niches in the professional sports marketplace, and, though they are popular with segments of the sports-fan population, they do not enjoy the mass following that male-dominated team sports command.

The question thus remains: why have women's team sports, including professional basketball, not flourished? One answer, grounded in persistent notions of femininity, is that the sports in which women are succeeding, though intensely competitive, do not involve personal bodily contact, or physical conflict, and thus do not cross the vague cultural line between the "masculine" and the "feminine." To state the case in a less jargonized manner, though Americans have come to accept their daughters competing in sports, they still do not like to see them crashing into one another in the ways they are used to seeing their sons collide on the playing field.

Another cultural obstacle to successful team sports for women is implicit in the "gendering" of sports names. Distinguishing between "basketball" and "women's basketball," suggests that the latter, somehow, is merely a feminine version of the "real" game that, implicitly, is the better game. The notion that female athletes are somehow intrinsically inferior is, of course, silly. A visit to a gymnastics meet or a fast-pitch softball game will quickly dispel that idea for any sports fan with eyes.

Commercially successful team sports for women probably await the erosion of these cultural biases. The continuing success of women in the individual sports can only help to wear them down.

When Tom Leiweke joined the Nuggets as president in 1991, he vowed that he would restore the team's popularity, "even if Major League Baseball comes to Denver." The arrival of the Colorado Rockies baseball team in 1993 created a big-league competitive problem not only for the Nuggets but for every other professional team in the area as well. And it fulfilled a decades-old civic ambition.[85]

9

"Isn't This Great?"
Baseball in the Mile High City

In early April, Denver's weather alternates between seductive previews of spring and cruel aftershocks of winter. Nature was in a generous mood on April 9, 1993, and served up a glorious, sunny afternoon for the Colorado Rockies' first home game, an 11-4 victory over the Montreal Expos. It was a storybook setting for a storybook game. More than eighty thousand fans—the largest crowd ever at a major league baseball game—jammed into venerable Mile High Stadium to cheer their new team. In the bottom of the first inning, Rockies leadoff batter Eric Young drew three balls and two strikes from Expo pitcher Kent Bottenfield (who donned a Rockies uniform before the 1993 season ended), and then drove Bottenfield's sixth pitch, a fastball, over the left-field fence for a home run (fig. 9-1). Later, in the fifth inning, Rockies pitcher Bryn Smith, backing up a play at third base, turned to nearby fans and exclaimed, "Isn't this great?"[1]

Great, indeed.

The Colorado Rockies' home opener marked the successful culmination of a decades-long effort to bring major league baseball to the Rocky Mountain region. The game also signified more than that effort, for the story of baseball runs through Denver's, and Colorado's, history like a connective tissue, binding past to present and linking Coloradans to powerful forces at work throughout American society.

9-1. Eric Young hit a home run as the Colorado Rockies' leadoff hitter in their first home game at Mile High Stadium, April 9, 1993. "EY" remained a favorite of Colorado fans even after he was traded to the Los Angeles Dodgers. Copyright 1993, Emmett Jordan/Rich Clarkson and Associates.

FROM GOLD RUSH TO GILDED AGE:

THE GENTLEMEN'S GAME, 1860–1880

Baseball, played on an expanse of green, may evoke pastoral images, but it is really a town game. A group of New York City clerks in the 1840s developed the basics of the game played in schoolyards and major league stadiums today. By the 1860s, baseball spread throughout the East, and some of the people who journeyed to Colorado in the gold excitement of 1859 doubtless had seen, if not actually played, a game. There probably were some sandlot games in the first couple of years of settlement in Denver, enough to suggest the possibility of more formal, organized play, because on March 12, 1862, *Rocky Mountain News* publisher William Newton Byers summoned anyone interested to attend a meeting at Whipple's cabinet shop for the purpose of forming a baseball club. Twenty-eight of Denver's most prominent young men turned out, including Byers's business associate, Horace E. "Hod" Rounds, and Baxter B. Stiles, a future mayor. Clearly, Denver's first organized baseball team was a gentlemen's team, representing the young city's elite. The group constituted themselves as the Colorado Base Ball Club (baseball was two words back then), and began forming teams and, presumably, practicing. At last, on April 26, 1862, the first "official" baseball game took place in Denver. "McNeil's side" administered a 20-7 thrashing to "Hull's side." It was a poorly played game, especially by Hull's team. The *Rocky Mountain News* reported that some of Hull's players' positions "were not well selected, and to that fact, and very poor batting, may be attributed the great difference in the score."[2]

Despite this unpromising start, local newspaper reports of early Denver games tended to be favorable. One enthusiastic scribe even claimed that Denver's players were the equal of any found in Chicago and would soon rival even New York City teams, though the Civil War and the lack of railroad connections to the East ensured that the comparison could not be tested anytime soon. Nevertheless, local braggadocio found its way into the eastern press. The *New York Clipper,* the leading sports newspaper of the day, in 1862 observed that Denver had "quite a good club," and looked forward to the day when they might have a "friendly encounter" with a New York nine.[3]

Although the Colorado Base Ball Club of 1862 and its teams and players were the earliest foundation of the game in Denver, they could not sustain interest in the face of the greater excitements of the Civil War and of local Indian conflicts (including battles with the Cheyenne and Arapaho Indians that led to the infamous Sand Creek Massacre of November 1864). With the return of peace, however, Denverites took up baseball with renewed enthusiasm.

Denver's population in 1870 numbered 4,759, only ten more than had been counted in 1860. However, other than a small, if growing, elite of permanent residents, the city's population turned over time and again in that decade. In such a transient society, social institutions that lent a semblance of stability and permanence were of great importance in forging a community and building a sense, even if temporary, of individual belonging. Churches, social clubs, schools, and saloons played those roles, and so did baseball. As historians Duane A. Smith and Mark S. Foster have noted, "[B]aseball united diverse and often fragmented groups of newly arrived Coloradans. Immigrants and tenderfoots, with a little help from an old-timer, could watch, enjoy, and judge the game and immediately feel themselves a part of the community."[4]

Denver's first post–Civil War team, the Young Bachelors Base Ball Club, appeared in 1866. The Young Bachelors included a number of prominent young businessmen, some members of the original Colorado Base Ball Club, as well as clerks and tradesmen, showing that, though the players still played baseball as a gentlemen's game, the sport was becoming a less elitist, more socially diverse activity, mirroring the city's changing and increasingly diverse population.[5]

A second team, the Rocky Mountain Base Ball Club, took the field in 1867, but a 79-43 win over the Young Bachelors, an embarrassment to both the winners and the losers, led to a shakeup. (High scores were, in part, a product of the early game's etiquette that required the pitcher, or "hurler," to lob the ball to the area the batter, or "striker," desired. Any attempt by the hurler to deceive the striker was considered ungentlemanly. Lack of fundamental skills, rock-strewn playing fields, and the absence of gloves also made for high run counts.) The better players from both clubs formed a new team, the Occidentals, and opened membership to any man, regardless of class or occupation. In addition to following the trend toward social diversity in Denver baseball, the Occidentals also marked a step toward semiprofessional play. Team members were not paid for their services, but their sponsor, the Occidental Billiard Hall, did provide their uniforms and equipment.[6]

The Occidentals played through the 1869 season and dominated baseball in Denver and surrounding regions. In 1867, when an Omaha team failed to show up for a challenge game, the *Rocky Mountain News* grandiosely claimed for them the championship of the entire West, "including Colorado, Nebraska, Iowa, Kansas, and western Missouri," declaring that "too much praise cannot be awarded to these bold, fearless, and youthful champions." A stirring accolade, indeed, for the beneficiaries of a forfeit, but a predictable one for a fledgling city already determined to assert itself as a regional metropolis.[7]

By the 1870s baseball also became a means by which seething town rivalries were acted out, especially against Denver. The *Rocky Mountain News* in 1874 took note of a heated three-way rivalry between Denver, Golden, and Central City. "We are a little impatient for them to commence breaking each other's head," said a notice in the Denver paper. Early challengers to Denver's baseball dominance appeared in Central City, Valmont, Longmont, Silverton, Kit Carson, Trinidad, and Greeley, and sported colorful names such as the Stars, the Unknowns, and the Resolutes. There were also Stockings—Blue, Brown, and White. Without doubt, though, the Greeley Calamities had the best name of all.[8]

The mighty Occidentals disbanded after the 1869 season and were succeeded by a less talented team, the White Stockings, who lost a championship game to the Central City Stars in 1870. Denver's hopes in 1871 rested with yet another nine, the McCooks, named in honor of territorial governor Edward McCook. At season's end, the Denver team met Kit Carson's squad to decide that year's championship. Kit Carson outclassed the McCooks sartorially, taking the field in handsome uniforms of blue breeches and stockings topped by white blouses. Unfortunately for Kit Carson, their play did not live up to the quality of their garb, as the more drably dressed McCooks thrashed them 66-31 to bring the state championship back to Denver.[9]

Town rivalry helped accelerate the transformation of baseball in Colorado from the gentlemanly, amateur game of the 1860s to the semi-professional and professional game of later years. To improve their chances, towns and team sponsors began to augment their lineups with professional players. Of course, as rivalries heated up, gambling inevitably became a part of the game, as wagering fans added their own excitement to the games. The disapproving *Rocky Mountain News* took note of the change in baseball, complaining that "there are influences at work which will greatly change its attractive features. For a year or two past the gambling element has worked its way into the conduct of the sport, and ever since its gradual decline has been manifest. The game has degenerated until it smacks of the tricks and tactics of the prize ring."[10]

BEGINNINGS OF PROFESSIONAL BASEBALL, 1880–1900

Despite the *Rocky Mountain News's* distaste for the game, amateur baseball proliferated in the late 1870s and early 1880s as Excelsiors, Eclipses, Metropolitans, Resolutes, Pacifics, Queen City, Clippers, Athletics, and others vied with one another for local and state honors. Most games, including so-called championships, were challenge matches. The Denver Brown Stockings, fielded by the Denver Baseball Club, a corporation led by businessman David Moffat, lost the 1881 championship to the Denver and Rio Grande Sporting Club of Colorado Springs. (Brown Stockings was a popular and recurring name among Denver teams. The 1879 Brown Stockings, owned by saloon keeper Charles Leichsenring, father-in-law of George Tebeau, who was to play a crucial role in Denver baseball history, was the city's first professional team.)[11]

Early Denver baseball teams played many of their games on the Broadway Grounds, a plot of land belonging to druggist and, later, water-company owner Walter Cheesman. The site, at Colfax Avenue and Broadway, was also known as Cheesman's million-dollar pasture because, as the city grew up around it, he kept a cow there to preserve for tax purposes the property's agricultural character. In later years the Broadway Grounds not only hosted ball games but also became the home of the annual Festival of Mountain and Plain. By the early 1880s, however, the Broadway Grounds could not contain Denver's burgeoning and increasingly organized baseball scene.[12]

In June 1882 the Brown Stockings joined with the Colorado Springs Reds (the new name of the Rio Grande team) and the Leadville Blues to form the Colorado Baseball League. The new league was small and, as quickly became apparent, wildly uneven in terms of talent, but it was the first baseball league in Colorado and marked an important step toward institutionalizing and professionalizing the game in the state. Denver's 1882 Browns, sponsored by a new Denver Baseball Association, were an amateur team. Indeed, the association did not want professionals in the lineup and stated clearly that there were "no provisions . . . to provide salaries for anyone." Unfortunately, the Browns' insistence on remaining an amateur team ran up against a powerful new tide in Colorado baseball. The mighty Leadville Blues, stocked with imported professional players, swept aside all opposition and captured the league title with thirty-four wins, eight losses, and a tie.[13]

Denver baseball enthusiasts tried in 1883 to answer Leadville's challenge yet stay true to amateurism. With *Rocky Mountain News* editor James T. Smith in the lead, another new club emerged to sponsor Denver's principal team. Formed in June, the Denver Baseball and Athletic Association abandoned the upper-class bias of the gentlemen's game and invited "all persons who are interested in sports activities of any kind" to join. The association leased a new field, north of downtown on the Larimer Street trolley line, where they played as the Browns and the Reds, before settling on Athletics as their nickname. Led by outfielder David E. Rowe, a player with major league professional experience, the Athletics brought respectable baseball back to Denver. In one winning streak, extending from the end of the 1883 season into the 1884 campaign, the team swept twenty straight games. They finished the 1884 season with twenty-seven wins, nine losses, and the state league championship.[14]

The 1884 Athletics were the last nonprofessional team to carry Denver's banner. In March 1885, *News* editor Smith joined with sporting-goods dealer George F. Higgins to head a new Denver Baseball Club with the avowed purpose of fielding a professional team, the Denvers. The new Denver organization also joined with the Pueblo Pastimes and the Leadville Blues in Colorado's first professional league, the Rocky Mountain League. The Denvers played a fifty-three-

9-2. The 1886 Denvers won the first Western League pennant, Denver's first championship in a multistate professional league. "From that time on," historian Duane Smith notes, "Denver was the heart of professional baseball in Colorado." Courtesy, Jay Sanford Collection.

game schedule, including twenty league games and thirty-three exhibition matches. Players' salaries for the 1885 season averaged about four hundred dollars.

The Denvers' season got off to an inauspicious start when, after an early-season loss to the Pastimes, team manager R. F. Ross fled town (possibly due to difficulties involving a lady) with seventy-five dollars of the day's ninety-dollar gate receipts. The Denvers must have thought highly of Ross's baseball skills, however, because the team welcomed him back as manager at midseason. The Denvers did not win a league game until July, but went on to win twelve while losing eight, good enough for the pennant. As the team's fortunes improved through the season, more and more fans came out to their new field at Thirty-Second Avenue and Larimer Street. By September, as the

Denvers closed in on the league title, crowds as large three thousand were there to cheer them.[15]

The 1885 Denvers rounded out the year with a postseason exhibition series against out-of-state teams, including the St. Joseph Reds, the St. Louis Enterprise, the Chicago Spaldings, and George Tebeau's Leavenworth team. That series reflected an important new departure for professional baseball in Denver because, in September, the Denvers joined the newly formed Western League, which included teams in St. Joseph, Missouri; Leadville; Leavenworth and Topeka, Kansas; and Lincoln, Nebraska.[16]

The Denvers celebrated a second championship in 1886 by winning the Western League pennant (fig. 9-2). At season's end they had a four-game lead over second-place St. Joseph. "From that time on," notes Colorado and baseball historian Duane Smith, "Denver was the heart of professional baseball in Colorado."[17]

If that is so, Denver's baseball heart was soon broken. The Denvers finished third in the Western League in 1887. The league dropped Denver from the circuit for the 1888 season, and when they returned for 1889 the Denvers finished with a disappointing record of only fifty-one wins and seventy losses.[18]

A few early Denver professional ballplayers went on to major league careers, but none had a greater impact on the sport nationally, and in Colorado, than George "White Wings" Tebeau. Tebeau at one time or another owned teams in Denver, Kansas City, and Louisville and was a founder of both the American League and the American Association. He came to Denver in 1885 with the Leavenworth team and returned in 1886 to lead the Denvers. Tebeau left Denver in 1887 for Cincinnati where he began a six-year major league career and earned a place in history as the first rookie to hit a home run in his first big-league at bat. He returned to Denver in 1890 and took over Broadway Park, located on the west side of Broadway between Sixth and Seventh Avenues. Built in 1889 by the Denver Tramway Company to attract riders to its new Colfax Avenue line, Broadway Park became the home of professional baseball in Denver until the 1920s (fig. 9-3). (Fires gutted the original structure during the winter of 1899–1900, and the remains were demolished sometime in early 1900. A second ballpark soon rose in its place.) Under Tebeau's control, the

9-3. Broadway Park, at Sixth Avenue and Broadway, was the home of professional baseball in Denver from 1889 through 1921. Fire destroyed the original structure in 1899. The stadium shown here in 1910 was built in its place. Courtesy, Jay Sanford Collection.

park eventually boasted grandstand and bleacher seating for ten thousand and something of a novelty, a tiny clubhouse for players outside center field. As both ballpark and team owner, Tebeau was baseball's center of gravity in Denver until his death in 1923. He also played a major role in the evolution of modern major league baseball. In 1900 he joined with Western League president Byron "Ban" Johnson to found baseball's second permanent major league, the American League.[19]

The late 1880s also saw Denver's first effort to land a major league team. Plagued by disappointing home crowds, Chris Van der Ahe, owner of the St. Louis Whites, toyed with the idea of moving to Denver in 1888. Nothing came of the idea, but for the first time both locals and big-league interests had given at least passing thought to Denver as something more than an amateur and minor league baseball outpost. Visits by major league teams seemed to underscore that notion. The Philadelphia Phillies came first in 1887, followed the next

year by Cap Anson's Chicago White Stockings. Boston, St. Louis, and
Cleveland visited in 1889, and the White Stockings returned in 1891
for spring training and played exhibition games at Broadway Park
against George Tebeau's Denver Baseball Club.[20]

Although professional baseball set its first roots in Denver, the
proliferation of playing fields showed that amateur baseball still prospered in the city. In addition to the Larimer Street field, the downtown area added Wynkoop Field, at Wynkoop Street and Thirty-Sixth
Avenue, and Five Points Field, bounded by Welton and California
Streets and Twenty-Third and Twenty-Fourth Avenues. Still the host
of amateur and neighborhood games, Five Points Field today is
Denver's oldest active ball field. As the city spread south and east,
ballplayers in the new "suburbs" enjoyed the Exposition Baseball
Grounds, built in 1882 on the east side of Broadway at Exposition
Avenue, across the street from the National Mining and Industrial
Exposition Building. By the late 1880s, fine new homes for Denver's
burgeoning middle class surrounded the field, creating a situation
ripe for conflict. Homeowners became annoyed by rowdy baseball
games, especially on Sundays, and complained to city officials about
the "noisy, rough characters such a place naturally calls around." Ironically, little more than three decades later, the same neighborhood
became the site of an even larger ballpark.[21]

As was the case everywhere in the United States at the time,
objections to Sunday baseball in Denver may have been a reflection
of a persistent strain of Puritanism. Or, it may have been a sentiment
of middle-class citizens who, enjoying greater amounts of leisure time
throughout the week themselves, saw no particular need for others to
use the Lord's day for baseball. Most likely, though, it was simple
cussedness. In Colorado, and throughout the West, Sunday had always been a day—for many hardworking miners and others, the only
day—for leisure and recreation, and baseball was a warm-weather
mainstay. With tongue barely concealed in cheek, one newspaper, the
Pueblo Chieftain, answered objections to Sabbath-day baseball, commenting that "good boys go to church on Sunday in Pueblo and bad
youths play base ball. It's curious how much healthier looking the
bad boys are than the good ones." Eventually, easterners adopted the
West's tolerant attitude toward Sunday baseball. Indeed, a Brooklyn,

New York, newspaper argued that Sunday baseball would help create a better moral climate, especially at nearby Coney Island, "as it will keep men away from the dancing halls, gin mills and other low dives that infest the island."[22]

Compared to the amateur game, professional baseball in Denver fared poorly in the 1890s. To be sure, in 1892, the Denver Blues defeated the Chicago Reds in the first professional women's baseball game played in Denver, but the event was more a symptom of changing gender mores than of the health of the game. George Tebeau managed to field Western League teams in 1890 and 1891, but they did not perform well. The cruel economic depression of the mid-1890s dealt another blow, as declining revenue matched declining player talent. Hard times affected the entire Western League, as twenty-three cities joined and left the eight-team loop during the decade. Tebeau assembled semiprofessional teams, sponsored by the Denver Athletic Club, in 1893 and 1894, but they rarely drew more than fifteen hundred paying fans, and usually many fewer. Finally, Tebeau gave up on fielding a professional team in Denver, for the time being, and in 1896 signed as a player with the National League's Cleveland Spiders, joining his brother, Oliver "Patsy" Tebeau, the team's player-manager. The 1896 season proved Tebeau's best as a major league player, as he turned in an impressive .326 batting average.[23]

New Beginnings, New Failures

George Tebeau was back in Colorado in 1900, ready to try his hand again at running a professional team. The appearance of the new American League helped set the stage for the revival of the Western League and for professional baseball's return to Denver. The two major leagues played almost entirely east of the Mississippi River, with St. Louis the westernmost city. That fact left the entire Missouri Valley open to new minor league organization. In 1900 a new Western League came together and included Des Moines, Omaha, St. Joseph, Sioux City, Pueblo, and Denver. Tebeau owned the Denver franchise.

With Broadway Park as their home, Tebeau's team took the field at various times as the Roughriders, the Skyscrapers, the Grizzlies, the Giants, the Mountaineers, the Cowboys, or the Cubs, all nicknames given them by newspapers in different Western League

9-4. George "White Wings" Tebeau was a dominant force in professional baseball in Colorado from 1890 until his death in 1923. In addition to his Denver baseball interests, Tebeau at one time or another owned teams in Kansas City and Louisville, Kentucky, and was a cofounder of both the American League and the American Association. Tebeau is pictured here with the 1900 Denver Bears, who won that year's Western League pennant. The team included future Hall of Fame player Joe Tinker. Courtesy, Jay Sanford Collection.

towns. However, George Tebeau, an avid bear hunter, liked the name *Bears*. Eventually, that name stuck and remained the identity of Denver's principal minor league teams until 1984.

Tebeau loaded his team with young, inexperienced players who would work for lower pay than more experienced men (fig. 9-4). The Bears' 1900 lineup did include one notable name, future Hall of Famer Joe Tinker, an infielder who became part of the Chicago Cubs' famous double-play combination of Tinker-to-Evers-to-Chance. Tebeau gamely predicted a pennant for Denver in 1900 and, perhaps to his surprise, was proved right. After a slow start, the Bears finished well and narrowly edged Des Moines for the title. Denver fans evidently appreciated the 1900 team's performance, as more than one hundred thousand filled the seats at Broadway Park during the season.[24]

Following the 1900 season Tebeau, ever alert to opportunities to turn a profit, sold off most of his best players and then sold the team to his friend, Denver insurance man Durand C. Packard. The next season, which featured the first night game played in Colorado, began a decade of dismal baseball, as the Bears turned in winning records only twice, in 1904 and 1905, and never finished better than second place. Poor fielding and bad pitching became the Bears' hallmark. A local sportswriter said of one pitcher that "his delivery was found as easily as a kid finds a jam pastry."[25]

George Tebeau, back in charge of the Bears as co-owner in 1905, claimed that the team's decline on the field owed to the fact that he alone among Western League owners obeyed the league's salary cap limiting team payrolls to eighteen hundred dollars per month. In fact, baseball players at the beginning of the century typically did not earn large sums. A major league star might make about twenty-five hundred dollars per year, which was a livable salary, but one of Tebeau's players earned only about nine hundred dollars in a season. Better minor league ballplayers might pick up a few extra dollars in coins tossed onto the field by appreciative fans rewarding a home run or a stolen base, but all of them expected to have off-season jobs.[26]

George Tebeau held on to the Bears until 1910, when he sold the team to James C. McGill, a Denver businessman, and John F. Gunthorpe. The new owners hired Jack Hendricks, a veteran ballplayer with two years' experience in the major leagues and many more in the minors, as field manager. Hendricks was a fiery competitor and got more out of his 1910 team of marginal players than expected. The Bears finished in second place that year. The following season

Hendricks took his team out of town for spring training and then put them through a three-week exhibition schedule that included two wins in a three-game series against the Boston Red Sox. The Bears went on to win 111 of 165 games in 1911 to take the Western League pennant. President William Howard Taft came to Denver in October to present to Hendricks a trophy and the keys to a new automobile. After his tour in Denver, Jack Hendricks went on to a successful career managing in the major leagues.[27]

If there was a golden age of early-twentieth-century baseball in Denver, the 1911 pennant marked its beginning, for it was the first of three consecutive Western League championships for the Bears. Hendricks's teams dominated the league through the 1913 season, playing the "inside game," which emphasized strong pitching, the hit-and-run, bunting, and base stealing.

Then everything fell apart. Jack Hendricks moved on to the major leagues, and the loss of his leadership showed immediately. An upstart, would-be third major league, the Federal League, raided some of the Bears' best talent, and within a couple of years other players left for military service in World War I. By the end of the 1917 season, declining attendance at Bear home games gave Western League officials a pretext for dropping Denver from the league.[28]

As had happened in the 1890s, amateur and semiprofessional baseball helped fill the void left by this most recent death of professional ball in Denver. Area cigar manufacturers sponsored several teams, most notably those representing M&O Cigars. M&O teams from Denver, Greeley, and Phoenix won four *Denver Post* Tournaments, an invitational tourney begun in 1915 pitting the best semipro and amateur teams in the state and region.[29]

Town ball also remained popular throughout Colorado in the first two decades of the twentieth century. Town teams were especially popular in northeastern Colorado, and clubs representing Sterling, Haxtun, Holyoke, Sedgwick, Julesburg, and Fleming even organized a Corn Belt Baseball League. Although the games tested town rivalries, they were also important social occasions. Fans traveled with their teams in caravans or on special trains, took along the town band, and often enjoyed a picnic or dinner before or after the game. Playing conditions at Plains-town ball fields may not have been up to profes-

9-5. The Boston Red Sox's great fastball pitcher Smoky
Joe Wood began his baseball career with a town team in
Ouray, Colorado. He played for George Tebeau's Ameri-
can Association team in Kansas City before joining the
Red Sox in 1908. Courtesy, Jay Sanford Collection.

sional standards, but at least they were more or less level and relatively free of injury-threatening hazards. The same cannot be said of
many mountain towns, especially in the rugged San Juans. After a 16–
4 loss to Telluride in 1908, a player from Savage Basin allowed that
though "the infield was fairly level," the outfield "had many tree stumps
sticking up."[30]

Town baseball produced perhaps the most important major
league star to emerge from Colorado in the first years of the twentieth

century, Smoky Joe Wood (fig. 9-5). Wood started his playing career at Ouray, at one time played on George Tebeau's Kansas City team, and became a pitching star for the Boston Red Sox in their glory years. In 1912 he won thirty-four games and lost only five, with an earned run average of 1.91. He went on to lead the Red Sox to that year's World Series championship with three wins. Pitching rival Walter "Big Train" Johnson said, "[T]here is no man alive can throw harder than Smoky Joe Wood." Unfortunately, Wood injured his arm during spring training in 1913, and never fully recovered. After his playing career, Wood went on to coach Yale University's baseball team.[31]

BEARS, WHITE ELEPHANTS, AND MONARCHS: 1920–1946

George Tebeau made a final effort to reestablish professional baseball in Denver in 1920. After the Western League turned down his bid for readmission, but still needing to fill the stands at his Broadway Park, Tebeau joined with *Denver Post* executive Frank Ricketson and the owners of six other teams in Colorado, Wyoming, and Nebraska to establish his own short-lived Midwest Professional League. Tebeau's team, the "Bronchos," won the league pennant in 1920, but both the team and the league collapsed after the season.[32]

Two years later, a group of Denver businessmen bought the Western League's Missouri Miners and moved the team from Joplin to Denver. Rechristened as the Bears, the team survived for a decade. Finding the Bears a home field for their first season, however, proved challenging. The owners first approached George Tebeau, but his terms for leasing Broadway Park were too high. Instead, the Bears looked to the site of Union Park, a small field at Center Avenue and Broadway, built in 1901 just north of the old Exposition Baseball Grounds and demolished in 1920. However, Union Park had grandstand and bleacher seating for only four thousand and needed other improvements. With only seven weeks left before the 1922 season began, the Bears' owners raised twenty thousand dollars and hired contractor Henry Samson to do the work. Samson finished the new grandstands, and what passed for a playing field, just before the season started. When the facility opened it had seating for eight thousand and a new name, Merchants Park, in honor of a local baking company that had made a sizable donation to the project (fig. 9-6). The playing field

9-6. Merchants Park, located at Exposition Avenue and Broadway, was home to the Denver Bears from 1921 until 1948. The park also hosted the *Denver Post* Tournament. Some fans preferred to watch ball games from their cars, parked just outside right field, rather than endure the rickety wooden grandstands. Courtesy, Jay Sanford Collection.

had some rather odd dimensions. Left field was 390 feet deep; center field stretched to 457 feet; but right field was only 318 feet. The short right field was an accommodation to the growing importance of automobiles in American society. Indeed, Merchants Park may have anticipated a later form of popular amusement, the drive-in theater, by providing drive-in baseball. A parking area on the perimeter of right field allowed motorists to enjoy the games from the relative comfort of their car seats instead of the rickety grandstands. With these and other endearing, and unendearing, quirks, Merchants Park became and remained the home of professional baseball in Denver until 1948.[33]

During their decade of play, this incarnation of the Bears never won a Western League pennant, but they were a respectable, competitive team most seasons. The team batting average was often greater than .300, a record at least partly attributable to Merchants Park's grassless outfield. The Bears also had good pitching in the 1920s and early 1930s, despite the already well-known problems of pitching at high altitude. Team owner Milton Anfenger, who acquired complete ownership of the Bears in 1923, held on to his best players through most of the decade, but by the end of the 1920s that stability in the clubhouse turned into decay as older players' skills declined and the team fell to the bottom of the league. Yearly attendance in the early 1920s topped 150,000, but fell to fewer than 50,000 in the early thirties, as poor play, the lure of radio and movies, and the economic impacts of the Great Depression drew fans away from the ballpark. During the 1930 season, Anfenger tried, with only brief success, to lure more fans to the park by installing lights and playing night games, at that time something of a novelty. Anfenger held on through the 1932 season, but finally had to fold the team when the Western League again dropped Denver.[34]

In addition to the Bears, Denver fans also got a taste of major league baseball when barnstorming teams, including teams led by New York Yankee greats Babe Ruth and Lou Gehrig, came to town. Ruth appeared in 1922 and again in 1927, and in one game put on a hitting exhibition, going five for five, including two home runs.[35]

Amateur and semiprofessional baseball once again had to fill the vacuum left by the Bears' collapse. In fact, semipro teams such as the Coors Brewers and the M&O Cigars provided part-time employment for out-of-work professional ballplayers. However, baseball was not the only game in town during the 1930s, as softball also became a widely popular spectator and participant sport. More than three hundred thousand fans turned out for games played around Denver in 1934, and the *Rocky Mountain News* began sponsoring a yearly all-star softball game. The sport became so popular that local newspapers gave it more coverage than they devoted to semipro baseball.[36]

The survival of high-quality baseball in Denver, Colorado, and the Rocky Mountain region in the 1930s owed much to the *Denver Post* Tournament. Two employees of the *Denver Post*'s circulation department, Frank Newhouse and Jabe Cassady, conceived the idea of a baseball tournament as a promotional gimmick and sold it to the paper's owners, Frederick G. Bonfils and Harry H. Tamman. The tournament began in 1915 and pitted eight invited Colorado teams. A team representing the town of Brush, led by St. Louis Browns pitcher Rolla "Lefty" Mapel, won the inaugural tournament with an 8-2 victory over La Junta. During the 1920s the tournament became a regional event, drawing teams from Kansas, Oklahoma, Texas, and Arizona. In the 1927 tournament, Babe Ruth and Lou Gehrig became ringers for local teams. Ruth's Piggly Wiggly grocery stores team defeated Gehrig's Denver Buicks 15-8.[37]

The *Denver Post* Tournament earned a significant place in baseball and American history in 1934 when it invited the Kansas City Monarchs, a Negro League team, to compete. African Americans played professional baseball almost from the beginnings of the game. However, as the spirit of Jim Crow infected American society, racism forced them out of white-dominated professional ball by 1891. Baseball, however, remained a vital part of life and culture in black communities. Amateur and semipro teams played one another, sometimes barnstorming the country for months at a time. By the 1920s, the rise of the Negro Leagues created an African American counterpart to the white major leagues.

John "Bud" Fowler was the first African American professional baseball player in the United States and, specifically, in Colorado. Fowler began his professional career with the International Association and moved among teams and leagues from Canada to Oklahoma until 1885 when he joined the Keokuk Iowas of the Western League. Keokuk folded in July 1885, and the Pueblo Pastimes recruited Fowler solely on his reputation. Although Fowler's new teammates were somewhat surprised to learn that he was an African American, he stayed with Pueblo for the rest of the season. About the time Fowler went to Pueblo, the *Sporting News* wrote of him that "he is one of the best general players in the country, and if he had a white face would be playing with the best of them." After the 1885 season the same publication noted that "the poor fellow's skin is against him. With his splendid abilities he would long ago have been on some good club had his color been white instead of black. Those who know say there is no better second baseman in the country." After the 1885 season, Fowler moved to Denver and operated a theatrical company for a few months. After he left Colorado, he played on both integrated and African American teams in the Midwest and New York until 1899.[38]

Other black players in Colorado in the 1880s and 1890s included William Castone and George Taylor, who played on several integrated teams such as the Solis Cigars, Evans and Littlefield, and the Pastimes. Brothers Zack and Bill Dean played for the Pueblo Blues, an all-black team, and the Pueblo Rovers. A black catcher named Watts also played in Pueblo in the 1880s.[39]

Denver in 1890 had a prosperous African American community of about 6,000 among a total population of about 132,000. The *Denver Republican* claimed that more black men in Denver owned homes, proportionately, than in any other northern city. During the last decade of the nineteenth century, this successful community supported two teams, the Black Diamonds and the Colorado Champions. A third team, the Lipton Teas, began playing in the early 1900s.[40]

Although Denver's African American teams represented and played for their community, racism in the surrounding, predominantly white city colored their experiences. *Rocky Mountain News* reports of African American baseball games conveyed a contemptuous and sneering attitude. For example, the *News* described a game between the Black Diamonds and the Colorado Champions as pitting "the darktown aggregation from the East" against "the Nightshades from the West." A report of a game between a black Denver team and one visiting from St. Louis noted that spectators "laughed a great deal and regarded the efforts of the colored nines as they would a good minstrel performance."[41]

Despite a racist atmosphere, African American baseball endured in Denver. In 1910 an African American Athletic Club fielded a team named the Denver Rockies. That early Rockies baseball team played through the following decade. Denver and other Colorado towns had several African American teams during the 1920s and the 1930s, including the Goalstone Brothers, Joe Alpert Clothiers, the Denver Monarchs, and the White Elephants. Coors Brewery also sponsored a black team during the 1934 season.[42]

Sponsored by Denver businessman A. H. W. Ross, the White Elephants were the most important African American team in Colorado. The White Elephants played for twenty-one seasons, from 1915 through 1935, with such notable players as Lefty Banks, "Boogie-Woogie" Pardue, Ike Bell, Maceo Brodnax, and Tom "Pistol Pete" Albright. Albright played in the Negro Leagues in 1925 and 1937, but hated the extensive travel required and returned to Denver after both tours. "Bubbles" Anderson was the only native Coloradan to advance to the Negro Leagues. He played second base for the Kansas City Monarchs, the Birmingham Black Barons, the Washington Potomacs, and the Indianapolis ABCs.[43]

Negro League teams occasionally played exhibition games in Colorado during the 1920s and the 1930s. The Kansas City Monarchs played a barnstorming exhibition series against the Denver Bears in September 1922. The teams met for one game each in Sterling, Fort Morgan, and Greeley and played the final two games in Denver. The Monarchs won the series three games to two. The St. Louis All-Stars visited Denver the following year, for a three-game exhibition series against the Milliken Whiz-Bangs, a team of locals assembled for the series. The All-Stars' roster included future Negro League great James "Cool Papa" Bell, who pitched in the series (Bell later became an outfielder). The All-Stars took the series two games to one.[44]

Although the Ku Klux Klan dominated state and local politics in the mid-1920s, white fans evidently appreciated the high caliber of baseball played by African American teams, especially the Negro League nines. The *Rocky Mountain News,* reporting on the 1923 St. Louis All-Stars' visit, noted that Denver fans were well impressed and promised that "a warm welcome will await them if they ever return to play in Denver." The Kansas City Monarchs' John Jordan "Buck" O'Neil recalled with some warmth his visits to Denver in the 1930s. "Great baseball town, Denver," he said. "We would bring another team along with us and play in Goodland and Topeka and eventually come to Denver, or we'd play a semi-pro team they had . . . that was very good. They had great crowds, probably more whites than blacks. We even had them standing in the outfield, so we had to make special grounds rules."[45]

Baseball became an important institution in other minority communities as well. Several towns, including Denver and Fort Lupton, fielded Japanese teams. Hispanic teams, some sponsored by the Great Western Sugar Company, played in and around Greeley and Fort

9-7. Oliver "The Ghost" Marcelle, perhaps the best third baseman ever to play in the Negro Leagues, was the first to suggest inviting Negro League teams to play in the *Denver Post* Tournament. The presence of African American players in the tournament marked the beginning of the desegregation of baseball in America. Courtesy, Jay Sanford Collection.

Collins. In addition, the Fort Lewis School in Durango and the Teller Institute in Grand Junction sponsored Indian teams.[46]

In 1995, Buck O'Neil recalled a Kansas City Monarch game in Denver, against a semipro team, in which the great pitcher Satchel Paige made a racist opponent eat his words. After two opposing batters hit slow, infield base hits, one Denver player loudly called Paige "an overrated darkie." According to O'Neil, Paige intentionally walked the next batter to load the bases and then called his infielders in and

9-8. Legendary pitcher Satchel Paige played in the *Denver Post* Tournament in 1934, 1936, and 1937. Other Negro League stars in the tournament included Josh Gibson, Walter "Buck" Leonard, and James "Cool Papa" Bell. Courtesy, Jay Sanford Collection.

had them kneel on the ground around the pitcher's mound. Paige then struck out the next three batters with nine pitches. "Overrated darkie, huh?" Paige exclaimed. "Satch," O'Neil recalled, "he was natural as rain."[47]

O'Neil's story has an apocryphal ring to it. More important, though, is the fact that by the time that game was said to have occurred, in 1939, the idea of African American teams playing white or integrated teams in Denver was nothing new.

In 1934 Negro League veteran Oliver "The Ghost" Marcelle approached *Denver Post* sportswriter Poss Parsons with the idea of inviting his former team, the Kansas City Monarchs, to play in the paper's annual baseball tournament (fig. 9-7). Parsons, who then managed the tournament, liked the idea and issued the invitation.[48]

The Monarchs played well throughout the tournament, the first time in the twentieth century that a black team faced a white team in anything but an exhibition game. However, the Kansas City team lost in the championship round to the House of David team. The House of David was a religious cult, based in Michigan. They were vegetarians, wore beards, and had long hair, and they did not admit African Americans into their ranks. In order to attract attention, the group sponsored a talented barnstorming baseball team. The House of David's racism did not bar them from playing and touring with the Kansas City Monarchs, so they were familiar with their rivals for the *Denver Post* championship. In fact, in order to ensure victory they set aside their racial rules and added pitcher Satchel Paige to their lineup for the tournament. Paige led them to a 2-0 victory in the championship game.[49]

Satchel Paige returned to Denver for the 1936 tournament, but with another team, the Negro National League All-Stars, composed of members of the Pittsburgh Crawfords, the Homestead Grays, and the Washington, D.C., Elites. Among the All-Stars were catcher Josh Gibson, first baseman Walter "Buck" Leonard, and outfielder Cool Papa Bell (fig. 9-8). They were, according to baseball historian Jay Sanford, "the best team ever to appear in the *Denver Post* Tournament." *Denver Post* sportswriter Leonard Cahn noted at the time that "it has been many a year since Denver has seen the likes of them. They're the cream in your coffee, the icing on your cake, the champagne in your cocktail. They're class." The All-Stars swept through the tournament undefeated, including the championship game against the House of David.[50]

The Negro League All-Stars returned to Denver after the tournament to play a two-game exhibition series against a team of white major league stars led by forty-year-old Rogers Hornsby, a seven-time major league batting champion. In the first game, Hornsby came to the plate four times against pitcher Satchel Paige, but reached base only once, on a fielding error. Paige struck him out twice, and he flied out once. The Negro League players won both games by scores of 6-3 and 6-4.[51]

Another black all-star team, led by Satchel Paige and sponsored by Dominican Republic dictator Raphael Trujillo, appeared in the 1937 *Denver Post* Tournament. In an early-round game, the Trujillo All-Stars faced a team of white players, the Pampa, Texas, Oilers. Some of the Texans resented having to play the black team and began baiting them with racist taunts. Finally, a bench-clearing brawl occurred when Cool Papa Bell spiked an Oiler baseman. When the fracas ended, four All-Stars were thrown out of the game, but no white players were ejected. The All-Stars went on to win the tournament.[52]

The Ethiopian Clowns, a barnstorming team whose pregame shows were similar to the antics of basketball's Harlem Globetrotters, in 1941 became the last black team to win the *Denver Post* Tournament. In the final year of the tournament, 1947, the Coors Brewers defeated the Cincinnati Crescents, who included the aging Cool Papa Bell.[53]

History properly credits Jackie Robinson and Brooklyn Dodgers general manager Branch Rickey for reintegrating major league baseball in 1947. However, when Robinson walked onto Ebbets Field for the first time on April 15, 1947, he was continuing, not initiating, the work of breaking down Jim Crow barriers in baseball. As in the broader civil rights movement in America, desegregation was a protracted, often dangerous struggle waged in thousands of corners of American society. When Poss Parsons and Oliver Marcelle agreed that the Kansas City Monarchs ought to play in the 1934 *Denver Post* Tournament, they advanced the cause of racial justice in America one small step, and helped set Jackie Robinson on the path to Ebbets Field.

The *Denver Post* suspended its annual baseball tournament during World War II. After the war, the series returned for only two more seasons, 1946 and 1947. A semblance of professional baseball reappeared in Denver in 1941 with yet another incarnation of the Western League (this one an enlargement of the old Nebraska State League). This version included Denver, Sioux City, Sioux Falls, Cheyenne, Pueblo, and Norfolk, Nebraska. The quality of play was poor. According to historian Mark Foster, the league was staffed with players "who could not make class C rosters." A *Rocky Mountain News* reporter went further, calling the 1941 edition of the Denver Bears "a disgrace to the fine name of baseball." Mercifully, both the league and the Denver team disappeared after the season.[54]

Denver fans did enjoy some fairly good baseball during the war years. At the urging of Colorado senator Edwin Johnson, Denver-area semipro teams joined with teams representing military installations in the region to form the Victory League. Teams from the Buckley and Lowry air bases, the Fitzsimons hospital, and Fort Logan met squads sponsored by M&O Cigars, Coors, and the Dave Cook sporting-goods stores. Some thirty-one players with major league experience played in the league between 1942 and 1946, but the quality of play, according to one sportswriter, was "something short of top-notch minor league baseball." Still, Victory League games were a welcome complement to local high school games, the other major source of baseball entertainment during the war.[55]

1947–1984

Although the renewed *Denver Post* Tournament and the final season of the Victory League had to suffice in 1946, efforts were already under way to bring professional baseball back to Denver. Senator Johnson became president of the revived Western League that year and was determined that Denver would be one of the league's stops. Will Nicholson, who later became mayor of Denver (1955–1959), and Eddie Nicholson (unrelated) stepped forward as the owners of a new Bears team. The 1947 Bears played in Merchants Park, which underwent some badly needed renovations. One of the contractors, Gerald Phipps, resodded the infield with turf taken up from his family's Denver estate. The 1947 Bears were not exactly a powerhouse and finished in fifth place in the six-team league with a record of fifty-four wins and seventy-five losses. Nonetheless, minor league professional baseball had returned to Denver to stay until major league ball replaced it four and one-half decades later.[56]

Not long after the 1947 season, the Nicholsons decided to get out of baseball and sold the Bears to Robert, Lee, and Earl Howsam in a deal brokered by Robert Howsam's father-in-law, Senator

9-9. When Bears Stadium opened in 1948 it was the biggest and best facility in the Western League. Expanded several times, and renamed Mile High Stadium in the 1960s, it was the home of professional baseball in Denver until 1995 and has been the Denver Broncos' home field since 1960. Courtesy, Jay Sanford Collection.

Johnson. One of the new owners' first decisions was to leave Merchants Park. Even with the recent renovation, the old ballpark was decrepit and lacked enough seating capacity to be profitable. Instead, the Howsams and Senator Johnson set out to build a new stadium for the Bears. Johnson bought an old dump site, at Twentieth Avenue and Federal Boulevard, from the City of Denver for $33,000 and personally guaranteed $150,000 in bonds to finance construction. When the new Bears Stadium opened in midseason 1948, it was the largest and best stadium in the Western League, with seating for 18,500 (fig. 9-9). The gamble on the new stadium paid off quickly, as 285,000 fans turned out for Bear games at Merchants Park and Bears Stadium in 1948. Nevertheless, that attendance paled in comparison to the 1949 record of 463,000. At midcentury, the new Bears were the best-supported team in the Western League, and Denver had begun to earn a national reputation as the capital of minor league baseball.[57]

Bob Howsam's 1950 Bears finished with seventy-five wins and seventy-nine losses. Future major leaguers Chuck Tanner and Pete Whisenant batted better than .300, but the pitching staff turned in a dismal earned run average of more than 5.00, and critics complained that the team's fielders had hands of stone. In one game, a line drive struck first baseman Dallas "Moose" Womack squarely between the eyes. As Bear historian Mark Foster observes, "[H]ow he survived over 100 games in the infield is a mystery."[58]

Despite their losing record and their sometimes unintentionally exciting play, the Bears continued to draw good crowds in the early 1950s, nearly doubling the nearest Western League rival's attendance. The team's box-office success owed much to Howsam's ceaseless promotional efforts, which included various community, college, company, club, ladies, and children's days and evenings.[59]

Howsam also solidified support in Denver's African American community by adding the first black players, second baseman Curt Roberts and outfielder Bill Bruton, to the Bears' roster in 1951. One businessman responded by urging African American Denverites to turn out for ball games and "show the Bears management and team our appreciation for the fine democratic team representing our great city." Howsam also actively recruited Hispanic players from the Mexican League and from Panama, including talented pitchers who helped the Bears to success in the early 1950s.[60]

With improved talent on the field, the Bears won the Western League pennant in 1952—Denver's first championship since 1913—and took it again in 1954. Ironically, though, as the Bears advanced to the top of the league in the mid-1950s, attendance at Bears Stadium fell off, slipping to 232,686 in 1954. Other forms of popular entertainment cut into the team's box-office take, as fans substituted television and movies, including drive-ins, for an afternoon or evening at the ballpark. The diffusion of the fast-growing city's population out to new suburbs also made for a longer trek to the stadium. However, many fans and sportswriters believed that Denver and the Bears had outgrown the Western League and needed to move up to a higher classification, and a higher caliber of competition, in the minor leagues.[61]

Late in 1954 Bob Howsam bought the rights to the American Association's defunct Kansas City franchise. With that move the Bears advanced to AAA status in the minor leagues and also became part of the New York Yankees' farm system. The move seemed to be the tonic needed for the Bears' ailing box office, as attendance in 1955 rebounded to 426,248. With future Yankee manager Ralph Houk in charge in the dugout, the Bears finished in second place in their first American Association season. Late-season call-ups of key players Bobby Richardson, Don Larsen, and "Rip" Coleman probably kept the team from winning the pennant.[62]

The mid-1950s were something of a golden age for the Denver Bears. The 1957 team again won the American Association pennant and went on to defeat the International League's Buffalo Bisons in the Junior World Series. The Bears of that period clearly were the best organization in minor league baseball. Their superiority is illustrated by the presence of a number of future major league stars, including the Yankees' Whitey Herzog, Tony Kubek, and Ralph Terry. Another future notable was "Marvelous" Marv Thornberry, who became renowned for his fielding errors with the generally inept 1962 New York Mets. While he was in Denver, however, Thornberry was a star hitter, racking up 118 home runs and 386 runs batted in from 1955 through 1957. Future Los Angeles Dodger manager Tommy Lasorda also had a tour pitching for the Bears in 1956. In one game, Lasorda deliberately threw at a St. Paul batter, provoking a memorable dugout-clearing brawl in which even manager Ralph Houk threw punches. When St. Paul manager Max Macon retreated to the fence on the third base side, an irate Denver fan clobbered him in the head with her purse.[63]

Despite the Bears' successes on the ball field, attendance again declined in the late 1950s, slipping to only 164,233 in 1959. Falling gate receipts forced Bob Howsam to try some dramatic moves to lure fans back to the stadium—moves that ultimately cost him control of the team.[64]

In July 1959 Howsam joined forces with Branch Rickey, the great front-office man of the Brooklyn Dodgers and the St. Louis Cardinals, to found the Continental League. Charter cities in the new would-be major league included Denver, Houston, Minneapolis–St. Paul,

New York City, and Toronto. Atlanta, Buffalo, and Dallas joined the list later. The plan called for the Continental League to begin play in 1961 as a AAA minor league. However, in 1964 it would become a third major league. Major league baseball, determined to thwart competition, crushed the upstart Continental League before it ever fielded a team by expanding into Minneapolis, Houston, and New York as well as planting a second team in Los Angeles and another in Washington, D.C. Eventually, every Continental League city but Buffalo obtained a major league team.[65]

As part of the abortive Continental League plan to bring major league baseball to Denver, Howsam borrowed money to build the south-stands addition to Bears Stadium. When the Continental League scheme collapsed, Howsam was left in debt and with even more empty seats to fill. His next effort to fill the stadium was his decision to join the new American Football League as owner of the Denver Broncos. Denver quickly adopted the new football team, but it was not enough to save Howsam financially. Finally, in 1961, Howsam sold Rocky Mountain Empire Sports, the holding company for both the Bears and the Broncos, to a consortium led by Cal Kunz and Gerald Phipps. Phipps became the teams' principle owner in 1965.

Bob Howsam went on to an important career in major league baseball. He joined the St. Louis Cardinals as general manager in 1964 and presided over that team's World Series win that year. He moved on to the Cincinnati Reds' front office in 1967 and helped build the "Big Red Machine" of the 1970s that won five division titles, two National League pennants, and two World Series. Bob Howsam retired in 1985, returned to Colorado, and was a behind-the-scenes player in the effort to win a major league franchise for Denver.

The 1960s were a sad time for the Denver Bears. Fan support, measured by attendance, continued to fall. Only 141 fans turned out for a championship game in 1961 against the Louisville Colonels. Hard times also plagued the entire American Association, and the league suspended operations between 1963 and 1968, forcing the Bears to affiliate with the Pacific Coast League, where the team had no natural rivals to prompt fan interest. Poor play did not help matters during the Pacific Coast League interlude. With poor hitting, bad fielding, and inept pitching, says historian Mark Foster, the Bears "frightened nobody but the stockholders." Attendance in 1963 bottomed out at 112,106.[66]

Changing major league affiliations also added to the air of instability in the franchise. The Yankees ended their connection with the Bears after the 1958 season. After a year with no parent club, the Bears in 1960 joined the Detroit Tigers' system for three years, affiliated with the Milwaukee Braves in 1963 and 1964, and switched to the Minnesota Twins for the rest of the decade.[67]

To turn things around, owner Gerald Phipps in 1965 hired an energetic new general manager, James H. Burris. Burris set out to promote fan interest, much as Bob Howsam had done in the 1950s, with attractions such as fireworks nights and exhibition games against the parent Minnesota Twins. Burris's efforts reversed the long decline in attendance, though it never topped 200,000 again in the 1960s.[68]

Perhaps the only highlight of the 1960s was Billy Martin's brief tenure as manager in 1968. After the Bears won only eight of their first thirty games that year, general manager Jim Burris hired the fiery Martin from the Twins' coaching staff. The job in Denver was the first of Martin's many managing jobs. During his short stay with the Bears, he began to coach the aggressive style of baseball, emphasizing daring base running, that became known as "Billy Ball." Under Martin, the 1968 Bears won sixty-five games, lost fifty, and finished with a total of seventy-three wins and seventy-two losses. After his success with the Bears, Martin returned to the Twins in 1969 as manager.[69]

Another hopeful development was the revival of the American Association in 1969. The Bears finished at the bottom of the league that year, but stormed back in 1970 to win the Western Division title. The Omaha Royals, however, denied them the 1970 league pennant. They won the league championship in 1971 and advanced to the Junior World Series, losing there to the Rochester Red Wings. The Bears slipped to the league basement the next three seasons, but rebounded with a division title in 1975 and back-to-back pennants in 1976 and 1977.[70]

The late 1970s and early 1980s brought a measure of stability and renewed fan support to the Bears. After a merry-go-round of affiliations with the Washington Senators, Texas Rangers, Houston

Astros, and Chicago White Sox, the Bears in 1976 began a successful six-year association with the Montreal Expos. A steady flow of talented players passed through Denver in this period, including Tim Raines, Andre Dawson, Randy Bass, and Tim Wallach. The 1980 Bears dominated the American Association with a record of ninety-two wins and only forty-four losses. More than a half-million fans came to Mile High Stadium that season.[71]

The Bears finished second and third in their division the next two seasons and reclaimed first place in 1983. By then, though, major changes were in the works for professional baseball in Denver. Serious efforts were under way to bring major league baseball to town. And after 1983 the Bears ceased to be the Bears.

Gerald Phipps ended his quarter-century ownership of the Denver Bears in 1984 when he sold the team to Denver real estate promoter John Dikeou. Dikeou had major league ambitions and hoped to use the Bears as a basis for landing an American or National League franchise. As part of his campaign, Dikeou changed the team's name to the Zephyrs, after the historic Denver-Chicago Zephyr train. The name change enraged many fans. Denver's leading sports columnist, Dick Connor, vowed never to use the name in print, and he never did.[72]

The Zephyrs' last years in Denver were successful and included three more first-place finishes. Another crop of future major league stars passed through town in the late 1980s and early 1990s, including Barry Larkin, LaVell Freeman, Jim Olander, Eric Davis, and 1992 National League batting champion Gary Sheffield. Almost 600,000 fans attended regular-season and postseason games in 1991 when the Zephyrs won the Triple A Classic, minor league baseball's championship series. The Zephyrs played their last home game in Denver on September 1, 1992, a 9-3 win over the Oklahoma City '89ers. The crowd sang "Auld Lang Syne" after the game. In the off-season, owner John Dikeou moved the team to New Orleans.[73]

The next professional baseball game played in Denver was to be a major league game.

EXPANSION

Although the Bears/Zephyrs pursued American Association pennants from the 1970s to the early 1990s, powerful business and political interests sought the demise of minor league baseball in Denver. Millionaires, politicians, and ordinary fans shared the dream of bringing major league baseball to Colorado. By the early 1990s, that dream became a civic goal, as voters in the Denver metropolitan area agreed to tax themselves to build a new stadium if the lords of baseball granted them a franchise. That vote was one important turning point among many on Colorado's labyrinthine, sometimes Byzantine, journey from the minor to the major leagues.

More than a quarter century passed between the collapse of Bob Howsam's Continental League scheme until the next serious effort to bring major league baseball to Colorado. By the mid-1970s, groups of Denver baseball boosters had begun haunting major league owners' meetings, promoting Denver as a desirable future major league city. Unfortunately, they had no wealthy owner waiting in the wings to buy a team. Then, in 1976, billionaire oilman Marvin Davis decided that he wanted to own a baseball team. A large man with large tastes, Davis stood atop Denver's financial and social pyramid. Each year the glitterati of the business and entertainment worlds traveled to Denver to attend the Davises' Carousel Ball. When he decided to try to buy a team, Davis told Larry Varnell, one of Denver's unofficial baseball ambassadors, "You find the team, I'll write the check."[74]

Davis first tried to buy the Chicago White Sox in 1976. In 1977 he went after the Baltimore Orioles. Finally that year, Davis began a frustrating three-year effort to buy the Oakland Athletics from their erratic owner, Charles O. Finley. The A's had been baseball's best team in the early 1970s, winning five division titles and three World Series. By 1977, however, Finley stripped the club of its best, and highest-paid, talent. Without the likes of Reggie Jackson, Jim "Catfish" Hunter, Vida Blue, and Rollie Fingers, the A's fell to the bottom of the American League West, and Finley was anxious to unload the franchise. In mid-December 1977, Davis thought he had a deal to buy the team. However, the deal fell apart over difficulties in negotiating a buyout of the A's lease at the Oakland Coliseum, and because of legal questions of whether Finley could even sell the team while his assets were tied up in a divorce suit.[75]

Rumors of a Davis-Finley deal continued to swirl during the next two years and gained substance in November 1979 when Oakland Coliseum officials let it be known that they would accept a $4 million cash buyout of Finley's lease. By early January 1980, press reports claimed that Davis and Finley were ready to sign a deal that would send the A's to Denver. Once again the deal fell through. This time the culprit was Al Davis, the mercurial owner of the Oakland Raiders. As Marvin Davis and Finley prepared to conclude their deal, Al Davis announced that he was moving his football team to Los Angeles. Oakland and Alameda County officials were not about to lose both of their major league sports franchises, and so refused to finalize the termination of Finley's lease.[76]

This attempt was Marvin Davis's last serious effort to buy a major league team. Frustrated and angry, he said, "I'm tired of being kicked around and I'm through with it." Charles Finley finally sold the Oakland A's to Walter J. Haas, Jr., chairman of Levi Strauss and Co., who promised to keep the team in Oakland.[77]

Denver's major league aspirations lay dormant until 1983, when John Dikeou entered the picture. Dikeou was one of Denver's wealthiest, but least-known, businessmen. His father, a Greek immigrant, came to Denver and built a popcorn stand into a vending-machine business and, finally, successful real estate investments. A private and shy man, Dikeou was not given to the flashy lifestyle of Marvin Davis. He and his brothers still ran the family business from a small office at Eighteenth Street and Welton. Dikeou may have had the money and the desire to lead Denver into the major leagues, but ultimately lacked the force of personality to see it through.[78]

However, if one man's money and personality had been the key ingredients for bringing major league baseball to Colorado, Marvin Davis would have become the owner of the Denver Athletics. In fact, though John Dikeou was not destined to become Denver's major league owner, he did begin the decade-long campaign that made Denver a National League city, a campaign that evolved into a broad-based civic enterprise.

John Dikeou began his bid in the fall of 1983 when he quietly introduced himself to major league baseball owners and officials. His efforts soon became much more public when he opened a Denver baseball office, staffed by associates Richard Betcke and Tony Citarella, to begin full-time promotion of Denver as a potential major league

city and himself as a potential owner. The Dikeou team's most imagi-
native early public relations move was to establish a fictitious baseball
team, the Denver Z's, complete with uniforms. Soon, mail poured in
from all over the country from souvenir buyers and would-be employees.[79]

Dikeou continued his public relations campaign at the 1984 major
league winter meeting in Houston. Denver advertising men Lew Cady
and Greg Akiyama, along with former *Boulder Daily Camera* sportswriters Leo and Bill Hirsch, published a daily newspaper, the *Denver
Zephyr,* to increase Dikeou's and the city's profile at the meetings.[80]

Dikeou's next step was his purchase of the Denver Bears to establish himself as a bona fide, if minor league, baseball owner. His
unpopular decision, in January 1985, to change the team's name to
the Zephyrs was calculated to emphasize Dikeou's role as a new baseball presence, breaking with Denver's minor league past.[81]

In the meantime, another set of players entered the picture.
Denver's young mayor, Federico Peña, took office in 1983 as the oil
boom, which had driven Colorado's economy for almost a decade,
collapsed. As the economy drifted into recession, Peña set out to jump-
start recovery through a number of large-scale capital construction
projects, including a new convention center and a new airport. The
mayor also included major league baseball, and a new stadium for it,
on his wish list. Peña made major league baseball an official city goal
in 1984 when he established the Denver Baseball Commission,
headed by attorney Steve Katich, a Peña campaign loyalist. Peña and
Katich recruited John McHale, Jr., son of the president of the Montreal
Expos, to head the commission's major league contact committee.
The commission began work with a small staff and seventy-five thousand dollars in seed money granted by AT&T.[82]

Although they shared the same goal, the Dikeou group and the
Denver Baseball Commission never worked well together. For one
thing, Dikeou was a political opponent of Peña. In addition, some of
the commission's people took Dikeou lightly and expected Marvin
Davis to weigh in again. It was not a promising partnership, and eventually other business and political forces pushed both aside.

Problems between Dikeou and the Denver Baseball Commission did not seem to matter during 1985, however, because for a time

it seemed as if Denver would get its major league team sooner than anyone hoped. Several teams, including the Pittsburgh Pirates, the Seattle Mariners, the San Francisco Giants, the Chicago White Sox, even the Oakland A's, were said to be on their way to town. Denver seemed to prove its readiness when seventy-six thousand fans filled Mile High Stadium for a Chicago Cubs–Montreal Expos exhibition game. The most likely prospect for a move to Denver was the Giants, whose owners began negotiations with the City and County of Denver to bring the team to Mile High Stadium for three years while they pressured San Francisco to build a new stadium. If the Giants did not get their new stadium, they would stay in Denver. San Francisco threatened legal action to block the move and later gave the Giants a favorable new lease to end the threat of a move. The following year, Chicago White Sox executives played a similar game, expressing interest in moving their team to Denver or St. Petersburg, Florida, all the while pressing for a new stadium in Chicago. Baseball owners by the mid-1980s clearly had learned the economic value of threatening relocation. The era of venue blackmail was under way.[82]

With luring a team through relocation proving to be a chimera, Denver's baseball hopes turned more and more to winning an expansion franchise. However, major league baseball seemed to be in no hurry to accommodate Denver's, and a host of other cities', hopes. The National League and the American League each added two teams in 1969 (the Montreal Expos; the San Diego Padres; the Seattle Pilots, which moved to Milwaukee after one season and were renamed the Brewers; and the Kansas City Royals) and the American League added two more in 1977 (the Toronto Blue Jays and the Seattle Mariners). More than a dozen cities, in addition to Denver, were actively promoting themselves as prospective major league towns in the mid-1980s, including Buffalo, Miami, Tampa, St. Petersburg, Orlando, Washington, D.C., Indianapolis, Phoenix, Vancouver, New Orleans, Nashville, Sacramento, and the New Jersey Sports and Exposition Authority.[83]

In mid-1985, baseball began to dangle the prospect of expansion before the anxious contenders. In July, Commissioner Peter Ueberroth teased the hopefuls by declaring that "expansion is coming and quicker than most people expect. I do have a date in mind," he hinted, "but it is not public information. But I agree we should move quickly toward expansion." However, Ueberroth then added that none of the prospective expansion cities met his major criteria, which included total government support, strong local ownership, and a large market and fan base. Ueberroth was talking from both sides of his mouth, raising the prospect of expansion but telling the contenders that they were not qualified. Expansion obviously was not looming around the corner, and the bidders had a lot of work to do.[84]

In October 1985, the commissioner's office sent out a letter to prospective expansion cities, further detailing criteria for expansion and inviting representatives to attend a meeting in New York in November. The enhanced criteria included local ownership, preferably an individual with net personal worth of more than $100 million; a baseball-only stadium with natural grass and state-of-the-art electronics; strong support from local government, including tax incentives; and guaranteed sale of at least ten thousand season tickets. At the November meeting, each city's delegation put on a brief dog-and-pony show, introducing local officials and prospective owners, making a case for themselves, and enduring questioning by the owner-members of baseball's Long Range Planning Committee. The Denver group came away from the encounter with the realization that a new stadium was probably a must.[85]

The City of St. Petersburg's decision in 1986 to build a new stadium, the Suncoast Dome, and the proposed construction of a new facility in Phoenix raised the ante for Denver. Both were warm-weather cities with growing population bases, and new stadiums would make them formidable challengers. However, just as baseball seemed to begin inching toward expansion, and with rival cities stepping up the competition, Denver's efforts flagged in 1986 and 1987. The Denver Baseball Commission had raised more than $1 million during its first two years, but important revenue sources, such as AT&T, began to dry up, forcing the commission to curtail its activities. However, key changes within baseball and significant political developments soon reenergized Denver's pursuit of an expansion franchise.[86]

Late in 1986 Yale University president A. Bartlett Giamatti became president of the National League, succeeding Chub Feeney, a remnant of baseball's old guard. Giamatti was an energetic man who embraced change, and in March 1987 he informed National League owners that he wanted to begin serious discussions about expansion. Commissioner Peter Ueberroth carefully endorsed Giamatti's initiative, saying that "attention should be paid to what he has to say." By midsummer 1987, Giamatti appointed a league committee composed of Chub Feeney, Phillies owner Bill Giles, Bob Lurie of the Giants, and the Cubs' John Madigan to begin fact-finding on the question of expansion.[87]

As the National League took these first tentative steps toward thinking about expansion, a new level of political pressure appeared to push baseball in that direction. In November 1987 a group of U.S. senators formed a special Senate Task Force on the Expansion of Major League Baseball. The task force initially included fourteen senators and the delegate from the District of Columbia, representing prospective expansion cities. More joined later. Colorado senator Timothy Wirth, who had conceived of the task force, became the group's chairman. The task force's stated goal was to encourage major league baseball to add six new teams by the year 2000. Left unstated, for the time being, was the task force's, and the Congress's, power to examine and perhaps modify baseball's cherished antitrust exemption if the lords of the game did not satisfy the demand for expansion. (Baseball's antitrust exemption stemmed from a 1922 United States Supreme Court ruling that found that a professional baseball player's athletic activity was not an item of "trade or commerce in the commonly accepted use of the words.")[88]

The Senate Task Force met for the first time with Commissioner Ueberroth in December 1987, and came away empty-handed. Ueberroth refused to state when, or if, baseball actually planned to expand. In fact, he took the occasion to fire a shot directly at Denver, at John Dikeou, and, perhaps, at Senator Wirth. The commissioner singled out Denver as a city not ready for major league baseball because it had no solid local ownership lined up, and because it still did not have a baseball-only stadium. Ueberroth underscored the importance of the stadium question by noting that "any tenant who plays 81 to 85 dates in a stadium shouldn't be second fiddle to any other sport in any way, shape or form," a clear reference to the Denver Broncos' status as primary tenant at Mile High Stadium.[89]

In the succeeding months, franchise hunters and members of the Senate Task Force became increasingly frustrated with what they saw as baseball's foot-dragging. They especially wanted baseball to state a timetable for expansion. In the spring of 1988 that frustration began to vent itself in Washington, as members of the task force began talking about the antitrust exemption. After a highly visible meeting with the leader of the players' union, Donald Fehr, Virginia senator John Warner, who backed a franchise for the nation's capital, warned that "baseball had better get its act together, because if Congress gets into the batter's box, we'll hit the ball and we have no idea where it will go." In response, Commissioner Ueberroth huffed, "I have never responded to threats and I don't think I'll start now." However, in June, the commissioner said that two new franchises were possible as early as 1990 and two more in 1992. Ueberroth's statement was not a firm timetable, or even a firm commitment to expansion, but it was the closest anyone of importance in baseball had come to those goals.[90]

Denver officials responded to the movement in baseball by beginning serious discussions about building a new stadium. The work included looking at potential sites, and the all-important question of how to pay for a new ballpark. By year's end, city planners narrowed the list of possible sites to five: two at the Mile High Stadium–McNichols Arena complex, two in the lower downtown area, and one at Stapleton Airport, which would be available once Denver's new airport opened. However, the more difficult problem of financing the stadium was unresolved. The City of Denver could not pay for the project itself, and private financiers were not lining up to pay for it.[91]

To Denver mayor Federico Peña's chagrin, the answer to the problem of paying for a new stadium came from the Dikeou camp, and from the statehouse. Late in 1988, real estate developer Neil Macey, a friend of Dikeou, and an opponent of Peña, concluded that the city's efforts to build a stadium were going nowhere and that a broad-based political and financial foundation was needed. Macey, with Dikeou's approval, approached the state legislature with a plan to create a metropolitan stadium district to finance and build a stadium. The district would collect a one-tenth of 1 percent sales tax to pay for the facility. The excise was modeled on a tax recently approved by voters to finance a metropolitan cultural-facilities district.[92]

The state legislature passed the bill, sponsored by Aurora representative Kathi Williams, based on Macey's plan. The measure called for a referendum, in August 1990, in the six-county metropolitan Denver area to approve the proposed sales tax. The tax would go into effect and the stadium would be built only if major league baseball awarded Denver a franchise. The bill required that "every reasonable effort" be made to pay half the costs of the project from private funds—a mandate that proved hollow. A new eighteen-member Colorado Baseball Commission, representing the entire state, would manage the referendum campaign and take over the task of winning an expansion franchise. A separate metropolitan stadium board would oversee construction of the stadium and negotiate its lease to its major league occupant. Governor Roy Romer named John McHale, Jr., who had been the Denver Baseball Commission's major league contact man, to chair the stadium board, and Sam Suplizio, a Grand Junction businessman with ties to baseball, became vice chairman. The governor also appointed John Dikeou to head the new Colorado Baseball Commission, and Neil Macey became its executive director.[93]

The stadium bill came at a fortuitous moment, putting Colorado back in the forefront of prospective major league cities just as baseball began taking more definite steps toward expansion during 1989 and 1990. Growing impatience among members of the Senate Task Force, coupled with rumors of a plan by cable television operators to launch a new major league, put more pressure on baseball to make a definite commitment to expansion and to set a timetable for it. By the end of June 1989, A. Bartlett Giamatti, who had succeeded Peter Ueberroth as commissioner, stated that the National League was committed to two new franchises and that a timetable would be announced within three months of the conclusion of upcoming negotiations for a new basic agreement with the players' union. Soon, National League president Bill White named a new league expansion committee including himself, Douglas Danforth (Pittsburgh Pirates), John McMullen (Houston Astros), and Fred Wilpon (New York Mets). Later, at the major league owners' winter meetings, White announced that the expansion committee would meet with representatives from candidate cities during 1990.[94]

More good news for Denver came in 1989 when voters in Phoenix rejected a plan for a new publicly financed stadium. Phoenix was Denver's only regional rival for an expansion franchise, and the failure of the stadium referendum there severely damaged the city's chance of landing a team. However, there was bad news, too. Commissioner Giamatti, viewed as a major driving force for expansion, died suddenly in September 1989. His successor, Fay Vincent, promised that the expansion process would go on without change, but no one was certain that Vincent had the will or the clout to push it as vigorously as Giamatti.

Another blow, this one direct, to the Denver baseball campaign fell in February 1990 when John Dikeou resigned as chairman of the Colorado Baseball Commission. Other board members, including Sam Suplizio, had complained that Dikeou had reneged on promises to finance the stadium referendum campaign and had not been aggressive enough in drumming up other funding sources. Dikeou pointed out that he and his family had poured some $5 million into baseball for Denver, but said that he was resigning because "some people on the commission thought I was a hindrance to their fund-raising efforts." Although Dikeou would remain, for the moment, as the prospective owner-in-waiting, his withdrawal from the Colorado Baseball Commission proved the first sign of his weakening grasp on that role.[95]

The news was not all bad in the first months of 1990. Senator Tim Wirth stepped up the pressure on baseball with a letter to Commissioner Vincent promoting a Denver franchise that would represent the entire Plains and Rocky Mountain region. Cosigning the letter were forty-one senators and congressmen from states as far from Colorado as New Jersey. Eighteen senators signed the letter, including at least one from every state bordering Colorado, except Arizona, as well as the Dakotas and Idaho. Clearly, Wirth had lined up a powerful political coalition in Congress in support of Denver's bid, one that baseball could not ignore.[96]

More good news came in April 1990 when National League expansion committee chairman Douglas Danforth invited candidate cities and ownership groups to make formal inquiries about expansion, that is, to begin the application process. Two months later, in

June, baseball owners announced the long-awaited timetable for expansion. In the first step, candidates would make formal presentations to the expansion committee in September 1990. In December the committee would announce a short list of finalist cities. The committee would then visit each city and make their final recommendation for the two new franchises in June 1991. The winners would be announced formally in September 1991. An expansion draft would be conducted in November 1992, and the new teams would take the field in April 1993.[97]

The Colorado Baseball Commission clearly had a lot of work to do in the summer of 1990. They had to mount the political campaign for the stadium referendum, coming up in August, and prepare Denver's presentation for the expansion committee in September. And neither project seemed to be going well.

The baseball commission had to rely on private donations to pay for the stadium referendum campaign. However, contributions continued to lag after John Dikeou's departure, and by summer the situation looked grim. In July, however, cable television magnate Bill Daniels donated one hundred thousand dollars to the campaign and challenged other area businesspeople to match it. Daniels's money gave the campaign a timely and much needed jump start. Other money started to come in, and the commission was able to mount a formidable campaign. The lack of any significant organized opposition helped the effort, too.[98]

Other problems and shocks threatened to undermine the stadium campaign and Denver's entire expansion effort in the summer of 1990. Perhaps the most important was John Dikeou's decision to withdraw as the prospective principal owner of a Denver franchise. Dikeou's own financial difficulties, and his inability to assemble a strong partnership, including failure to bring the Coors family on board, led to his decision. Thus, on the eve of the stadium referendum, Denver had no ownership anchor. In addition, after years of insisting that any expansion city had to provide a baseball-only stadium, reports surfaced that some owners were softening on that demand. And some stadium board and commission members were arguing among themselves over whether apparent weak support for the referendum might require postponing the ballot issue. Finally, just days before the vote, the baseball owners announced that the expansion franchise fee, the price of admission to the major leagues, would be $95 million for each new team. The expansion fee was shocking, especially compared to the $6 to $7 million assessed new teams in the 1977 expansion.[99]

In the short term, these shocks had little impact on the stadium issue. The baseball commission and other stadium supporters marshaled an assortment of arguments in favor of the measure, from economic stimulus to civic and regional pride, to convince voters in the six-county metropolitan area to approve the stadium tax by a margin of 54 percent to 46 percent. Ironically, the referendum won most strongly in suburban Jefferson and Arapahoe Counties, but lost—by fewer than six hundred votes—in Denver, where the stadium was to be built.[100]

Now, with less than one month left before the proposal had to be submitted to the National League expansion committee, Colorado had the promise of a new baseball stadium, but no owner for the team. Governor Roy Romer intervened in his typically aggressive manner to solve that problem.

Romer took the lead in trying to organize a new ownership group after John Dikeou dropped out. Many in the baseball effort looked to the Coors family, and, indeed, the Golden brewers had flirted with involvement but resisted signing on. Amway chairman Richard DeVos toyed with the idea, quickly backed off, and eventually backed Orlando's bid. In August 1990, as the stadium campaign neared its end, Romer asked businessmen Dick Robinson, Trygve Myhren, and Jim Baldwin to identify potential owners. The list they compiled included the *Rocky Mountain News;* cable television leaders Bob Magness and Gene Schneider; Greeley meat packer Charles Monfort; Cary Teraji, who had been a partner of John Dikeou; a California group led by former Oriole and Angel all-star Doug DeCinces; Jerry McMorris, head of a large regional trucking company, Northwest Transport Services; the Hensel-Phelps Construction company, whose interest was based mainly on the desire to build the new stadium; and a Denver-Memphis group including Steve Ehrhart, president of the World Basketball League, and Mike Nicklous, owner of the minor league Memphis Chicks. Ehrhart and Nicklous had been recruited by Denver attorney Paul Jacobs, a member of the influential firm of Holme, Roberts, and Owen, which had ties to powerful business and political interests in Colorado and around the country.[101]

The governor summoned all potential owners to a meeting the day after the stadium referendum and asked those genuinely interested to submit proposals. Only the Ehrhart-Nicklous group gave Romer a serious ownership proposal, so at a second meeting, on August 23, 1990, the governor named them as the designated general partners who would assemble the final ownership group. It was a move of no little bravado, for as Romer told Paul Jacobs, "I have no authority to do this but I'm going to do it anyway because if I don't do it, it's not going to get done."[102]

A few days later, Steve Ehrhart brought Michael "Mickey" Monus and John Antonucci into the ownership group. Indeed, Ehrhart had been something of a stalking horse for Monus and Antonucci all along. Monus and Antonucci were the principal financial backers of the World Basketball League, which Ehrhart led. They were partners in a real estate development company, and Monus was the head of the Phar-Mor discount drugstore chain, which in 1990 seemed to be well on its way to becoming the largest such chain in the country. Monus and Antonucci, whom the Denver press quickly tagged as the Drugstore Cowboys, were to be the financial deep pockets of the ownership group. Together, they pledged $30 million to the baseball partnership. By then the partnership had taken on a stronger local character, as the Coors and Monfort families joined as limited partners. The list of limited partners also included Jerry McMorris, the *Rocky Mountain News,* KOA Radio, Hensel-Phelps, and financier Oren Benton.[103]

Attorney Paul Jacobs delivered Denver's baseball expansion application to major league headquarters in New York on September 4, 1990. Twelve days later Jacobs, Ehrhart, Antonucci, Mayor Peña, and Governor Romer made Colorado's case in front of the National League expansion committee. Then the wait began.

The baseball hopefuls waited three months for the committee to announce the list of finalists from which the two expansion cities would be chosen. When the announcement came on December 18, 1990, Denver was on the list, along with Buffalo, Miami, Orlando,

Tampa–St. Petersburg, and Washington, D.C. Notably, Denver was the only western city still in the running.

The next major hurdle would be the expansion committee's visit in March 1991. In the meantime, however, the baseball group worked to strength Colorado's case by promoting advance season-ticket sales. By the end of February twenty thousand seats had been pledged, backed up by fifty-dollar deposits. In addition, the Coors family increased its commitment to a total of $30 million by purchasing naming rights for the new stadium. On March 14 the owners and the stadium board agreed to lease terms that Steve Ehrhart described, in an understatement, as "outstanding for us." Under the agreement the stadium would be financed totally with public funds, despite the authorizing legislation's mandate that "every reasonable effort" be made to pay for half of its costs with private money. The baseball franchise would manage the stadium and pay all operating costs. However, all of the money from naming rights and all revenue from concessions, parking, luxury boxes, and advertising would go to the team. The team would pay no rent on the stadium until 2000 and a fee of 2.5 percent of net taxable income thereafter. It was the best lease deal of any major league sports franchise.[104]

The National League expansion committee came to Denver on March 26, 1991. Their visit began with a helicopter tour of the city. As they flew over East High School, the school band saluted them from a baseball-shaped formation. They flew on to the site of Coors Field where a group of kids played a baseball game on a diamond chalked in for the day. The group flew over to Mile High Stadium, landed for a quick tour there, and then motored to the Governor's Mansion for lunch. After lunch the committee and Colorado's baseball delegation moved on to the United Bank Center for formal discussions. As they entered the building, a crowd of five thousand greeted them with cheers and a rendition of "Take Me Out to the Ballgame." The "spontaneous" demonstration was risky because the committee had specifically told cities not to stage welcoming rallies. Nonetheless, the committee members were genuinely touched by the demonstration. "I never get an ovation like this back in Pittsburgh," said Pirates owner Douglas Danforth. Afterward, in the closed-door meeting, the committee went over the ownership roster and its finances, and looked over the recently signed lease agreement. The meeting lasted almost an hour longer than scheduled, and Paul Jacobs noticed that the committee members asked detailed questions and made suggestions on matters that struck him as being about "things that are operational once you have a team," not "what you have to do to get a team."[105]

The expansion committee's visit proved the decisive moment in Colorado's bid. The owners came away with a more positive impression of the ownership group than they had before. And they now truly understood the depth of popular support for the bid. Phillies owner Bill Giles said, later, that Denver ranked only in "the top three or four when we started the process. The combination of the population and the ownership group was not perceived all that high until we met them and talked to them. They went up a lot in our estimation. And you could just feel the electricity of the people. . . . That was a big plus."[106]

While Colorado waited for the expansion committee's final decision, the would-be owners announced that the team, if Denver got it, would be called the Colorado Rockies. The name was not instantly popular. A *Denver Post* poll showed that a solid majority favored Denver as the identifying locality, and a plurality supported calling the team the Bears. The fact that the stadium referendum lost, narrowly, in Denver may have figured in the Colorado designation. Former Denver Bear and Bronco owner Gerald Phipps called the Rockies name "a terrible choice," though he understood the goal of giving the team a regional identity. Steve Ehrhart answered criticism of the new name with the lame explanation that people might confuse a Denver Bears major league baseball team with the Chicago Bears football team—not an optimistic assessment of the average person's ability to distinguish one city, or one sport, from another. Notably, the owners did not seem concerned that their team might be confused with the former Colorado Rockies, the National Hockey League team that played in Denver in the 1970s.[107]

Finally, in June 1991, the National League expansion committee announced its recommendation that the two new franchises be awarded to Denver and Miami. On July 5, after last-minute haggling by the American League over the future expansion draft, the major league owners finalized the decision. National League president Bill White flew to Denver for the announcement and predicted that the new Colorado Rockies would become "one of the most successful new franchises ever."[108]

Colorado's campaign for a major league baseball franchise was a civic enterprise. To be sure, self-interested political figures—Governor Romer, Mayor Peña, Senator Wirth, and leaders of the state legislature—and powerful social and business figures such as John Dikeou, the Coors and Monfort families, and the Drugstore Cowboys from Ohio had led the effort. However, it also relied on citizens who voted to tax themselves to build Coors Field and who packed a bank lobby to serenade the lords of baseball. If a solid majority of metropolitan Denver citizens had not believed that baseball was going to be good for them, economically and otherwise, the enterprise would have failed—as had the 1976 Olympic project—and Denver would have remained a minor league town.

Why was winning a major league baseball team so important? The economic argument had been significant in winning strong public support. And Coors Field and baseball have proved important ingredients in a virtual renaissance of lower downtown Denver, a phenomenon that has defied the trend in other cities where new stadiums have not contributed significantly to economic growth.

Ultimately, though, having a major league baseball team was important to Denver and Colorado for the same reasons that having a Super Bowl champion football team and a Stanley Cup hockey team are important. Major league sports teams are important symbols of personal and civic identity; they lend to their fans and their home-towns and states a sense of significance. Denver, until 1991, was the capital of the time zone without a major league baseball team, the region that television broadcast schedules skip over. But in June 1991 Denver became a Major League city.

Even more than the other major league sports, baseball is one of those cords of memory that bind American society and culture together. It is, after all, the national game. The memories of Matthewson, Ruth, Gehrig, Robinson, DiMaggio, Williams, Maris, and Rose are national memories evoking not only the game but important times in the nation's life as well. For all its importance as a community institution, minor league baseball could never match the connection to the cords of popular culture and memory that a major league team bestows.

PLAY BALL

Having won the franchise, the Colorado Rockies' owners now had to build an organization and a team. And they had to do so in an environment of upheaval within the ownership itself.

To anchor the organization and begin building a team, the owners in September 1991 hired Bob Gebhart as senior vice president and general manager. Gebhart could not come to Denver immediately, however, because his current team, the Minnesota Twins, where he was player-personnel director, was involved in the American League playoffs. The delayed proved worthwhile for Gebhart, as the Twins ultimately won the World Series.

Once he was in Denver, Gebhart began the slow process of assembling a team. In December free agent Ryan Turner, an outfielder, became the first man to sign a Rockies contract. Said Turner at the time, "I think I may be destined to be a trivial pursuit question." In fact, Turner ended up on the roster of one of the Rockies' farm teams, the Central Valley Rockies of the California League, but never contributed significantly to the parent team, and was gone from the Rockies' organization by the 1995 season. The Rockies participated in the amateur draft in June 1992 and selected pitcher John Burke, of the University of Florida, in the first round and picked up pitchers Mark Thompson and Roger Bailey in later rounds.[109]

As Gebhart took these first steps toward fielding a team, controversy and chaos struck in the front office. John McHale, Jr., the head of the stadium board who negotiated the Rockies' lease on Coors Field, left the board in July 1991. Then, in September, McHale took a job with the Rockies as executive vice president in charge of baseball operations. The appearance of a conflict of interest was clear. There were investigations, and threats from the legislature to restructure the lease and the stadium bill. Eventually, the storm cleared after Colorado attorney general Gale Norton found that the stadium lease was both legal and proper, absolving McHale of feathering his own nest.[110]

A more serious crisis erupted late in July 1992 when Mickey Monus flew to Denver and informed John Antonucci and Paul Jacobs

9-10. The Colorado Rockies' first manager, Don Baylor, was one of only a few African American managers and executives in major league sports. Copyright 1997, David Gonzales/Rich Clarkson and Associates.

that "I have to get out of baseball. I'm no longer acceptable to baseball." Monus was in serious financial and legal trouble. Eventually, Phar-Mor's board of directors removed Monus from the corporation, and he was prosecuted and convicted of embezzlement charges. Attorney Paul Jacobs had Monus transfer control of his Rockies stock to him and team financial consultant Steve Kurtz to keep it from becoming ensnared in Monus's legal problems, but that move did not prevent a major financial headache for the franchise. When Monus's troubles became public, a Pittsburgh bank canceled a $20 million line of credit given to him and John Antonucci. That line represented the Drugstore Cowboy's financial interest in the Rockies, and its cancellation effectively ended Antonucci's role as an owner, though he stayed on, temporarily, as the team's chief executive officer.[111]

The Rockies had secured letters of credit to pay the $95 million expansion fee, and there was no immediate danger that the league would cancel the franchise, but the loss of its two principal owners put a major hole in the team's financial structure. New general partners had to come forward quickly. During the month of August 1992, Jerry McMorris, a limited partner, took the lead in assembling a new general partnership with Oren Benton and Charles Monfort. McMorris took over management of the franchise and quickly moved Steve Ehrhart, who had been Monus's and Antonucci's front man, out of the club president's office and assigned him to a meaningless job as stadium development director.[112]

With the ownership shakeup completed, the Rockies got on with the work of building a team. A major step came on October 27, 1992, when Bob Gebhart hired Don Baylor as the team's manager (fig. 9-10). Baylor brought nineteen years of major league playing and coaching experience to the job. After finishing high school in his hometown of Austin, Texas, Baylor signed with the Baltimore Orioles' organization in 1967 and joined the parent club in 1970. He moved on to the Oakland A's, the California Angels, the Yankees, and the Red Sox, where he ended his playing career in 1988. Baylor was a more than adequate hitter and finished his career with 338 home runs and 1,276 runs batted in. And he was fearless at the plate, holding the major league record for being struck by 267 pitches. After his playing career, Baylor turned to coaching and worked on the staffs of the Milwaukee Brewers, the St. Louis Cardinals, and the Minnesota Twins, where Gebhart became acquainted with him. Gebhart was struck by Baylor's strong leadership and teaching abilities. "I used to watch him in the clubhouse," Gebhart said, and "I never forgot what I saw."[113]

Baylor's former managers hailed his appointment. Said Earl Weaver, of the Orioles, "[H]e played the game the way it's supposed to be played, and he was great in the clubhouse. As far as a person who knows baseball and has paid his dues, the Rockies couldn't have picked a better man." Gene Mauch, Baylor's manager with the Angels, observed that "the surprise to me is that it took this long for him to get a big league job. I thought he would be veteran manager by now." Mauch's surprise is revealing, because when the Rockies hired Baylor in 1992, he became one of only a handful of African American managers and coaches in the major leagues.[114]

Jackie Robinson once said, "I won't be satisfied until there is a black manager in the dugout." Robinson did not live to see that happen. No African American managed in a major league organization until 1961 when the Pirates put Gene Baker in charge of one of their minor league teams. Finally, in 1975, three years after Jackie Robinson's death, the Cleveland Indians made Frank Robinson the first African American manager in the major leagues. Don Baylor became major league baseball's sixth African American manager, joining Frank Robinson, Larry Doby (the first black player in the American League), Maury Wills, Cito Gaston, Hal McRae, and Felipe Alou. More than four decades after baseball's desegregation, only a half-dozen blacks had managed major league clubs, there were no black owners, and only a few held top front-office jobs. National League president Bill White was the ranking African American in all of baseball.[115]

With Baylor on board, the Rockies were ready for the expansion draft, which took place on November 17, 1992. The Rockies and the other expansion team, the Florida Marlins, took turns picking players left unprotected by all of the National and American League teams. The Rockies made Atlanta Braves pitcher David Neid their first pick. Other players who became mainstays on the Rockies' rosters during the first several seasons included second baseman Eric Young (Dodgers), who hit the first home run as the first batter in the first inning of the first home game; third basemen Charlie Hayes (Yankees) and Vinny Castilla (Braves); pitchers Darren Holmes (Brewers) and Curtis Leskanic (Twins); and catcher Joe Girardi (Cubs). The Rockies also acquired outfielder Dante Bichette in a trade with the Brewers, and signed free agents Andres Galarraga, a first baseman, and outfielder Ellis Burks. Bichette, Galarraga, Burks, and Castilla became the foundations of the Rockies' potent batting offense, the "Blake Street Bombers."[116]

One of baseball's supposed traditions has it that expansion teams, because they are made up of players cast off by other teams, cannot play competitively for several seasons and expect to lose at least one hundred games their first year. Don Baylor rejected that notion. Because the 1992 expansion draft drew from both leagues, and because of free agency, many high-quality players joined the Rockies and the Marlins. In the Rockies' first half-decade of play, the team played well, if not at championship levels, and many individual players turned in exceptional performances. Unfortunately, poor pitching too often negated a potent offense.

The 1993 Rockies had the best first-season record of any National League expansion team, winning sixty-seven games and losing ninety-five to defy the one-hundred-loss "rule." The highlight of the year, following Eric Young's leadoff home run in the first game, was Andres Galarraga's National League batting championship. The "Big Cat" finished the season with a .370 average, tying Tony Gwynn's 1987 record for the highest average since Stan Musial's .376 average in 1948. The Rockies had their first winning season in 1995 (77-67) and earned the wild-card spot in the National League Championship Series, becoming the first expansion team to advance to the playoffs so quickly. Their performance that year also earned Don Baylor the National League's manager of the year honors. The team had another winning year in 1996 (83-79), but did not qualify for postseason play. In 1997, right fielder Larry Walker won honors as the National League's most valuable player (fig. 9-11). Walker, who joined the Rockies in 1995, batted .366, including forty-nine home runs and 130 runs batted in. He also had thirty-three stolen bases and a Gold Glove–award season on defense with his play in right field. Dante Bichette and Ellis Burks had been contenders for most valuable player in 1995 and 1996, but lost because most of their offensive output had been at Coors Field. Baseball writers, who voted the award each year, penalized them because they believed playing at high altitude gave the Rockies' players a batting advantage. Walker, on the other hand, was just as potent on the road as at home. Owner Jerry McMorris hoped that Walker's award would help end the bias against Rockies players. "Every Rockie in the future," McMorris said to Walker, would be "thankful to you for kicking that door down to where the Rockies players can get proper recognition."[117]

Don Baylor's tenure as the Rockies' manager ended after the 1998 season when the team won only seventy-seven games while losing eighty-five. The season, which included fifteen losses in the first nineteen games, was especially disappointing because team officials believed the 1998 team, including pitcher Darryl Kile, a high-priced free-agent acquisition, was the best in the franchise's six-year

9-11. Larry Walker's hitting and fielding earned him most valuable player honors in the National League in 1997. Copyright 1997, David Gonzales/Rich Clarkson and Associates.

history. The Rockies replaced Baylor with Florida Marlin manager Jim Leyland, who coached that team to the 1997 World Series Championship. Leyland's three-year, $6 million contract made him the highest-paid manager in baseball. However, the Rockies' management did not bring in any major new talent for the 1999 season, leaving Leyland with essentially the same team that had played so unspectacularly in 1998.[118]

When major league baseball came to Denver, the game hit a home run in the Rockies. The Rockies quickly became baseball's most successful franchise, at least as measured by fan support. The more than 80,000 who attended the first home game in April 1993 were only the first wave in a tide of humanity that swept into Mile High Stadium and Coors Field. The final tally for 1993 was 4,483,350 in attendance at the Rockies' home games, more than 400,000 over the Toronto Blue Jays' previous record set just the year before when that team went to and won the World Series. The Rockies' attendance record may never be equaled given major league baseball's insistence on smaller, more intimate stadiums. In the two seasons played at Mile High Stadium, crowds of more than 70,000 turned out twenty-one times. Rockies attendance continued to outstrip other major league teams after the move to Coors Field, which has 25,000 fewer seats than Mile High Stadium. Almost 3.4 million fans came to Coors Field in the strike-shortened 1995 season, and more than 3.8 million attended in 1996 and 1997. Major league baseball recognized the Rockies' success in the grandstands by awarding Denver the 1998 All-Star Game.[119]

10

HOCKEY IS ALL THE RAGE

Ice hockey is an exciting, fast-paced, often violent game. With the exception that felonies are discouraged, it has few rules readily apparent to the novice fan. Indeed, when the Quebec Nordiques of the National Hockey League (NHL) moved to Denver in May 1995 and became the Colorado Avalanche, few Coloradans knew much about the state's newest major league sport. Little more than a year later, however, Colorado was hockey crazy, as the Avalanche stormed through the NHL playoffs and won the Stanley Cup, the trophy commemorating the league championship. When the "Avs" returned to Denver after their dramatic overtime win over the Florida Panthers in game four of the championship series, a crowd of more than four hundred thousand jammed Denver's Civic Center to celebrate the team's, and Colorado's, first major league championship.

To say that Colorado was delighted with its first big league championship would be an understatement. To say that Colorado was surprised that a hockey team delivered that long-coveted prize would also be something of an understatement. The story of the Colorado Avalanche graphically illustrates the character and the changing political and economic realities of major league sports in Colorado and the United States. The brief history of the Avalanche franchise in Colorado has included franchise relocation, the economic impacts of free agency and escalating player salaries, and the ever closer connection between major league sports and corporate empires, including the entertainment communications industry.

It is important to remember, though, that the story of hockey in Colorado did not begin in 1995. Indeed, few realized in 1995 that organized professional and collegiate hockey in Colorado had a history dating back more than a half century.

ORIGINS

In December 1901, the *Denver Times* reported that "hockey is all the rage in Leadville." The Cloud City "is congenial ground for the great English game," the *Times* noted, "as every man, woman and child . . . knows how to skate." The twenty-seven members of Leadville's hockey club divided themselves into two teams, the Whites and the Maroons. Although the two squads enjoyed a "sharp rivalry" that kept both "up to a high standard," they also sought outside competition from the Denver Wheel Club, Denver University, and Colorado College. Although this *Denver Times* article is brief, it reveals much about the origins of hockey and its development in Colorado.[1]

In *Sports in the Western World,* historian William J. Baker identifies two antecedents of hockey. One was the Indian game of lacrosse. Indians of the northern Plains and Canada played lacrosse year-round and in the winter sometimes added excitement to their matches by foraying onto frozen lakes and rivers. White settlers in Canada began playing Indian teams in the 1840s, but did not record a win until 1851. Thereafter, white teams proliferated, and lacrosse soon became Canada's "official" sport. By the 1880s, Canadian whites effectively barred Indian competition by limiting organized club play to amateurs, a designation denied to Indians because their games usually netted the winners a cash prize. Unlike Indians, whites played lacrosse only in the summer and fall months. "Outdoors on frozen lakes," Baker notes, "lacrosse on ice skates proved as awkward as did similar attempts to play winter soccer, cricket, and baseball."[2]

Lacrosse's popularity, and long winters, made Canada a potential host for the game historian Baker sees as the direct English progenitor of hockey. Long before the nineteenth century, East Anglians played a game called bandy, an adaptation of field hockey played on frozen ponds and canals. Bandy players used curved sticks to propel a flat, circular object toward a goal. English migrants undoubtedly carried their game to North America where the long Canadian winters made for an ideal playing environment. Canada's Amateur Hockey Association claimed in 1941 that a group of English soldiers played the first recorded hockey game in Kingston, Ontario, in 1855. That claim is probably as historically sound as placing the "first" baseball game in Cooperstown, New York, in 1839. Yet, it is accurate insofar as hockey took root in the second half of the nineteenth century as Canada's most popular winter sport.[3]

The early game was simple compared to the modern version. Two sticks frozen into the ice about six feet apart served as the goal. Pucks were as likely to be made of wood as rubber. Players, including goal tenders, whose job, then as now, was to block the puck from penetrating the goal, wore no protective gear. When a Winnipeg goalie appeared for a game wearing cricket pads on his shins, a hostile Montreal crowd greeted him with derisive howls. Montreal fans were not entirely opposed to innovation, however, and in 1900 one brought fish netting to hang on the goal sticks, making it easier to determine when a goal was scored.[4]

By the late 1870s, Montreal became the center of hockey's development in Canada. In the winter of 1879–1880, a group of students formed the McGill University Hockey Club. The McGill club's rules, which featured nine men to a team, a square rubber puck, and no forward passing, quickly became widely accepted. By the 1890s almost one hundred hockey clubs competed in the Montreal area. From there, hockey spread throughout Canada and was especially popular in Regina, Calgary, Vancouver, Winnipeg, and Quebec.[5]

The appearance of the sport's most coveted prize illustrates that collegiate and amateur hockey was a well-developed, institutionalized sport in Canada during the last decade of the nineteenth century. In 1893 Sir Frederick Arthur Stanley, a former English governor-general of Canada, commissioned a silver bowl, its interior finished in gold, set on a base of ebony, to be awarded annually to the champion Canadian team. The Montreal Amateur Athletic Association became the first team to claim the Stanley Cup by defeating the Ottawa Capitals before a crowd of five thousand. Amateur teams held on to the cup for the next decade and a half, but in 1910 the new National

Hockey Association, a predecessor of the modern National Hockey League, took it, and the cup has remained a professional sports trophy ever since.[6]

Collegians and other amateurs in the United States began playing organized hockey during the 1890s. Intramural squads at Yale and Johns Hopkins Universities took to the ice in 1893. Five years later, Brown University shut out Harvard, 6-0, in the first American intercollegiate hockey game. By that time, too, a four-team United States Amateur Hockey League had been founded in New York City.[7]

Professional hockey appeared in the United States and Canada early in the twentieth century. Like football, professional hockey first took root in working-class towns. The first such team was J. L. Gibson's Portage Lakes, organized in 1903 in Portage Lake, Michigan. The following year, the Lakes joined with several other teams to form the International Professional Hockey League. The league survived for only four seasons, but during its life it attracted many of the best players, especially from Canada, and forced the Canadian amateur associations to professionalize. Professional teams and leagues appeared and disappeared on both sides of the U.S.-Canada border over succeeding years, but in 1917 the National Hockey Association merged with another league to form the National Hockey League. The new NHL had four teams, two in Montreal and one each in Montreal and Ottawa. By 1926 the league had expanded to twenty teams, six of them in the United States (in Boston, New York, Chicago, Detroit, and Pittsburgh). However, the NHL had expanded too rapidly, and over the next two decades more than a dozen franchises folded. By the end of World War II only six teams remained. Moreover, the shakeout shifted the league's geographic center of gravity from Canada to the United States where New York, Chicago, Detroit, and Boston hosted four teams, while Montreal and Toronto were home to the two remaining Canadian franchises. Canadians, however, continued to outnumber Americans among the ranks of NHL players.[8]

The National Hockey League remained a small fiefdom for more than two decades. Three men, James Norris, Arthur Wirtz, and Conn Smythe (or their heirs), controlled four of the league's six teams—the Chicago Blackhawks, the Detroit Red Wings, the New York Rangers, and the Toronto Maple Leafs—and saw no urgent reason to change things. NHL players generally were a compliant lot, happy with the minimum salary of seven thousand dollars for playing seventy games in 1957. That year the players did organize a short-lived union to demand a percentage of the league's small television revenues. The fledgling union fell apart after the owners agreed to share some of their broadcast money.[9]

By the late 1960s, the league was ready to follow the rapidly growing and shifting population of North America south and west. Six new teams joined the NHL in 1967 and another four by the 1972–1973 season. Another would-be major hockey league, the World Hockey Association (WHA), challenged the NHL beginning in 1972. With twelve original teams, the WHA at first seemed to be a formidable contender, especially after its Winnipeg franchise signed NHL great Bobby Hull away from the Chicago Blackhawks and another NHL star, Gordie Howe, went to Houston. By 1979, however, the realities of hockey's small fan base and sparse broadcast revenues whittled the WHA field to six teams. Negotiations between the two leagues in 1979 led to the merger of four of the remaining WHA teams into the National Hockey League. The merger increased the NHL's presence in Canada by adding the Winnipeg Jets, the Edmonton Oilers, and the Quebec Nordiques to the loop, and the New England Whalers added to the league's U.S. component. By 1998 the National Hockey League included twenty-six teams playing in four divisions arrayed from the Atlantic to the Pacific and from Canada to Florida.[10]

Since World War II, several regional and national minor leagues have maintained a professional hockey presence in non-NHL cities, including Denver. Some, like the United States Hockey League, were one-season wonders. Others, including the WHA, the Central Hockey League, the Western Hockey League, and the International Hockey League, were more durable. Each made at least one stop in Colorado.[11]

Collegiate Hockey in Colorado

Early press references to hockey in Colorado are scarce, but it is clear that Coloradans learned to play and watch the game long before the first professional team played in the state. An item in Leadville's

Evening Chronicle in January 1884 reported on a match between two squads of the Leadville Shinny Club led by Sam Leonard and W. G. Niblock. (In addition to the Indian women's field hockey game, the term *shinny* has also been used for ice hockey.) The game reportedly was "well-played on both sides, but victory perched on the banner of the Niblock forces." After the game "the club repaired to Mart Duggan's where they sat down to an excellent supper at the expense of the losing side."[12]

Whether it was the Leadville Shinny Club of 1884 or the club seeking challengers in 1901, hockey in Colorado clearly began as an amateur game played by young gentlemen. That the turn-of-the-century Leadville team looked to the University of Denver and Colorado College for competition suggests that some of the young gentlemen attending those schools were playing hockey by then. Although Denver and Colorado Springs collegians probably played intramural and other opponents by the early years of the twentieth century, school records date the beginning of intercollegiate hockey to 1939 at Colorado College and 1949 at the University of Denver. Both schools quickly built and sustained championship-caliber hockey programs that, in turn, helped build a solid, if small, fan base for the sport in Colorado.

In 1938 hockey enthusiasts in Colorado Springs, backed by local businesses, formed eight teams and organized the Pikes Peak Hockey League. One of the new teams represented Colorado College. The Broadmoor Hotel's World Arena (later renamed as the Broadmoor Ice Palace), recently converted from an indoor horse-riding facility to an ice rink, hosted the new league's games. The Broadmoor arena remained Colorado College's home ice for fifty-five years. However, Colorado College's first hockey season was not terribly promising. After losing their first game 8-1, to the Giddings Department Store team, the "Tigers," led by player-coach John Atwood, lost eight more matches and won only three.[13]

The Pikes Peak collegians' hockey fortunes improved significantly in the 1938–1939 season when they won eight games and lost only three. Among the Tigers' eight wins were victories in their first two intercollegiate games, an 8-5 defeat of the Colorado School of Mines and an 8-3 thumping of the University of Colorado. An important element in CC's sudden improvement was the arrival of the school's first Canadian player, Ernie Young of Saskatoon, Saskatchewan. Five more Canadians joined Young the following year, including Wilmer "Spike" Wilson, who led the Tigers in scoring for three seasons, and goalie Bob Scarlett, who later briefly coached a professional hockey team in Denver. With this corps, Colorado College quickly developed into a major force in collegiate hockey and by the winter of 1942 was regarded, along with the University of Southern California, the University of Illinois, and Dartmouth, as one of college hockey's "Big Four." Their worst season in this early period was the 1941–1942 campaign that ended with a .500 record of six wins, six losses, and three ties. By then, teams such as the Newton Lumberjacks, the Coca Cola Bottlers, the Colorado Springs Merchants, and the Alexander Filmers had given way to an all-collegiate schedule of games featuring Michigan, Yale, Illinois, Dartmouth, and a raft of California schools.[14]

World War II forced the cancellation of the 1942–1943 and 1943–1944 seasons. When play resumed with an abbreviated schedule in 1944–1945, the Tigers, still missing their prewar starters, won only one game, lost three, and tied one. The following season was little better, ending with only three wins and eight losses, but the ingredients for renewed success were in place with the return of several veteran players, the arrival of reinforcements from Canada, and the hiring of a new coach, Cheddy Thompson, a naturalized Canadian and U.S. Army Air Corps veteran, who led the Tigers for a decade. The 1946–1947 season saw a return to winning play with fourteen wins and only five losses. The Tigers had only one losing season (nine wins and twelve losses in 1952–1953) during Thompson's tenure.[15]

Thompson and Colorado College made Colorado Springs the virtual capital of collegiate hockey in this era. With the Broadmoor Hotel, the college in 1948 hosted the NCAA hockey championship tournament. The hotel's Ice Palace evidently proved a congenial setting for the annual game, as it was held there for the next ten years. In that span, the Tigers vied for the championship seven times, winning it in 1950 and finishing in second place in 1952 (the year the United States Hockey Coaches Association named Thompson coach of the year) and 1955.[16]   •

Colorado College also became a founding member in 1951 of the Mid-West Collegiate Hockey League, predecessor of the modern Western Collegiate Hockey Association (WCHA), which included the University of Denver, three Michigan schools, and the Universities of Minnesota and North Dakota. The Tigers won three league titles in the 1950s (1952, 1955, 1957), but did not return to championship form again for almost four decades. Indeed, between 1957 and 1997 Colorado College had only nine winning seasons. Despite the poor win-loss record, several Colorado College hockey players went on to professional careers, including ten who advanced to the NHL, most notably Doug Lidster, a 1983 graduate who played with the 1994 Stanley Cup–winning New York Rangers. Beginning with the 1993–1994 season, the Tigers once again became a major power in regional and national collegiate hockey, winning three WCHA titles and, in 1996, advancing to the NCAA championship game, which they lost to Michigan, and the 1997 semifinals.[17]

Colorado College has played more games against its in-state hockey rival, the University of Denver, than against any other opponent. And over the years, DU has had the Tigers' number, turning in a record of 132-75-7.[18]

DU's Pioneer hockey team played their first season in 1949–1950. Coached by Vern Taylor, former all-star goalie for the Duluth Hornets and more recently manager of the Broadmoor Ice Palace, the Pioneers debuted against the University of Saskatchewan on December 19, 1949. They lost 17-0. Gene Amole, who became a radio and newspaper legend in Denver, broadcast the game on station KMYR. It was the second hockey game Amole had ever seen. Amole recalled that "the next night, the Canadians took pity on DU and played their bench, winning again, 9 to 1." The Pioneers also fell victim that season to Brown, Colorado College, British Columbia, North Dakota, and Alberta, losing thirteen of seventeen games. DU bested only the University of Wyoming in four games. Taylor's 1950–1951 team improved their record to eleven wins, eleven loses, and one tie. Their victories that year included wins over Princeton, Minnesota, and Michigan.[19]

Twenty-four-year-old Neil Celley took over as the Pioneers' coach the next season. A member of the 1948 U.S. Olympic hockey team, Celley came to DU straight from the University of Michigan where, as his team's most valuable player, he led the Wolverines to their first national hockey championship in 1951. During the regular season that year he scored a hat trick (three goals) against the Pioneers. The following December he coached his DU squad in a 5-4 win over Michigan. Celley established DU as a legitimate hockey power, and a local sports favorite, with five straight winning seasons. By the end of Celley's first season, *Rocky Mountain News* writer Jack Foster declared that the Pioneer skaters had "captured the town's fancy as few outfits ever have." He also identified an important ingredient in their success. "Most of them," he noted, "are Canadian kids."[20]

The arrival of head coach Murray Armstrong in 1956 heralded the beginning of DU hockey's golden age, though the 1956–1957 season's record of twelve wins, fourteen losses, and two ties might have suggested otherwise. In fact, that was one of only three losing seasons in Armstrong's twenty-one years at DU. Armstrong, an NHL veteran who played for the Toronto Maple Leafs, the Detroit Red Wings, and the New York Americans, had coached in Canadian minor league hockey before coming to Denver. He built on the foundation of success built by Celley, including recruiting more talented Canadian players. Gene Amole once asked him what he did to attract so many players from one area in particular, Thunder Bay, Ontario. Armstrong answered simply, "I tell them it is warm down here."[21]

Under Armstrong, the Pioneers won five NCAA championships (1958, 1960, 1961, 1968, 1969), eight Western Collegiate Hockey Association regular-season titles (1959, 1960, 1961, 1963, 1964, 1968, 1972, 1973), and ten WCHA playoff championships (1960, 1961, 1963, 1964, 1966, 1968, 1969, 1971, 1972, 1973). His 1960–1961 team was his best, compiling a record of thirty wins, one loss, and one tie, including the NCAA and WCHA championships. That squad also defeated the 1960 U.S. Olympic team. Armstrong's Pioneers also found themselves involved in an early thaw in Cold War–era tensions. In January 1959 the DU team played the Soviet Union's national team in an exhibition at the Broadmoor. The hard-fought East-West game ended in a tie after a Soviet player scored with only a minute and eighteen seconds left in the game. The appreciative, black-tie crowd of more than three thousand hailed both teams with a standing ovation. A rematch fifteen years later end with a 9-1 Soviet victory.[22]

Since Armstrong's retirement, after the 1976–1977 season, the Pioneers have had fifteen winning and six losing seasons under coaches Marshall Johnston (1977–1981), Ralph Backstrom (1981–1990), Frank Serratore (1990–1994), and George Gwozdecky (1995–). The best years were 1978, when DU won the WCHA regular-season championship, and 1986, when it won the WCHA regular-season and playoff titles.[23]

Winger John MacMillan, who played for the Detroit Red Wings and the Toronto Maple Leafs from 1960 to 1965, was the first DU player to move on to professional hockey. More than forty others have followed him. Perhaps the most notable was forward Craig Patrick (1967–1971), who played eight seasons in the NHL before becoming general manager of the New York Rangers (1981–1986) and the Pittsburgh Penguins (1989–). Patrick's Penguins have twice won the Stanley Cup. Patrick, who was DU's athletic director from 1987 to 1989, became a member of the United States Hockey Hall of Fame in 1996.[24]

PROFESSIONAL HOCKEY

College hockey in Colorado never won the wide public following or the media attention devoted to other college and professional sports. Nonetheless, the successful hockey programs at Colorado College and the University of Denver created a core of knowledgeable fans for professional teams to lure, though it would take exceptionally talented, well-financed, and reasonably well-managed professional teams to succeed in Colorado. The 1995–1996 Avalanche team clearly met those criteria. However, professional hockey had an almost half-century history in Denver before that grand, Stanley Cup–winning season.

Colorado's first professional hockey team, the Denver Falcons, a United States Hockey League franchise, played for only one season, 1950–1951. Owned by Charles Boettcher III and Will and Eddie Nicholson (former owners of the Denver Bears baseball team), the Falcons shared the ice at the DU Arena with the collegian Pioneers. Former New York Ranger player William Osser "Bill" Cook, called the "greatest right winger ever to blast the puck into the nets," coached the team. Before coming to Denver, Cook coached his Minneapolis Millers to a championship. The United States Hockey League collapsed after the 1950–1951 season, and the Falcons disappeared.[25]

Seven years later a group of prominent political and business leaders tried unsuccessfully to launch another professional hockey team in Denver. Then-governor Steve McNichols and former governor Ed Johnson (who had played a key role in reviving professional baseball in Denver after World War II) joined with businessmen Eugene Clift, Palmer Burch, Mel Gatz, Robert E. Lee, and John F. Ehrhart and Denver city government officials Carl Becker and Charles Byrne to form Mile High Hockey, Inc. The corporation, which hoped to sell one hundred thousand shares of stock, purchased the Cincinnati franchise of the International Hockey League (IHL) in August 1958. The team, to be called the Viscounts, not only never took the ice but also never existed. Two weeks after the corporation announced its franchise, president Eugene Clift announced that the team could find neither a coach nor players. Clift blamed "rigid financial requirements imposed on Denver" by the league for the failure to put a team together.[26]

Clift vowed to assemble a team for the following season and did so, but with only slightly more success. The new team, the Denver Mavericks, were also an IHL team. Clift hired as general manager former Colorado College player Bob Scarlett. After college, Scarlett had played minor league hockey and then moved into sports management, in baseball, working as assistant general manager of the Colorado Springs Sky Sox and the Amarillo Gold Sox. The University of North Dakota's Bob May signed on as head coach and, with Scarlett, began recruiting players. The Mavericks tapped into local talent and signed a number of DU and Colorado College players, including Murray Massier, the most valuable player on DU's 1958 NCAA championship team. May also brought in players from North Dakota. With a front office, players, and a coach, the Mavericks seemed to get off to a much better start than the ill-fated Viscounts. However, by early December 1959 the team had to notify the league that it could not afford to play the remainder of the season. The IHL then transferred the franchise to new owners in Minneapolis, and the Mavericks became the Millers.[27]

Three and one-half years later, in June 1963, a new team and a new league appeared in Denver. The Denver Invaders, a Western Hockey League (WHL) team owned by the Toronto Maple Leafs of the NHL, set up shop in the Denver Coliseum to take on WHL rivals from San Francisco, Portland, Seattle, Los Angeles, and Vancouver. Coach Rudy Pilous predicted before the season that the Invaders would qualify for the league playoffs. In fact, the Invaders won the league regular-season championship. However, Denver's one-year (or less) jinx for hockey also applied to the Invaders. When the parent Maple Leafs negotiated a better arena deal in British Columbia, the Invaders retreated to Canada.[28]

Denver's next professional hockey entry, the Spurs, had more staying power and lasted for seven and one-half seasons. Originally a WHL franchise, the Spurs played in two other leagues and experienced two ownership changes before the team's demise in 1976. Founded in 1968 by Timothy Collins, the Spurs came under the control of the NHL's St. Louis Blues in 1971. The change to major league management proved an elixir for the Spurs, as they won the WHL regular-season championship and the league's Lester Patrick Cup in the playoffs. During the off-season the Blues' management hatched a scheme to groom Denver and the Spurs for eventual entry into the NHL. As part of the plan, the Blues sold the Spurs to St. Louis real estate developer Ivan L. Mullenix. However, as part of the deal, the Blues' organization would continue to manage the Denver team and guide it toward admission to the NHL. As he announced his purchase of the Spurs, Mullenix declared that he planned to apply for an NHL franchise "in the near future." However, he said that a new arena would be necessary, a view seconded by the Blues' Sid Salomon, who said that "a new sports arena would culminate our efforts and insure another successful professional effort in the Mile High City." The Spurs-Blues' management hoped that the pending referendum on a multiuse facility for the proposed 1976 Winter Olympics would produce the desired new venue. In fact, Denver voters approved the measure, and the city went on to build McNichols Arena, which became the home of Denver's professional hockey and basketball teams.[29]

Mullenix moved the Spurs to the Central Hockey League in 1974, but stayed in pursuit of a major league franchise. Then in March

1975 the hope of making Denver a National Hockey League town was seemingly realized when the NHL granted Mullenix a conditional franchise for the 1975–1976 season. However, Mullenix instead chose, apparently for financial reasons, to take the Spurs into the new World Hockey Association, formed as a would-be major league rival to the NHL. That decision was the beginning of the end for the Spurs. Disappointed fans abandoned the Spurs, and, as attendance and revenue fell, the team fell into financial trouble. Finally, on January 2, 1976, the Spurs left Denver on a road trip and never returned. While they were away, the WHA agreed to transfer the franchise to Ottawa. Mullenix left behind debts of more than $2 million owed to a Denver bank and the city government. The City of Denver got some small satisfaction by seizing hockey and office equipment left behind at McNichols Arena. Season-ticket holders—sixteen hundred of them— were left holding worthless tickets. The former Spurs, playing as the Ottawa Civics, lasted only a few more weeks before Mullenix dissolved the franchise.[30]

The National Hockey League lost little time in moving into Denver in place of the departed Spurs. In August 1976 the league approved the sale of the bankrupt and talent-poor Kansas City Scouts to oilman Jack Vickers, who promptly moved the team to Denver and renamed them the Colorado Rockies. Vickers hired NHL and World Hockey Association veteran coach Johnny Wilson to coach the Rockies, the first of seven men to lead the team during its six seasons in Denver. The team had only one potential star player, winger Wilf Paiement, a twenty-one year old with a mercurial temper and a penchant for criticizing his teammates in the newspapers. The others, Wilson recalled, "were just a bunch of hard-working guys with a lot of mileage on them." One of them, defenseman Steve Durbano, "was a strange guy to handle. Every once in a while," Wilson said, "you had to take him aside and explain to him what hockey was all about. He was trying to injure guys in practice."[31]

The Rockies' dearth of talent showed in their 1976–1977 record of twenty wins, forty-six losses, and fourteen ties, the second worst in the league. Unfortunately, the team never improved and in its best year, 1980–1981, won only twenty-two games in its eighty-game schedule. Years later, Johnny Wilson said that "after that first year, I don't think Jack [Vickers] was completely sold that Denver was a place for an NHL franchise."[32]

During the two years he owned the Rockies, Vickers lost about $5 million. He hoped to stem his cash hemorrhage by demanding that the City of Denver renegotiate his lease at McNichols Arena. Under the existing lease, Vickers did not share in concessions, parking, or other revenue sources at the arena. He wanted a share of those monies, or perhaps even a management agreement that would give him control of McNichols. At the end of the 1977–1978 season, when the Rockies earned a spot in the NHL playoffs despite a dismal 19-40-21 record, Vickers even threatened to move the team if Mayor William McNichols did not agree to a more favorable lease. Asked years later why he had not negotiated a better lease in the first place, Vickers explained that because his purchase of the Kansas City Scouts had to be worked out quickly, he "didn't have the time to sit down with the city and work out all the details ahead of time, but I got a lot of promises—promises that weren't lived up to." It is ironic that Vickers, a veteran of the oil business, traditionally a rough-and-tumble, even cutthroat industry, complained about the City of Denver's hardball business tactics. Nevertheless, when Mayor McNichols made it clear that the city would not agree to Vickers's demands, the Rockies' owner decided to sell the team. "The thing that drove us off," he said, "was that the city got so greedy as to all the parking, concessions, advertising." Clearly, by the late 1970s, when fiscal conservatives were chanting the mantra of "running government like a business," Vickers shared the increasingly common view among sports-franchise owners that government should subsidize their enterprises.[33]

•   Jack Vickers unloaded the Rockies in July 1978, selling the team to Arthur Imperatore, owner of a New Jersey trucking company. Imperatore immediately announced his plan to keep the Rockies in Denver for only two more seasons and then move the team to a new arena under construction at the Meadowlands in New Jersey. However, the National Hockey League quickly quashed Imperatore's plan, though the league's enmity in the matter focused on Jack Vickers. "This is a slap in the face at Denver," said Philadelphia Flyers chairman Ed Snider. "It's unbelievable. There is no way we are ever going to let Jack Vickers ruin what is a great hockey territory." Snider added,

"Vickers is going to get what he deserves, which is a beating, when he tries to put this nonsense to a vote."[34]

Arthur Imperatore heard the NHL's message loud and clear and quickly backed away from his plan to move the Rockies to New Jersey. In August 1978 the league's board of governors approved the team's sale to Imperatore, supposedly with "no strings attached." However, NHL president John Ziegler noted that the governors "made it quite clear that they want the Colorado franchise to remain in Denver." Imperatore issued a statement saying that "we have met with the league's board of governors and have heard the considered argument of many that Denver ought to be a viable city for professional hockey. We are now prepared to do our utmost to maintain the Colorado Rockies in Denver. We are committed to building a championship team in Denver."[35]

The Rockies' future in Denver seemed secure, at least for the time being; but that security did not translate into better performance on the ice. The 1978–1979 team went through two coaches, Pat Kelly and Aldo Guidolin, and finished with the worst record in the league, 15-53-12. After the season the management bought full-page ads in the Denver newspapers apologizing for the sorry performance.[36]

Imperatore tried to restore fan confidence by hiring one of the most successful coaches in the NHL, Don Cherry. A cocky, acerbic man, Cherry had played eighteen years of minor league hockey and one game in the NHL. After he retired from play, Cherry worked in construction and car sales, but in 1971 unemployment forced him back onto the ice with a minor league team, the Rochester Americans. Midway through the season Cherry became the team's coach, and added the title of general manager the next year. He turned an undertalented team into a playoff contender and soon caught the notice of the NHL. The Boston Bruins hired him in 1974. Cherry's Bruins advanced to the Stanley Cup finals in 1976–1977 and 1977–1978. By 1979, conflicts with the Bruins' management had Cherry looking for a new job.[37]

Don Cherry lasted only one year in Denver. Conflicts with management, especially with general manager Ray Miron over personnel decisions, and a poor 19-48-13 record led to his dismissal after the 1979–1980 season. Cherry blamed Miron for the Rockies' poor performance that year. "It was incredible," he recalled. "I couldn't get a goaltender. I had the Swedish Sieve, Hardy Astron, whose only problem as a goalie was pucks." Miron, he said, "was knifing me in the back after the first exhibition game. I knew then I wasn't going to last long." Cherry added, "[I]f somebody sat down and said, 'Let's have a blueprint how to ruin a franchise,' this was how. It was chaos from the word go." Cherry's firing was unpopular, but team president Armand Pohan (Imperatore's stepson) defended the move and attacked Cherry in kind. "It is a tribute to Don Cherry's genius as a self-promoter," Pohan said, "that he could coach Colorado to a last-place finish, to a worse record than Johnny Wilson or Pat Kelly, with a better team, and still be considered a local hero." Obviously, chaos and bitterness were the major characteristics of the Rockies' organization.[38]

In December 1980, halfway through the 1980–1981 season, Arthur Imperatore sold the Rockies to Peter Gilbert, owner of a cable television company headquartered in Buffalo, New York. Gilbert at first seemed committed to keeping the franchise in Denver and building a competitive team. "I don't ever want to move the team," he declared. "That's not even something I would think about. I think Denver can be a great hockey city, and what I want to do is hold the Stanley Cup in my hands after we win it." To underscore his commitment to Colorado, Gilbert hired former lieutenant governor Mark Hogan as chairman of the board and former University of Denver hockey coach Murray Armstrong, who was still popular, as a team consultant.[39]

Peter Gilbert's commitment to keeping the Rockies in Colorado soured within a year. Gilbert voiced the same complaints Jack Vickers had about the team's lease at McNichols Arena, even though the city had renegotiated a deal with Arthur Imperatore. Gilbert inherited that lease when he bought the team. Declining ticket sales also eroded the team's financial situation. "As it stands now," Gilbert said, "we can't make it with the lease we have. . . . I thought Denver was a progressive city, but the city administration is not. I'm doing my part. The city government and the fans are not." In November 1981 press reports indicated that he wanted to move the team to the New Jersey Meadowlands. Gilbert confirmed those reports in December when he asked the league for permission to make the move. Although fans and politicians rallied to try to convince the league to block the move, Mayor William McNichols's failure to attend, or send representatives, to a crucial league meeting in Washington, D.C., gave league officials the impression that the City of Denver did not care if the Rockies left town. League president John Ziegler noted that the city's absence from the meeting "stands out like a sore thumb."[40]

By 1982 the National Hockey League was no longer committed to maintaining a franchise in Colorado and would not block the Rockies' move. In May, Peter Gilbert sold the team to an investment group headed by John McMullen, an owner of the Houston Astros baseball team. With the league's approval, McMullen moved the team to New Jersey where they became the Devils.[41]

When the Rockies and the NHL left town in 1982, Denver again became a minor league hockey town. In July 1982, two months after the Rockies' departure, Denver car deal Doug Spedding acquired a Central Hockey League franchise. Spedding's team, the Colorado Flames, survived only one season, and Colorado had no professional hockey team again until 1986. In November 1986, Aurora mayor Dennis Champine and Mike Ilitch, Jr., became owners of the Denver Rangers, an International Hockey League team. In September 1988, after Ilitch pulled out of the partnership, Champine sold the team to Richard Gerry and Denver Nuggets owner Sidney Schlenker. However, the new owners could not salvage the financially weak franchise and folded it in June 1989. Finally, in 1994, another IHL franchise, the Denver Grizzlies, took the ice at McNichols Arena. The Grizzlies quickly attracted a large following, and crowds, averaging twelve thousand per game, cheered them as they won the IHL championship in their only season in Denver. However, in 1995, the Grizzlies moved to Salt Lake City to make way for Colorado's second National Hockey League franchise.[42]

Far to the north, in Quebec City, Marcel Aubut, owner of the Quebec Nordiques, was in serious financial trouble. He made it clear to the provincial government that the team could not remain there unless the government committed to a major financial subsidy, including building a $125 million arena for the team. When Quebec's governor, Jacques Parizeau, rejected the demands, Aubut put the team on the market, declaring that the government's small offer of assistance "was not in line with what it takes to keep a professional NHL club in Quebec City." In May 1995, COMSAT Video Enterprises, owner of the Denver Nuggets basketball team, agreed to the $70 million purchase price and announced the Nordiques' move to Denver for the 1995–1996 season.[43]

The National Hockey League had wanted to plant a team in Denver for some time and had courted COMSAT as the prospective Denver owner since 1993. COMSAT expected to be given an expansion franchise, but instead now had a team on the very edge of championship caliber. Team leaders included centers Joe Sakic, a seven-year veteran, and rookie of the year Peter Forsberg, a national hero in his native Sweden. Forsberg had led the Swedish national hockey team to a gold medal in the 1994 Olympics. The team's fiery coach, Marc Crawford, played for six seasons with the Vancouver Canucks and coached in the Canucks' and Toronto Maple Leafs' organizations before taking over the Nordiques in 1994. The Nordiques' 30-13-5 record in 1994–1995 earned Crawford coach of the year honors. Kevin Johnston, a sportswriter for Quebec's *Journal Le Soleil,* said of the departing Nordiques, "[T]his is a team that is maybe one player and a little bit of experience away from being the best in the league. . . . The people in Denver should consider themselves very fortunate."[44]

Colorado's hockey fans evidently felt fortunate to have a new NHL franchise in Denver. By the time COMSAT announced the team's new name—the Colorado Avalanche—in August 1995, twelve thousand fans had purchased season tickets. Apparently, the NHL had guessed correctly that Colorado would support a major league hockey team, even though Denver had a much smaller population base than the other eight cities hosting four major league teams (New York, Chicago, Philadelphia, Boston, Detroit, Los Angeles, Miami, and Dallas).[45]

As the 1995–1996 season got under way, general manager Pierre LaCroix engineered key trades that made the Colorado Avalanche into a championship squad. In October, LaCroix sent winger Wendel Clark, a contract holdout, to the New Jersey Devils for Claude Lemieux, whom a *Rocky Mountain News* writer described as "one of the toughest, nastiest, most abrasive players in the league." Lemieux, a right winger, led the Devils to the Stanley Cup championship in 1995 and won the NHL Conn Smythe Trophy as most valuable player in that year's playoff series. LaCroix also added a talented defenseman, Sandis Ozolinsh, a native of Latvia. However, the most important trade came in December 1995, when the Avalanche landed the best goal tender in the league.[46]

Patrick Roy (pronounced "Wah") had played his entire NHL career with the Montreal Canadiens, who drafted him in 1982. Montreal fans called him "St. Patrick" and the "Brick Roy" for his spectacular goal defense that gave up an eleven-season average of only 2.77 goals per game. Roy had twice won the Conn Smythe Trophy, leading the Canadiens to the Stanley Cup in 1986 and 1993. Despite his talent and his popularity in Montreal, Roy left the Canadiens on bitter terms. Even the finest goalie in the league can have a bad game, and Roy had one early in December 1995, against the Detroit Red Wings, who scored nine goals against him in less than two periods of play before coach Mario Tremblay took him out of the game. Roy was incensed and believed that Tremblay had left him in the game in order to embarrass him. As he left the ice, Roy told team president Ronald Corey, "[T]hat's my last game in Montreal" and demanded to be traded. Within a week Roy donned the Avalanche jersey.[47]

Thus reinforced, the Avalanche stormed through the 1995–1996 NHL season. They won the Pacific Division title with a record of forty-seven wins, twenty-five losses, and ten ties, thirteen games better than their nearest division rival, the Calgary Flames. The Avalanche won their Western Conference quarterfinal series against the Vancouver Canucks four games to two, and went on to defeat the Chicago Blackhawks in the semifinals, again four games to two. The Western Conference final series also went to six games before the Avs beat the Detroit Red Wings, the team destined to become Colorado's most ferocious hockey rival. That win set the stage for the Stanley Cup series against the Eastern Conference champions, the Florida Panthers.[48]

The Panthers never really had a chance, as the Avalanche swept the series in four games (fig. 10-1). Patrick Roy gave up only four goals in the entire series. Peter Forsberg scored a hat trick in the first period of game two, and Joe Sakic had five points (one goal and four assists) for the series. (Sakic's eighteen goals through all of the playoffs

10-1. Colorado Avalanche captain Joe Sakic hoists the Stanley Cup in 1996. The hockey team's NHL championship was Denver's first major league title. Courtesy, Tim DeFrisco.

earned him the Conn Smythe Trophy as most valuable player.) In game two, the Avalanche buried the Panthers by the score of 8-1. Patrick Roy uttered the Panthers' epitaph after game three. Florida fans liked to shower opposing teams with fake rats whenever their team scored a goal (a custom that began after a Florida player killed a real rat in the team's locker room). After game three, which Florida lost three to two, Roy said, "Thank god they scored two goals. Those fans would have left with all those rats in their pockets. I would have been sad for them." The Panthers' best effort came in game four when goalie John Vanbiesbrouck held the Avalanche scoreless through three periods of regulation play and more than forty-four minutes of overtime. Finally, defenseman Uwe Krupp, who injured his knee severely in the first game of the season and returned to action for only the last five games of the year, nailed a slap shot for the winning goal.[49]

Game four was played in the Miami Arena, and afterward many Florida fans gamely applauded the new Stanley Cup champions. Back in Denver, ecstatic fans jammed bars and spilled into the streets of lower downtown in celebration of Colorado's first major league championship. A few half-wits lit bonfires and climbed light poles, but the victory party for the most part was peaceful, if not orderly. Two days later, a crowd of up to 450,000 greeted the champions with a parade and rally at Civic Center. Fan Dan Egan drove to Denver from Alamosa, about 250 miles, for the event. Egan reflected the satisfaction of long-time Colorado sports fans. "I've waited a long time for a championship," he said. "I cheered the striped-socks Broncos of Frank Tripucka and Charlie [sic] Johnson. That goes back a few years."[50]

After the Stanley Cup triumph, *Sports Illustrated* predicted that "playing for the Stanley Cup is going to become an annual event in Colorado" and that the Avalanche would be "the NHL's next dominant team." Predictions of an Avalanche dynasty evaporated, however, over the next two seasons. The Avalanche finished atop the Pacific Division again in 1996–1997 with a record of forty-nine wins, twenty-four losses, and nine ties, the best record in the league. The team seemed to be on the way to another Stanley Cup after defeating the Chicago Blackhawks in the Western Conference quarterfinals and the Edmonton Oilers in the semifinals. Then, the Detroit Red Wings, the Avalanche's bitter rivals, stopped them four games to two in the conference finals.[51]

Long before the playoffs began that season, the Avalanche lost something or left it on the ice at Joe Louis Arena in Detroit. A photograph of Claude Lemieux on his knees, covering his head with his arms against the fists of Detroit's Darren McCarty, told the story of the Avalanche's undoing. Ten days earlier, Lemieux hit Detroit player Kris Draper from behind, sending him crashing into the side boards and crushing his jaw. McCarty's attack on Lemieux in the March 26, 1997, game was Detroit's vengeance, and the Avalanche never fully recovered the swaggering confidence of the Stanley Cup season. The loss to Detroit in the conference finals merely completed the humiliation. The Red Wings went on to win the 1997 Stanley Cup.[52]

Although the Avalanche again won the Pacific Division in 1997–1998, they made an even earlier, and more embarrassing, exit from the playoffs. With the second-best record in the conference, the Avalanche faced the seventh-ranked Edmonton Oilers in the first round of the playoffs. After taking a three games to one lead in the series, the Avalanche lost three straight to a much more determined Oiler squad led by goalie Curtis Joseph, who shut the Avalanche out for more than eight consecutive periods of play through the last three games of the series. Patrick Roy again provided the epitaph for the series. "I feel like we didn't have as much passion as the year we won the Cup. We all wanted to win, but not at every price. I wonder if this is the price you pay for winning the Stanley Cup?"[53]

Two years earlier, in the afterglow of the Stanley Cup victory, *Rocky Mountain News* columnist Bob Kravitz heaped praised on the Avalanche for "the professionalism and grace and selflessness and passion they showed in the effort to earn the sport's greatest prize." Now Kravitz called them "just another one-time Stanley Cup wonder." Three weeks after the season, Marc Crawford rejected a two-year contract extension and quit as coach. His record with the Nordiques/Avalanche included 165 wins, 88 losses, 41 ties, and one Stanley Cup. General manager Pierre LaCroix replaced Crawford with Bob Hartley, coach of the team's minor league affiliate, the Hershey Bears.[54]

The Avalanche played well under Hartley in the 1998–1999 season but did not return to championship form. They won their division and advanced through the quarterfinal and semifinal conference playoffs, but lost to the Dallas Stars in the Western Conference championship series, four games to three.

The Avalanche's decline following their Stanley Cup year may have been the result of a loss of passion or of the mysterious ebb and flow of fortune in sports. However, other problems affecting the franchise were symptomatic of trends at work throughout major league sports, including venue issues, the role of government and public finance in professional sports, the impact of free agency, and the growing power of the entertainment communications industry. For the Avalanche, the focal points of this web were the team's plan to build a new arena and the future of one player.

When COMSAT acquired the Nordiques in 1995, the company announced that both the hockey club and the Denver Nuggets would soon play in a new multiuse complex with a sports arena and a state-of-the-art television and movie production facility to be called the Pepsi Center (COMSAT already had a naming-rights agreement with the soft drink company for an estimated $38 million). The company originally planned to build the arena itself and transfer ownership to the City of Denver to avoid property taxes on the structure, paying Denver an annual fee of $2 million instead. That proposal fell through, however, when a Colorado Supreme Court ruling in April 1995 made it clear that COMSAT would be liable for taxes on its franchise property housed at the arena even though the facility itself was public property.[55]

COMSAT then proposed building and owning the arena and asked Denver to exempt the facility from property taxes altogether and to rebate to the company all sales taxes. Because the arena would be a private facility, Denver would no longer collect the seat tax, worth nearly $4 million, charged for Nugget and Avalanche games at McNichols Arena. The city would also give up other revenue sources from parking, concessions, and advertising. Mayor Wellington Webb was prepared to deal with COMSAT and its subsidiary, Ascent Entertainment, created in November 1995, as the Nuggets' and Avalanche's operating company, but he was not willing to allow the teams to walk away from McNichols Arena without compensation for the city. Webb also wanted Ascent to promise to pay prevailing wage scales on the construction project and to guarantee a percentage of the project for businesses owned by women and minorities.[56]

Negotiations between Ascent and the city took two years and at times dissolved into public acrimony. City officials were irked in July 1996 when a National Basketball Association official threatened to lend that league's weight to any effort by Ascent to break its leases at McNichols. The league asserted that it had the right to require NBA team owners to leave facilities it considered substandard. City officials pointed out that though the Avalanche had signed only a two-year lease, the Nuggets were obliged to play at McNichols for another ten years, a fact that gave the city considerable leverage in its talks with Ascent. Denver officials became convinced that Ascent was dragging its feet on the negotiations while putting out feelers in suburban cities for possible better deals. At one point, Mayor Webb demonstrated his displeasure with Ascent by staging a press conference at which he blasted the company for having a "take it or leave it" attitude while "fiddle-faddling around" with the negotiations. Webb underscored his anger by drinking a can of Coca-Cola during the session.[57]

Ascent's problems worsened a few weeks after the end of the 1996–1997 hockey season when Avalanche captain Joe Sakic became a free agent. The New York Rangers shocked Sakic's employers, and the rest of the NHL, by offering him a $21 million contract. Ascent had lost $57 million in the previous two years and faced the problem of financing a new arena, the cost of which had grown from about $125 million to about $160 million while negotiations with Denver dragged on. Now the company would have to dig deep into its corporate pockets to keep Sakic or else lose the team's leader and one of the best players in the league.[58]

Ascent and the City of Denver resolved the arena issue, and Joe Sakic signed a new contract with the Avalanche in a series of dramatic deals in August 1997. First, Mayor Wellington Webb and Ascent's chief executive Charlie Lyons signed an agreement paying Denver a smaller annual income from the hockey and basketball franchises but guaranteeing that income for a longer period of time. Ascent would build, own, and manage the new Pepsi Center and pay the city a yearly fee of from $1 million to $2 million derived from sales taxes. Ascent also promised not to move the Nuggets or the Avalanche from Denver for twenty-five years. Sweeteners for Ascent included a sales tax rebate of $2.25 million for construction materials and Denver's commitment to pay up to $4.5 million of the costs of infrastructural improvements, such as roads, to serve the arena. In addition, because the arena site lay within the Platte Valley urban-renewal area, Denver would refund all property taxes on the arena and on team property there. The City of Denver retained control of McNichols Arena and could demolish it if it wished (a likely prospect as the site became the most probable location of a new football stadium). Although McNichols remained standing, Ascent would have first refusal of major events. Ascent broke ground on the Pepsi Center in November 1997, and expected to open the arena in time for the Avalanche to start the 1999–2000 season there.[59]

At the same time, Ascent suddenly found itself flush with the money to re-sign Joe Sakic, and do almost anything else it wanted. Two cable television companies, Fox Sports Rocky Mountain and Tele-Communications Incorporated (TCI), came on the scene like deus ex machinas in a classical Greek play to rescue the company from its financial plight. Fox Sports Rocky Mountain agreed to pay Ascent $100 million over seven years for the broadcast rights to all Avalanche and Nuggets games. TCI's Liberty Media subsidiary paid Ascent $15 million to become a partner in the Pepsi Center. TCI's investment exactly matched the signing bonus paid to Joe Sakic to keep him with the Avalanche, a fact that Ascent's Charlie Lyons wrote off as mere coincidence.[60]

The Pepsi Center, Joe Sakic's contract, and Ascent's deals with Fox and TCI epitomized significant trends in professional sports at the end of the twentieth century. Sports venues, the stadiums and arenas where teams play, represent the difference between successful and less successful franchises. Every team owner is determined to maximize revenue from tickets, parking, concessions, advertising, and, especially, high-priced luxury boxes, and to minimize costs, often by securing public subsidies. The need to generate as much money as possible is largely the result of free agency. When professional sports leagues functioned as full-fledged cartels with absolute control over their players, salaries could be held in check, and lucrative television contracts guaranteed handsome profits for all. Free agency upset sports' cartel structure and introduced a frenzied form of competition among owners to land the best talent at whatever the cost. High player salaries, after all, could be recouped from bigger television contracts and from venue income.

Ascent Entertainment and its partnerships with TCI and Fox signify another trend in modern sports. The big-money television contracts of the 1960s triggered the growth of professional sports into a multibillion-dollar industry, and the flood of television money, in turn, prompted players to pursue free agency to win a larger share of industry earnings. However, until recent years, owners and leagues and the television networks stayed in separate camps, feeding off one another. But COMSAT's purchase of the Nordiques represented the move of broadcasters, especially cable operators, into ownership. Whether that trend will help contain costs or increase them is not yet clear, but it does mean that more and more teams are simply parts of large corporate entertainment packages, which can mean that owners may have less personal interest in teams and the communities that support them than in the financial bottom line.

Denver businessman Donald Sturm's purchase of the Avalanche and Nuggets in 1999 did not substantially alter these trends. In April 1999, Ascent agreed to sell the teams and the Pepsi Center to Wal-Mart heirs Nancy and William Laurie for $400 million. However, Ascent stockholders challenged the deal, claiming that the sale price was too low. Stockholders also criticized Ascent president Charlie Lyons's role in the deal that would make him a minority owner. After stockholders filed a lawsuit to block the sale, Ascent and the Lauries agreed to cancel it, and Charlie Lyons stepped aside as Ascent's president. In July, Ascent accepted bids from other potential buyers including Sturm, a group led by ski industry mogul George Gillette and John Elway, and Thara Saud, who claimed to be a Saudi Arabian princess. In a second step in the process, the Lauries had a chance to beat the highest bid. Sturm's offer of $461 million topped the others and convinced the Lauries to walk away. Though the Avalanche and Nuggets passed from corporate to private ownership, they became part of Sturm's diverse portfolio, which includes banks, real estate, and telecommunications interests. As he assumed control of the franchises and began the task of integrating them into his business empire, the new owner was not intimidated by the costs of free agency. Informed by Nuggets officials that the team needed to spend $5 million on free agents in 1999, Sturm replied, "So why don't we spend $10 million?"[61]

Ascent's agreement with Denver for the Pepsi Center was both emblematic of and a departure from perhaps the most important and controversial trends in modern professional sports. Franchise owners, whether individuals or corporations, have learned to manipulate communities and governments to win massive public subsidies for their stadiums and arenas. Almost every major league sports city has experienced the process of venue blackmail. At its worst, a team owner may brazenly shop his team to the city offering the best package of subsidies. Sometimes owners simply threaten to leave town in order to get a better facility or lease arrangement. And sometimes they threaten to sell a team to someone else who will move it. Denver was the beneficiary of the latter variety of venue blackmail. When the Quebec government did not meet Marcel Aubut's demands, he sold the Nordiques to COMSAT, who moved them to Colorado.

However, there were important differences in Ascent's dealings with Denver over the Pepsi Center. Often when team owners demand a new stadium or arena, they also demand public financing. In the case of the Pepsi Center, however, COMSAT/Ascent planned all along to finance construction itself, and sought only comparatively modest tax breaks and subsidies, a commitment that stands in sharp contrast to Coors Field and to the new football stadium for the Broncos, both largely tax financed. (The Broncos are committed to paying only 25 percent of the football stadium's cost, and the Colorado Rockies contributed nothing to the construction of Coors Field.)

During the sometimes acrimonious discussions with the City of Denver that led to the Pepsi Center deal, the Avalanche's two-year lease at McNichols Arena hung over the negotiations like a bludgeon. However, though Ascent briefly flirted with suburban cities and counties, the company never made an explicit threat to leave Denver. In fact, after the deal was finished, Ascent's Charlie Lyons revealed that he had rejected several offers to sell both the Avalanche and the Nuggets to buyers in other cities, including Houston, Port-land, and Nashville. They were, he said, "serious offers that involved moving the teams." Asked why Ascent did not give up on Denver and sell one or both of the teams, Lyons explained that though "in the short term, an owner can make a lot of money by moving," the "whole trend of franchise free-agency is not good for the business of sports in the long-term." Sounding like an owner from a bygone age, Lyons said, "[I]n the long run, there has to be a good-faith, trusting relation-ship between fans and owners of sports teams."[62]

CONCLUSION

After the Denver Broncos won Super Bowl XXXIII in January 1999, public and media attention focused, as it had a year earlier, on the question of whether or not John Elway would retire from football. Most fans hoped that the chance to win an unprecedented third consecutive Super Bowl would lure him to the field again. Elway's decision to retire disappointed those hopes. Nevertheless, this latest "Elway Watch" underscored the Broncos', and sports', powerful hold on popular culture in Colorado. However, sports' penetration of life in Colorado runs deeper and broader than the influence of one man or one team. In all their professional, amateur, and recreational dimensions, sports have shaped personal and civic identity; mirrored and helped redefine social norms, especially of race and gender; influenced politics and public policy; and even reshaped institutions of higher education.

Broncomania—the fervent, idolatrous devotion of Bronco fans to their team—has antecedents in nineteenth-century rock-drilling contests, fire-cart races, and baseball games. These pioneer sports were as important to the sense of civic esteem of mining-town residents as the Broncos are to Coloradans today. The city fathers of Leadville understood that fact when they set out in 1882 to build the best baseball team in the state as a way to restore flagging civic spirit in the then economically distressed town. Although the tendency of some of today's People Who Wear Orange to make their identity and sense of self-esteem a reflection of their favorite team approaches the pathological, the underlying connection between sport and identity is not new.

It is commonplace today to liken to religion the ardent sports fan's attachment to a favorite team. Certainly, the most successful athletes, and some coaches, are treated virtually as demigods, their autographs and other artifacts sought and treasured as icons. Nonetheless, modern sport is not religion, as the contrast with the traditional sports of American Indians in Colorado shows. To the Utes, the Cheyenne, and the Arapaho, sports often functioned as a connection between man, the physical world, and the sacred. The hoop and pole game, for example, not only sharpened a young man's hunting skills but also symbolized the origins of the buffalo hunt, the basis of life among the Plains Indians.

From the time when only Indians populated Colorado, and certainly from the settling of the mining towns by white migrants, women participated in and used sports to create spheres of life separate from male society. The Ute women's shinny game was such a separate sphere, a social event when they could play, visit, and trade among themselves. For white women in the mining towns, sport, especially skiing, was not so much a separate sphere of life as a necessary means of travel and communication. Like the men, though, mining-town women soon turned necessary activity into recreation. Thus, sports became the means by which women learned to challenge not only their physical skills but also traditional gender roles and restraints. Dora Ellen Thornworth Rinehart's bicycling exploits at the end of the nineteenth century would challenge the strength and abilities of the strongest and best-equipped male bicyclist today. Back then, she also undermined notions of female weakness and delicacy. The safety bicycle liberated women. With a frame and saddle height lower than the high-wheeled "ordinary," a lady could mount the safety bicycle without risking immodesty. More important, the bicycle gave women independent mobility. Although organized women's sports today, especially at the professional level, still do not command the levels of public and business support that men's sports enjoy, few object to girls and women being athletically active. That acceptance of women in sports, imperfect as it may be, mirrors the larger terrain of life women have won in America, in business and professions, politics, education, and the arts.

As with issues of gender, sports in Colorado have also mirrored the profound, but incomplete, transformation of racial attitudes across America. The appearances of Negro League baseball players, including Satchel Paige and Cool Papa Bell, in the *Denver Post* Tournament in the 1930s helped pave the way for the reintegration of major league baseball, which Jackie Robinson carried forward more than a decade later. Since then, the ranks of African American and Hispanic players in both professional and collegiate sports have grown, and they now outnumber white players on some teams. Despite the successes of minorities on the playing field, they have had little success in entering the ranks of management and ownership. Peter Bynoe's brief tenure as part owner and Bernie Bickerstaff's time as general manager of the Denver Nuggets are the only instances of significant minority management of a Colorado professional team. When the Colorado Rockies hired Don Baylor as the team's first manager, the major story was not that the Rockies had hired a talented manager but that they had hired a talented African American manager. Less encouraging was the University of Colorado's failure to live up to its 1994 promise to actively recruit and consider minority candidates for future football head-coaching vacancies. More disappointing was the failure of the sports media and others in 1999 to even notice the lapse, as the university's search for Rick Neuheisel's replacement turned up no serious minority candidates.

Neuheisel's departure from Colorado epitomized the transformation of organized sport from amateur activity to multimillion-dollar industry. Modern professional and collegiate sports trace their origins to amateur play, usually among middle-class males. However, as soon as some of those players, or their sponsors, realized that there was a dollar to be made by selling tickets or playing for pay, those games became businesses. By the late twentieth century, those businesses grew to influence and sometimes redefine politics, public policy, and important institutions, including, especially, higher education.

In 1961 when the University of Denver dropped intercollegiate football from its athletic program, the university explained that it could no longer justify the sport's expense. Thirty-eight years later, DU built the $55 million Ritchie Center, a state-of-the-art athletic facility to house the school's hockey, basketball, swimming, gymnastics, and other sports programs, made necessary by the university's decision to compete in the NCAA's Division I, the elite level of intercollegiate athletics. With a 205-foot tower crowned by a gold-leaf–clad steeple, the Ritchie Center is a grand athletic cathedral. Like Rick Neuheisel's departure for the University of Washington and a lucrative new contract, it reflects the enormous costs of high-level college sports. The Neuheisel story and the Ritchie Center are further evidence of the high-stakes business nature of supposedly amateur collegiate athletics and of how sports have altered the mission of higher education. Today, greatness in a university is often measured in terms of its football team's successes, not the quality of its academic departments.[1]

Organized and recreational sports have reshaped Colorado's political terrain. Denver's great parks system and Colorado's extensive network of state and national parks represent a century-old commitment by government not only to preserve open space and natural resources but also to support recreation. Denver's parks are busy year-round with bicyclists, runners, soccer matches, tennis players, golfers, and baseball games. State and national parks also host sports and field recreation.

Government's commitment to subsidizing recreation helped transform recreational skiing into a powerful multimillion-dollar industry. Colorado's great ski resorts have enjoyed easy and inexpensive use of national-forest property for ski runs and facilities. The ski industry's formerly easy relationship with government is becoming more difficult, however, as concerns have grown over skiing's environmental impacts. Environmentalists now actively challenge resort expansionists whose plans appear to threaten wildlife habitats or other scarce resources. Indeed, the burning by arsonists in 1998 of controversial new facilities at Vail suggests that some environmentalists' hostility to ski-area expansion has become extreme and dangerous. State transportation officials worry more each year about traffic congestion along Interstate 70 through the mountains and the costs of remedying it.

Recent conflicts over ski-industry expansion are not the first to pit sports enthusiasts and businesspeople against environmentalists.

In 1972 Coloradans debated the proposed 1976 Winter Olympics, then voted to deny the use of public funds to finance the event. That decision effectively ended hopes of staging the games in the state. The struggle over the Olympics pitted two different visions of Colorado. One was a gospel of unlimited growth. An elite of well-intentioned, if ultimately arrogant and inept, business and political leaders believed, as Coloradans had believed for generations, that any and all business opportunities were good for all of Colorado. The other view, represented mainly by a younger set of political, intellectual, and environmental activists, argued that unregulated economic development threatened the state's natural environment and the quality of life of its citizens. The referendum's outcome drove the Olympics from Colorado and launched the careers of new political leaders, including Richard Lamm and Patricia Schroeder. The Olympic debate reshaped the state's politics for a generation and embedded environmentalism in Colorado's culture and politics. It was not, however, a complete and permanent rejection of the gospel of growth.

In the successful campaigns to win public financing for Coors Field and to replace Mile High Stadium, supporters argued that the new facilities would be economic boons, at least for the Denver metropolitan area. Despite the contrary experiences of other cities that had financed new sports venues, many voters accepted that claim. Others believed that without the new stadiums, Colorado either would not get its major league baseball team or might lose the Broncos, which would diminish the state's major league status and harm it economically. Of course, having major league sports franchises, especially successful ones, remained a powerful source of civic identity and self-esteem. In short, civic and economic boosterism was still potent in the 1990s.[2]

In the end, what is the most important Colorado sports story? Is it all the debate, spilled ink, and airtime devoted to organized professional and collegiate athletics? Is it Broncomania? No. Far more important is the satisfaction that tens of thousands of Coloradans earn every day from their own athletic efforts. The woman runner pushing herself mile after mile creates in her soul a sense of power and self-esteem far stronger and more meaningful than that of even the most ardent spectator in the grandstands at Mile High Stadium. The child learning to hit a baseball or kick a soccer ball hones not only his physical skills but also his sense of confidence and individuality. The middle-age professor, a bit overweight and ungainly afoot, mounts his Italian racing bicycle. With the wind and the Colorado sun in his face, he is once again young, graceful, and fast.

Sports have always been a part of life in Colorado. Through them we build powerful bonds to the land, to our communities, and find strength and energy in ourselves.

NOTES

PREFACE

1. *Sporting News* 221:26 (June 30, 1997): 14–22.

2. *Denver Post,* February 1, 1998, p. 1c.

3. Allen Guttmann, *A Whole New Ball Game: An Interpretation of American Sports* (Chapel Hill: University of North Carolina Press, 1988), 1–6.

4. Elliott J. Gorn and Warren Goldstein, *A Brief History of American Sports* (New York: Hill and Wang, 1993), xii.

CHAPTER 1

1. Robert Emmitt, *The Last War Trail: The Utes and the Settlement of Colorado* (Norman: University of Oklahoma Press, 1954), 44–49, 50, 53.

2. Frank Gilbert Roe, *The Indian and the Horse* (Norman: University of Oklahoma Press, 1955), 73, 79; Robert Delaney et al., *The Southern Utes: A Tribal History* (Ignacio, Colo.: Southern Ute Tribe, 1972), 67–68; Jan Pettit, *Utes: The Mountain People* (Boulder: Johnson Books, 1990), 97; James Russell, "Conditions and Customs of Present-Day Utes in Colorado," *Colorado Magazine* 6:3 (May 1929): 197; Emmitt, *Last War Trail,* 35; *Colorado Miner* (July 19, 1879): 1; *Denver Times,* December 28, 1900, p. 12.

3. Marshall Sprague, *Massacre: The Tragedy at White River* (Boston: Little, Brown, 1957), 145–46; Emmitt, *Last War Trail,* 123; *Colorado Magazine* 32:4 (October 1955): 254.

4. Charles S. Marsh, *People of the Shining Mountains: The Utes of Colorado* (Boulder: Pretty Publishing, 1982), 89; Emmitt, *Last War Trail,* 124–25.

5. Emmitt, *Last War Trail,* 132–35, 155–66.

6. Robert W. Delaney, *Ute Mountain Utes* (Albuquerque: University of New Mexico Press, 1989), 53–54; Carl Abbott, Stephen J. Leonard, and David McComb, *Colorado: A History of the Centennial State,* rev. ed. (Boulder: Colorado Associated University Press, 1982), 125.

7. Elliott J. Gorn and Warren Goldstein, *A Brief History of American Sports* (New York: Hill and Wang, 1993), 5; Allen Guttmann, *A Whole New Ball Game: An Interpretation of*

American Sports (Chapel Hill: University of North Carolina Press, 1988), 13–22.

8. Guttmann, *Whole New Ball Game,* 19–21.

9. Stewart Culin, *Games of the North American Indians,* vol. 2 (Washington, D.C.: Government Printing Office, 1907; Lincoln: University of Nebraska Press, Bison Books edition, 1992), 427–30, 438–39. See also Edward S. Curtis, *The North American Indian,* vol. 6 (1911; New York and London: Johnson Reprint, 1970), 142.

10. Culin, *Games of the North American Indians,* 427, 442, 478; George Bird Grinnell, *The Cheyenne Indians: The History and Ways of Life,* 2 vols. (Lincoln: University of Nebraska Press, 1972), 325.

11. Culin, *Games of the North American Indians,* 421, 442.

12. Ibid., 442.

13. Culin, *Games of the North American Indians,* 420, 443; Joseph B. Oxendine, *American Indian Sports Heritage* (Champaign, Ill.: Human Kinetics Books, 1988), 113–18.

14. Culin, *Games of the North American Indians,* 420, 439–40.

15. Ibid., 443.

16. John Stands-in-Timber and Margot Liberty, *Cheyenne Memories* (New Haven: Yale University Press, 1967), 28–30.

17. Ibid., 30.

18. Pettit, *Utes: The Mountain People,* 95.

19. Oxendine, *American Indian Sports Heritage,* 35, 64; Jerald C. Smith, "The Native American Ball Games," in *Sport in the Socio-Cultural Process,* ed. Mabel Marie Hart (Dubuque, Iowa: William C. Brown, 1976), 353.

20. Oxendine, *American Indian Sports Heritage,* 37; Culin, *Games of the North American Indians,* 563.

21. Smith, "The Native American Ball Games," 352–53.

22. Ibid., 353.

23. Culin, *Games of the North American Indians,* 616; Anne M. Smith, *Ethnography of the Northern Utes* (Albuquerque: Museum of New Mexico Press, 1974), 233; Pettit, *Utes: The Mountain People,* 95, 97.

24. Culin, *Games of the North American Indians,* 616–17; Grinnell, *Cheyenne Indians,* 325–26; Smith, *Ethnography of the Northern Utes,* 233–34; Pettit, *Utes: The Mountain People,* 97.

25. Culin, *Games of the North American Indians,* 647–48, 658; Smith, "The Native American Ball Games," 353; Oxendine, *American Indian Sports Heritage,* 55–56.

26. Oxendine, *American Indian Sports Heritage,* 56–58; Culin, *Games of the North American Indians,* 649.

27. Culin, *Games of the North American Indians,* 704–6; Grinnell, *Cheyenne Indians,* 330–31; Curtis, *The North American Indian,* 157.

28. Grinnell, *Cheyenne Indians,* 331.

29. Culin, *Games of the North American Indians,* 619.

30. Oxendine, *American Indian Sports Heritage,* 67, 89.

31. Peter Nabokov, *Indian Running* (Santa Barbara: Capra Press, 1981), 14, 9.

32. Oxendine, *American Indian Sports Heritage,* 76–77; Nabokov, *Indian Running,* 23.

33. Nabokov, *Indian Running,* 26.

34. *Rocky Mountain News,* July 4, 1993, p. 6a.

CHAPTER 2

1. Central City *Daily Register,* November 23, 1880, p. 4; *Rocky Mountain News,* December 10, 1880, p. 3.

2. Carl Abbott, Stephen J. Leonard, and David McComb, *Colorado: A History of the Centennial State,* rev. ed. (Boulder: Colorado Associated University Press, 1982), 59, 71, 335.

3. Duane A. Smith, *Rocky Mountain Mining Camps: The Urban Frontier* (Lincoln: University of Nebraska Press, 1967), 28.

4. Smith, *Rocky Mountain Mining Camps.*

5. Ronald C. Brown, *Hard-Rock Miners: The Intermountain West, 1860–1920* (College Station: Texas A&M University Press, 1979), 21; Abbott, Leonard, and McComb, *Colorado,* 109.

6. Brown, *Hard-Rock Miners,* 54–56; Rodman Wilson Paul, *Mining Frontiers of the Far West, 1848–1880* (Albuquerque: University of New Mexico Press, 1963), 94.

7. Leadville *Herald-Democrat,* reprinted in *Denver Republican,* August 10, 1889, p. 2.

8. Victor I. Noxon, "Hardrock Drilling Contests in Colorado," *Colorado Magazine* 11:3 (May 1934): 84, 85.

9. Ibid., 81–82; *Rocky Mountain News,* August 14, 1899, p. 3; *Denver Times,* September 17, 1899, p. 9.

10. *Rocky Mountain News,* October 19, 1895, p. 8.

11. Marshall Sprague, *Money Mountain: The Story of Cripple Creek Gold* (New York: Ballantine Books, 1953), 154–62.

12. Malcolm J. Rohrbough, *Aspen: The History of a Silver-Mining Town* (New York: Oxford University Press, 1986), 45–46; John Willard Horner, *Silver Town* (Caldwell, Idaho: Caxton Printers, 1950), 181.

13. Rohrbough, *Aspen,* 45–46, 140; *Rocky Mountain News,* August 15, 1877, p. 4; *Rocky Mountain News,* August 16, 1877, p. 4.

14. *Rocky Mountain News,* August 15, 1877, p. 4.

15. Abbott Fay, *Ski Tracks in the Rockies: A Century of Colorado Skiing* (Louisville, Colo.: Cordillera Press, 1984), 3; Calvin Queal, "Colorado Skiing: A Century of Sport," *Denver Post Empire Magazine* (November 9, 1969): 12; E. John B. Allen, *From Skisport to Skiing: One Hundred Years of an American Sport, 1840–1940* (Amherst: University of Massachusetts Press, 1993), 14.

16. E. R. Warren, "Show-Shoeing in the Rocky Mountains," *Outing* 9 (January 1887): 350; Allen, *From Skisport to Skiing,* 29.

17. Warren, "Snow-Shoeing in the Rocky Mountains," 350; Jack A. Benson, "Before Skiing Was Fun," *Western Historical Quarterly* 8:4 (October 1977): 433; Allen, *From Skisport to Skiing,* 44; James K. Hastings, "A Winter in the High Mountains, 1871–1872," *Colorado Magazine* 27:3 (July 1950): 229; Duane Vandenbusch, *The Gunnison Country* (Gunnison, Colo.: B&B Printers, 1980), 423.

18. Warren, "Snow-Shoeing in the Rocky Mountains," 350; Queal, "Colorado Skiing," 12; Charles F. Gardiner, *Doctor at Timberline* (Caldwell, Idaho: Caxton Printers, 1938), 29; Allen, *From Skisport to Skiing,* 44.

19. Vandenbusch, *The Gunnison Country,* 423.

20. Ibid.; *Track and Timberline* 374 (February 1950): 19.

21. "Snowshoe Post-Routes," *Colorado Magazine* 17:1 (January 1940): 36; Benson, "Before Skiing Was Fun," 432, 435–36; Vandenbusch, *The Gunnison Country,* 247, 423; Sarah Platte Decker Chapter, Daughters of the American Revolution, Durango, Colorado, *Pioneers of the San Juan Country,* 2 vols. (Colorado Springs: Out West Printing, 1940–1942), 1:47, 2:184–85; Allen, *From Skisport to Skiing,* 37.

22. Fay, *Ski Tracks in the Rockies,* 3; Vandenbusch, *The Gunnison Country,* 423; Benson, "Before Skiing Was Fun," 434.

23. Benson, "Before Skiing Was Fun," 432; Jack Schaefer, *Heroes Without Glory: Some Good Men of the Old West* (Boston: Houghton Mifflin, 1965), 255; Gardiner, *Doctor at Timberline,* 31.

24. Gardiner, *Doctor at Timberline,* 28; Benson, "Before Skiing Was Fun," 433; Vandenbusch, *The Gunnison Country,* 425, 426.

25. Gardiner, *Doctor at Timberline,* 31–32.

26. *Rocky Mountain News,* July 6, 1891, p. 5; Jack A. Benson, "Before Aspen and Vail: The Story of Recreational Skiing in Frontier Colorado," in *Sport in the West,* ed. Donald J. Mrozek, (Manhattan, Kans.: *Journal of the West,* Sunflower University Press, 1983), 57; Vandenbusch, *The Gunnison Country,* 424.

27. Benson, "Before Aspen and Vail," 52; Vandenbusch, *The Gunnison Country,* 424.

28. Warren, "Snow-Shoeing in the Rocky Mountains," 351–52; Vandenbusch, *The Gunnison Country,* 427–28.

29. Warren, "Snow-Shoeing in the Rocky Mountains," 352; Vandenbusch, *The Gunnison Country,* 428.

30. Warren, "Snow-Shoeing in the Rocky Mountains," 352–53.

31. *Denver Times,* March 11, 1901, p. 9; *Denver Post Empire Magazine* (January 17, 1954): 14; Fay, *Ski Tracks in the Rockies,* 12.

32. Edward Blair, *Leadville: Colorado's Magic City* (Boulder: Pruett Publishing, 1980), 136; Eugene Floyd Irey, "A Social History of Leadville, Colorado, During the Boom Days, 1877–1881" (Ph.D. diss., University of Minnesota, 1951), 158; C. H. Hannington, "Early Days of Central City," *Colorado Magazine* 19:1 (January 1942): 14; Lynn Irwin Perrigo, "A Social History of Central City, Colorado, 1859–1900" (Ph.D. diss., University of Colorado, 1936), 332.

33. *Denver Times,* December 24, 1901, p. 10.

34. Perrigo, "A Social History of Central City," 522–23; Duane A. Smith, *Rocky Mountain Boom Town: A History of Durango* (Albuquerque: University of New Mexico Press, 1980), 71, 216.

35. *Pep and Punch* 20:10 (March 1948): 1; *Pep and Punch* 20:6 (November 1947): 1; Lynn I. Perrigo, "The Cradle of Colorado: Early Central City in the Reminiscences of Pioneers, 1935" (Las Vegas, N.M.: Denver Public Library, Western History Department, 1973): 36; *Denver Times,* May 14, 1891, p. 6.

36. Paul, *Mining Frontiers of the Far West,* 68, 69, 128; Brown, *Hard-Rock Miners,* 8.

37. Arthur Cecil Todd, *The Cornish Miner in America* (Glendale, Calif.: Arthur H. Clark, 1967), 71; Hannington, "Early Days of Central City," 8; Perrigo, "The Cradle of Colorado," 31; Horner, *Silver Town,* 238, 249; *Rocky Mountain News,* September 10, 1881, p. 3.

38. Irey, "A Social History of Leadville," 157; Benjamin G. Rader, *American Sports: From the Age of Folk Games to the Age of Televised Sports,* 3d ed. (Englewood Cliffs, N.J.: Prentice-Hall, 1996), 66–67.

39. Irey, "A Social History of Leadville," 156; Smith, *Rocky Mountain Mining Camps,* 216; Horner, *Silver Town,* 231.

40. Central City *Daily Register,* November 11, 1871, p. 4; *Rocky Mountain News,* April 25, 1885, p. 3; Smith, *Rocky Mountain Mining Camps,* 219.

41. Blair, *Leadville,* 135; Smith, *Rocky Mountain Boom Town,* 71.

42. Smith, *Rocky Mountain Mining Camps,* 215; Perrigo, "A Social History of Central City," 329–30; Mabel Barbee Lee, *Cripple Creek Days* (Garden City, N.Y.: Doubleday, 1958), 114–15.

43. Toby Smith, *Kid Blackie: Jack Dempsey's Colorado Days* (Ouray, Colo.: Wayfinder

Press, 1987), 9.

44. *Herald Democrat* (Leadville), June 1, 1900, clipping in William J. Irwin Scrapbooks, courtesy of Terry L. Irwin, Colma, Calif.; *Herald Democrat,* January 8, 1998, pp. 5, 6.

45. Perrigo, "A Social History of Central City," 329–30; Rohrbough, *Aspen,* 131.

46. *Rocky Mountain News,* August 20, 1879, p. 5; Irey, "A Social History of Leadville," 156–57; Georgina Brown, "Horses . . . Sport of the Carbonate Kings," *Mountain Diggings* 3:1 (April 1973): 14–21; Don L. Griswold and Jean H. Griswold, *The Carbonate Camp Called Leadville* (Denver: University of Denver Press, 1951), 219.

47. On the origins and development of baseball in the nineteenth century see Harold Seymour, *Baseball: The Early Years* (New York: Oxford University Press, 1960); William J. Baker, *Sports in the Western World,* rev. ed. (Urbana and Chicago: University of Illinois Press, 1988); Benjamin G. Rader, *Baseball: A History of America's Game* (Urbana and Chicago: University of Illinois Press, 1994); and Mark S. Foster, "Playing by the Rules: The Evolution of Baseball in the Nineteenth Century," *Colorado Heritage* (spring 1995): 44–51.

48. Duane A. Smith, *Song of the Hammer and Drill: The Colorado San Juans,* 1860–1914 (Golden: Colorado School of Mines Press, 1982), 159; Duane A. Smith, "Might Casey Matches the Mountains: The Origins of Baseball in Colorado," *Colorado Heritage* (spring 1995): 8.

49. Smith, "Mighty Casey Matches the Mountains," 5–6.

50. Perrigo, "A Social History of Central City," 330.

51. Rohrbough, *Aspen,* 51–52; Smith, "Mighty Casey Matches the Mountains," 12–13.

52. Hannington, "Early Days of Central City," 14; Rohrbough, *Aspen,* 51–52, 200.

53. Smith, "Mighty Casey Matches the Mountains," 13.

54. Duane A. Smith, "Baseball Champions of Colorado: The Leadville Blues of 1882," *Journal of Sports History* 4:1 (spring 1977): 55.

55. Ibid., 56; Smith, "Mighty Casey Matches the Mountains," 10.

56. Smith, "Baseball Champions of Colorado," 60, 65, 68; Smith, "Mighty Casey Matches the Mountains," 10.

57. Smith, "Mighty Casey Matches the Mountains," 11; Irvin Moss and Mark Foster, *Home Run in the Rockies: The History of Baseball in Colorado* (Denver: A. B. Hirschfeld Press, 1994), 88; *Denver Post,* September 26, 1958, p. 31.

58. Blair, *Leadville,* 202.

CHAPTER 3

1. *Denver Post,* July 14, 1989, p. 2b; July 26, 1989, p. 8b; *Rocky Mountain News,* July 14, 1989, p. 11.

2. *Denver Post,* July 14, 1989, p. 2b; July 26, 1989, pp. 1b, 8b.

3. *Denver Post,* July 26, 1989, p. 1b.

4. Ibid.; *Rocky Mountain News,* July 27, 1989, p. 73; July 28, 1989, p. 68; July 31, 1989, p. 32.

5. *Denver Post,* July 27, 1989, pp. 1b, 2b; *Rocky Mountain News,* July 27, 1989, p. 19.

6. *Rocky Mountain News,* October 10, 1983, p. 131.

7. *Rocky Mountain News,* January 19, 1869, p. 4; February 2, 1869, p. 4; February 18, 1869, p. 4; March 2, 1869, p. 4; March 4, 1869, p. 4; March 16, 1869, p. 4; April 20, 1869, p. 4.

8. *Rocky Mountain News,* May 14, 1869, p. 4; *Rocky Mountain News,* April 10, 1966, reprint in *Colorado Prospector* 13:5 (May 1982): 8; *Rocky Mountain News,* July 4, 1880, p. 5.

9. *Official Souvenir for the League of American Wheelmen, Annual Meeting, Denver, August*

13–18, 1894, 1, in Denver Pubic Library, Western History Department; *Denver Times,* January 17, 1900, p. 12.

10. *Colorado Sun,* April 23, 1893, p. 16.

11. Ibid.; *Official Souvenir,* 20.

12. *Colorado Sun,* April 23, 1893, pp. 14–15; *Denver Times,* June 17, 1900, p. 20; *Denver Post,* April 9, 1920, p. 24; *Rocky Mountain News,* August 8, 1971, reprint in *Colorado Prospector* 13:5 (May 1982): 1, 12; *Rocky Mountain News,* April 8, 1984, p. 19.

13. *Cycling West,* January 1, 1894, clipping in Denver Public Library, Western History Department, Denver Wheel Club Scrapbooks, 1891–1895.

14. *Colorado Sun,* April 23, 1893, p. 15; *Official Souvenir,* 20; Thomas J. Noel, *The Denver Athletic Club, 1884–1984* (Denver: Denver Athletic Club, 1984), 20, 30, 31.

15. *Rocky Mountain News,* April 1, 1869, p. 4.

16. *Colorado Sun,* April 23, 1893, p. 15; *Rocky Mountain Herald,* April 22, 1972, p. 1.

17. Colorado Historical Society, Denver Athletic Club Scrapbooks, 6–21; Noel, *Denver Athletic Club,* 30; Denver Public Library, Denver Wheel Club Scrapbooks, 1891–1895; *Denver Post Empire Magazine* (April 2, 1978): 37, 39.

18. *Rocky Mountain News,* April 25, 1897, reprint in *Colorado Prospector* 13:5 (May 1982): 3.

19. *Official Souvenir,* 20; *League of American Wheelmen Bulletin* 1:23 (August 23, 1894): 1, clipping in Denver Public Library, Frank W. Tupper Scrapbook, 1889–1896, 1:153; *Colorado Transcript* (Golden), May 16, 1894, p. 7.

20. *Denver Times,* September 19, 1896, reprint in *Colorado Prospector* 13:5 (May 1982): 4; *Denver Times,* August 26, 1898, p. 13; *Denver Republican,* September 19, 1900, reprint in *Colorado Prospector* 13:5 (May 1982): 6.

21. *Official Souvenir,* 21.

22. *Colorado Sun,* April 23, 1893, p. 17.

23. *Cycling West,* September 1, 1893, p. 6; March 25, 1897, p. 19.

24. *Cycling West,* March 10, 1898, p. 14; April 14, 1898, p. 14.

25. *Cycling West,* April 15, 1897, pp. 9–10.

26. *Cycling West,* April 15, 1897, p. 10; "Useful Information for the Bicyclist," reprint in *Colorado Prospector* 13:5 (May 1982): 10; *Cycling West,* January 13, 1898, p. 18.

27. *Cycling West,* May 19, 1898, p. 17; February 10, 1898, p. 13.

28. *Denver Evening Post* cartoon, May 22, 1899; Eugene Frank Rider, "The Denver Police Department: An Administrative, Organizational, and Operational History, 1858–1905," (Ph.D. diss., University of Denver, 1971), 495; *Denver Times,* August 7, 1896, reprint in *Colorado Prospector* 13:5 (May 1982): 11.

29. *Cycling West,* June 24, 1897, p. 12; July 15, 1897, p. 9.

30. Rider, "The Denver Police Department," 436–37, 470; *Cycling West,* April 15, 1897, p. 41.

31. *Denver Times,* August 7, 1896, reprint in *Colorado Prospector* 13:5 (May 1982): 1, 11.

32. *Rocky Mountain News,* May 23, 1898, p. 3.

33. Denver Public Library, Western History Department, Denver Wheel Club Scrapbooks, 1891–1895, clippings; *Denver Times,* October 26, 1896, p. 1; November 10, 1896, p. 1; January 17, 1900, p. 12.

34. *Denver Times,* August 25, 1896, reprint in *Colorado Prospector* 13:5 (May 1982): 5; Andrew W. Gillette, "The Bicycle Era in Colorado," *Colorado Magazine* 10 (November 1933): 214–16; LeRoy R. Hafen and Ann W. Hafen, *Colorado: A Story of the State and Its People* (Denver: Old West Publishing, 1944), 306.

35. Gillette, "The Bicycle Era in Colorado," 216.

36. *Denver Post,* May 22, 1899, p. 5.

37. *Denver Times,* August 25, 1896, reprint in *Colorado Prospector* 13:5 (May 1982): 5; *Littleton Independent,* September 17, 1965, reprint in *Colorado Prospector* 13:5 (May 1982): 6.

38. *Cycling West,* July 8, 1897, p. 9; Gillette, "The Bicycle Era in Colorado," 217; *Rocky Mountain News,* April 10, 1966, reprint in *Colorado Prospector* 13:5 (May 1982): 8.

39. *Denver Times,* October 19, 1899, p. 11; *Rocky Mountain News,* August 8, 1971, reprint in *Colorado Prospector* 13:5 (May 1982): 1, 12; *Rocky Mountain News,* December 30, 1901, p. 3; *Denver Times,* December 11, 1901, p. 6; *Denver Times,* September 22, 1900, clipping in Denver Public Library, Western History Department, "Bicycle Riding. Denver."

40. *Cycling West,* February 25, 1897, p. 12.

41. *Rocky Mountain News,* June 14, 1965, p. 5; August 4, 1991, pp. 54, 58; *Denver Post Contemporary Magazine* (October 5, 1969): 9; *Denver Post,* August 23, 1986, p. 1b; *City Edition,* April 4, 1984, pp. 1, 7.

42. *Rocky Mountain News,* October 10, 1983, p. 131.

43. *Rocky Mountain News,* May 25, 1992, p. 40.

44. Ibid.

45. *Rocky Mountain News,* February 25, 1993, p. 20; March 1, 1993, pp. 20, 21; *Denver Post,* February 25, 1993, p. 3b.

46. *Rocky Mountain News,* March 1, 1993, p. 20; March 2, 1993, p. 11; *Denver Post,* March 2, 1993, p. 4b.

47. *Rocky Mountain News,* March 2, 1993, p. 11; *Denver Post,* March 2, 1993, p. 4b.

48. *Denver Post,* June 13, 1993, cited in Lisa McGrath, "A History of Bicycling in Colorado" (1994), unpublished manuscript in author's possession.

49. *Denver Post,* May 8, 1980, p. 81; July 7, 1989, p. 3e.

50. *Rocky Mountain News,* September 24, 1984, p. 16; June 8, 1992, p. 10; David M. Schwartz, "Over Hill, Over Dale, on a Bicycle Built for . . . Goo," *Smithsonian* 25:3 (June 1994): 82.

51. Schwartz, "Over Hill, Over Dale," 77–78; Whitman W. Thompson, "Fat Tires: The Origins and Explosion of Mountain Biking," unpublished manuscript in author's possession, 3–5.

52. Schwartz, "Over Hill, Over Dale," 77–78.

53. *Rocky Mountain News,* September 24, 1984, p. 16; April 18, 1993, 10a, 30a, 31a; *Denver Post,* November 4, 1996, 1b, 5b; Thompson, "Fat Tires," 8.

54. Schwartz, "Over Hill, Over Dale," 86; *Rocky Mountain News,* October 21, 1991, p. 10; August 20, 1995, p. 30a; *Denver Post,* May 27, 1992, p. 8d; May 23, 1993; *Denver Post Summertime West,* p. 6; July 3, 1994, p. 12b.

55. *Rocky Mountain News,* June 28, 1993, p. 8a.

56. *Rocky Mountain News,* September 24, 1984, p. 17; September 8, 1993, p. 16a; September 19, 1993, p. 26a; *Denver Post,* September 14, 1995, p. 2b; author's conversation with Jefferson County Open Space official Stanton La Breche, February 6, 1996; *Denver Post,* March 29, 1996, p. 2b.

57. Schwartz, "Over Hill, Over Dale," 80.

58. Karen DeBacker, "Peddling Bikes Now Big Business," *Executive Denver and Corporate Connection* 9:8 (December 1994): 26–28; *Rocky Mountain News,* September 9, 1994, p. 54a; *Rocky Mountain News,* April 29, 1996, p. 6a.

59. *Denver Post,* July 17, 1993, p. 2c; June 26, 1994, pp. 1g, 15g; *Rocky Mountain News,* June 8, 1993, p. 33a; June 19, 1993, p. 50a; December 3, 1993, p. 68a; December 21, 1995,

p. 78a; December 29, 1996, p. 7b; *Denver Post,* February 21, 1999, 5b, 7b.

60. Denver Public Library, Western History Department, Frank W. Tupper Scrapbooks, 1889–1896, 2:172.

CHAPTER 4

1. John B. Allen, *From Skisport to Skiing: One Hundred Years of American Sport, 1840–1940* (Amherst: University of Massachusetts Press, 1993), 11.

2. Ibid., 47–62.

3. John Rolf Burroughs, *Steamboat in the Rockies* (Fort Collins, Colo.: Old Army Press, 1978), 187–88; Jack A. Benson, "Before Aspen and Vail: The Story of Recreational Skiing in Colorado," in *Sport in the West,* ed. Donald J. Mrozek (Manhattan, Kans.: *Journal of the West,* Sunflower University Press, 1983), 57.

4. Burroughs, *Steamboat in the Rockies,* 188; Benson, "Before Aspen and Vail," 57–58.

5. Benson, "Before Aspen and Vail," 58–59; Abbott Fay, *Ski Tracks in the Rockies: A Century of Colorado Skiing* (Louisville, Colo.: Cordillera Press, 1984), 9.

6. Calvin Queal, "Colorado Skiing: A Century of Sport," *Denver Post Empire Magazine* (November 9, 1969): 12.

7. Fay, *Ski Tracks in the Rockies,* 9; Burroughs, *Steamboat in the Rockies,* 188–89; Queal, "Colorado Skiing," 12.

8. Fay, *Ski Tracks in the Rockies,* 9–10; Benson, "Before Aspen and Vail," 60.

9. Benson, "Before Aspen and Vail."

10. Stephen J. Leonard and Thomas J. Noel, *Denver: Mining Camp to Metropolis* (Niwot: University Press of Colorado, 1990), 153–54; Fay, *Ski Tracks in the Rockies,* 15–16.

11. Mary Ellen Gilliland, *Summit: A Gold Rush History of Summit County, Colorado* (Silverthorn, Colo.: Alpenrose Press, 1980), 307–08; Fay, *Ski Tracks in the Rockies,* 75.

12. Allen, *From Skisport to Skiing,* 84.

13. Gilliland, *Summit,* 307.

14. Allen, *From Skisport to Skiing,* 96–98; Douglas Reynolds, "White and Green, One Formula for Making Money: The Birth and Maturation of Colorado's Ski Industry" (1994), unpublished manuscript.

15. Allen, *From Skisport to Skiing,* 98–103, 121–22; *Denver Post,* quoted in Reynolds, "White and Green," 9.

16. Fay, *Ski Tracks in the Rockies,* 16, 25; Allen, *From Skisport to Skiing,* 109; Leonard and Noel, *Denver,* 154; Steve Patterson and Kenton Forrest, *Rio Grande Ski Train* (Denver: Tramway Press, 1984), 25; Queal, "Colorado Skiing," 13.

17. Fay, *Ski Tracks in the Rockies,* 21, 26; Queal, "Colorado Skiing," 12; Leonard and Noel, *Denver,* 153–54.

18. Fay, *Ski Tracks in the Rockies,* 23; Queal, "Colorado Skiing," 12–13.

19. Fay, *Ski Tracks in the Rockies,* 21–23.

20. Allen, *From Skisport to Skiing,* 113, 143–44.

21. Anne Gilbert, "Re-Creation Through Recreation: Aspen Skiing from 1870 to 1970" (Aspen: Aspen Historical Society, 1995), 14–17; Sally Barlow-Perez, *A History of Aspen* (Aspen: WHO Press, 1991), 37–38; Fay, *Ski Tracks in the Rockies,* 26.

22. Gilbert, "Re-Creation Through Recreation," 17–19; Barlow-Perez, *A History of Aspen,* 38.

23. Gilbert, "Re-Creation Through Recreation," 17; Barlow-Perez, *A History of Aspen,* 38–39.

24. *Aspen Times,* November 26, 1936, quoted in Gilbert, "Re-Creation Through Recreation," 18.

25. Gilbert, "Re-Creation Through Recreation," 19.

26. Ibid., 20; Queal, "Colorado Skiing," 13.

27. Gilbert, "Re-Creation Through Recreation," 20–21.

28. Robert Benchley, "How to Aspen" (1936), quoted in Gilbert, "Re-Creation Through Recreation," 23–24; Allen, *From Skisport to Skiing,* 139; Barlow-Perez, *A History of Aspen,* 41.

29. Gilbert, "Re-Creation Through Recreation," 25–27; Barlow-Perez, *A History of Aspen,* 39; Fay, *Ski Tracks in the Rockies,* 79.

30. Gilbert, "Re-Creation Through Recreation," 27–31; Barlow-Perez, *A History of Aspen,* 39; *Western Colorado and Eastern Utah* 1:7 (January 1939): 8, 9, 20; *Rocky Mountain News,* July 18, 1939, p. 7.

31. Gilbert, "Re-Creation Through Recreation," 31–33; Barlow-Perez, *A History of Aspen,* 39–40.

32. Charles Minot Dole, *Adventures in Skiing* (New York: Franklin Watts, 1965), 90–91; Jack A Benson, "Skiing at Camp Hale: Mountain Troops During World War II," *Western Historical Quarterly* 15:2 (April 1984): 163–64. Dole dates his conversation with Langley to February 1939. This date is unlikely since the Soviet-Finnish war did not begin until November 1939. Benson's account relies on Dole and thus repeats the error.

33. Benson, "Skiing at Camp Hale," 166–67.

34. Ibid., 167, 168.

35. Ibid., 169; Flint Whitlock, *Soldiers on Skis: A Pictorial Memoir of the Tenth Mountain Division* (Boulder: Paladin Press, 1992), 6–7.

36. KRMA-TV, "Soldiers of the Summit" (Council for Public Television, 1987), video; Barlow-Perez, *Aspen,* 43–44.

37. Whitlock, *Soldiers on Skis,* 19–29.

38. Benson, "Skiing at Camp Hale," 172–173; Whitlock, *Soldiers on Skis,* 42–43.

39. Benson, "Skiing at Camp Hale," 173; Whitlock, *Soldiers on Skis,* 55–181; *New York Times,* April 8, 1996, p. 8a.

40. Charlie Meyers, *Colorado Ski Country,* Colorado Geographic Series, no. 4 (Helena and Billings: Falcon Press, 1987), 18–19; Fay, *Ski Tracks in the Rockies,* 73–80; *New York Times,* April 8, 1996, p. 8a.

41. Meyers, *Colorado Ski Country,* 43; Barlow-Perez, *A History of Aspen,* 41–42; Gilbert, "Re-Creation Through Recreation," 49–50.

42. Gilbert, "Re-Creation Through Recreation," 50.

43. Ibid., 50–51.

44. Ibid., p. 51; Fay, *Ski Tracks in the Rockies,* 36.

45. Gilbert, "Re-Creation Through Recreation," 52.

46. Ibid., 53–54; Barlow-Perez, *A History of Aspen,* 47.

47. Gilbert, "Re-Creation Through Recreation," 55–58; Barlow-Perez, *A History of Aspen,* 49; Paul I. Hauk, *Aspen Mountain Ski Area Chronology* (Glenwood Springs, Colo.: United States Department of Agriculture, Forest Service, 1978), 2–3.

48. Hauk, *Aspen Mountain,* 2–3; Gilbert, "Re-Creation Through Recreation," 57.

49. Gilbert, "Re-Creation Through Recreation," 58–59; Barlow-Perez, *A History of Aspen,* 49; Dick Durrance and John Jerome, *The Man on the Medal: The Life and Times of America's First Great Skier* (Aspen: Durrance Enterprises, 1995), 93–106.

50. Gilbert, "Re-Creation Through Recreation," 65.

51. Ibid., 70–75; Barlow-Perez, *A History of Aspen,* 53–62; Meyers, *Colorado Ski Country,* 43.

52. Gilbert, "Re-Creation Through Recreation," 77.

53. Ibid., 78–80; Barlow-Perez, *A History of Aspen,* 64.

54. Gilbert, "Re-Creation Through Recreation," 80–82; Barlow-Perez, *A History of Aspen,* 63.

55. Gilbert, "Re-Creation Through Recreation," 90–93; Barlow-Perez, *A History of Aspen,* 64–65.

56. Gilbert, "Re-Creation Through Recreation," 89; *Denver Post,* July 14, 1996, p. 3f.

57. Barlow-Perez, *A History of Aspen,* 83–84.

58. Hunter S. Thompson, introduction to *To Aspen and Back: An American Journey,* by Peggy Clifford (New York: St. Martin's Press, 1980), xvi.

59. Ibid.

60. Edna Strand Dercum, *It's Easy, Edna, It's Downhill All the Way,* 2d ed. (Carbondale, Colo.: Sopris Press, 1991), 43–45.

61. Gilliland, *Summit,* 64, 72; Meyers, *Colorado Ski Country,* 64; Dercum, *It's Easy, Edna,* 4.

62. Dercum, *It's Easy, Edna,* 1, 30, 38–39.

63. Queal, "Colorado Skiing," 14; Dercum, *It's Easy, Edna,* 46–47; Meyers, *Colorado Ski Country,* 64; Gilliland, *Summit,* 310–311.

64. Douglas Reynolds, "Ralston Purina's Recreational Kingdom: A Look at the History of Summit County Skiing," (unpublished manuscript, 1994), 9–10; Queal, "Colorado Skiing," 14; Gilliland, *Summit,* 311–12; Dercum, *It's Easy, Edna,* 70–71.

65. Reynolds, "Ralston Purina's Recreational Kingdom," 10; Gilliland, *Summit,* 313; Dercum, *It's Easy, Edna,* 125–26.

66. Reynolds, "Ralston Purina's Recreational Kingdom," 10–12.

67. Charles R. Goeldner and R. L. Wobbekind, *The Colorado Ski Industry: Highlights of the 1993–1994 Season* (Boulder: Business Research Division, Graduate School of Business Administration, University of Colorado at Boulder, 1994), 12–15; Gilliland, *Summit,* 315.

68. Reynolds, "Ralston Purina's Recreational Kingdom," 13.

69. Dercum, *It's Easy, Edna,* 99–124; Meyers, *Colorado Ski Country,* 64.

70. Meyers, *Colorado Ski Country,* 64; Dercum, *It's Easy, Edna,* 211.

71. Paul I. Hauk, *Keystone Ski Area Chronology* (Glenwood Springs, Colo.: United States Department of Agriculture, Forest Service, 1979), 4; Reynolds, "Ralston Purina's Recreational Kingdom," 21–23.

72. Meyers, *Colorado Ski Country,* 64; Dercum, *It's Easy, Edna,* 208.

73. Dercum, *It's Easy, Edna,* 208; Hauk, *Keystone,* 8; Reynolds, "Ralston Purina's Recreational Kingdom," 23.

74. *Denver Post,* February 7, 1971, in Reynolds, "Ralston Purina's Recreational Kingdom," 24; Hauk, *Keystone,* 1.

75. Paul I. Hauk, *Arapahoe Ski Area Chronology* (Glenwood Springs, Colo.: United States Department of Agriculture, Forest Service, 1979), 6; Reynolds, "Ralston Purina's Recreational Kingdom," 25.

76. Goeldner and Wobbekind, *The Colorado Ski Industry, 1993–1994,* 12.

77. Meyers, *Colorado Ski Country,* 61; *Denver Post,* December 17, 1981, quoted in Reynolds, "Ralston Purina's Recreational Kingdom," 27.

78. Goeldner and Wobbekind, *The Colorado Ski Industry, 1993–1994,* 4, 12; Reynolds, "Ralston Purina's Recreational Kingdom," 28.

79. Goeldner and Wobbekind, *The Colorado Ski Industry, 1993–1994,* 7–8; Reynolds,

"Ralston Purina's Recreational Kingdom," 29.

80. Goeldner and Wobbekind, *The Colorado Ski Industry, 1993–1994,* 10; Reynolds, "Ralston Purina's Recreational Kingdom," 30–31.

81. Goeldner and Wobbekind, *The Colorado Ski Industry, 1993–1994,* 4.

82. Meyers, *Colorado Ski Country,* 58–60; Reynolds, "Ralston Purina's Recreational Kingdom," 14–15.

83. Reynolds, "Ralston Purina's Recreational Kingdom," 15–16; Fay, *Ski Tracks in the Rockies,* 51; Gilliland, *Summit,* 316; Meyers, *Colorado Ski Country,* 60; Charles R. Goeldner and Karen Dicke, *Colorado Ski and Winter Recreation Statistics, 1980* (Boulder: Business Research Division, Graduate School of Business Administration, University of Colorado, 1981), 11.

84. Charles R. Goeldner and Andy Dudiak, *The Colorado Ski Industry: Highlights of the 1989–90 Season* (Boulder: Business Research Division, Graduate School of Business Administration, University of Colorado at Boulder, 1990), 15.

85. Reynolds, "Ralston Purina's Recreational Kingdom," 18–19; Goeldner and Wobbekind, *The Colorado Ski Industry, 1993–1994,* 18.

86. Charles R. Goeldner and Yvonne Sletta, *The Breckenridge Skier* (Boulder: Business Research Division, Graduate School of Business Administration, University of Colorado, 1975), 4, 5, 9, 16, 20; Charles R. Goeldner, *The Aspen Skier: 1977–1978 Season* (Boulder: Business Research Division, Graduate School of Business Administration, University of Colorado, 1978), 7, 13.

87. Goeldner and Wobbekind, *The Colorado Ski Industry, 1993–1994,* 15.

88. June B. Simonton, *Vail: Story of a Colorado Mountain Valley* (Denver: Knudsen Printing, 1987), 66.

89. Fay, *Ski Tracks in the Rockies,* 49; William Oscar Johnson, "A Vision Fulfilled: From One Man's Dream, Vail Has Grown Into America's Biggest Ski Resort," *Sports Illustrated* (January 30, 1989): 77.

90. Johnson, "A Vision Fulfilled," 77; Simonton, *Vail,* 61, 62.

91. Simonton, *Vail,* 58; Johnson, "A Vision Fulfilled," 77; Paul I. Hauk, *Vail Ski Area Chronology* (Glenwood Springs, Colo.: United States Department of Agriculture, Forest Service, 1979), 1–2.

92. Johnson, "A Vision Fulfilled," 77.

93. Simonton, *Vail,* 62; Hauk, *Vail,* 2.

94. Simonton, *Vail,* 62; Johnson, "A Vision Fulfilled," 77.

95. Simonton, *Vail,* 66.

96. Simonton, *Vail,* 62–63; Hauk, *Vail,* pp. 3–4.

97. Simonton, *Vail,* 62–63; Hauk, *Vail,* 3–4.

98. Simonton, *Vail,* 65, 67.

99. *Denver Post,* December 29, 1961, clipping in Hauk, *Vail,* 98; Meyers, *Colorado Ski Country,* 32; Simonton, *Vail,* 68; Thomas J. Noel, *Buildings of Colorado* (New York: Oxford University Press, 1997), 469.

100. Johnson, "A Vision Fulfilled," 77; Simonton, *Vail,* 75.

101. Fay, *Ski Tracks in the Rockies,* 49; I. William Berry, *The Great North American Ski Book* (New York: Charles Scribner's Sons, 1982) 54, 57.

102. Johnson, "A Vision Fulfilled," 78; Hauk, *Vail,* 8, 9.

103. Johnson, "A Vision Fulfilled," 78; Hauk, *Vail,* 8, 9.

104. Johnson, "A Vision Fulfilled," 78; Fay, *Ski Tracks in the Rockies,* 60; Berry, *The Great North American Ski Book,* 59; Simonton, *Vail,* 120–27.

105. Goeldner and Dicke, *Colorado Ski and Winter Recreation Statistics, 1980,* 4; Goeldner and Wobbekind, *The Colorado Ski Industry, 1993–1994,* 13–15.

106. Johnson, "A Vision Fulfilled," 81.

107. Berry, *The Great North American Ski Book,* 54; Johnson, "A Vision Fulfilled," 82.

108. Johnson, "A Vision Fulfilled," 78.

109. *Rocky Mountain News,* September 11, 1996, pp. 1b, 3b; February 17, 1997, 1b, 5b.

110. *Rocky Mountain News,* July 24, 1996, 1b, 4b, 5b; July 28, 1996, 1b, 8b, 9b; *Denver Post,* July 24, 1996, 1c, 8c; July 27, 1996, p. 1b.

111. Donald Worster, *Rivers of Empire: Water, Aridity and the Growth of the American West* (New York: Pantheon Books, 1985).

112. *Rocky Mountain News,* July 5, 1996, p. 10a.

113. *Denver Post,* June 15, 1996, p. 1b.

114. Gilliland, *Summit,* 314.

115. Simonton, *Vail,* 72.

116. Annie Gilbert Coleman, "Whiteout: The Ethnicity of Skiing in the American West," paper presented at the Western History Association Conference, October 12, 1995, Denver, Colorado, 4.

117. According to the ski-industry organization Colorado Ski Country USA, 71.7 percent of skiers visiting Colorado resorts in 1997–1998 earned more than $50,000 per year; more than 18 percent commanded incomes of more than $200,000. These figures underscore the relative absences of minorities in skiing, as whites far outnumber minorities in these upper-income ranges (*Rocky Mountain News,* February 19, 1999, p. 26).

Chapter 5

1. Thomas G. Paterson, "Fixation With Cuba: The Bay of Pigs, Missile Crisis, and Covert War Against Fidel Castro," in *Kennedy's Quest for Victory: American Foreign Policy, 1961–1963,* ed. Thomas G. Paterson (New York: Oxford University Press, 1989), 135.

2. *Rocky Mountain News,* April 4, 1971, p. 1.

3. *Rocky Mountain News,* April 23, 1949, p. 30; Denver Olympic Organizing Committee (DOOC), *Final Report, December 29, 1972* (Denver Public Library, Western History Department), 75; Pete Homan, "Colorado's Rejection of the 1976 Winter Olympics," unpublished manuscript in author's possession (1994), 2.

4. DOOC, *Final Report,* 75.

5. Ibid., 75–76.

6. Ibid., 76–77.

7. Laura Lee Katz Olson, "Power, Public Policy, and the Environment: The Defeat of the 1976 Winter Olympics in Colorado" (Ph.D. diss., University of Colorado, 1974), 94–95.

8. Colorado Olympics Commission, Minutes of Meetings of the Board of Directors, November 12, 1965, Files of the Denver Olympic Committee, tape 3ER, quoted in Olson, "Power, Public Policy, and the Environment," 94.

9. Olson, "Power, Public Policy, and the Environment," 99–100; *Rocky Mountain News,* June 24, 1966, p. 85; DOOC, *Final Report,* 81.

10. DOOC, *Final Report,* 79; Olson, "Power, Public Policy, and the Environment," 97.

11. DOOC, *Final Report,* 79.

12. Ibid., 82.

13. Olson, "Power, Public Policy, and the Environment," 100–101.

14. DOOC, *Final Report,* 84.

15. Ibid., 85.

16. Ibid., 86.

17. Ibid., 58, 86–87.

18. *Rocky Mountain News,* April 7, 1971, p. 8; Mark S. Foster, "Colorado's Defeat of the 1976 Winter Olympics," *Colorado Magazine* 53:2 (spring 1976): 166; Olson, "Power, Public Policy, and the Environment," 106.

19. Jerry Kirshenbaum, "Voting to Snuff the Torch," *Sports Illustrated* 37:21 (November 20, 1972): 49; Rick Reese, "The Denver Winter Olympics Controversy" (Salt Lake City: Rick Reese, 1984; typescript in Denver Public Library, Western History Department), 9; Foster, "Colorado's Defeat of the 1976 Winter Olympics," 167.

20. Foster, "Colorado's Defeat of the 1976 Winter Olympics," 165.

21. Olson, "Power, Public Policy, and the Environment," 108–9.

22. Ibid., 112.

23. Ibid., 111.

24. Ibid., 110–11; DOOC, *Final Report,* 93.

25. Olson, "Power, Public Policy, and the Environment," 121–24, 126–27.

26. Ibid., 125, 126.

27. Ibid., 127–29.

28. *Rocky Mountain News,* April 7, 1971, p. 6.

29. *Rocky Mountain News,* April 6, 1971, p. 8; Foster, "Colorado's Defeat of the 1976 Winter Olympics," 173.

30. *Denver Post,* March 9, 1971, quoted in Foster, "Colorado's Defeat of the 1976 Winter Olympics," 176.

31. DOOC, *Final Report,* 88, 92, 100.

32. Ron Wolf, "Who Owns the Olympics?: Colorado's Financial Elite Plan 1976 Snow Job for Public," *Straight Creek Journal* 1:29 (August 24, 1972): 3; Kirshenbaum, "Voting to Snuff the Torch," 46.

33. DOOC, *Final Report,* 103.

34. Foster, "Colorado's Defeat of the 1976 Winter Olympics," 164.

35. *Rocky Mountain News,* April 4, 1971, p. 8; Foster, "Colorado's Defeat of the 1976 Winter Olympics," 166–67.

36. DOOC, *Final Report,* 102–5.

37. Ibid., 106.

38. Foster, "Colorado's Defeat of the 1976 Winter Olympics," 175; DOOC, *Final Report,* 107; Olson, "Power, Public Policy, and the Environment," 133, 142.

39. Foster, "Colorado's Defeat of the 1976 Winter Olympics," 175–76.

40. Olson, "Power, Public Policy, and the Environment," 144.

41. *Rocky Mountain News,* April 9, 1971, p. 8.

42. DOOC, *Final Report,* 46; Olson, "Power, Public Policy, and the Environment," 142; *Rocky Mountain News,* April 6, 1971, p. 8.

43. *Rocky Mountain News,* April 6, 1971, p. 8.

44. Olson, "Power, Public Policy, and the Environment," 146–48, 156–63; *Rocky Mountain News,* April 6, 1971, p. 8; DOOC, *Final Report,* 118.

45. Olson, "Power, Public Policy, and the Environment," 148–53.

46. Ibid., 152–56.

47. Ibid., 156–59; *Rocky Mountain News,* April 7, 1971, p. 8.

48. *Rocky Mountain News,* April 7, 1971, p. 8; *Denver Post Bonus Section,* September 25, 1972, p. 2.

49. DOOC, *Final Report,* 53–57; Olson, "Power, Public Policy, and the Environment,"

163–68; *Denver Post Bonus Section,* September 25, 1972, p. 2.

50. Olson, "Power, Public Policy, and the Environment," 135–37, 168–73; *Denver Post Bonus Section,* September 25, 1972, p. 6.

51. DOOC, *Final Report,* 9. Olson claims that in the period 1965–1971 the State of Colorado contributed $505,000 and the City and County of Denver $225,000 of the DOC's total income of $1,043,000 ("Power, Public Policy, and the Environment," 211).

52. Olson, "Power, Public Policy, and the Environment," 212; *Denver Post,* May 13, 1970, p. 23.

53. Olson, "Power, Public Policy, and the Environment," 215.

54. Ibid., 216–17.

55. Ibid., 218.

56. *Denver Post,* January 12, 1971, and *Rocky Mountain News,* January 27, 1971, both quoted in Foster, "Colorado's Defeat of the 1976 Winter Olympics," 177.

57. Olson, "Power, Public Policy, and the Environment," 231–34; *Rocky Mountain News,* April 12, 1972, clipping in Denver Public Library, Western History Department, Citizens for Colorado's Future (CCF), Records, 1971–1972, file folder 3, clippings, 1972.

58. Olson, "Power, Public Policy, and the Environment," 26–27, 30; Kirshenbaum, "Voting to Snuff the Torch," 46.

59. Morten Lund, "Their New Alps, Our New Alps: The Coming Despoliation of Colorado," *Ski Magazine* (December 1971): 80; Foster, "Colorado's Defeat of the 1976 Winter Olympics," 166; Reese, "The Denver Winter Olympics Controversy," 14.

60. Foster, "Colorado's Defeat of the 1976 Winter Olympics," 177–78; Olson, "Power, Public Policy, and the Environment," 174, 176.

61. Olson, "Power, Public Policy, and the Environment," 174–75; Foster, "Colorado's Defeat of the 1976 Winter Olympics," 178.

62. Foster, "Colorado's Defeat of the 1976 Winter Olympics," 178–79; Olson, "Power, Public Policy, and the Environment," 175–77.

63. Olson, "Power, Public Policy, and the Environment," 176; Foster, "Colorado's Defeat of the 1976 Winter Olympics," 179; *Denver Post Bonus Section,* September 25, 1972, p. 5.

64. Foster, "Colorado's Defeat of the 1976 Winter Olympics," 179–80; Olson, "Power, Public Policy, and the Environment," 176–77; John Parr, "Face to Face With the Olympic Gods," *Capital Ledger* 1:3 (March 1972): 11.

65. *Denver Post,* March 16, 1972, clipping in CCF Records, file folder 3, clippings, 1972; Foster, "Colorado's Defeat of the 1976 Winter Olympics," 182; Olson, "Power, Public Policy, and the Environment," 177.

66. Olson, "Power, Public Policy, and the Environment," 188, 189; Foster, "Colorado's Defeat of the 1976 Winter Olympics," 182.

67. Richard D. Lamm, "Promotional Pollution: The Case for Not Holding the 1976 Winter Olympics in Colorado," typescript text in CCF Records, file folder 1, articles, n.d., 1971, 1972.

68. Olson, "Power, Public Policy, and the Environment," 182–84, 187.

69. Poll by William R. Hamilton Associates for the DOC, in ibid., 259.

70. *Denver Post Bonus Section,* September 25, 1972, p. 5.

71. Olson, "Power, Public Policy, and the Environment," 194, 255; *Denver Post Bonus Section,* September 25, 1972, p. 3.

72. Olson, "Power, Public Policy, and the Environment," 197, 198, 202; Richard O'Reilly, "Olympic Column Wipeout," *Unsatisfied Man* 2:8 (April 1972): 1; Kirshenbaum,

"Voting to Snuff the Torch," 45.

73. Olson, "Power, Public Policy, and the Environment," 195; Senate Committee on Interior and Insular Affairs, *1976 Denver Winter Olympics,* 92d Cong., 2d sess., 1972, 45.

74. Foster, "Colorado's Defeat of the 1976 Winter Olympics," 182–83, 184–85; Kirshenbaum, "Voting to Snuff the Torch," 50–51.

75. DOOC, *Final Report,* 114; Olson, "Power, Public Policy, and the Environment," 178.

76. Olson, "Power, Public Policy, and the Environment," 189, 190; *Rocky Mountain News,* April 8, 1971, p. 8.

77. *Denver Post Bonus Section,* September 25, 1972, pp. 3, 7; DOOC, *Final Report,* 117; Olson, "Power, Public Policy, and the Environment," 192–94.

78. *Denver Post,* November 8, 1972, p. 95.

79. *Rocky Mountain News,* March 8, 1988, p. 10s.

80. *Denver Post,* November 8, 1972, p. 95.

81. Olson, "Power, Public Policy, and the Environment," 205; *Denver Post,* November 8, 1972, p. 95; *Denver Post,* November 12, 1972, p. 50.

82. *Denver Post,* November 12, 1972, p. 50.

83. *Rocky Mountain News,* March 8, 1988, p. 3s.

84. Benjamin G. Rader, *American Sports: From the Age of Folk Games to the Age of Televised Sports,* 3d ed. (Englewood Cliffs, N.J.: Prentice-Hall, 1996), 280.

CHAPTER 6

1. *Rocky Mountain News,* November 29, 1997, p. 1c; March 6, 1998, pp. 1c, 8c; *Sporting News* 221:33 (August 18, 1997): S–23.

2. *Denver Post,* December 15, 1996, p. 1b; *Rocky Mountain News,* December 15, 1996, pp. 1c, 23c; *Rocky Mountain News,* November 29, 1998, p. 1c.

3. Ronald A. Smith, *Sports and Freedom: The Rise of Big-Time College Athletics* (New York: Oxford University Press, 1988), 74.

4. Ibid.

5. Benjamin G. Rader, *American Sports: From the Age of Folk Games to the Age of Televised Sports,* 3d ed. (Englewood Cliffs, N.J.: Prentice-Hall, 1996), 174, 175; Elliott J. Gorn and Warren Goldstein, *A Brief History of American Sports* (New York: Hill and Wang, 1993), 155, 231.

6. Smith, *Sports and Freedom,* 126.

7. William J. Baker, *Sports in the Western World,* rev. ed. (Urbana and Chicago: University of Illinois Press, 1988), 131; Gorn and Goldstein, *Brief History of American Sports,* 158–59, 163.

8. Rader, *American Sports,* 180.

9. William E. Davis, *Glory Colorado! A History of the University of Colorado, 1858–1963* (Boulder: Pruett Press, 1965), 36.

10. *Rocky Mountain News,* April 23, 1880, p. 2; Frederick S. Allen et al., *The University of Colorado, 1876–1976: A Centennial Publication of the University of Colorado* (New York: Harcourt Brace Jovanovich, 1976), 49; Davis, *Glory Colorado,* 36.

11. *Rocky Mountain News,* April 12, 1885, p. 1.

12. Davis, *Glory Colorado,* 68.

13. Ibid., 67; Fred Casotti, *CU Century: One Hundred Years of Colorado University Football* (Denver: Original Publications, 1990), 13–14.

14. Davis, *Glory Colorado,* 68–69; Casotti, *CU Century,* 13–14; *Rocky Mountain News Sunday Magazine* (January 5, 1992): 16m.

15. Davis, *Glory Colorado,* 69; Casotti, *CU Century,* 15.

16. Davis, *Glory Colorado,* 116.

17. Ibid.

18. Ibid., 117–18; Silvia Pettem, *Boulder: The Evolution of a City* (Niwot: University Press of Colorado, 1994), 98, 144–45.

19. Davis, *Glory Colorado,* 118; Casotti, *CU Century,* 15.

20. Davis, *Glory Colorado,* 118.

21. Ibid.; William E. Davis, " 'P.I.' Folsom: The Man Who Built CU Football," *Denver Post Empire Magazine* (September 26, 1965): 14.

22. Ibid., 13.

23. Davis, *Glory Colorado,* 120.

24. Casotti, *CU Century,* 18.

25. James E. Hansen II, *Democracy's College in the Centennial State: A History of Colorado State University,* 126–27.

26. Hansen, *Democracy's College,* 128; *Rocky Mountain News,* April 19, 1959, p. 71.

27. Hansen, *Democracy's College,* 141.

28. Ibid., 267–68; *Rocky Mountain News,* April 19, 1959, p. 65.

29. Davis, *Glory Colorado,* 205; *Denver Times,* June 18, 1903, p. 7.

30. Davis, *Glory Colorado,* 208–9; Casotti, *CU Century,* 22; Hansen, *Democracy's College,* 269.

31. Davis, *Glory Colorado,* 209, 366–67.

32. Davis, *Glory Colorado,* 206–11, 240; Davis, " 'P.I.' Folsom," 16–18; Casotti, *CU Century,* 22–23.

33. Hansen, *Democracy's College,* 269; Davis, *Glory Colorado,* 206.

34. Casotti, *CU Century,* 24; Hansen, *Democracy's College,* 274.

35. Davis, *Glory Colorado,* 326–27.

36. Casotti, *CU Century,* 24–29, 37; Davis, *Glory Colorado,* 324–30.

37. Davis, *Glory Colorado,* 369; Casotti, *CU Century,* 32–34.

38. Davis, *Glory Colorado,* 369; Casotti, *CU Century,* 33.

39. Davis, *Glory Colorado,* 369–70.

40. *Denver Post,* February 5, 1932, p. 33; Casotti, *CU Century,* 36–42, 164; Davis, *Glory Colorado,* 370, 425–26, 429.

41. Casotti, *CU Century,* 42–43.

42. Ibid., 45–50, 164; Davis, *Glory Colorado,* 430–31.

43. Casotti, *CU Century,* 46; Davis, *Glory Colorado,* 425.

44. Casotti, *CU Century,* 50.

45. Ibid., 50–52; Davis, *Glory Colorado,* 434–35.

46. Hansen, *Democracy's College,* 280, 323, 325–26.

47. Ibid., 326, 341–42.

48. Ibid., 358–59.

49. Ibid., 359.

50. Casotti, *CU Century,* 52–55; Davis, *Glory Colorado,* 498–500, 503, 568.

51. Casotti, *CU Century,* 55–56; Davis, *Glory Colorado,* 567–68.

52. Davis, *Glory Colorado,* 565–67; Allen et al., *University of Colorado,* 148.

53. Casotti, *CU Century,* 57; *Rocky Mountain News,* May 23, 1956, p. 60.

54. Casotti, *CU Century,* 57–79; Davis, *Glory Colorado,* 568–69, 621, 717, 720–21.

55. Davis, *Glory Colorado,* 621; Casotti, *CU Century,* 61–62.

56. Casotti, *CU Century,* 75–76.

57. Davis, *Glory Colorado,* 721–22; Casotti, *CU Century,* 79–80.

58. Davis, *Glory Colorado,* 721.

59. Ibid., 722.

60. Ibid.

61. Hansen, *Democracy's College,* 359, 361; *Denver Post,* November 23, 1948, p. 32; November 27, 1955, p. 84; *Rocky Mountain News,* April 19, 1959, p. 65; Davis, *Glory Colorado,* 719.

62. *Denver Post Empire Magazine* (January 12, 1997): 12–16; *Colorado State University Alumni* (winter 1996–1997): 6–7; see also *Denver Post,* November 7, 1998, pp. 1d, 11d.

63. Hansen, *Democracy's College,* 421–22.

64. Ibid., 426.

65. *Rocky Mountain News,* January 10, 1961, pp. 5, 6.

66. Ibid., 6; Hansen, *Democracy's College,* 423.

67. Hansen, *Democracy's College,* 423–25.

68. Casotti, *CU Century,* 80–87; Davis, *Glory Colorado,* 723.

69. Davis, *Glory Colorado,* 725–28; Casotti, *CU Century,* 88–89; *Denver Post,* March 18, 1962, p. 23a.

70. Davis, *Glory Colorado,* 728; Casotti, *CU Century,* 90, 92.

71. *Denver Post,* March 18, 1962, p. 23a; Davis, *Glory Colorado,* 725; Casotti, *CU Century,* 87.

72. William E. "Bud" Davis, "Colorado Football's Galloping Disaster: Memoirs of a Big-Time Coach," *Harper's Magazine* 231:1385 (October 1965): 50, 51; Davis, *Glory Colorado,* 728; Casotti, *CU Century,* 90.

73. Davis, "Colorado Football's Galloping Disaster," 52–53; Casotti, *CU Century,* 92–93.

74. *Rocky Mountain News,* March 23, 1962, p. 92; Davis, *Glory Colorado,* 730.

75. Davis, *Glory Colorado,* 729; David Chamberlain, "A Fan's Lament," *Rocky Mountain Magazine* 1:6 (September 1979): 24; Casotti, *CU Century,* 93–100.

76. Casotti, *CU Century,* 100, 163.

77. Ibid., 100–102.

78. Ibid., 103–13.

79. Ibid., 114.

80. Ibid., 114–15.

81. Ibid., 116–22.

82. Ibid., 122–27.

83. Ibid., 128–30.

84. Ibid., 130–31.

85. Ibid., 131–33.

86. Hansen, *Democracy's College,* 426.

87. *Denver Post,* January 4, 1962, pp. 61, 62; Hansen, *Democracy's College,* 427.

88. *Denver Post,* January 4, 1962, p. 61; Hansen, *Democracy's College,* 426.

89. *Denver Post,* August 19, 1966, pp. 57, 61; Hansen, *Democracy's College,* 427.

90. Hansen, *Democracy's College,* 428; *Rocky Mountain News,* September 8, 1967, pp. 84, 87.

91. *Rocky Mountain News,* January 14, 1969, p. 5; Hansen, *Democracy's College,* 428–29.

92. Hansen, *Democracy's College,* 428–29; *Rocky Mountain News,* January 14, 1969, p. 5.

93. Hansen, *Democracy's College,* 482; *Denver Post,* December 23, 1969, pp. 41, 42.

94. *Denver Post,* December 23, 1969, pp. 41, 42.

95. *Rocky Mountain News,* February 2, 1973, pp. 86, 88.

96. *Rocky Mountain News,* February 20, 1978, p. 44.

97. Hansen, *Democracy's College,* 482; *Rocky Mountain News,* December 8, 1981, pp. 66, 72.

98. *Rocky Mountain News,* December 8, 1981, pp. 66, 72.

99. *Rocky Mountain News,* January 29, 1989, p. 12s.

100. *Rocky Mountain News,* December 30, 1990, pp. 1s, 8s.

101. *Rocky Mountain News,* November 25, 1992, pp. 71, 79.

102. Ibid., 79.

103. *Rocky Mountain News,* June 10, 1982, p. 133.

104. Casotti, *CU Century,* 167; *Westword,* August 17, 1979, p. 9.

105. *Rocky Mountain News,* November 30, 1993, p. 3a; *Denver Post,* January 9, 1994, p. 1a.

106. *Denver Post,* September 7, 1975, p. 28; *Rocky Mountain News,* April 20, 1978, p. 39; *Westword,* August 17, 1979, p. 9; *Denver Post,* January 9, 1994, pp. 12a, 15a; see also *Denver Post,* December 8, 1998, p. 12d.

107. *Rocky Mountain News,* October 18, 1983, p. 17; *Denver Post,* April 23, 1989, pp. 1c, 4c; *Rocky Mountain News,* November 30, 1993, p. 3a; *Denver Post,* January 9, 1994, p. 13a.

108. *Denver Post,* January 9, 1994, p. 1a.

109. *Colorado Statesman,* October 14, 1905, p. 1.

110. Rick Reilly, "What Price Glory," *Sports Illustrated* (February 27, 1989): 32–34; *Rocky Mountain News,* February 24, 1989, p. 7.

111. Reilly, "What Price Glory," 32–33.

112. Ibid., 34.

113. *Rocky Mountain News,* May 15, 1988, pp. 14s–16s; December 31, 1994, pp. 4b, 5b, 7b.

114. *Rocky Mountain News,* May 15, 1988, p. 15s; December 31, 1994, p. 5b.

115. *Rocky Mountain News,* February 6, 1997, p. 22a.

116. *Rocky Mountain News,* May 15, 1988, p. 14s.

117. *Rocky Mountain News,* February 24, 1989, p. 7.

118. *Rocky Mountain News,* December 9, 1994, p. 6b.

119. Ibid.

120. Bill McCartney, with Dave Diles, *From Ashes to Glory,* rev. ed. (Nashville: T. Nelson, 1995), xiv, 111.

121. Ibid., 236.

122. Ibid., 237–39; Casotti, *CU Century,* 154–55.

123. McCartney, *From Ashes to Glory,* 237.

124. Ibid., 239–40.

125. Ibid., 240–42.

126. *Rocky Mountain News,* August 26, 1992, pp. 62, 75; February 8, 1992, p. 92; February 9, 1992, p. 7.

127. *Denver Post,* January 10, 1999, pp. 1c, 4c; *Rocky Mountain News,* January 10, 1999, p. 4c.

128. *Rocky Mountain News,* January 10, 1999, pp. 1c, 3c, 4c.

CHAPTER 7

1. *Denver Post,* January 26, 1998, pp. 1aa, 4aa.

2. *Rocky Mountain News,* August 15, 1959, p. 47, reprinted, January 21, 1990, p. 10.

3. *Rocky Mountain News,* April 19, 1959, p. 65.

4. Thomas J. Noel, *The Denver Athletic Club, 1884–1984* (Denver: Denver Athletic Club, 1984), 23–26; *Rocky Mountain News,* April 22, 1934, p. 5; April 19, 1959, p. 65.

5. On the founding of the American Football League and the Denver Bronco franchise, see Dick Connor, *The Denver Broncos* (Englewood Cliffs, N.J.: Prentice-Hall, 1974), 9–10; Larry Gordon and Dick Burnell, *Barely Audible: A History of the Denver Broncos*

(Denver: Graphic Impressions, 1975), 8–9; Woodrow Paige, Jr., *Orange Madness: The Incredible Odyssey of the Denver Broncos* (New York: Thomas Y. Crowell, 1978), 25–26; Lou Sahadi, *Broncos! The Team That Makes Miracles Happen* (New York: Stein and Day, 1978), 1–3; Bob Collins, Chet Nelson, and Jackie Kutsko, *Broncos: From Striped Socks to Super Bowl and Beyond* (Colorado Springs: Pikes Peak Publishers, 1980), 16–23; James Gerzewski, ed., *Denver Broncos, 1960–1984 Silver Anniversary* (Denver: Special Productions, 1985), 12; Joseph Hession and Michael Spence, *Broncos: Three Decades of Football* (San Francisco: Foghorn Press, 1987), 23; Colorado Historical Society, Oral History of Colorado Project, Gerald Phipps Interview, December 19, 1973, 24–25.

6. Denver Broncos, "Denver Broncos vs. Dallas Texans, October 30, 1960: Official Souvenir Program," 1; Connor, *The Denver Broncos,* 10; Hession and Spence, *Broncos,* 25.

7. Gerzewski, *Denver Broncos,* 12–13; Gordon and Burnell, *Barely Audible,* 10; Denver Broncos, "Denver Broncos vs. Dallas Texans," 20.

8. Denver Broncos, "Denver Broncos vs. Dallas Texans," 32; Sahadi, *Broncos,* 7.

9. Collins et al., *Broncos,* 23, 25.

10. Sahadi, *Broncos,* 4, 9; Hession and Spence, *Broncos,* 67–68; Connor, *The Denver Broncos,* 23; Denver Broncos, "Denver Broncos vs. Dallas Texans," 30.

11. Collins et al., *Broncos,* 26, 33; Gordon and Burnell, *Barely Audible,* 76; Denver Broncos, "Denver Broncos vs. Dallas Texans," 11, 17, 36.

12. Connor, *The Denver Broncos,* 10; Gerzewski, *Denver Broncos,* 13.

13. Sahadi, *Broncos,* 229.

14. Collins et al., *Broncos,* 34.

15. Colorado Historical Society, Phipps Interview, 27; Connor, *The Denver Broncos,* 12; Collins et al., *Broncos,* 38; Hession and Spence, *Broncos,* 35.

16. Connor, *The Denver Broncos,* 15; Sahadi, *Broncos,* 13; Gerzewski, *Denver Broncos,* 15–25.

17. Connor, *The Denver Broncos,* 19, 20; Paige, *Orange Madness,* 29.

18. Gordon and Burnell, *Barely Audible,* 33.

19. Hession and Spence, *Broncos,* 47.

20. Ibid., 48; Gordon and Burnell, *Barely Audible,* 36.

21. Hession and Spence, *Broncos,* 53.

22. Connor, *The Denver Broncos,* 24.

23. Colorado Historical Society, Phipps Interview, 32–33; Gordon and Burnell, *Barely Audible,* 17.

24. Ibid., 18; Connor, *The Denver Broncos,* 24.

25. Collins et al., *Broncos,* 5; Sahadi, *Broncos,* 22; *Denver Post,* February 22, 1999, p. 15d.

26. Sahadi, *Broncos,* 22.

27. Gordon and Burnell, *Barely Audible,* 36.

28. Paige, *Orange Madness,* 30.

29. Rader, *American Sports,* 252.

30. Gordon and Burnell, *Barely Audible,* 21–22; *Rocky Mountain News,* December 11, 1967, p. 55.

31. Gordon and Burnell, *Barely Audible,* 23; Gerzewski, *Denver Broncos,* 35; Colorado Historical Society, Phipps Interview, 47–48.

32. Gordon and Burnell, *Barely Audible,* 21.

33. Connor, *The Denver Broncos,* 28.

34. Ibid., 30; Collins et al., *Broncos,* 63; Sahadi, *Broncos,* 27, 229.

35. Collins et al., *Broncos,* 65.

36. *Rocky Mountain News,* December 11, 1967, p. 55.

37. Hession and Spence, *Broncos,* 65; Gordon and Burnell, *Barely Audible,* 44.

38. Gordon and Burnell, *Barely Audible,* 44; *Rocky Mountain News,* January 11, 1998, p. 24n.

39. Paige, *Orange Madness,* 32.

40. Hession and Spence, *Broncos,* 78.

41. Collins et al., *Broncos,* 85; *Rocky Mountain News Sunday Magazine* (December 8, 1991): 14m.

42. *Denver Post,* January 2, 1972, p. 67; Connor, *The Denver Broncos,* 33.

43. *Rocky Mountain News Sunday Magazine* (December 8, 1991): 12m–16m.

44. Collins et al., *Broncos,* 88.

45. Sahadi, *Broncos,* 29.

46. Hession and Spence, *Broncos,* 89, 90.

47. Gordon and Burnell, *Barely Audible,* 146.

48. Connor, *The Denver Broncos,* 40.

49. *Denver Post Empire Magazine* (September 29, 1974): 9, 14; author's conversation with Prof. James E. Hansen, April 1997, Fort Collins, Colo.

50. Collins et al., *Broncos,* 108.

51. Author's telephone conversation with Larry Zimmer, June 30, 1997.

52. Sahadi, *Broncos,* 38; Paige, *Orange Madness,* 37.

53. *Rocky Mountain News,* December 19, 1976, p. 96.

54. *Rocky Mountain News,* December 22, 1976, p. 92.

55. *Rocky Mountain News,* December 24, 1976, p. 48.

56. Ibid.

57. *Rocky Mountain News,* February 1, 1977, pp. 1, 56.

58. Sahadi, *Broncos,* 50.

59. Paige, *Orange Madness,* 41–43.

60. Ibid., 45.

61. Sahadi, *Broncos,* 52–59.

62. Ibid., 47.

63. Ibid., 164.

64. Hession and Spence, *Broncos,* 170.

65. *Rocky Mountain News,* December 18, 1977, p. 6; *Rocky Mountain News,* January 26, 1990, p. 8; Paige, *Orange Madness,* 14.

66. Paige, *Orange Madness,* 12, 167.

67. Ibid., 10, 194 96.

68. Ibid., 130.

69. Sahadi, *Broncos,* 191; *Denver Post,* January 18, 1998, p. 7j.

70. Paige, *Orange Madness,* 206.

71. Ibid., 247.

72. Hession and Spence, *Broncos,* 128–40; *Rocky Mountain News,* March 10, 1981, p. 65.

73. *Rocky Mountain News,* February 25, 1981, pp. 1, 78.

74. *Rocky Mountain News,* February 27, 1981, pp. 86, 88; February 26, 1981, p. 103.

75. *Rocky Mountain News,* March 10, 1981, pp. 1, 60, 61, 65.

76. *Rocky Mountain News,* June 17, 1982, pp. 111, 112; *Rocky Mountain News Sunday Magazine* (February 26, 1989): 16m–23m.

77. Dan Reeves, with Dick Connor, *Reeves: An Autobiography* (Chicago: Bonus Books, 1988), 36.

78. Ibid., 24.

79. Rick Reilly, "A Great Run: After Fourteen Seasons in Denver, John Elway Hasn't

Lost a Step," *Sports Illustrated* 85:27 (December 30, 1996–January 6, 1997): 34; Russell Martin, *The Color Orange: A Super Bowl Season with the Denver Broncos* (New York: Henry Holt, 1987), 151.

80. Reeves, *Reeves,* 17.

81. Ibid., 18–19.

82. Ibid., 19–21.

83. *Rocky Mountain News,* December 29, 1986, pp. 10c–12c; Martin, *The Color Orange,* 253–55; Hession and Spence, *Broncos,* 145.

84. *Rocky Mountain News,* January 26, 1990, p. 8.

85. *Rocky Mountain News,* January 26, 1987, p. 7.

86. *Rocky Mountain News,* January 26, 1990, p. 8.

87. *Rocky Mountain News,* February 1, 1988, p. 8.

88. *Rocky Mountain News,* January 29, 1990, pp. 1, 6; *Sports Illustrated* 88:4 (February 2, 1998): 58.

89. *Rocky Mountain News,* January 29, 1990, p. 6.

90. Stephen J. Leonard and Thomas J. Noel, *Denver: Mining Camp to Metropolis* (Niwot: University Press of Colorado, 1990), 481.

91. Martin, *The Color Orange,* 229.

92. *Rocky Mountain News,* March 20, 1984, p. 1; March 21, 1984, p. 96; *Denver Post,* July 13, 1996, p. 2a.

93. *Rocky Mountain News,* March 21, 1984, p. 96; March 24, 1984, p. 114.

94. *Rocky Mountain News,* March 24, 1984, p. 114.

95. *Rocky Mountain News,* March 21, 1984, p. 92; Martin, *The Color Orange,* 62.

96. *Rocky Mountain News,* December 29, 1992, pp. 39, 45, 49.

97. Ibid., 47, 48.

98. *Rocky Mountain News,* January 3, 1999, p. 6c; January 18, 1999, p. 1c; January 31, 1999, p. 59n.

99. *Rocky Mountain News,* February 1, 1995, pp. 2b, 3b, 8b.

100. *Rocky Mountain News,* January 26, 1993, pp. 39, 40.

101. Ibid., 38.

102. Ibid., 34, 39, 40.

103. *Denver Post,* July 22, 1994, p. 7d; August 17, 1994, p. 1d; *Rocky Mountain News,* February 2, 1995, p. 6b.

104. *Rocky Mountain News,* May 21, 1995, p. 8b.

105. *Rocky Mountain News,* December 30, 1994, pp. 1b, 2b, 3b.

106. *Rocky Mountain News,* February 1, 1995, p. 1b; *Denver Post,* October 18, 1996, p. 8d.

107. *Rocky Mountain News,* January 5, 1997, pp. 3C, 18c; *Denver Post,* January 5, 1997, pp. 1cc, 2cc.

108. *Denver Post,* January 5, 1997, p. 2cc.

109. *Sports Illustrated* 88:4 (February 2, 1998): 58.

110. *Denver Post,* January 5, 1997, p. 2cc; *Rocky Mountain News,* January 12, 1998, p. 51.

111. Quoted in *Denver Post,* November 18, 1995, p. 2c.

112. *Denver Post,* November 18, 1995, pp. 1c, 2c; July 13, 1996, p. 2a.

113. Mark S. Rosentraub, *Major League Losers: The Real Cost of Sports and Who's Paying for It* (New York: Basic Books, 1997), 8–11.

114. *Denver Post,* March 9, 1996, pp. 1a, 12a.

115. *Denver Post,* November 9, 1995, pp. 1d, 10d; May 15, 1996, p. 3b; July 18, 1997, p. 27a.

116. *Denver Post,* March 5, 1997, pp. 1a, 14a.

117. *Denver Post,* March 8, 1997, pp. 1b, 6b.

118. *Denver Post,* July 13, 1996, p. 2a.

119. *Denver Post,* January 2, 1998, pp. 1a, 2a; *Rocky Mountain News,* February 11, 1998, pp. 1a, 6a; April 22, 1998, pp. 5a, 18a.

120. *Denver Post,* July 30, 1995, p. 9b; March 9, 1996, p. 12a.

121. *Denver Post,* September 22, 1996, pp. 1a, 22a.

122. *Rocky Mountain News,* September 15, 1996, p. 4a; August 1, 1996, p. 5a; *Denver Post,* October 4, 1996, pp. 1b, 5b.

123. *Denver Post,* July 18, 1997, pp. 1a, 27a.

124. Ibid.

125. Rosentraub, *Major League Losers,* 129–78.

126. *Rocky Mountain News,* July 30, 1995, p. 9b; *Denver Post,* November 9, 1995, p. 10d.

127. *Rocky Mountain News,* November 4, 1998, p. 7a.

128. *Rocky Mountain News,* January 18, 1999, p. 11n; December 28, 1998, p. 1c; September 23, 1998, pp. 16c–17c.

129. *Rocky Mountain News,* January 21, 1999, pp. 4n, 6n.

130. *Rocky Mountain News,* February 1, 1999, pp. 1n, 17n.

131. *Rocky Mountain News,* February 2, 1999, p. 2w.

132. Ibid.

Chapter 8

1. James Naismith, *Basketball: Its Origin and Development,* (Lincoln: University of Nebraska Press, 1996), 109.

2. Ibid.

3. Benjamin G. Rader, *American Sports: From the Age of Folk Games to the Age of Televised Sports,* 3d ed. (Englewood Cliffs, N.J.: Prentice-Hall, 1996), 101.

4. Naismith, *Basketball,* 29–60, 54, 85–86.

5. Ibid., xv.

6. Ibid., 124–25. On Naismith in Denver, see Kevin Simpson, "Hoop Heritage of the Wild, Wild West," in *Rocky Mountain Basketball: Naismith to Nineteen Ninety,* by the Denver Organizing Committee (Englewood, Colo.: Westcliffe Publishers, 1989), 16–19.

7. *Rocky Mountain News,* February 1, 1896, p. 8.

8. *Rocky Mountains News,* April 22, 1934, Sports Section, p. 4; *Denver Post,* February 16, 1972, Zone 1, p. 13.

9. *Rocky Mountain News,* April 22, 1934, Sports Section, p. 4.

10. *Rocky Mountain News,* April 19, 1959, p. 66.

11. Ibid.

12. Adolph H. Grundman, "Pigs, Jellymakers, and Graybeards: When Denver Was a Basketball Mecca," *Colorado Heritage* (autumn 1994): 35; Bud Maloney, "Colorado's AAU Tournaments," in *Rocky Mountain Basketball,* 21; *Rocky Mountain News,* January 28, 1970, p. 65.

13. Grundman, "Pigs, Jellymakers, and Graybeards," 37–38.

14. Ibid., 38–39; Maloney, "Colorado's AAU Tournaments," 22–26.

15. Grundman, "Pigs, Jellymakers, and Graybeards," 38–41; Maloney, "Colorado's AAU Tournaments," 24.

16. Grundman, "Pigs, Jellymakers, and Graybeards," 41–43.

17. Ibid., 43; Denver Nuggets, *1996–1997 Media Guide* (Denver: Denver Nuggets, 1996), 186.

18. On the social origins of professional basketball, see Ted Vincent, *The Rise and Fall of American Sport: Mudville's Revenge* (Lincoln: University of Nebraska Press, 1994), 247–50.

19. Ibid., 279–89.

20. Carl Skiff, "The Year the Pros Played for Nothing," *Denver Post Empire Magazine* (January 16, 1972): 48, 50.

21. Ibid., 50, 51.

22. Ibid., 48, 51.

23. Ibid., 51, 53.

24. Ibid., 53.

25. Vincent, *The Rise and Fall,* 289; Rader, *American Sports,* 256; Michael L. LeBlanc, ed., *Professional Sports Team Histories: Basketball* (Detroit, Washington, D.C., and London: Gale Research, 1994), 3.

26. *Rocky Mountain News,* April 25, 1950, p. 38; Vincent, *The Rise and Fall,* 304; Skiff, "The Year the Pros Played for Nothing," 53.

27. *Rocky Mountain News,* June 15, 1976, p. 53.

28. Mike Monroe, *Hardwood Gold: The Rise and Fall and Rise of the Denver Nuggets* (Dallas: Taylor Publishing, 1994), 69–70; Terry Pluto, *Loose Balls: The Short, Wild Life of the American Basketball Association* (New York: Simon and Schuster, 1990), 39–43.

29. Monroe, *Hardwood Gold,* 70–71; Denver Nuggets, *1993–1994 Media Guide* (Denver: Denver Nuggets, 1993), 91.

30. Pluto, *Loose Balls,* 58–59; Monroe, *Hardwood Gold,* 72–73.

31. Pluto, *Loose Balls,* 64–65, 90; Monroe, *Hardwood Gold,* 73–74.

32. Pluto, *Loose Balls,* 46–47.

33. LeBlanc, *Professional Sports Team Histories,* 16, 17.

34. Monroe, *Hardwood Gold,* 74.

35. Ibid., 74–75; Pluto, *Loose Balls,* 181–82.

36. Monroe, *Hardwood Gold,* 75; Pluto, *Loose Balls,* 181–82.

37. Monroe, *Hardwood Gold,* 76–77; LeBlanc, *Professional Sports Team Histories,* 245.

38. LeBlanc, *Professional Sports Team Histories,* 245; Monroe, *Hardwood Gold,* 77; Denver Nuggets, *1993–1994 Media Guide,* 91.

39. Monroe, *Hardwood Gold,* 77; LeBlanc, *Professional Sports Team Histories,* 245–46.

40. Pluto, *Loose Balls,* 395–96.

41. Ibid., 396; Tom Hohensee, "Denver Nuggets," in *Rocky Mountain Basketball,* 86.

42. Denver Nuggets, *1996–1997 Media Guide,* 186, 337; Monroe, *Hardwood Gold,* 78; Pluto, *Loose Balls,* 396–97.

43. Pluto, *Loose Balls,* 396–97; Zeke Scher, "The Nuggets: Reborn?" *Denver Post Empire Magazine* (October 16, 1977): 11.

44. Denver Nuggets, *1996–1997 Media Guide,* 186, 193–94; Monroe, *Hardwood Gold,* 82–83.

45. Pluto, *Loose Balls,* 398–99; Monroe, *Hardwood Gold,* 83–86.

46. Monroe, *Hardwood Gold,* 86–88; Pluto, *Loose Balls,* 330–31, 390–94.

47. Monroe, *Hardwood Gold,* 88–90; Pluto, *Loose Balls,* 25–29.

48. Monroe, *Hardwood Gold,* 90; Denver Nuggets, *1996–1997 Media Guide,* 194.

49. Monroe, *Hardwood Gold,* 93–95; Pluto, *Loose Balls,* 421–33; Zeke Scher, "How the SOBs Got Into the NBA," *Denver Post Empire Magazine* (October 17, 1976): 12; *Rocky Mountain News,* June 18, 1976, pp. 110, 114; *Denver Post,* September 15, 1976, p. 63.

50. *Rocky Mountain News,* February 2, 1979, pp. 1, 80; Denver Nuggets, *1996–1997 Media Guide,* 157, 181, 182, 186; Monroe, *Hardwood Gold,* 97–100, 109.

51. *Rocky Mountain News,* February 2, 1979, p. 82; Denver Nuggets, *1996–1997 Media Guide,* 181, 182.

52. *Rocky Mountain News,* April 19, 1982, p. 10s.

53. Monroe, *Hardwood Gold,* 122, 124–25.

54. *Rocky Mountain News,* April 19, 1982, p. 11s; Monroe, *Hardwood Gold,* 124, 127.

55. Monroe, *Hardwood Gold,* 107–9, 112–14.

56. Ibid., 117–19; Denver Nuggets, *1996–1997 Media Guide,* 180.

57. Monroe, *Hardwood Gold,* 129–30.

58. Ibid., 131–32.

59. Ibid., 130–33.

60. *Rocky Mountain News,* July 16, 1989, p. 79.

61. Monroe, *Hardwood Gold,* 55–56; *Rocky Mountain News,* August 11, 1992, pp. 43, 51.

62. Monroe, *Hardwood Gold,* 57–62; *Rocky Mountain News,* June 9, 1991, pp. 63, 76–77; February 13, 1997, p. 6c.

63. *Rocky Mountain News,* June 9, 1991, p. 76; Monroe, *Hardwood Gold,* 62, 63.

64. *Rocky Mountain News,* June 9, 1991, p. 76.

65. Monroe, *Hardwood Gold,* 62–63, 141; *Denver Post,* September 7, 1990, pp. 1a, 12a, 13a, 1d, 8d; *Rocky Mountain News,* June 9, 1991, p. 76.

66. *Denver Post,* September 7, 1990, pp. 1d, 8d; Monroe, *Hardwood Gold,* p. 63.

67. *Rocky Mountain News,* June 9, 1991, p. 77; April 23, 1992, pp. 77, 84.

68. *Rocky Mountain News,* August 11, 1992, pp. 43, 51.

69. *Rocky Mountain News,* April 23, 1992, p. 77.

70. Monroe, *Hardwood Gold,* 41–52, 173–82.

71. *Rocky Mountain News,* pp. 1b, 4b.

72. *Denver Post,* July 16, 1996, pp. 1d, 2d; July 17, 1996, pp. 1d, 8d.

73. *Denver Post,* February 11, 1997, pp. 1d, 8d; April 20, 1997, p. 22c.

74. *Rocky Mountain News,* February 13, 1997, p. 6c.

75. *Denver Post,* December 24, 1997, p. 5d; *Rocky Mountain News,* February 5, 1998, pp. 1c, 8c; April 10, 1998, p. 3c; April 20, 1998, pp. 1c, 20c; April 21, 1998, pp. 1c, 6c.

76. "Nuggets Name D'Antoni Head Coach," Denver Nuggets website, http://www.nba.com/nuggets/dantoni_coach.html, February 17, 1999; *Rocky Mountain News,* January 21, 1999, p. 1c; *Denver Post,* January 17, 1999, p. 1c.

77. *Denver Post,* August 13, 1997, pp. 1a, 17a.

78. Michael N. Danielson, *Home Team: Professional Sports and the American Metropolis* (Princeton: Princeton University Press, 1997), 58; Denver Nuggets, *1996–1997 Media Guide,* 4; Monroe, *Hardwood Gold,* 190.

79. Danielson, *Home Team,* 287.

80. *Colorado Woman News* (June 1995): S1; University of Colorado, *Silver and Gold Record,* January 11, 1996, p. 5; *ABL Courtside* 1:2 (1997): 4.

81. *Denver Post,* July 7, 1996, p. 5c; September 3, 1996, p. 10c.

82. *ABL Courtside* 1:2 (1997): 17; Colorado Xplosion, *1997–1998 Media Guide* (Denver: Colorado Xplosion, 1997), 59–60; *Denver Post,* July 7, 1996, p. 5c; *Rocky Mountain News,* February 27, 1997, pp. 3c, 11c.

83. *Rocky Mountain News,* February 2, 1998, April 2, 1998, April 28, 1998, cites at website http://www.archives.InsideDenver.com.

84. *Rocky Mountain News,* December 23, 1998, p. 3c.

85. Monroe, *Hardwood Gold,* 142.

CHAPTER 9

1. Irvin Moss and Mark Foster, *Home Run in the Rockies: The History of Baseball in Colorado* (Denver: A. B. Hirschfeld Press, 1994), 1; Alan Gottlieb, *In the Shadow of the Rockies: An Outsider's Look Inside a New Major League Baseball Team* (Niwot, Colo.: Roberts Rinehart Publishers, 1994), 7; Bob Kravitz, *Mile High Madness: A Year With the Colorado Rockies* (New York: Times Books, 1994), 52.

2. Moss and Foster, *Home Run,* 81–82; Jay Sanford, "African-American Baseballists and the *Denver Post* Tournament," *Colorado Heritage* (spring 1995): 20; Duane A. Smith and Mark S. Foster, *They Came to Play: A Photographic History of Colorado Baseball* (Niwot: University Press of Colorado, 1997), 3.

3. Moss and Foster, *Home Run,* 82; Duane A. Smith, "Mighty Casey Matches the Mountains: The Origins of Baseball in Colorado," *Colorado Heritage* (spring 1995): 6.

4. Stephen J. Leonard and Thomas J. Noel, *Denver: Mining Camp to Metropolis* (Niwot: University Press of Colorado, 1990), 12, 30; Smith, "Mighty Casey Matches the Mountains," 6; Smith and Foster, *They Came to Play,* 3.

5. Mark S. Foster, *The Denver Bears: From Sandlots to Sellouts* (Boulder: Pruett Publishing, 1983), 3.

6. Ibid., 4.

7. Moss and Foster, *Home Run,* 84; Smith, "Mighty Casey Matches the Mountains," 8.

8. *Rocky Mountain News,* June 26, 1874, p. 4; Smith, "Mighty Casey Matches the Mountains," 6–7.

9. Moss and Foster, *Home Run,* 84–85; Smith, "Mighty Casey Matches the Mountains," 8–9.

10. Foster, *The Denver Bears,* 6.

11. Ibid.

12. Mark S. Foster, "Mile High Greenfields: Denver's Notable Ballparks," *Colorado Heritage* (spring 1995): 37.

13. Foster, *The Denver Bears,* 6–8.

14. Ibid., 8–9; Moss and Foster, *Home Run,* 86.

15. Foster, *The Denver Bears,* 10–12; Moss and Foster, *Home Run,* 87–88.

16. Foster, *The Denver Bears,* 12; Moss and Foster, *Home Run,* 88.

17. Moss and Foster, *Home Run,* 88; Foster, *The Denver Bears,* 12; Smith, "Mighty Casey Matches the Mountains," 16.

18. Moss and Foster, *Home Run,* 88.

19. Ibid.; Smith and Foster, *They Came to Play,* 61; Foster, "Mile High Greenfields," 38; Benjamin G. Rader, *Baseball: A History of America's Game* (Urbana and Chicago: University of Illinois Press, 1994), 78–81; Allen DuPont Breck, *William Gray Evans, 1855–1924: Portrait of a Western Executive* (Denver: University of Denver, Department of History, 1964), 113–14.

20. Moss and Foster, *Home Run,* 89; Sanford, "African-American Baseballists," 20.

21. Foster, "Mile High Greenfields," 38; Nancy L. Widmann, "Denver's Merchants Park" (unpublished manuscript in author's possession, 1994), 4.

22. Smith, "Mighty Casey Matches the Mountains," 11–12.

23. Foster, *The Denver Bears,* 14–15; Moss and Foster, *Home Run,* 89–90; Thomas J. Noel, *The Denver Athletic Club, 1884–1984* (Denver: Denver Athletic Club, 1984), 28. Colorado's most recent women's professional baseball team, the Silver Bullets, played from 1994 through 1997. Managed by former major league pitching star Phil Niekro,

the team played exhibition schedules against women's and men's semiprofessional and amateur teams. The club folded before the 1998 season when the Coors company withdrew financial support. See Dave Kindred, *The Colorado Silver Bullets: For the Love of the Game: Women Who Go Toe-to-Toe With the Men* (Atlanta: Longstreet Press, 1995); *Rocky Mountain News,* June 26, 1994, pp. 30a–34a; *Rocky Mountain News,* August 22, 1997, April 20, 1998, cites at website http://www.InsideDenver.com.

24. Foster, *The Denver Bears,* 18–19; Moss and Foster, *Home Run,* 92.

25. Foster, *The Denver Bears,* 19, 21–23; Moss and Foster, *Home Run,* 92–93.

26. Moss and Foster, *Home Run,* 92–93; Smith and Foster, *They Came to Play,* 57.

27. Foster, *The Denver Bears,* 25–27.

28. Moss and Foster, *Home Run,* 95–96.

29. Sanford, "African-American Baseballists," 22, 25.

30. Smith and Foster, *They Came to Play,* 4, 24.

31. Ibid., 27, 83; Harold Seymour, *Baseball: The Golden Age* (New York: Oxford University Press, 1971), 120, 163.

32. Moss and Foster, *Home Run,* 96.

33. Ibid., 96; Foster, "Mile High Greenfields," 39; Widmann, "Merchants Park," 4, 8.

34. Moss and Foster, *Home Run,* 96–97; Foster, *The Denver Bears,* 38–40, 42–43, 46; Widmann, "Merchants Park," 11–12.

35. Foster, *The Denver Bears,* 46.

36. Ibid., 47, 49–50.

37. Sanford, "African-American Baseballists," 21, 25.

38. Ibid., 28–29; Robert Peterson, *Only the Ball Was White: A History of Legendary Black Players and All-Black Professional Teams* (New York: Oxford University Press, 1970), 20–21, 337.

39. Sanford, "African-American Baseballists," 28–29.

40. Dennis L. Green, "African-American Baseball Players in Denver" (unpublished manuscript in author's possession, 1994), 6; Sanford, "African-American Baseballists," 29.

41. Green, "African-American Baseball Players in Denver," 4; Moss and Foster, *Home Run,* 91.

42. Green, "African-American Baseball Players in Denver," 36; Sanford, "African-American Baseballists," 28–29.

43. Sanford, "African-American Baseballists," 29.

44. Ibid., 30; Green, "African-American Baseball Players in Denver," 8–10.

45. Ibid., 10; *Rocky Mountain News,* March 30, 1995, p. 4b.

46. KRMA Television, "They Came to Play: A History of Baseball in Colorado, 1860–1960" (Denver: KRMA TV, 1994), video.

47. *Rocky Mountain News,* March 30, 1995, p. 4b.

48. Sanford, "African-American Baseballists," 29.

49. Ibid., 26, 30.

50. Ibid., 31.

51. Green, "African-American Baseball Players in Denver," 22–24.

52. Smith and Foster, *They Came to Play,* 49.

53. Sanford, "African-American Baseballists," 34.

54. Foster, *The Denver Bears,* 50–51.

55. Ibid., 51; Moss and Foster, *Home Run,* 99.

56. Moss and Foster, *Home Run,* 100.

57. Ibid.

58. Foster, *The Denver Bears,* 60.

59. Ibid.

60. Moss and Foster, *Home Run,* 101.

61. Ibid., 102–3.

62. Ibid.

63. Ibid., 104–5.

64. Ibid., 105.

65. David Whitford, *Playing Hardball: The High Stakes Battle for Baseball's New Franchises* (New York: Doubleday, 1993), 22–23.

66. Moss and Foster, *Home Run,* 107; Foster, *The Denver Bears,* 94.

67. Moss and Foster, *Home Run,* 105.

68. Ibid., 107.

69. Foster, *The Denver Bears,* 89–90.

70. Ibid., 98–111; Moss and Foster, *Home Run,* 108–9.

71. Moss and Foster, *Home Run,* 108–9, 110–11.

72. Ibid., 30, 110–11.

73. Ibid., 105, 111–12; *Rocky Mountain News,* September 2, 1992, p. 7.

74. Whitford, *Playing Hardball,* 25–26.

75. Ibid., 26–27; Moss and Foster, *Home Run,* 25–26.

76. Moss and Foster, *Home Run,* 26; Whitford, *Playing Hardball,* 27–28.

77. Whitford, *Playing Hardball,* 28; Moss and Foster, *Home Run,* 26.

78. Moss and Foster, *Home Run,* 27; Whitford, *Playing Hardball,* 38–39.

79. Moss and Foster, *Home Run,* 28–29.

80. Ibid., 29.

81. Ibid., 30

82. Ibid., 32–33, 35; Whitford, *Playing Hardball,* 34; Kravitz, *Mile High Madness,* 57.

83. Moss and Foster, *Home Run,* 28–29; Colorado Rockies Baseball Club, *Inaugural Season Media Guide* (Denver: Colorado Rockies Baseball Club, 1993), 104.

84. Moss and Foster, *Home Run,* 33.

85. Ibid., 31–33; Whitford, *Playing Hardball,* 35–41.

86. Moss and Foster, *Home Run,* 33, 35; Whitford, *Playing Hardball,* 31.

87. Moss and Foster, *Home Run,* 35–36.

88. Ibid., 30; Whitford, *Playing Hardball,* 59; Benjamin G. Rader, *American Sports: From the Age of Folk Games to the Age of Televised Sports,* 3d ed. (Englewood Cliffs, N.J.: Prentice-Hall, 1996), 163–64.

89. Moss and Foster, *Home Run,* 37.

90. Ibid., 38, 39; Whitford, *Playing Hardball,* 68–69.

91. Moss and Foster, *Home Run,* 39.

92. Whitford, *Playing Hardball,* 47–48; Moss and Foster, *Home Run,* 39.

93. Moss and Foster, *Home Run,* 39, 40, 42; Whitford, *Playing Hardball,* 49–52.

94. Moss and Foster, *Home Run,* 40–41, 42.

95. Ibid., 44.

96. Whitford, *Playing Hardball,* 85–86.

97. Moss and Foster, *Home Run,* 44.

98. Ibid., 46.

99. Ibid., 46–47; Whitford, *Playing Hardball,* 105.

100. Moss and Foster, *Home Run,* 49.

101. Ibid., 48–49, 50–51; Whitford, *Playing Hardball,* 87–96.

102. Whitford, *Playing Hardball,* 97; Moss and Foster, *Home Run,* 51.

103. Moss and Foster, *Home Run,* 51–52, 55; Whitford, *Playing Hardball,* 101–3.

104. Whitford, *Playing Hardball,* 115, 124–26, 130; Moss and Foster, *Home Run,* 57.

105. Moss and Foster, *Home Run,* 58, 62; Kravitz, *Mile High Madness,* 63–64; Whitford, *Playing Hardball,* 132.

106. *Rocky Mountain News,* June 16, 1991, p. 61.

107. Moss and Foster, *Home Run,* 49, 59.

108. Ibid., 63.

109. Ibid., 65, 66, 71.

110. Whitford, *Playing Hardball,* 124–26, 191–222; Moss and Foster, *Home Run,* 66–68.

111. Whitford, *Playing Hardball,* 228; Moss and Foster, *Home Run,* 72.

112. Moss and Foster, *Home Run,* 73; Whitford, *Playing Hardball,* 229; *Rocky Mountain News,* March 24, 1996, pp. 1b, 10b–12b; March 25, 1996, pp. 1b, 13b–14b.

113. Colorado Rockies, *Inaugural Season Media Guide,* 12–13.

114. Ibid., 13.

115. *Denver Post,* March 22, 1997, p. 1c; *Rocky Mountain News,* October 28, 1992, p. 78; Rader, *Baseball,* 153.

116. Moss and Foster, *Home Run,* 75, 76.

117. Kravitz, *Mile High Madness,* 247; Colorado Rockies, *1997 Media Guide,* 47, 142, 153; *Rocky Mountain News,* November 8, 1995, pp. 1b, 2b; November 14, 1997, pp. 1c, 2c.

118. *Rocky Mountain News,* September 28, 1998, pp. 1c, 7c; October 6, 1998, pp. 1c, 3c.

119. Colorado Rockies, *1997 Media Guide,* 142; *Rocky Mountain News,* September 18, 1993, p. 4a.

CHAPTER 10

1. *Denver Times,* December 24, 1901, p. 10.

2. William J. Baker, *Sports in the Western World,* rev. ed. (Urbana and Chicago: University of Illinois Press, 1988), 159.

3. Ibid., 159–60.

4. Ibid., 161.

5. Ibid., 160.

6. Ibid., 161.

7. Ibid.

8. Ibid.; Randy Roberts and James Olson, *Winning Is the Only Thing: Sports in America Since 1945* (Baltimore: Johns Hopkins University Press, 1989), 51; Michael N. Danielson, *Home Team: Professional Sports and the American Metropolis* (Princeton: Princeton University Press, 1997), 23; Richard A. Swanson and Betty Spears, *History of Sport and Physical Education in the United States,* 4th ed. (Madison, Wis., and Dubuque, Iowa: Brown and Benchmark, 1995), 264. Daniel S. Mason, "The International Hockey League and the Professionalization of Ice Hockey, 1904–1907," *Journal of Sport History* 25:1 (spring 1998): 1–17.

9. Olson and Roberts, *Winning Is the Only Thing,* 65–66.

10. Ibid., 143–44; Swanson and Spears, *History of Sport,* 264; Colorado Avalanche, *Colorado Avalanche: 1997–1998 Yearbook* (Denver: Colorado Avalanche, 1997), 322.

11. Colorado Avalanche, *Colorado Avalanche: 1997–1998 Yearbook,* 348–49.

12. *Evening Chronicle,* January 21, 1884, quoted in Don L. Griswold and Jean Harvey Griswold, *History of Leadville and Lake County, Colorado: From Mountain Solitude to Metropolis,* 2 vols. (Boulder: Colorado Historical Society in cooperation with the University

Press of Colorado, 1996), 1375.

13. Colorado College, *Tiger Hockey: 1997–1998 Media Guide* (Colorado Springs: Colorado College, 1997), 4, 66.

14. Ibid., 4, 48, 66; *Rocky Mountain News,* August 11, 1959, p. 51.

15. Colorado College, *Tiger Hockey,* 4, 66.

16. Ibid., 4.

17. Ibid., 4–5, 70–76.

18. Ibid., 52.

19. University of Denver, *1997–1998 Hockey Media Guide* (Denver: University of Denver, 1997), 61, 67; *Rocky Mountain News,* June 4, 1996, p. 5a.

20. University of Denver, *1997–1998 Media Guide,* 49, 61, 67; *Rocky Mountain News,* March 1, 1952, p. 23.

21. University of Denver, *1997–1998 Media Guide,* 61; *Rocky Mountain News,* June 4, 1996, p. 5a.

22. University of Denver, *1997–1998 Media Guide,* 49, 61, 67–70; *Rocky Mountain News,* January 11, 1959, p. 48.

23. University of Denver, *1997–1998 Media Guide,* 49, 61.

24. Ibid., 76, 89.

25. Colorado Avalanche, *1996–1997 Colorado Avalanche Media Guide* (Denver: Colorado Avalanche, 1996), 258; *Rocky Mountain News,* July 23, 1950, p. 33.

26. *Rocky Mountain News,* August 7, 1958, p. 67; August 21, 1958, p. 74.

27. Ibid., August 21, 1958, p. 74; August 11, 1959, p. 51; August 21, 1959, p. 99; December 4, 1959, p. 108.

28. *Denver Post,* October 9, 1963, p. 60; March 30, 1972, p. 64; Colorado Avalanche, *1996–1997 Media Guide,* 258.

29. *Denver Post,* February 16, 1968, p. 55; May 3, 1971, p. 49; March 30, 1972, pp. 61, 64; *Rocky Mountain News,* August 17, 1972, pp. 74, 81; Colorado Avalanche, *1996–1997 Media Guide,* 258.

30. Colorado Avalanche, *1996–1997 Media Guide,* 258; *Rocky Mountain News,* March 12, 1975, p. 88; January 3, 1976, pp. 5, 8; January 29, 1976, p. 1; March 10, 1976, p. 8; June 8, 1976, p. 5; *Denver Post,* May 25, 1975, pp. 49, 50.

31. Colorado Avalanche, *1996–1997 Media Guide,* 258; *Denver Post,* May 24, 1997, p. 8c; *Rocky Mountain News,* September 1, 1976, p. 84; May 15, 1977, p. 67; September 26, 1993, p. 35b.

32. *Rocky Mountain News,* September 26, 1993, p. 35b; *Denver Post,* May 24, 1997, p. 8c.

33. *Denver Post,* May 12, 1978, p. 67; *Rocky Mountain News,* September 26, 1993, p. 35b.

34. *Rocky Mountain News,* July 13, 1978, p. 5; July 14, 1978, p. 54; September 26, 1993, p. 35b; *Denver Post,* November 4, 1979, p. 90.

35. *Rocky Mountain News,* August 10, 1978, p. 1.

36. *Rocky Mountain News,* September 26, 1993, p. 35b.

37. *Denver Post,* November 4, 1979, p. 89.

38. Ibid.

39. *Rocky Mountain News,* September 26, 1993, p. 36b.

40. Ibid.

41. Ibid.; May 28, 1982, pp. 1, 122.

42. Colorado Avalanche, *1996–1997 Media Guide,* 258.

43. *Denver Post,* May 25, 1995, p. 1a; Danielson, *Home Team,* 121.

44. *Denver Post,* May 25, 1995, p. 10a; *Rocky Mountain News,* May 25, 1995, pp. 1b, 13b;

June 6, 1996, pp. 1n, 2n; June 7, 1996, pp. 10n, 11n; Bob Kravitz, *Avalanche: Capturing the Cup* (Boulder: Johnson Books, 1996), 34–39.

45. Colorado Avalanche, *1996–1997 Media Guide,* 258; *Denver Post,* May 25, 1995, p. 11a.

46. Kravitz, *Avalanche,* 45–46.

47. Ibid., 46; *Denver Post,* June 16, 1996, p. 11d; Colorado Avalanche, *1997–1998 Yearbook,* 77–79.

48. Colorado Avalanche, *1996–1997 Media Guide,* 102, 178–79.

49. *Denver Post,* June 11, 1996, pp. 1aa, 3aa; *Rocky Mountain News,* June 12, 1996, p. 28n; Colorado Avalanche, *1996–1997 Media Guide,* 38, 75, 179, 188; *Sports Illustrated* 84:24 (June 17, 1996): 57.

50. *Denver Post,* June 13, 1996, p. 3aa.

51. *Sports Illustrated* 84:24 (June 17, 1996): 51; Colorado Avalanche, *1997–1998 Yearbook,* 136–37.

52. *Rocky Mountain News,* May 27, 1997, p. 6n.

53. *Rocky Mountain News,* April 22, 1998, p. 7n; May 5, 1998, pp. 1c–3c.

54. *Rocky Mountain News,* June 12, 1996, p. 3n; May 5, 1998, p. 2c; June 3, 1998, pp. 1c, 2c.

55. *Denver Post,* August 13, 1997, pp. 17a, 1c, 3c.

56. *Rocky Mountain News,* July 30, 1996, p. 6a; *Denver Post,* July 30, 1996, p. 5b.

57. *Denver Post,* July 27, 1996, pp. 1a, 12a; July 30, 1996, pp. 1b, 5b; *Rocky Mountain News,* July 30, 1996, p. 6a.

58. *Denver Post,* August 13, 1997, p. 1a.

59. Ibid., 1a, 17a; *Rocky Mountain News,* August 13, 1997, p. 5a.

60. *Denver Post,* August 13, 1997, 1a, 19a; *Rocky Mountain News,* August 14, 1997, pp. 1b, 20b.

61. *Rocky Mountain News,* April 27, 1999, p. 1b; July 27, 1999, pp. 1b, 5b; July 28, 1999, pp. 1b, 6b, 7b; *Denver Post,* July 27, 1999, pp. 1a, 15a; July 28, 1999, pp. 1a, 19a, 1d.

62. *Denver Post,* November 4, 1997, p. 1d.

CONCLUSION

1. *Denver Post,* February 22, 1999, pp. 1a, 9a, 10a.

2. Michael N. Danielson, *Home Team: Professional Sports and the American Metropolis* (Princeton: Princeton University Press, 1997); Mark S. Rosentraub, *Major League Losers: The Real Cost of Sports and Who's Paying for It* (New York: Basic Books, 1997).

BIBLIOGRAPHIC ESSAY

The following emphasizes monographic literature on the history of sports in the United States and Colorado. See the notes for specific sources, including primary materials, used in this study.

GENERAL WORKS: COLORADO

Readily available standard works on Colorado history include LeRoy R. Hafen, ed., *Colorado and Its People: A Narrative and Topical History of the Centennial State,* 4 vols. (New York: Lewis Historical Publishing, 1948), which, though old, contains useful topical chapters; Robert Athearn, *The Coloradans* (Albuquerque: University of New Mexico Press, 1976); Carl Ubbelohde, Maxine Benson, and Duane A. Smith, *A Colorado History,* 7th ed. (Boulder: Pruett Publishing, 1995); and Carl Abbott, Stephen J. Leonard, and David McComb, *Colorado: A History of the Centennial State,* 3d ed. (Niwot: University Press of Colorado, 1994). On Denver, see Thomas J. Noel and Stephen J. Leonard, *Denver: Mining Camp to Metropolis* (Niwot: University Press of Colorado, 1990).

GENERAL WORKS: SPORTS HISTORY

The scholarly literature on the history of sports in the United States is large, growing, and increasingly specialized. Important general works include William J. Baker, *Sports in the Western World,* rev. ed.

(Urbana and Chicago: University of Illinois Press, 1988); Benjamin G. Rader, *American Sports: From the Age of Folk Games to the Age of Televised Sports*, 3d ed. (Englewood Cliffs, N.J.: Prentice-Hall, 1996); Elliott J. Gorn and Warren Goldstein, *A Brief History of American Sports* (New York: Hill and Wang, 1993); Douglas A. Noverr and Lawrence E. Ziewacz, *The Games They Played: Sports in American History, 1865–1980* (Chicago: Nelson-Hall, 1983); David K. Wiggins, ed., *Sport in America: From Wicked Amusement to National Obsession* (Champaign, Ill.: Human Kinetics Books, 1995); Ted Vincent, *The Rise and Fall of American Sport: Mudville's Revenge* (Lincoln: University of Nebraska Press, 1994); Richard A. Swanson and Betty Spears, *History of Sport and Physical Education in the United States*, 4th ed. (Madison, Wis., and Dubuque, Iowa: Brown and Benchmark, 1995); Randy Roberts and James Olson, *Winning Is the Only Thing: Sports in America Since 1945* (Baltimore: Johns Hopkins University Press, 1989); and Allen Guttmann, *A Whole New Ball Game: An Interpretation of American Sports* (Chapel Hill: University of North Carolina Press, 1988). For sports in the American West, see Donald J. Mrozek, ed., *Sport in the West* (Manhattan, Kans.: *Journal of the West,* Sunflower University Press, 1983). The *Journal of Sports History,* published quarterly by the North American Society for Sports History, has a diverse content, but is especially useful for the social history of sport.

AMERICAN INDIAN SPORTS

The classic work on American Indian sports is Stewart Culin's *Games of the North American Indians,* 2 vols., originally published by the Smithsonian Institution in 1907 (Lincoln: University of Nebraska Press, Bison Books, 1992). See also Edward Curtis's massive twenty-volume study, *The North American Indian* (1911; New York and London: Johnson Reprint, 1970). A more recent monographic study is Joseph B. Oxendine, *American Indian Sports Heritage* (Champaign, Ill.: Human Kinetics Books, 1988). Jerald C. Smith examines shinny and other ball games in "The Native American Ball Games," in *Sport in the Socio-Cultural Process,* ed. Mabel Marie Hart (Dubuque, Iowa: William C. Brown, 1976). Frank Gilbert Roe studies the importance of horses in Indian culture in *The Indian and the Horse* (Norman: University of Oklahoma Press, 1955). See Peter Nabokov, *Indian Running* (Santa

Barbara: Capra Press, 1981), on the cultural and economic impor-
tance of running. On the Utes and the Cheyenne, see missionary
James Russell's report, "Conditions and Customs of Present-Day Utes
in Colorado," *Colorado Magazine* 6:3 (May 1929): 104; Robert Emmitt,
The Last War Trail: The Utes and the Settlement of Colorado (Norman:
University of Oklahoma Press, 1954); Marshall Sprague, *Massacre: The
Tragedy at White River* (Boston: Little, Brown, 1957); Robert W. Delaney,
James Jefferson, and Gregory Thompson, *The Southern Utes: A Tribal
History* (Ignacio, Colo.: Southern Ute Tribe, 1972); Charles S. Marsh,
People of the Shining Mountains: The Utes of Colorado (Boulder: Pruett
Publishing, 1982); Robert W. Delaney, *Ute Mountain Utes* (Albuquer-
que: University of New Mexico Press, 1989); Jan Pettit, *Utes: The Moun-
tain People* (Boulder: Johnson Books, 1990); John Stands-in-Timber
and Margot Liberty, *Cheyenne Memories* (New Haven: Yale University
Press, 1967); and George Bird Grinnell's *Pawnee, Blackfoot, and Cheyenne: History and Folkways of the Plains* (New York: Charles Scribner's
Sons, 1961) and *The Cheyenne Indians: The History and Ways of Life,* 2
vols. (Lincoln: University of Nebraska Press, 1972).

MINING CAMP SPORTS

There is extensive literature on mining and mining towns in
Colorado and the American West. Among the better overviews are
Rodman W. Paul, *Mining Frontiers of the Far West, 1848–1880* (Albu-
querque: University of New Mexico Press, 1963); Duane A. Smith,
Rocky Mountain Mining Camps: The Urban Frontier (Lincoln: University
of Nebraska Press, Bison Books, 1974); Ronald C. Brown, *Hard-Rock
Miners: The Intermountain West, 1860–1920* (College Station: Texas
A&M University Press, 1979). On Leadville, see Don L. Griswold
and Jean Harvey Griswold, *The Carbonate Camp Called Leadville* (Den-
ver: University of Denver Press, 1951), and *History of Leadville and Lake
County, Colorado: From Mountain Solitude to Metropolis,* 2 vols. (Boulder:
Colorado Historical Society in cooperation with the University Press
of Colorado, 1996); Eugene Floyd Irey, "A Social History of Leadville,
Colorado, During the Boom Days, 1877–1881" (Ph.D. diss., Univer-
sity of Minnesota, 1951); and Edward Blair, *Leadville: Colorado's Magic
City* (Boulder: Pruett Publishing, 1980). For Cripple Creek, see
Marshall Sprague, *Money Mountain: The Story of Cripple Creek Gold*

(New York: Ballantine Books, 1953); Mabel Barbee Lee, *Cripple Creek Days* (Garden City, N.Y.: Doubleday, 1958); and Robert L. Brown, *Cripple Creek: Then and Now* (Denver: Sundance Publications, 1991). Lynn Irwin Perrigo looks at life in Central City in "A Social History of Central City, Colorado, 1859–1900" (Ph.D. diss., University of Colorado, 1936) and "The Cradle of Colorado: Early Central City in the Reminiscences of Pioneers, 1935" (Las Vegas, N.M.: Denver Public Library, Western History Department, 1973). See also C. H. Hannington, "Early Days of Central City," in *Colorado Magazine* 19:1 (January 1942): 3–14. John Willard Horner's *Silver Town* deals with Georgetown (Caldwell, Idaho: Caxton Printers, 1950). For southwestern Colorado, see Sarah Platte Deck Chapter, Daughters of the American Revolution, Durango, Colorado, *Pioneers of the San Juan Country,* 2 vols. (Colorado Springs: Out West Printing, 1940, 1942); Duane Vandenbusch, *The Gunnison Country* (Gunnison, Colo.: B&B Printers, 1980); and Duane A. Smith, *Rocky Mountain Boom Town: A History of Durango* (Albuquerque: University of New Mexico Press, 1980), and *Song of the Hammer and Drill: The Colorado San Juans, 1860–1914* (Golden: Colorado School of Mines Press, 1982).

On skiing in the Colorado mining towns, see E. R. Warren, "Snow-Shoeing in the Rocky Mountains," *Outing* 9 (January 1887): 350–54; John L. Dyer, *The Snow-Shoe Itinerant: An Autobiography of the Rev. John L. Dyer* (Cincinnati: Cranston and Stowe, 1890); Charles F. Gardiner, *Doctor at Timberline* (Caldwell, Idaho: Caxton Printers, 1938); "Snowshoe Post-Routes: From the *Colorado Graphic* of April 18, 1891," *Colorado Magazine* 17:1 (January 1940): 36–38; Calvin Queal, "Colorado Skiing: A Century of Sport," *Denver Post Empire Magazine* (November 9, 1969): 11–17; Jack A. Benson, "Before Skiing Was Fun," *Western Historical Quarterly* 8:4 (October 1977): 431–41; Jack A. Benson, "Before Aspen and Vail: The Story of Recreational Skiing in Frontier Colorado," in *Sport in the West,* ed. Donald J. Mrozek, 52–61 (Manhattan, Kans.: *Journal of the West,* Sunflower University Press, 1983); John Rolfe Burroughs, *Steamboat in the Rockies* (Fort Collins, Colo.: Old Army Press, 1978); Sureva Towler, *The History of Skiing at Steamboat Springs* (Steamboat Springs, Colo.: Routt County Research, 1987); Hal K. Rothman, " 'Powder Aplenty for Native and Guest Alike': Steamboat Springs, Corporate Control, and the Changing Meaning of Home," *Montana: The Magazine of Western History* 48:4 (winter 1998): 2–17; Malcolm J. Rohrbough, *Aspen: The History of a Silver-Mining Town, 1879–1893* (New York: Oxford University Press, 1986); and E. John B. Allen, *From Skisport to Skiing: One Hundred Years of an American Sport, 1840–1940* (Amherst: University of Massachusetts Press, 1993).

For mining-town baseball, see Duane A. Smith, "Baseball Champions of Colorado: The Leadville Blues of 1882," *Journal of Sports History* 4:1 (spring 1977): 51–71; Duane A. Smith, "Mighty Casey Matches the Mountains: The Origins of Baseball in Colorado," *Colorado Heritage* (spring 1995): 5–18; Irvin Moss and Mark Foster, *Home Run in the Rockies: The History of Baseball in Colorado* (Denver: A. B. Hirschfeld Press, 1994); and Duane Smith and Mark Foster, *They Came to Play: A Photographic History of Colorado Baseball* (Niwot: University Press of Colorado, 1997).

The literature on other mining-town sports is sparse. See Victor I. Noxon, "Hardrock Drilling Contests in Colorado," *Colorado Magazine* 11:3 (May 1934): 81–85; Georgina Brown, "Horses . . . Sport of the Carbonate Kings," *Mountain Diggings* 3:1 (April 1973): 14–25; Arthur Cecil Todd, *The Cornish Miner in America* (Glendale, Calif.: Arthur H. Clark, 1967), which includes a description of Cornish wrestling; and Toby Smith, *Kid Blackie: Jack Dempsey's Colorado Days* (Ouray, Colo.: Wayfinder Press, 1987), on boxing.

BICYCLING

On bicycling, see Robert A. Smith, *A Social History of the Bicycle: Its Early Life and Times in America,* which focuses on the bicycling boom of the late nineteenth century (New York: American Heritage Press, 1972); Andrew W. Gillette, "The Bicycle Era in Colorado," *Colorado Magazine* 10 (November 1933): 213–17; Thomas J. Noel, *The Denver Athletic Club, 1884–1984* (Denver: Denver Athletic Club, 1984); and James Whiteside, "It Was a Terror to the Horses: Bicycling in Gilded-Age Denver," *Colorado Heritage* (spring 1991): 2–16.

RECREATIONAL SKIING

On the history of skiing in Colorado, begin with the sources cited for mining-town skiing. Abbott Fay's *Ski Tracks in the Rockies: A Century of Colorado Skiing* (Louisville, Colo.: Cordillera Press, 1984) is a useful overview. See also Charlie Meyers, *Colorado Ski Country* (Helena and Billings, Mont.: Falcon Press, 1987), and I. William Berry, *The Great North American Ski Book* (New York: Charles Scribner's Sons, 1982).

The Tenth Mountain Division brought many of the ski industry's key figures to Colorado during World War II. See Charles Minot Dole, *Adventures in Skiing* (New York: Franklin Watts, 1965); Curtis W. Casewit, *Mountain Troopers: The Story of the Tenth Mountain Division* (New York: Thomas Y. Crowell, 1972); Jack A. Benson, "Skiing at Camp Hale: Mountain Troops During World War II," *Western Historical Quarterly* 25:2 (April 1984): 163–74; KRMA (Denver) Television's video, "Soldiers of the Summit" (Denver: Council for Public Television, 1987); and Flint Whitlock, *Soldiers on Skis: A Pictorial Memoir of the Tenth Mountain Division* (Boulder: Paladin Press, 1992).

Steve Patterson and Kenton Forest, *Rio Grande Ski Train* (Denver: Tramway Press, 1984), is an interesting look at the train and the development of Winter Park.

Several useful books chronicle the development of Aspen. Sally Barlow-Perez, *A History of Aspen* (Aspen: WHO Press, 1980), is a compact overview introducing the major characters in Aspen's ski history. See also Paul I. Hauk, *Aspen Mountain Ski Chronology* (Glenwood Springs, Colo.: United States Department of Agriculture, Forest Service, 1978), especially for the federal licensing process. Peggy Clifford, *To Aspen and Back: An American Journey* (New York: St. Martin's Press, 1980), looks at the social impacts of skiing. Anne Gilbert, *Re-Creation Through Recreation: Aspen Skiing from 1870 to 1970* (Aspen: Aspen Historical Society, 1995), is a good scholarly treatment of Aspen's social and economic transformation.

On Vail, see Sandra Dallas, *Vail* (Boulder: Pruett Publishing, 1969); Paul I. Hauk, *Vail Ski Area Chronology* (Glenwood Springs, Colo.: United States Department of Agriculture, Forest Service, 1979); June B. Simonton, *Vail: Story of a Colorado Mountain Valley* (Denver: Knudsen Printing, 1987); and William Oscar Johnson, "A Vision Fulfilled: From One Man's Dream, Vail Has Grown Into America's Biggest Ski Resort," *Sports Illustrated* (January 30, 1989): 70–82.

For the Summit County ski areas (Breckenridge, Arapahoe Basin, Keystone), see Paul I. Hauk, *Keystone Ski Area Chronology* and

Arapahoe Basin Ski Area Chronology (Glenwood Springs, Colo.: United States Department of Agriculture, Forest Service, 1979); Mary Ellen Gilliland, *Summit: A Gold Rush History of Summit County, Colorado* (Silverthorn, Colo.: Alpenrose Press, 1980); and Edna Strand Dercum's delightful memoir, *It's Easy, Edna, It's Downhill All the Way,* 2d ed. (Carbondale, Colo.: Sopris Press, 1991).

Beginning in the 1970s, Charles R. Goeldner, of the Business Research Division, Graduate School of Business Administration, University of Colorado at Boulder, supervised a series of studies of the ski industry's growth and economic impacts. Also useful on the economy of skiing is Ford C. Frick and Dean C. Coddington, *The Contribution of Skiing to the Colorado Economy* (Denver: Browne, Bortz, and Coddington, 1982) and Frick's 1985 update of the same title.

1976 OLYMPICS

On the 1976 Winter Olympic controversy, begin with two articles by Mark S. Foster, "Colorado's Defeat of the 1976 Winter Olympics," *Colorado Magazine* 53:2 (spring 1976): 163–87, and "Little Lies: The Colorado 1976 Winter Olympics," *Colorado Heritage* (winter 1998): 22–33. Laura Lee Katz Olson's "Power, Public Policy, and the Environment: The Defeat of the 1976 Winter Olympics," is a detailed study of the issue and the emergence of environmental politics in the 1970s (Ph.D. diss., University of Colorado, 1974). Rick Reese assessed the failure of the Colorado Olympic effort for Utah organizers in "The Denver Winter Olympics Controversy" (Salt Lake City: Rick Reese, 1984; typescript in Denver Public Library, Western History Department). Important original sources include hearings by the United States Senate, Committee on Interior and Insular Affairs, *1976 Denver Winter Olympics* (92d Cong., 2d sess., 1972); Citizens for Colorado's Future, *Records, 1971–1972,* in the Denver Public Library, Western History Department; and the Denver Olympic Organizing Committee's *Final Report, December 29, 1972,* also in the Denver Public Library, Western History Department.

COLLEGE FOOTBALL

College athletics has spawned a large and growing literature. Among the better recent studies are Ronald A. Smith, *Sports and Free-*

dom: The Rise of Big-Time College Athletics (New York: Oxford University Press, 1988); Murray Sperber, *College Sports, Inc.: The Athletic Department vs. the University* (New York: Henry Holt, 1990); and John R. Thelin, *Games Colleges Play: Scandal and Reform in Intercollegiate Athletics* (Baltimore: Johns Hopkins University Press, 1994). The best source on the development of football and other athletics at Colorado State University is James E. Hansen II, *Democracy's College in the Centennial State: A History of Colorado State University* (Fort Collins: Colorado State University, 1977). Football at the University of Colorado is well chronicled in books by the school's longtime athletic information officer, Fred Casotti. See *Football CU-Style* (Boulder: Pruett Publishing, 1972); *The Golden Buffaloes: Colorado Football* (Huntsville, Ala.: Strode Publishers, 1986); and *CU Century: One Hundred Years of Colorado University Football* (Denver: Original Publications, 1990). See also university histories by William E. Davis, *Glory Colorado! A History of the University of Colorado, 1858–1963* (Boulder: Pruett Press, 1965), and Frederick S. Allen et al., *The University of Colorado, 1876–1976* (New York: Harcourt Brace Jovanovich, 1976). On Byron White, see Dennis J. Hutchinson, *The Man Who Once Was Whizzer White: Portrait of Justice Byron R. White* (New York: Free Press, 1998). J. David Kennebeck and Jeffrey M. Potts examine the CU football program, if uncritically, in *Decade of Excellence: An Illustrative Look at Colorado's Finest Football Era, 1985–1995* (Denver: MIM Publishing, 1997). Bill McCartney's autobiography (with Dave Diles), *From Ashes to Glory,* is revealing (Nashville: T. Nelson, 1995).

BRONCOMANIA

Journalists and fans have generated a number of books about the Denver Broncos. The quality is uneven at best, but several are useful. See Dick Connor, *The Denver Broncos* (Englewood Cliffs, N.J.: Prentice-Hall, 1974); Larry Gordon and Dick Burnell, *Barely Audible: A History of the Denver Broncos* (Denver: Graphic Impressions, 1975); Lou Sahadi, *Broncos! The Team That Makes Miracles Happen* (New York: Stein and Day, 1978); Woodrow Paige, Jr., *Orange Madness: The Incredible Odyssey of the Denver Broncos* (New York: Thomas Y. Crowell, 1978); Bob Collins, Chet Nelson, and Jackie Kutsko, *Broncos: From Striped Socks to Super Bowl and Beyond* (Colorado Springs: Pikes Peak Publishers, 1980); James Gerzewski, ed., *Denver Broncos, 1960–1984 Silver Anniversary* (Denver: Special Productions, 1985); Joseph Hession and Michael Spence, *Broncos: Three Decades of Football* (San Francisco: Foghorn Press, 1987); Russell Martin, *The Color Orange: A Super Season with the Denver Broncos* (New York: Henry Holt, 1987); and Dan Reeves, with Dick Connor, *Reeves: An Autobiography* (Chicago: Bonus Books, 1988). See also John Elway's autobiography, *Elway* (Chicago: Benchmark Press, 1998).

AMATEUR AND PROFESSIONAL BASKETBALL

James Naismith, basketball's inventor, recalls the game's beginnings, including his stay in Denver, in *Basketball: Its Origins and Development* (Lincoln: University of Nebraska Press, 1996). A useful overview of amateur and professional basketball in Colorado is the Denver Organizing Committee, *Rocky Mountain Basketball: Naismith to Nineteen Ninety* (Englewood, Colo.: Westcliffe Publishers, 1989). For amateur basketball and the AAU Tournament, see Adolph H. Grundman, "Pigs, Jellymakers, and Greybeards: When Denver Was a Basketball Mecca," *Colorado Heritage* (autumn 1994): 35–43. Terry Pluto chronicles the American Basketball Association in *Loose Balls: The Short, Wild Life of the American Basketball Association* (New York: Simon and Schuster, 1990). On the Denver Nuggets, see Mike Monroe, *Hardwood Gold: The Rise and Fall and Rise of the Denver Nuggets* (Dallas: Taylor Publishing, 1994).

PROFESSIONAL BASEBALL

The literature on baseball is the largest in the historiography of sport. Useful introductions to the game's history are Harold Seymour's trilogy, *Baseball: The Early Years, Baseball: The Golden Age,* and *Baseball: The People's Game* (New York: Oxford University Press, 1960, 1971, 1990); Benjamin G. Rader's *Baseball: A History of America's Game* (Urbana and Chicago: University of Illinois Press, 1994); and Geoffrey C. Ward and Ken Burns, *Baseball: An Illustrated History* (New York: Alfred A. Knopf, 1994), the companion book to Burns's celebrated television series. On the Negro Leagues, see Donn Rogosin, *Invisible Men: Life in Baseball's Negro Leagues* (New York, Tokyo, and London: Kodansha International, 1983), and Robert Peterson, *Only the Ball*

Was White: A History of Legendary Black Players and All-Black Professional Teams (New York: Oxford University Press, 1970).

The best overview of the history of baseball in Colorado is Irvin Moss and Mark Foster's *Home Run in the Rockies: The History of Baseball in Colorado* (Denver: A. B. Hirschfeld Press, 1994). See also Mark Foster, *The Denver Bears: From Sandlots to Sellouts* (Boulder: Pruett Publishing, 1983). The spring 1995 issue of the Colorado Historical Society's *Colorado Heritage* is devoted to the history of baseball in Colorado and includes Duane A. Smith, "Mighty Casey Matches the Mountains: The Origins of Baseball in Colorado" (4–18); Jay Sanford, "African-American Baseballists and the *Denver Post* Tournament" (20–34); and two articles by Mark S. Foster, "Mile High Greenfields: Denver's Notable Ballparks" (35–43) and "Playing by the Rules: The Evolution of Baseball in the Nineteenth Century" (44–51).

For the Colorado Rockies and the effort to bring major league baseball to Colorado, start with Moss and Foster, *Home Run in the Rockies.* See also David Whitford, *Playing Hardball: The High Stakes Battle for Baseball's New Franchises* (New York: Doubleday, 1993); Norm Clarke, *High Hard Ones: Denver's Road to the Rockies from Inside the Newspaper War,* which might more aptly be subtitled "how Norm Clarke brought major league baseball to Denver" (Denver: Phoenix Press of Denver, 1993); Alan Gottlieb, *In the Shadow of the Rockies: An Outsider's Look Inside a New Major League Baseball Team* (Niwot, Colo.: Roberts Rinehart Publishers, 1994); and Bob Kravitz, *Mile High Madness: A Year with the Colorado Rockies* (New York: Times Books, 1994).

On women's professional baseball, see Dave Kindred, *Colorado Silver Bullets: For the Love of the Game: The Women Who Go Toe-to-Toe with the Men* (Atlanta: Longstreet Press, 1995).

HOCKEY

For the history of hockey, see the general works on sports history. Michael N. Danielson discusses the move of the Quebec Nordiques to Colorado in *Home Team: Professional Sports and the American Metropolis* (Princeton: Princeton University Press, 1997). Bob Kravitz's *Avalanche: Capturing the Cup* chronicles the team's 1996 championship season.

INDEX